The Interactive Guide to QuarkXPress 4

Rick Wallace

que
E&T

The Interactive Guide to QuarkXPress 4

Library of Congress Catalog No.: 96-69466

ISBN: 1-57576-527-6

00 99 98   3 2 1

Interpretation of the printing code: the rightmost double-digit number is the year of the book's printing; the rightmost single-digit number, the number of the book's printing. For example, a printing code of 98-1 shows that the first printing of the book occurred in 1998.

This book was produced digitally by Macmillan Computer Publishing and manufactured using computer-to-plate technology (a film-less process) by GAC/Shepard Poorman, Indianapolis, Indiana.

Publisher: Robert Linsky

Acquisitions Editor: Randy Haubner

Managing Editor: Caroline Roop

Product Marketing Manager: Susan L. Kindel

Development Editor: Songlin Qiu

Technical Editor: Phil Gaskill

Production Editor: Susan Hobbs

Copy Editor: Asit J. Patel

Book Designer: Louisa Klucznik

Indexer: Sandra Henselmeier

Production Team: Tricia Flodder, Aleata Howard, Elizabeth SanMiguel, Megan Wade

Composed in *Stone Serif* and *MCPdigital* by Que® Education & Training

Dedication

To Dyckie and Hubert Wallace, the best roots a guy ever had.

About the Author

For more than 40 years, Rick Wallace has been working in communications, design, and the media. Since he bought one of the first IBM-PCs (they didn't even have hard drives), and since he bought one of the first Macintoshes (they not only didn't have hard drives, they had 9" screens), he has been fascinated with the process of using computers as tools for the practical communication of ideas.

Currently, a vice president at a prominent public affairs and advertising agency, Rick Wallace has applied information design principles to a wide range of public policy issues including oil spill recovery, forestry habitat, ecosystem studies, and the permitting and siting of industrial projects. He has also worked as a political campaign coordinator and in preparing presentations and witnesses for use in government regulatory hearings and courtrooms.

In the course of such projects, he has been involved in the creation and production of multimedia displays, newsletters and direct mail pieces, broadcast and print advertising, video documentaries, scientific conferences, and Web sites.

As an author, he has written numerous books and training programs on computer-related topics for graphic designers, lawyers, and real estate agents. As a journalist, he worked for 20 years in television and radio as an award-winning news director, assignment manager, reporter, and anchor.

Acknowledgments

Thanks goes to Cyndi Walker, a great North Carolina-based illustrator, who just happens to be my daughter. She did all the illustrations used in the exercises for this book and did them well, not to mention on time and within budget.

Lydia Mather, and her get-it-done practicality, has been a constant source of inspiration through our long professional association. She was the guinea pig for the predecessor to this book, *An Interactive Guide to PageMaker 6*.

The staff at Que Education & Training have been great book crafters, a statement that I hope you, the reader, will agree is true after you have used this book through a school term and experienced for yourself their dedication to detail and quality.

Trademark Acknowledgments

All terms mentioned in this book that are known to be trademarks or service marks have been appropriately capitalized. Que Education & Training cannot attest to the accuracy of this information. Use of a term in this book should not be regarded as affecting the validity of any trademark or service mark.

Microsoft and Windows are registered trademarks of Microsoft Corporation.

Contents at a Glance

Table of Contents

Introduction

Few things on this earth are, in fact, more practical than the craft of moving a publishing project from a glimmer of an idea, to laid out pages, to a finished product rolling off the printing press.

So, in *The Interactive Guide to QuarkXPress 4*, we have tried hard to be practical above all. It would have been easy to just expose you to the features of the program—to tell you to pull down this or that menu and to check off such and such items in a dialog box. But that would not have taught you much about the real world of getting a project to the printing press.

We have, in addition to teaching the basics of the software, tried to distill years of our own hard earned publishing experience into this book. In fact, much of what you will read comes from practical lessons we had to learn the hard way, by making mistakes. We would never want to make those mistakes again, and hope you don't have to either. That's one reason we've put together the book you have in your hands right now.

Key Features of this Book

You will, during this course, use QuarkXPress to create a series of design projects. These projects recreate experiences you will encounter when you move from the classroom into a professional studio environment— a stationery design, a price list, restaurant menus, a newsletter, several advertisements, a book, an annual report cover.

That's the most important feature of this book, the fact that you will learn by doing. In the process you will, we hope, learn a lot about the practical aspects of publishing from the desktop.

Chapter Features

Each chapter has been built around one of the design projects we mentioned and then organized into a series of sections that introduce you to key concepts, provide design notes, help you set up for the chapter exercises, and then help make sure you retain what you learned through a series of reviews and self-tests.

What You Will Learn

The first thing you will see in each chapter is a "What You Will Learn" section that gives you a road map to what's ahead. It describes what the chapter is all about, including a bulleted list of specific topics and software features covered in the chapter.

Getting Set Up

Also, at the beginning of each chapter, you will find notes on preparing for each chapter's design project, including the fonts you will need to have installed on your computer and other files you will need from the enclosed CD-ROM.

Design Notes

We have augmented each chapter's step-by-step design exercises with a section of design notes. These design notes give you important context and background for your work in QuarkXPress by explaining how the design project took shape as it did and how it meets specific practical objectives.

Review It

After you complete the chapter work, you will find a summary section that summarizes the key concepts you have just covered, including ten "essay" style open-ended questions that review and reinforce the information you have learned.

Check It

To provide further review and to help you identify any weak spots in your understanding before moving on, we have provided "Check It" self-test sections at the end of each chapter—a series of ten multiple choice and ten true/false questions.

Design It

More practical work—at the end of each chapter you will find a section of specific ideas for performing additional independent design work using QuarkXPress on your own outside the classroom.

Portfolio Builders

It can be pretty tough to land design work right out of the classroom. One of the major challenges is finding a good way to show a potential employer what you can do.

At the end of each of the five major parts of the book, you will find independent Portfolio Builder work sections that give you practical advice on constructing an effective portfolio of sample designs. In addition to specific assignments for portfolio projects, we have also interviewed a dozen design professionals who pass on their advice on how they build their portfolios and present them to potential clients during design audition interviews.

Organization of this Book

We have organized *An Interactive Guide to QuarkXPress 4* into five parts.

Part I: Getting a Quick Start

Take a tour through QuarkXPress and in two chapters get quickly up to speed on the basics—everything from opening a file to setting preferences. You will learn to zoom in and out for magnified views, use QuarkXPress palettes (especially the Tool palette), and the basic concepts behind text and picture boxes.

You will construct your first simple project, some business stationery, and in the process will import text and graphics, position items on a page, use the all-important Modify command, and print out a page.

Part II: Setting Type

In the course of designing a price list and redesigning a restaurant menu, you will learn all the basics of using QuarkXPress to set type.

You will gain hands-on experience in specifying and formatting typefaces and type sizes, setting type in various weights, as well as setting the spacing of letters, words, and lines (kerning and H&Js).

Paragraph formatting exercises include alignment and setting rules and tabs, in addition to space before/after.

You will also learn about QuarkXPress's powerful find/change command, and its spellchecker.

Part III: Working Systematically

Using exercises with menus, book chapters, and a newsletter, you learn about all of QuarkXpress's tools for automating production. You'll learn about character and paragraph styles, constructing indexes and tables of contents, assembling chapter files into books, and setting columns.

Most important of all, you will get major hands-on experience in using QuarkXPress's master page capability.

Part IV: Adding Graphics

In this part of the book, you add pictures to words. You learn about vector versus bitmapped graphics and more graphics importing techniques.

You will capture the basic design fundamentals of working with pictures—cropping, positioning, scaling, anchoring them to text.

QuarkXPress 4 now has drawing and sophisticated text wrap capabilities that set it apart from other desktop publishing programs. You will understand the fundamentals of working with text on a path and with Beziér lines and nodes. You will put those tools to work in building actual projects—including a series of magazine advertisements.

Part V: Getting Colorful

In three chapters, you will learn basic color printing theory, create your own colors palette, and apply the color. You will then see to it that the color will turn out as you designed it on the printing press.

We cover practical aspects of working with color including selection of spot colors, and when to use process colors instead. You will color text and graphics, and you will experience for yourself the issues of trying to get accurate screen color.

The last chapter is perhaps the most practical of all of them. You will walk step-by-step through everything you need to know in working with a commercial printer to get your project that last step from a design concept to a final product.

Additional Resources

Que E&T provides an instructor's disk and a CD-ROM.

The CD-ROM

We have included a great deal of supplemental material on the CD-ROM—all of it designed to provide a practical context for the core information in each chapter.

At each point in a chapter where you might need material from the CD-ROM you will find one of these icons in the text. You will, for example, see this icon near the beginning of each chapter in the "Getting Set Up" section when we ask you to copy all the files from that chapter's folder to your working hard drive.

Chapter-by-Chapter Folders

The CD-ROM in this book contains all the elements you need for each chapter's design projects. The disk works for whichever platform you happen to be using, either Macintosh or Windows 95.

Inside each chapter-level folder are all the text and graphics you will need to complete that chapter's design project.

You will also find within each chapter folder a series of QuarkXPress files. These work-in-progress "step" files show what that chapter's design project should look like at the end of each exercise within the chapter. You choose to use these step files in three different ways.

- In some chapters you begin the chapter by loading one of these step files, finishing a design project that we have already started for you.

- If you need to stop in mid-chapter you can pick up where you left off by loading the appropriate intermediate step file.

- If you are having trouble following some of the instructions, you can get back on track by loading the appropriate step file to compare it to your own

work. That's a good way to see for yourself what your design should look like at any given point in a chapter.

Each step file has a name that looks like **05BASE02.QXT**. The first number in the name indicates which chapter it is for, and the second number tells you its sequence in the chapter.

Fonts

In addition to the chapter folders, on the CD-ROM you will also find a folder full of all the fonts you will need to produce each design project in this book.

All the fonts used in this book come from the book *Digital Type Design Guide* (Hayden Books, 1995), by Sean Cavanaugh and they are provided on the companion CD with his permission. For information about obtaining additional fonts, set your Web-browser to WWW.MVD.COM/SEANC, or send an e-mail to 70471.160@compuserve.com.

Appendixes

Also on the CD-ROM are four electronic appendixes in Acrobat format.

- **Font Management (Appendixes A, B):** More than a tutorial on how to install fonts on your Macintosh or PC, we have tried to provide practical information on how to manage the hundreds of fonts you are likely to acquire as a desktop publisher.

- **Glossary (Appendix C):** A detailed glossary of desktop publishing terms used in the book.

- **DTP Master Checklist (Appendix D):** Unique, comprehensive checklist that you can use to guide yourself through the publishing proces from the initial conceptualization of a design project through the printing process.

The Instructor's Resource Disk

The instructor's disk contains a suggested course syllabus, teaching tips/strategies, answers to the exercises in "Review It" and "Check It" sections, test bank, as well as instructional resources.

1 Taking a Quick Tour

What You Will Learn

In this chapter, you begin your exploration of QuarkXPress 4.0 by learning about its fundamental controls and tools. Instead of constructing a desktop publishing project, you experiment with the program's various features and in the process you will:

➤ Open an existing QuarkXPress publication

➤ Save a document

➤ Control the magnification and size of your page view

➤ Get to know how the QuarkXPress palettes work

➤ Introduce yourself to the Tool palette

➤ Explore the difference between text boxes and picture boxes

➤ Move objects around on a page

➤ Add and delete pages

➤ Navigate between pages

➤ Learn about the concept of defaults

Part I

Getting a Quick Start

As you work your way through this chapter, you will use the sample document shown in Figure 1.1—a layout for some business stationery. When you get to Chapter 2, you will learn how to create a letterhead layout by using basic QuarkXPress techniques to build a duplicate of this one from scratch.

Annie's Elegant Rose Place

Landscape Design • Garden Maintenance
1267 Hoedown Highway • Teaneck, Oregon 29346 • 503-923-0050 • Fax: 503-923-0060

Figure 1.1

A sample business letterhead layout.

Prep and Design Notes

Before beginning, you will need to copy the files for this chapter from the CD-ROM to a work area on your hard drive, if your instructor has not already done so. They are all in the **Steps** folder in the folder labeled **01**.

You will also need to install the font called Goudy Sans. The typefaces used for the projects in this book can all be found on the CD-ROM. If you don't know how to install fonts, ask your instructor for help. Also, directions for font installation along with some helpful font management basics have been covered in Appendixes A and B, which can also be found on the CD-ROM.

All the fonts used in this book come from the book Digital Type Design Guide (Hayden Books, 1995), by Sean Cavanaugh and they are provided on the companion CD-ROM with his permission. For information about obtaining additional fonts, set your Web browser to www.mvd.com/seanc, or send an e-mail to seanc@compuserve.com.

In addition to font information, the Design Notes section at the beginning of each chapter will cover design concepts incorporated into each of the desktop publishing projects.

Opening a Publication

If you've ever opened up a document in a word processor or a spreadsheet program, you already know how to open a document in QuarkXPress.

Follow these steps to open the letterhead layout that will be the basis of your work in this chapter:

Opening a File

1. With QuarkXPress open, pull down the **File** menu and choose **O**pen (**File**>**O**pen) as shown in Figure 1.2.

   Alternately, as in almost any other software application, you could have double-clicked the file itself rather than first opening QuarkXPress.

   Notice that Figure 1.2 is from the Windows version of QuarkXPress. As with most of the illustrations in this book, the Windows 95 and Macintosh versions of the program may look a bit different, but they operate in a nearly identical fashion.

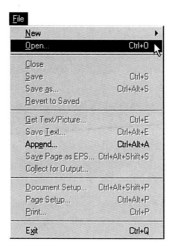

Figure 1.2

*The **F**ile>**O**pen menu command.*

Template Files

2. In the dialog box, select the file named **01BASE01.QXT**, as in Figure 1.3.

   Notice that the file has a three-letter extension of .QXT. Windows uses extensions to identify file types. Most QuarkXPress files have an extension of .QXD, which stands for QuarkXPress Document. The .QXT extension indicates that the file is a template. For convenience in this dual platform book, we have also adopted the extensions for use on the Macintosh versions of the files.

   *(Win95) Ironically, Macintosh users may find it easier than Windows users to see these extensions on the file names. Windows 95 normally hides these extensions from you. In order to see extensions in Windows 95, you go to Explorer and select **V**iew>**O**ptions, where you can turn off the checkbox for hiding MS-DOS file extensions.*

   Template files are exactly like regular QuarkXPress files with one exception. When you open them, they leave the original file untouched and they open a fresh copy of the file. Use them in situations where you have a regularly scheduled publication that uses certain standard elements, such as a newsletter or price sheet. That way, you can preserve and reuse your layout work over and over again.

QuarkXPress, in this case, opens a fresh copy of the letterhead. This fresh copy of the document will be titled something like Document1 with the final number in the name depending on how many new documents you have created in your current QuarkXPress work session.

You can turn any QuarkXPress document into a template simply by choosing that option in the Save As dialog when you save the file.

Automatic Double-Checks

3. Depending on your local setup, when you open the file you may see one of the dialog boxes shown here in Figures 1.4 and 1.5. Again, one illustration is from Windows (1.4) and the other is from the Mac (1.5) but the differences are cosmetic. They both say essentially the same thing.

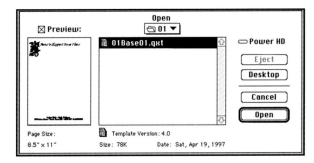

Figure 1.3

The file Open dialog box.

Whenever you open an existing publication, QuarkXPress tries to make sure that the document will look just as it did the last time it was saved. It automatically double-checks to see if you have QuarkXPress set up in the same way and if you have the needed fonts installed on your computer.

The warning in Figure 1.4 lets you know if the typographic settings in the file you are opening are different from the preferences you have set for your copy of QuarkXPress. You will almost always want to choose Keep Document Settings because changing those settings could cause the text line breaks to shift. That could spoil the layout work that has been done on the publication before it came to you.

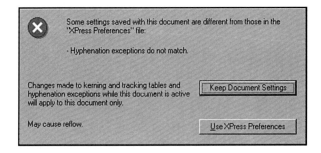

Figure 1.4

The mismatched preferences warning.

Select the Keep Document Settings option.

The Missing Fonts dialog box in Figure 1.5 warns you if you have opened a publication that requires fonts you do not have installed.

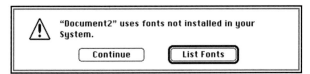

Figure 1.5

The Missing Fonts warning dialog box.

Clicking the List Fonts button takes you to the dialog box in Figure 1.6, where you can identify what fonts are missing. Generally, you probably will not want to click the Replace button. Replacing the font would cause the line breaks to change in the document, possibly throwing off the entire layout.

If you do not have the needed fonts on your machine, stop now and load them before going ahead.

Figure 1.6

The List Fonts dialog box.

Saving Your Work

4. Before moving on, use **File>Save** to name your new document and, more importantly, save your work. You can give it any name you like and save it in a working directory on your hard disk.

   In this case, the Save command is equivalent to the Save As command because this is a brand-new file that has never before been given a name. You would use Save As instead of Save when you need to select a new name or location for an existing publication, one that has been saved at least once before. That's particularly helpful when you are saving stages of your work, making backups as you go.

Zooming Your View

Desktop publishing requires a combination of precision and "big picture" design sense. That's why DTP programs like QuarkXPress come with plenty of tools to change the magnification of your view. High magnification makes it possible to achieve maximum precision when positioning an object on the page, whereas a full page view permits you to get an overall sense of your design.

In QuarkXPress, you can set the magnification view of your publication using several techniques: menus, keyboard shortcuts, the mouse, and a custom magnification control called the Access View Percent field. You will try out each technique in the following steps.

Menu and Keyboard Zooming

With the letterhead still on your screen, follow these steps:

1. Select **View** to see the various magnification choices you can make as in Figure 1.7.

2. Experiment on your own with the choices on this menu. Make sure you try the Actual Size and 200% views.

3. End up with a page view that lets you see the rose drawing. You'll be working with it in the next step.

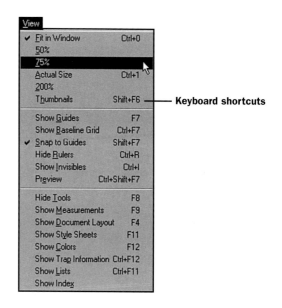

— **Keyboard shortcuts**

Figure 1.7

The various zoom levels accessed via the View menu.

Centering Your View

4. Now try some of the same views by using the keyboard shortcuts noted on the menu in Figure 1.7.

   Try all three of them. ⌘+1 (Mac) or Ctrl+1 (Win95) for Actual Size. Shift+F6 for a tiny Thumbnails view. Complete your experiments by choosing the Fit in Window view, ⌘+0 (Mac) or Ctrl+0 (Win95).

   Notice that's not the letter "O." It's a zero.

Windows Keyboard Menu Control

(Win95) In the Windows version of QuarkXPress, you have the option of choosing virtually any menu command directly from the keyboard. Hold down Alt to activate the menu, press an underlined letter on the menu, and then choose a command by pressing an additional underlined letter. Try this: Press Alt+V to get the View menu. The letter **F** then selects the **F**it in Window view.

Mouse Zooming

The most flexible (and often handiest) way to adjust your view is with any one of several mouse moves—especially if you already have your mouse in action because you are positioning or drawing objects, placing an imported graphic, or selecting some text.

1. Try out the Zoom tool. Hold down Ctrl (Mac) or Ctrl+Spacebar (Win95) keys and notice that your cursor turns into a magnifying glass.

2. Click this magnifying glass Zoom tool on a spot you want to zoom in on.

3. To select an area that you would like blown up to the maximum degree possible, click and drag out a marquee to specify the zoom area you want to see centered in a close-up as shown in Figure 1.8.

Figure 1.8

Using the Zoom tool to draw out a custom magnification view.

The click-and-drag move works by pointing the Zoom tool at a corner of the area you want to magnify. Click and hold the mouse button as you drag it to the opposite corner of the area, forming a rectangular selection marquee.

When you've outlined the area you want to have a closer look at, release the mouse. The area you outlined with the click-and-drag action is now centered in your screen.

4. Now give yourself a negative magnification adjustment tool by adding the Option key (Mac) or Alt key (Win95) to the key combinations in step 1.

Press Option+Ctrl (Mac) or Alt+Ctrl+Spacebar (Win95) and you get a minus sign in the Zoom tool instead of a plus sign. The minus sign means you now have a Zoom tool that zooms out instead of in.

Step down the magnification by clicking the negative magnifying glass on the page. Each click will make the view magnification smaller by one notch, following the order of the magnification levels available in the View menu.

(Win95) In the Windows version of QuarkXPress, you have a way to access several zoom levels directly through the mouse. Right-click the page and you will get a pop-up menu that offers, among other things, several zoom options.

End with your zoom level at Fit in Window using ⌘+0 (Mac) or Ctrl+0 (Win95).

View Percentage Field

You don't need to feel restricted by the standard views available from the menu or the keyboard. In addition to the Zoom tool approach, you can also directly type in a view percentage.

1. Locate the View Percent field, located in the lower left corner of the document window, just to the left of the page number indicator, as you see in Figure 1.8.

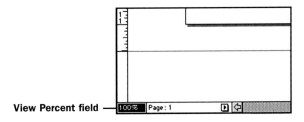

View Percent field —— 100% Page: 1

Figure 1.9

Locating the View Percent field.

2. Press Ctrl+V (Mac) or Ctrl+Alt+V (Win95) to activate the field, or simply click it with the mouse.

3. Type in a percentage amount and press Return (Mac) or ↵Enter (Win95). Your view will instantly zoom to the exact percentage you specify. (You don't actually need to type in the percent symbol to make this work, just the percentage amount.)

Introducing...Palettes

Chances are, by the time you got to this course, you have already used computers enough to understand how to use menus. But software programs for the graphic arts—page layout, painting, drawing—have a set of additional tools for implementing commands. They are called *palettes*, like artists' palettes. In fact, QuarkXPress even has a palette for colors, shown in Figure 1.10. You will get to know it and the other QuarkXPress palettes very well during this course.

Figure 1.10

The Colors palette, one of eight QuarkXPress palettes.

Why Palettes?

Why does QuarkXPress have both menus and palettes, even though they often perform the same functions? It's because menus, in many graphic arts situations, just aren't the ideal mechanism for accomplishing work. Page layout, for example, often requires a lot of fluid work with a mouse. If you are working in the page area of the screen, that means you must move the mouse all the way up to the menus. That may not seem like much trouble but the time it takes, and the distraction, adds up during intensive production work.

So that's why palettes help. They give you instant access to your tools because they float on your screen so you can move them right to where you are working. In fact, there's even a Tool palette in QuarkXPress.

The main reason, of course, for having palettes is to help you accomplish your work. The following table, Table 1.1, lists the palettes in the Window menu and explains what you can use each for.

Table 1.1 A quick guide to the functions of each of the QuarkXPress palettes

Palette Function	You can use it to...
Tools	Select tools for layout and drawing
Measurements	Precisely control the size, shape, rotation, and position of items
Document Layout	Create new pages and navigate to existing ones
Style Sheets	Customize and apply definitions for text formatting
Colors	Apply colors to objects and text
Trap Information	Set controls for how different inks overlap on press
Lists	Compose lists, such as tables of contents
Index	Create indexes of document contents

Turning Palettes On and Off

You control whether your palettes are visible or not through several different methods in QuarkXPress. With eight palettes opened at once, you could cover your entire screen, but if they were all open at once, you wouldn't have any room to work on your pages.

As with setting your page magnification, command central for palettes is the **View** menu, and you have a choice of using menu commands or keyboard shortcuts. Try out the palette controls in the following steps.

Menu Palette Control

1. Try the menu approach first. Pull down the **View** menu (see Figure 1.11).

    The wording you see for the palette section of the View menu changes, depending on whether the palette is hidden or showing.

    If a palette is open (your Tool palette is probably showing at this point), the menu will say something like "Hide **T**ools." But notice that all the other palette items on the menu begin with "Show"— Show Measurements, Show Colors, and so on.

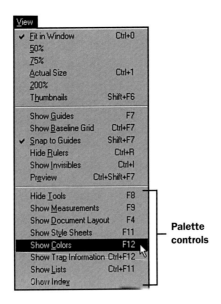

Figure 1.11

Use the View menu to turn palettes on and off.

2. Choose one of the palette controls on the menu that says "Show." In Figure 1.11, we selected Show Colors.

   When you release the mouse, the palette will open up.

3. Pull down the **V**iew menu again and note that the item for the palette you chose now reads "Hide," as in Hide Colors.

Positioning Palettes

4. You can move the palette to any position on your screen and it basically works just like any other window on your computer except that it floats on top of everything else.

   Click the bar at the top of the palette and drag your mouse, releasing the mouse button when you have the palette in the desired spot.

Close Box Palette Control

5. That same bar at the top of the palette holds a Close box that you can use to hide the palette again. For the Mac, it's a small square in the

upper-left corner. On the Windows side, it's a small square with an "x" in it in the upper right.

Click the Close box for the palette that you opened in step 2.

Keyboard Palette Control

6. There are a number of keyboard shortcuts for turning palettes on and off. You can see all of them in the **V**iew menu in Figure 1.11.

   Try it out for yourself. Turn the Colors palette on and off by pressing F12. (There are a few differences in the keyboard shortcuts for the Macintosh and Windows 95, but this one works on both kinds of computer.)

Trying Out the Tool Palette

The most important palette in QuarkXPress is the Tool palette. It's hard to imagine how you could accomplish anything at all without the Tool palette. Have a look at Figure 1.12 and Table 1.2 and you will get some idea of how many vital tools are controlled from here.

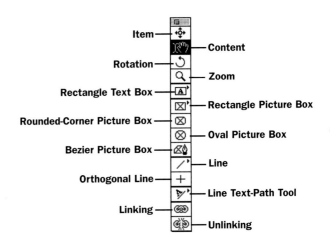

Figure 1.12

The Tool palette.

The following table lists the tools in the Tools palette and gives you a description of their functions.

Table 1.2   A mini-table overview of all the QuarkXPress tool functions

Tool	You can use it to...
Item	Select, resize, reshape, move items and paths
Content	Work with content of boxes including importing and editing text and graphics
Rotation	Spin items
Zoom	Control the view magnifications
Rectangle Text Box	Draw a rectangular box to hold text
Rectangle Picture Box	Draw a rectangular box to hold a graphic
Rounded-Corner Picture Box	Draw a rounded corner box to hold a graphic
Oval Picture Box	Draw an oval box to hold a graphic
Bezier Picture Box	Draw a picture box point by point
Line	Create straight lines of any angle
Orthogonal Line	Create straight vertical or horizontal lines
Line Text-Path	Create a line or path that can hold text
Linking	Link boxes of text so their contents flow from one to the other
Unlinking	Break a text link

In the following exercise, you won't use every tool, but you will learn the basics of using the Tool palette. Don't worry too much at this point about what each of the tools do or the references to text boxes and picture boxes. You will be working with those tools and items soon but the important thing right now is to become familiar with working with the Tool palette.

1. Begin by closing all the palettes except the Tools palette so you'll have room to work. Also, get into Fit in Window view so you have a full view of the letterhead elements. You can use **View>Fit in Window** or the keyboard shortcuts ⌘+0 (Mac) or Ctrl+0 (Win95).

Selecting a Tool

2. Try clicking several of the tools in the Tool palette to get the hang of selecting them with the mouse.

3. You can also select tools with keyboard shortcuts.

   Select the tool below the current one by pressing ⌘+Tab (Mac) or Ctrl+Alt+Tab (Win95).

   Select the tool above the current tool by pressing ⌘+◆Shift+Tab (Mac) or Ctrl+Alt+◆Shift+Tab (Win95).

Using Pop-Out Tools

4. There are many more tools available than are shown in the Tool palette and you access these tool variations through pop-out palettes.

   Click and hold the Rectangle Text Box tool to get a pop-out selection of tools as you see in Figure 1.13.

   Slide your pointer to the Oval Text Box tool (the fourth one on the pop-out) to select it and release the mouse button. That tool will take the place of the Rectangle Text Box tool.

5. Reverse the pop-out tool selection by clicking and holding the Oval Text Box tool until you get the pop-out.

   Select the Rectangle Text Box tool and release the mouse button to return it to its standard position in the Tool palette.

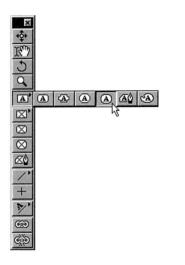

Figure 1.13

Pop-out tool options are available for text boxes, picture boxes, lines, and text-paths.

Customizing the Tool Palette

6. You can customize the Tool palette by adding or subtracting any of the pop-out tools from it.

Repeat step 4 except this time hold down Ctrl (Mac) or Ctrl (Win95) as you click and hold the Rectangle Text Box tool.

Keep the Control key pressed as you select the Oval Text Box tool and release the mouse button.

The Oval Text Box tool will be added to the palette just below the standard Rectangle Text Box tool.

7. You can remove any tool on the Tool palette by holding down Ctrl (Mac) or Ctrl (Win95) while clicking it.

Remove the Oval Text Box tool now.

Remove the Rounded-Corner Picture Box tool.

(It doesn't get deleted, by the way, just put back into the pop-out menu.)

8. Another way to customize the Tool palette is through the QuarkXPress preferences system. You will be using this system through this course to tell QuarkXPress how you want it to behave.

There are several different ways to set your preferences. For example there's a menu item at Edit>Preferences. However, there's a faster and more convenient way to set preferences for the Tool palette items.

Double-click any one of the tools.

You will be taken to the Document Preferences dialog box you see in Figure 1.14, with the Tool preferences section already chosen from among the five different tabs.

Tabs for different kinds of preferences

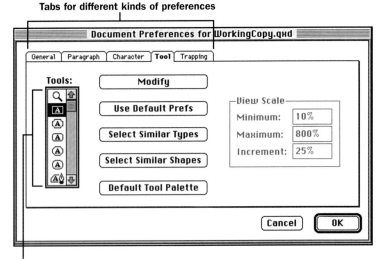

Scrolling list of tools

Figure 1.14

The Document Preferences dialog box.

Notice that the tool you double-clicked is selected in the scrolling list of tools. Depending on the tool, you will have available, a variety of buttons that make it possible for you to set a myriad of variables for each of the tools—colors, magnification levels, typeface, and so on.

9. To reconstruct your Tool palette—return it to the standard complement of tools, click the Default Tool Palette button, and then click OK.

When you come back to your document, you will see that the tools you added to the Tool palette are gone and it is exactly as it was when you first opened QuarkXPress.

Understanding Boxes, Lines, and Content

QuarkXPress has only three kinds of items it can use in a layout—lines, text boxes, and picture boxes. Admittedly, that's an oversimplification since each one of these items can take on a nearly infinite variety of shapes, colors, and other attributes. Nevertheless, it's true. There are only three fundamental building blocks you can use when desktop publishing with QuarkXPress.

Let me mention one more thing. Content. Text boxes and picture boxes have content. Text boxes hold type as in Figure 1.15, and picture boxes hold...well, pictures like the one in Figure 1.16.

Anne's Elegant Rose Place

Figure 1.15

A text box.

Figure 1.16

A picture box.

In addition to text boxes and picture boxes, this latest version of QuarkXPress offers a fancy new content wrinkle. Prior to version 4, you could not have type on a page unless it was in a text box. Now, lines can have content because QuarkXPress 4 offers a new feature called text on a path, shown in Figure 1.17. You put this new feature to work in Chapter 11.

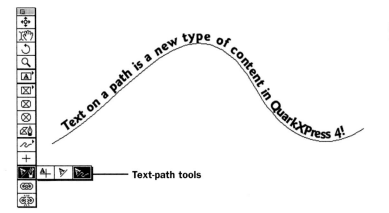

Text-path tools

Figure 1.17

Text on a path.

Content Tool vs. Item Tool

Items such as text or picture boxes behave differently from their contents. That's why we have both a Content tool and an Item tool.

In the following exercise, you put these two tools to work. This is a good way to get a solid grip on the difference between items and content.

1. Begin with the stationery file with which you have been working.

2. Access the magnifying glass tool by pressing Ctrl (Mac), or Ctrl+Spacebar (Win95). While still holding down those keys, click and drag a marquee around the rose sketch picture box and the text box containing the words "Anne's Elegant Rose Place."

   When you release the mouse button, you should have a close view of those two items like the one you see in Figure 1.18.

Using the Content Tool

3. Click the Content tool, the one that looks like a combined hand and a text editing cursor. It's the second one from the top. (If the Tool palette isn't showing, press F8 to unhide it.)

4. Click with the Content tool on the rose sketch picture box. Notice that the box becomes visible.

5. Without clicking, slide the Content tool over the picture box and see how the mouse pointer becomes a hand. Yet, when the mouse has been moved outside the edges of the box, it goes back to being a regular pointer.

Looking Through the Picture Box "Window"

6. Click the hand mouse pointer on the picture and drag the graphic around within the box, as you see in Figure 1.19.

   It helps to understand how this works. Think of the graphic as a picture that is revealed through a window, the window being the picture box. When you move the graphic around, you see a different view of it through the fixed position window of the picture box.

Using the Item Tool

7. Now use the Item tool. With the rose sketch still selected, hold down ⌘ (Mac), or Ctrl (Win95) and maneuver the pointer over the picture box. Notice that the mouse pointer changes to the quadruple arrowhead Item tool.

   (This technique works only if the box is selected. You can also switch to the tool by clicking on it in the Tool palette.)

8. With the Item tool active, click anywhere on the picture box and drag it, just as you did with the Content tool.

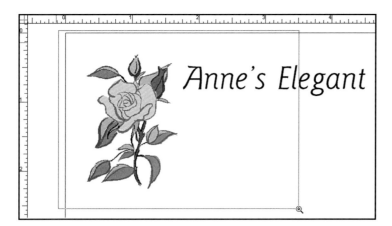

Figure 1.18

In the process of drawing out a marquee to get a close working view of the picture and text boxes.

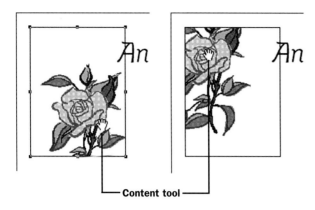

Content tool

Figure 1.19

Using the Content tool to move the graphic around inside the picture box "window."

This time, as you drag, instead of moving the graphic within the picture box, you move the picture box itself as in Figure 1.20.

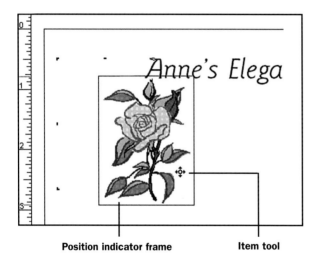

Position indicator frame   Item tool

Figure 1.20

Using the Item tool to move the entire picture box.

Tip

For a Better View, Wait for the Flash

If you click an item and drag immediately you will get only an empty position indicator frame. However, if you click and hold for a beat (actually half a second), the item will flash slightly. After that flash, you will have a full view of the item as you drag instead of just the position indicator frame.

Selecting Text Content

9. The distinction between a picture box item and its graphic contents holds true for text boxes as well.

   With the Content tool chosen, click the "Anne's Elegant Rose Place" text box. (To get the Content tool from the last step, release ⌘ (Mac), or Ctrl (Win95), or click on the Content tool in the Tool palette.)

   The text box will be selected and you will have a blinking cursor, just like in a word processor.

   Just like a word processor, notice that instead of a "hand," you now have an "I" shaped text cursor for a Content tool. That's why the item in the Tool palette has both a hand and the text cursor. QuarkXPress gives you the appropriate pointer needed, depending on the kind of box selected.

10. With the Content tool, double-click one of the words in the text. You will have a word selected, just like a word processor, as in Figure 1.21.

Text Content Tool

Figure 1.21

Using the Content tool in a text box.

11. Now use the Item tool on this text box. Hold down ⌘ (Mac) or Ctrl (Win95) to get a temporary Item tool. You could also click the Item tool in the Tool palette.

Accessing the Modify Command

12. At this point, you could move the text box item, as you did with the rose sketch picture box.

   Instead, double-click the text box. You will get a Modify dialog box like the one in Figure 1.22. This dialog box allows you to control virtually every aspect of the item—that's everything from its position, to its color, to the kind of framing line around it.

There's a Modify dialog box for every item on a QuarkXPress page. You can reach the box for the item you have selected by double-clicking on the item with the Item tool.

You can also get to the Modify dialog box for any selected item, whether or not you have the Item tool chosen, by using the Item>Modify menu. You can also do this by pressing ⌘+Ⓜ (Mac) or Ctrl+Ⓜ (Win95).

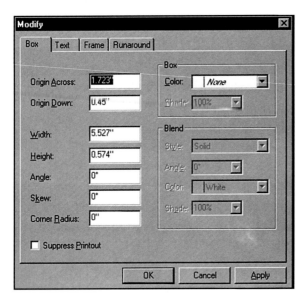

Figure 1.22

Modify any QuarkXPress item by activating this dialog box.

Tip

Use the Undo Command to Take Back the Last Action

Use ⌘+Ⓩ (Mac) or Ctrl+Ⓩ (Win95) if you need to undo your last move. Those are the keyboard shortcuts for the Edit>Undo command.

Adding and Deleting Pages

It would do you no good to have items, or even text and picture content for your items, if you didn't have a place to put them. You need pages to build a document, something on which you can arrange your items.

Follow the next several steps to learn how to add pages, navigate through them, and delete them.

1. Open the Document Layout palette. That's Ⓕ10 (Mac) or Ⓕ4 (Win95), or you can use the View>Show Document Layout menu command. The result will be the palette shown in Figure 1.23.

   Like most QuarkXPress palettes, you can expand or shrink the Document Layout palette by clicking and dragging the lower-right corner.

   The Document Layout palette shows you the relationships between your different pages. It's also one of the ways you can navigate between pages. Watch how the palette changes when you add new pages in the next few steps.

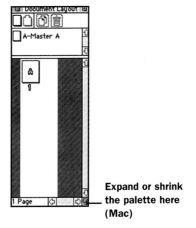

Expand or shrink the palette here (Mac)

Figure 1.23

The Document Layout palette.

2. Use Page>Insert to reach the dialog box shown in Figure 1.24.

   The top portion of the dialog box reads like a sentence. Insert so many pages before or after a certain page number, or at the end of the document.

   In this case, type **3** into the insert pages section of this dialog box.

   Notice that you can specify whether the new pages go after or before the current page. In this case, leave the setting at after and click OK.

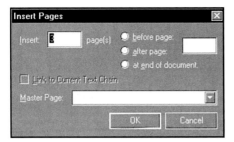

Figure 1.24

The Insert Pages dialog box.

3. Now have a look at the Document Layout palette. It should look like the one in Figure 1.25, with three extra pages added to it.

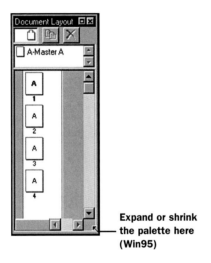

Expand or shrink the palette here (Win95)

Figure 1.25

Document Layout with three pages added.

4. Experiment with changing the size of the Layout palette.

   This sizing capability works just like any other window on your Macintosh or Windows 95 desktop. Although the palettes look slightly different, depending on which type of computer you are using, they both work the same.

   Change the size of the Layout palette by clicking the lower-right corner and dragging it, as indicated in Figures 1.23 (Mac) or 1.25 (Win95).

Tip

Use Master Pages to Speed Big Layout Jobs

You may have been wondering about the master page references in the dialog boxes and palettes you have seen in this section. Master pages are one of the most important productivity tools in QuarkXPress. They are designed to help you get a lot of work done in a hurry. They allow you to set up standard "master" pages—including page numbering, repeating art and text, text boxes for holding body text, and standard page measurements—that can be quickly applied to any of your document's body pages. You will learn how to put master pages to work for you in Chapters 8 and 9.

5. QuarkXPress gives you two indicators, which tell you the current page number, as you see in Figure 1.26.

   In the lower-left edge of the QuarkXPress window, just to the right of the view percentage indicator we discussed previously, you will see a page indicator.

Outlined (Mac) or Bold (Win95) type

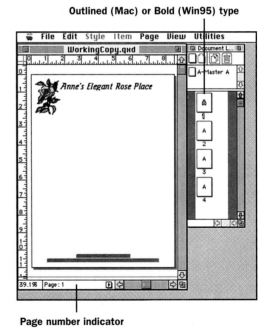

Page number indicator

Figure 1.26

Two ways to tell what page you are on in QuarkXPress.

6. Now that you have added pages, experiment with flipping between them.

In the Layout palette, double-click page 3. Notice how the page numbers change in the palette. On a Mac, the number for the current page will be in outlined type. In Windows 95, the type will be bold.

Also, the page number indicator in the lower-left edge of the QuarkXPress window will say page 3 instead of page 1.

7. Notice the small black arrowhead next to the page number indicator.

If you click the arrowhead, you will get a pop-up menu like the one in Figure 1.27.

Drag your mouse until page 2 has been highlighted in the pop-up menu and release the button. You will be taken to page 2.

(Mac) There's a bit of a difference between Macintosh and Windows pop-up menus. On the Mac, you need to hold down the mouse button to keep the menu open so you can select an item.

(Win95) In Windows, a pop-up menu stays open once you click on it. You don't need to keep holding down the mouse button in order to select an item.

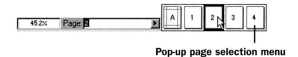

Pop-up page selection menu

Figure 1.27

Using the page indicator pop-up menu for page navigation.

In addition to the pop-up menu, you can also change pages by typing in a new page number in the page number indicator.

You can also use the **Page**>**Go** to command, which has a handy keyboard shortcut, ⌘+J (Mac) or Ctrl+J (Win95).

8. To delete a page, first click the page icon in the Document Layout palette to select it.

Select page 4.

Click the delete page symbol in the upper-right corner of the palette. As you see in Figure 1.28, it's a trashcan icon on the Mac (left) and a slashed "X" in Windows 95 (right).

QuarkXPress will give you a dialog box confirming that you really want to remove this page. Click OK.

Notice that you could have selected several pages by clicking them while holding down ⬆Shift and deleted multiple pages using this same technique.

Figure 1.28

Delete pages using these icons in the Document Layout palette.

9. Another way to delete pages is through the QuarkXPress menu.

Use **Page**>**Delete** to access the Delete Pages dialog box you see in Figure 1.29.

Fill in the blanks to delete pages 2 through 3 and click OK.

Notice that there's no confirming dialog box. The deletion takes place instantly when you use the menu method of page deletion.

Figure 1.29

The Delete Pages dialog box.

Understanding QuarkXPress Defaults and Preferences

Almost every aspect of QuarkXPress can be customized to your personal working style. You can, in other words, set defaults and preferences for how the program behaves.

You learn about specific default and preference settings for many items as we go through the class. For now, however, let's talk about the basic concept of the QuarkXPress default and preference system.

Preferences

A preference is any setting you make in one of QuarkXPress's preference dialog boxes.

You can use Edit>Preferences>Application or Edit>Preferences>Document to set a preference. For example, the Application Preferences dialog box is shown in Figure 1.30. You use the tabs, fields, and checkboxes in this dialog box to specify how you want QuarkXPress to behave.

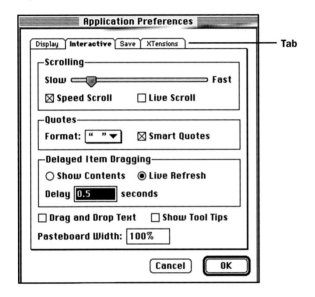

Figure 1.30

The Application Preferences dialog box.

Application preferences are the most broadly applied of the QuarkXPress defaults. Whatever settings you select here will apply to your current document, old documents that may have been created with completely different application preferences settings, and any future documents—until you change them.

The Document Preferences dialog box basically works the same way as the Applications Preferences dialog box but it contains a different set of tabs. Document preferences affect only the document that's open when you set them, although you can set document preferences that will apply to any new documents by making adjustments with no document open, as discussed in the next section.

Defaults (No Document Open)

The word default sometimes confuses people. Just remember, the point of a default is to tell the program what standard behavior should be in the absence of any other direction. It will perform the default action every time, except when you explicitly tell it to do something else.

You set defaults by setting some aspect of QuarkXPress with no document open.

If you were to look at all the menus in QuarkXPress without any document open, you would see that many items are grayed out. You can't set defaults for any of those items. You can, however, set defaults for any items that are showing as available in the menus when you have no document open.

That means you can set default preferences, default color definitions, default hyphenation and justification settings, and so on. But you can't set defaults for fonts or the color of frames.

Whatever settings you make with no document open will be saved by QuarkXPress when you shut down the program. Then, when you open the program again, the setting will have been remembered and will apply to any new documents you create.

Factory Fresh Defaults

When QuarkXPress saves a default, it stores that information in a special preferences file. That's the key to understanding how you can set all of your QuarkXPress defaults back to their original settings. To get back the preset defaults—the ones that were in place when the box left the factory—you delete QuarkXPress' preferences file. The next time you open QuarkXPress, the program will generate a new preferences file to replace the one you deleted, and will contain the standard, preset defaults.

(Mac) To reset Macintosh QuarkXPress defaults back to factory fresh settings, quit the program and open the folder where you have installed QuarkXPress, probably something like "QuarkXPress 4.0 Folder." Find the file named "XPress Preferences" and either rename it or discard it in the Trash.

(Win95) To reset Windows 95 QuarkXPress defaults, exit the program. In the folder where you have installed QuarkXPress, probably something like "QuarkXPress," rename or discard the file "XPress Preferences."

Summary

The exercises in this chapter should have given you a basic understanding of how QuarkXPress works—and built up your confidence that you can handle its features. In the next chapter, you will actually put those features to work and from scratch you will build the stationery design you used as a base for experimentation in this chapter.

Review It

As a review of what you have learned in this chapter, please answer the following questions.

1. What's the work advantage to setting up a QuarkXPress document as a template?

2. Name at least three ways you can set the magnification of your view in QuarkXPress.

3. What keyboard shortcut would you use to get the Zoom tool to create a custom magnification view?

4. Where can you find keyboard shortcuts for commands on the menus?

5. What's the advantage of having palettes?

6. How do you position palettes? Open and close them?

7. What are the three types of QuarkXPress defaults and preferences?

8. How are the Content and Item tools different?

9. How are picture boxes and text boxes alike?

_____

_____

10. How do you switch between any tool and the Item tool?

_____

_____

Check It

Multiple Choice

Please circle the correct answer for each of the following questions.

1. You can switch palettes on and off through_____.

   a.   Menus

   b.   Keyboard shortcuts

   c.   close box

   d.   all of the above

2. The keyboard shortcuts ⌘+Tab (Mac) or Ctrl+Alt+Tab (Win95) will_____.

   a.   rotate the tool selection

   b.   switch between open document windows

   c.   close the selected open window

   d.   activate the Zoom tool

3. Holding down the Control key while selecting a tool____.

   a.   opens up tool preferences

   b.   closes the Tool palette

   c.   adds an alternate tool to palette

   d.   selects Item tool

4. QuarkXPress has how many kinds of items?

   a.   Five

   b.   Two

   c.   Three

   d.   Four

5. In order to add text to a page, you can____.

   a.   use the Get Text command

   b.   draw a text box

   c.   select text box

   d.   all of the above

6. In order to edit text or position a picture in a box, you need the_____.

   a.   item tool

   b.   magnifying glass

   c.   content tool

   d.   box tool

7. The signal that the full view mode is on when you are sizing or moving an item is____.

   a.   a momentary flash

   b.   a gray shade on the box

   c.   blinking cursor

   d.   all of the above

8. The ⌘+Z (Mac) or Ctrl+Z (Win95) keyboard shortcut will____.

   a.   cancel a pending move

   b.   undo an action

   c.   turn on the Zapf Dingbats font

   d.   switch off Preview mode

9. Through the Ctrl+V (Mac) or Ctrl+Alt+V (Win95) keyboard shortcut, you can____.

   a. paste the Clipboard contents

   b. access the percentage view field

   c. turn on Preview mode

   d. close the View menu

10. You can navigate to a specific page by____.

   a. selecting it in the Layout palette

   b. using PgDn or PgUp

   c. using ⌘+← or → (Mac) or Ctrl+← or → (Win95)

   d. all of the above

True or False

Please circle *T* or *F* to indicate whether the statement is true or false.

T F **1.** You set a document default for QuarkXPress by holding down Option (Mac) or Alt (Win95) while selecting an item.

T F **2.** An application preference can be set with the **Edit>Preferences** command.

T F **3.** If you have a document open when you set a document default, the default will apply to all future documents.

T F **4.** Template files can contain text and pictures.

T F **5.** You can center a view on an item by selecting that item before changing the magnification.

T F **6.** Adding Option (Mac) or Alt (Win95) to the Zoom tool will double its magnification.

T F **7.** You can use the Modify command to modify the QuarkXPress magnification levels.

T F **8.** Adding pages to QuarkXPress documents is as simple as **Page>Insert**.

T F **9.** The pop-out menus on some tools control which tools show on the Tools palette.

T F **10.** No matter what tool you have active, you can temporarily get to the Item tool by holding down ⌘ (Mac) or Ctrl (Win95).

Design It

In upcoming chapters of the book, you will use the exercises in this section to launch into your own design work, putting your new skills to work in independent exercises. At this point, however, it would be a bit premature to give you a full design project. Here are some suggestions for some independent work that will help you solidify your new knowledge of QuarkXPress.

■ Use the Item tool to select a text box and reposition it.

■ Even though we haven't used it in a formal exercise, give the Rotation tool a spin by rotating the text box.

■ Switch to the Content tool and edit the text. Rename the store. Change the address and phone number.

■ Generally, get crazy and go down the Tools palette, using each one in turn on the stationery page to get the feel of how they work.

Creating a New Publication

What You Will Learn

Your overall goal in Part One is to get a quick start with Quark—to become functional just as soon as possible in a desktop publishing design studio. In this second of two introductory chapters, you will complete your quick start by actually going to work on a simple, easy-to-produce desktop publishing project.

Using the exercises in this chapter, you will create some personal letterhead stationery and, in the process, you will:

➤ Set up basic page information for the publication, including page size and margins

➤ Import text to start the layout

➤ Create a text box and enter text

➤ Select and format the text

➤ Create a picture box and import a graphic to enhance the letterhead design

➤ Position these elements on the page using several different techniques, including ruler guides and the Measurement palette

➤ Print your final page on a desktop printer

Anne's Elegant Rose Place

Landscape Design • Garden Maintenance
1267 Hoedown Highway • Teaneck, Oregon 29346 • 503-923-0050 • Fax: 503-923-0060

Figure 2.1

Your finished letterhead will look like this familiar document, the one you used for "Taking A Quick Tour" in Chapter 1.

The name and address on the letterhead has been set in the Goudy Sans font. As in Chapter 1, this font can be found on the CD-ROM that accompanies this book.

Font expert Sean Cavanaugh, who assembled the collection of fonts on the CD-ROM, describes Goudy Sans as a humanist sans serif font. By humanist, he means that the font has a drawn appearance, is not purely geometric. Serifs are the tiny flags at the ends of the stems of letters. Sans serif fonts have no flags.

In his book, *Digital Type Design Guide*, Sean says, "Of all the sans serifs, the Humanists are probably the most versatile and well-suited for a variety of tasks. For example, they work equally well as text faces as they do in headlines and subheads or in callouts and captions." He says that Goudy Sans is "the quirkiest of the Humanist sans serifs," noting that Goudy Sans actually "has very slight hints of serifs on most of its stems," even though it is generally considered a sans serif font.

He also points out that it's common, but not necessary, to combine different typefaces in a document, specifically sans serif designs with serifs. If you decide to take that route, he says, "most sans serifs, especially when used in heavier bold weights, combine well with most serif typefaces for accent." In other words, you can't go far wrong using sans serif type for headlines and serif type for body copy.

I chose Goudy Sans for this letterhead because of the flag stroke at the top of the capital letter "A," which makes a jaunty visual connection to the sketch of the rose.

Of course, the sketch of the rose was chosen because it clearly identifies the commercial purpose of the business, "Anne's Elegant Rose Place."

Prep Notes

If your computer lab instructor has not already done so, copy the files for this chapter from the CD-ROM to a work area on your hard drive. They are all in the **Steps** folder in the folder labeled **02**.

You will need the font Goudy Sans to be installed on your computer. The typefaces used for the projects in this book can all be found on the CD-ROM. If you don't know how to install fonts, ask your instructor for help. Also, some helpful font management basics have been covered in Appendixes A and B, which you will also find on the CD-ROM.

Creating a New Publication

The basic concept of starting a new QuarkXPress publication is a lot like starting a new document in your word processor or spreadsheet program. You use the File>New command. There are some nuances to the process, however, and you learn about them in the following exercise as you begin building your letterhead project.

1. In QuarkXPress, once you have used the new file command, you have a selection of items you can create.

    After you have opened the program, select File>New>Document as in Figure 2.2.

    Notice that we'll be showing you pictures from the Macintosh version of QuarkXPress. As we discussed in Chapter 1, the Macintosh and Windows versions are almost exactly alike except for the cosmetic differences created by the two different operating systems.

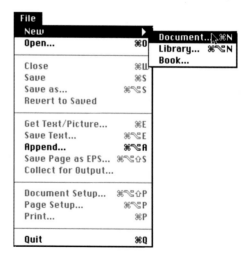

Figure 2.2

Using the menus to create a new QuarkXPress document.

Notice that you could have used a keyboard short-cut to go directly to the next step, ⌘+N (Mac) or Ctrl+N (Win95).

2. Examine the New Document dialog box. You can see a number of options for setting up your letter-head page, as in Figure 2.3.

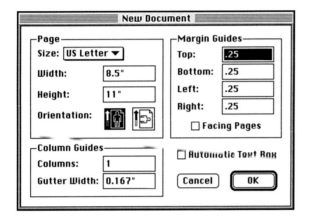

Figure 2.3

The New Document dialog box.

By default, some of the most important settings are already in place. The page **S**ize should be US Letter with a **W**idth of 8.5" and a **H**eight of 11". The Orientation should be vertical, which is **P**ortrait.

Setting Margins

3. For this letterhead project, you do need to make a change in the default Margin Guides settings. Start with the top margin.

If you are on a Macintosh, click in the field for top margin. Use Del to remove the old default set-ting of .5, and type in **.25**.

If you are working in a Win95 environment, instead of clicking in the top margin field, try the hot key feature of that operating system (not available on the Mac). Hold down Alt and press T. Use Del to remove the old default setting of .5, and type in **.25**. (By the way, you don't neces-sarily have to delete before typing. Notice that the old setting was highlighted when you selected that top margin field. You can just type right over the top of it.)

Tabbing Between Fields

4. Press Tab⇄ once and you will be transported to the next field, **B**ottom margin. Notice that the entire content of this field has been highlighted.

Whenever you see this kind of highlighting—it's one of the big advantages of tabbing between fields—you don't need to delete what's there. You can just type over the top of it to replace it.

Simply type **.25** to replace the default margin set-ting of .5.

Continue on tabbing and typing **.25** until all four margins are set at **.25** inches.

5. One more thing needs to be done in this New Document dialog box. Click the checkbox off for the **A**utomatic Text Box.

We'll be talking more about the Automatic Text Box feature in Chapter 3. It puts a text box on each new page you create in the document (as long as that page has the default master page assigned to it). The point is to make it easier in some design circumstances to flow text from one page to the other. We don't need it for this project, since this is a letterhead design.

OK Button

6. Notice that the OK button has a dark border around it.

Whenever you see that emphasis on a button, either on the Mac or in Win95, it means the "focus" is on that button. Instead of using the mouse to click OK, you can press Return (Mac) or ↵Enter (Win95) to accept the settings in the New Document dialog box and close it.

7. The view will probably be at 100%, too big to get an overview on most screens.

Press ⌘+0 (Mac) or Ctrl+0 (Win95) to get the Fit In Window view and you'll see that you've created a blank document with a narrow margin guide around its outside edge as in Figure 2.4.

Don't forget. The Fit In Window command is a zero, not the letter "o."

8. Save your letterhead project working file on your hard drive by using the same procedure you learned in Chapter 1.

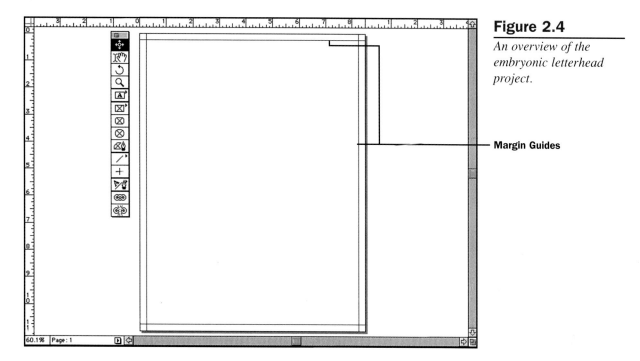

Figure 2.4

An overview of the embryonic letterhead project.

Margin Guides

● A current copy of the letterhead project has been included on your CD-ROM as file **02BASE01.QXT**.

Typing in Text

Almost nothing can go on a QuarkXPress page unless you first create a box to hold it. In this exercise, you draw a text box and then fill it with text. In later exercises, you will format the text, position the text box on the page, and learn how to create and use graphics boxes.

1. Open the letterhead project from the end of the last exercise.

    Set the view at Fit In Window and make sure the Tool palette is showing. Use F8 to bring it up, if necessary.

Choosing a Text Box Tool

2. Select the rectangular text box tool from the Tool palette as in Figure 2.5. It's the one with the letter "A" in it.

    You can either click it with the mouse or use ⌘+Tab or ⌘+Shift+Tab (Mac) or Ctrl+Alt+Tab or Shift+Ctrl+Alt+Tab (Win95) to maneuver to it.

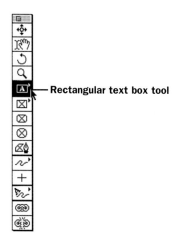

Rectangular text box tool

Figure 2.5

Selecting the text box tool.

Drawing a Text Box

3. Notice that the tool is a crosshair shape, like a plus sign.

    Click the top margin guide one-third of the way from the left edge of the page and drag the crosshair down and to the right until you have a box that reaches the right margin guide. It should be about a couple of inches high, as in Figure 2.6.

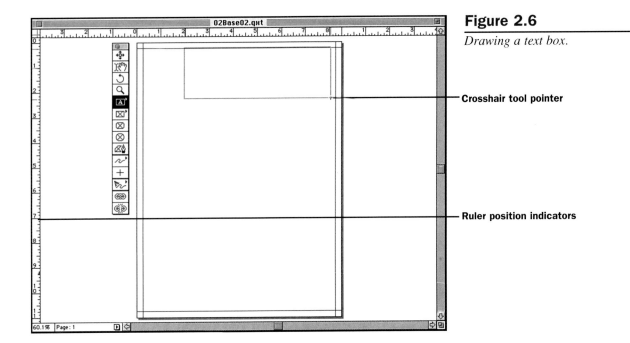

Figure 2.6

Drawing a text box.

— Crosshair tool pointer

— Ruler position indicators

As you draw your text box, observe the sliding dotted line indicators on the rulers at the top and left side of the QuarkXPress window. That will give you a pretty good idea of where you are on the page. However, don't be too concerned right now about exact dimensions. We'll set those in another step.

4. Release the mouse when you have the box drawn out to roughly the right dimensions and you will have a text box.

You can see that the text box is selected because the sizing handles at its corners and along its sides are visible.

Tool Reversion

5. Notice that the Tool palette, after you released the mouse, reverted to either the Content or the Item tool. You get one or the other, depending on which one you have most recently chosen. For example, if you had the Item tool in effect and then chose half a dozen different tools—but never the Content tool—and then drew a text box, then the tool would revert to the Item tool.

In fact, as you can see in Figure 2.7, that's what happened to us. We had our Item tool in effect at some point before drawing this box and the tool reverted to it instead of the Content tool.

If you aren't already there, navigate to the Content tool. That's what you need next to enter some text in this text box.

The fastest way to get there would be to simply press ⌘+Tab (Mac) or ⌘+Alt+Tab (Win95) to move down in the palette or add the ◆Shift key to the keyboard shortcut combination to move up in the palette. Of course, you could always just click on the Content tool, the second one down in the tool palette.

Tip

Retain Your Chosen Tool

Hold down the Option (Mac) or Alt (Win95) key while first selecting a tool. That will tell QuarkXPress that you want that tool to stay in effect so it won't switch back to the Item or Content tool every time you perform a move.

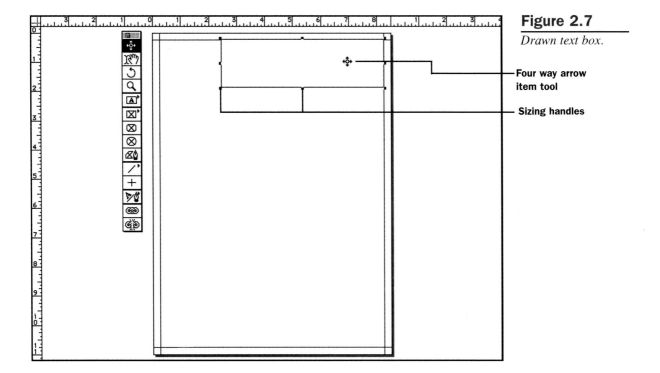

Figure 2.7

Drawn text box.

Four way arrow
item tool

Sizing handles

Typing Text

6. Since the text box was selected, as soon as you have the Content tool activated you will get a blinking text cursor inside the text box, ready to receive your typed text.

Type out the words `Annie's Elegant Rose Place`.

Ungreeking Text Display

7. Depending on the size of computer display you are using, the text you type may not be visible. Instead, it may display as a gray bar where the letters should be.

To see your text better at smaller sizes use the command **Edit>Preferences>D**ocument to reach the Document Preferences dialog you see in Figure 2.8. You can get there quickly with a keyboard shortcut, ⌘+Ⓨ (Mac) or Ctrl+Ⓨ (Win95).

Uncheck the Greek **B**elow setting and press Return (Mac) or ⏎Enter (Win95) to OK the change.

If your text was greeked before, just showing as a gray bar, it won't be greeked now, Figure 2.9.

Actually, the gray bar isn't real greeking as typographers usually use the term. Greeking often is actual type although the type usually spells out nonsense words that have been inserted as a placeholder on the page.

8. Save your work so you can pick up where you've left off at the beginning of the next exercise.

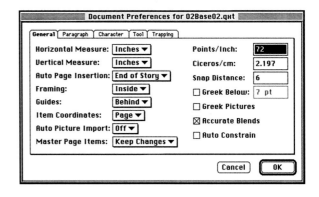

Figure 2.8

The Document Preferences dialog box.

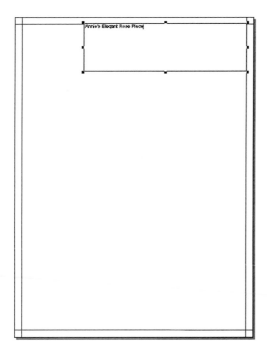

Figure 2.9

Letterhead with its first text.

● A copy of the letterhead project as it should look so far has been included on your CD-ROM as file **02BASE02.QXT**.

Formatting Text

Obviously, the text you just typed in just won't do for this letterhead. It should be much bigger and it should be in the special font we've called for in the design. The following steps will show you how to accomplish those design tasks, picking up from where you left off from the last exercise.

1. Choose the Content tool and click Annie's Elegant Rose Place text box at the top of the page.

Select All Text

2. Select all the text in the text box by pressing ⌘+Ⓐ (Mac) or Ctrl+Ⓐ (Win95).

All the text should be highlighted.

That is, it should be highlighted assuming you actually did select the Content tool in the last step. If you, maybe, had the Item tool selected, all the items on your page would be selected instead. In this case, that's just the text box.

Choosing a Typeface

3. Use a menu command to format the text— Style>Font, and choose Goudy Sans as in Figure 2.10.

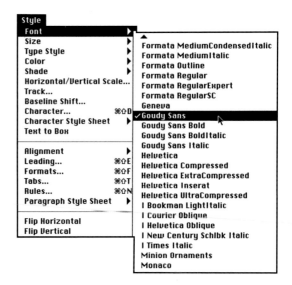

Figure 2.10

Assigning a typeface to text.

Choosing a Type Size

4. Now make the type bigger. With all the text still selected, use Style>Size and select the 36 point size from the list as in Figure 2.11.

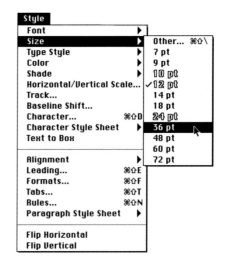

Figure 2.11

Choosing a type size.

Styling Type as Bold and Italic

5. Style the type as bold using the Style>Type Style command, selecting **Bold** from the list as in Figure 2.12.

6. Notice in Figure 2.12 that there are a number of keyboard shortcuts for the type styles. Use ⌘+Shift+I (Mac) or Ctrl+Shift+I (Win95) to set your type in the italic style. Your type should now look like Figure 2.13.

7. Save your work so you'll be ready to start the next exercise.

• The present state of the letterhead project has been saved as a template file on your CD-ROM. It's named **02BASE03.QXT**.

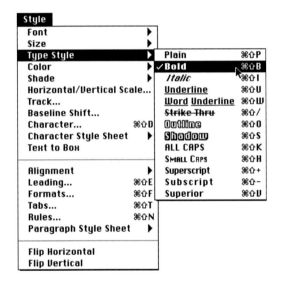

Figure 2.12

Choosing a type style.

Importing Text

For many projects you need to import text files that have been submitted to you for page layout. Even if you are generating the text, sometimes there's so much of it that it is easier to create the text initially in your word processor rather than type it directly into QuarkXPress. In such cases you need to be able to import word processor text and that's the process you will learn about in this next exercise.

1. As you have already learned, you need a box to put most anything (except a line or text on a line) on a QuarkXPress page.

   Select the Rectangle Text Box tool.

   Get to Fit in Window view using the ⌘+0 (Mac) or Ctrl+0 (Win95) keyboard shortcut.

2. Click the lower left corner of the margins, where the left margin and the bottom margin meet, and drag up and to the right to draw out a rectangle with the cross hair pointer.

   You want to draw out a text box that runs from left margin to right margin, and its bottom edge should rest on the bottom margin. Looking at the vertical ruler, this new text box should be about an inch high. Figure 2.14 shows how this text box should look.

3. Make sure you have the Content tool selected. Notice that a text insertion point is blinking in the new text box.

   This is crucial. You must have the text box selected with the Content tool before importing a word processor file. Otherwise QuarkXPress won't know where to put the imported text on your page.

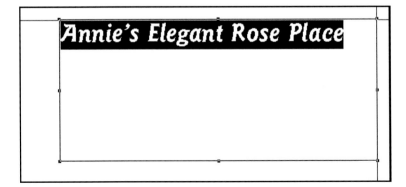

Figure 2.13

Type formatted properly for the top of the letterhead

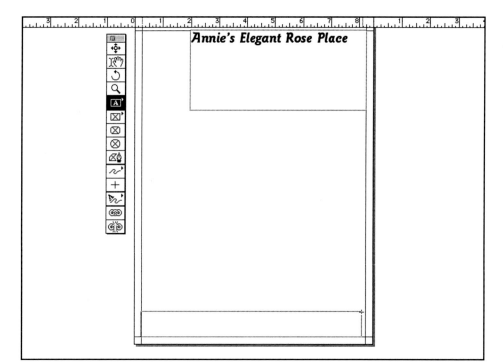

Figure 2.14

Drawing out a new text box for the rose shop address

4. Now you can bring in the word processor text. We have provided a file for you to import on the CD-ROM. You will find it in the Steps folder, in the folder called 02. It's called **ADDRESS.DOC**.

This file should have already been copied to a work area on your own computer from the CD-ROM at the beginning of this exercise. If it wasn't, do that now. Do not import the file directly from the CD-ROM.

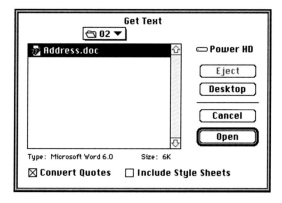

Figure 2.15

Getting the text to be imported.

> **Tip**
>
> **Don't Import From Removable Media**
>
> In general, no matter what program you are working in, it's a bad idea to import files from CD-ROMs, Zip drives, floppies, or other removable media. In many cases, and this is particularly true of graphics files in QuarkXPress, the program will ask you to have the CD-ROM available every time you open your publication. If you ever send the publication outside to a client or to a commercial printer you will be forced to send the CD-ROM with it.

Use the **File>G**et Text command and you will see the dialog box in Figure 2.15.

5. Click the file ADDRESS.DOC and click Open.

Remember, since there's a dark border on the Open button that means it has the focus and you could also simply press [Return] (Mac) or [↵Enter] (Win95). You could also double-click the file name to open it.

The text will come in with an extra line, probably, so just press [Del] (Mac) or [←Backspace] (Win95) to get rid of it.

6. Go to a closer view to have a look at this new text.

    Hold down Ctrl (Mac) or Ctrl+Spacebar (Win95) to get the Zoom tool and drag out a marquee around the text box so you can blow it up to a larger size as in Figure 2.16.

Selecting the Picture Box Tool

2. Of course, by now you know that you will need a QuarkXPress box in which to place the rose.

    Select the Rectangle Picture Box tool. It's the one with the "X" in it, right below the Text Box tool.

Figure 2.16

Pre-formatted address text.

Good news. The text has been formatted already. QuarkXPress "reads" whatever formatting you impose on the text in your word processor—in this case the type has been centered and set in 14-point Goudy Sans Italic.

7. As always at the end of an exercise, save your work so you'll be able to pick up where you left off.

    Note: At this point in your learning process we hope we have made our point that you should make a habit of saving your work as you go. We'll stop boring you with these reminders every single time.

On your CD-ROM, as usual, we have saved the present progress on the letterhead project for you. The name of the file for the exercises conducted so far is **02BASE04.QXT**.

Importing a Graphic

Just as you need to import text for many QuarkXPress projects, you also need to import pictures. They may be scans of photographs, clip art, or other electronic illustration material. In this case we need the rose for the upper left corner of this letterhead design. Use the following exercise to get that picture.

1. Set your view at Fit In Window, in case you have picked up from the last exercise where you ended up with a magnified view.

Drawing a Picture Box

3. Drawing a picture box works just like drawing a text box.

    Click the cross hair pointer in the upper left corner of the margins where the left margin meets the top margin and drag down and to the right until you have a box that's roughly about 2 inches wide by 2.5 inches tall.

    You can gauge the size by the vertical and horizontal rulers. Don't worry about being too precise because you'll make adjustments in an upcoming exercise.

    The picture box is selected because you just drew it. That's important. As with the text import process, before you can import a file you must select its box so QuarkXPress knows where to put it. Unlike Get Text, however, you can have either the Item or the Content tool selected when you use Get Picture.

Importing the Graphic

4. Now get the graphic, again very much the same kind of process you used to import your word processor text.

    Use **File>Get** Picture to reach the dialog in Figure 2.17. Although this Macintosh version of the dialog looks a bit different from the Windows version, all the same elements are there, including a thumbnail-sized preview of the picture.

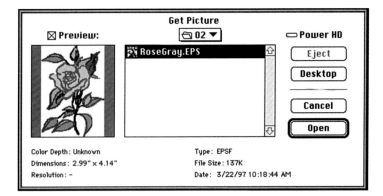

Figure 2.17
The Get Picture dialog box.

When you pull down the File menu notice two things. First, the Get Picture command has replaced the Get Text command because you have a picture box selected. Second, there's a keyboard shortcut you could use for Get Picture, ⌘+E (Mac) or Ctrl+E (Win95).

5. Double-click the file **ROSEGRAY.EPS** to Open it. In this case, even thought the button says "open," we are actually importing it.

The **ROSEGRAY.EPS** file should have already been copied to a work area on your computer. If not, you can copy it now. It is in the Steps folder in the subfolder named **02**.

When you return from the Get Picture dialog to your QuarkXPress page you will notice that the rose isn't completely showing.

Think of the picture box as a sort of window on your graphic, showing you just one part of it if the graphic is too big to fit completely through the window.

6. To size the graphic, reduce it so it shows completely. You can use the **Item>Modify** command.

All the letterhead elements have now been placed on the page, although they have yet to be sized and positioned properly. Our page looked like Figure 2.18 at this point.

The file **02BASE05.QXT** on your CD-ROM contains the letterhead as it should exist now with all the exercises completed so far.

Putting the Modify Command to Work

There aren't many QuarkXPress commands that do more work—and are therefore more important—than the Modify command. It's a sort of command center for setting everything from size to position, and from color to angle of rotation. And you can apply it to anything that goes onto a QuarkXPress page—including a text box, a picture box, or a line.

In this exercise, you will use the Modify command to perfectly size and position the rose graphic on your letterhead page.

1. Select the Item tool and click once on the rose graphic to select it.

Actually, you could also use the Content tool in this situation.

Activating Modify

2. Use **Item>Modify** to activate the Modify dialog box you see in Figure 2.19.

You could also use a keyboard shortcut for the Modify command, ⌘+M (Mac) or Ctrl+M (Win95). And, if you have the Item tool chosen, you can double-click an item to open up the Modify dialog box.

Using Dialog Box Tabs

3. The Modify command's dialog box offers different options depending on what kind of item you have chosen. It looks quite a bit different, for example, if you **Item>Modify** a line.

Figure 2.18

The letterhead with all the elements on the page.

The Modify command for a picture box has five layers of options, each one indicated by one of the tabs at the top of the box—Box, Picture, Frame, Clipping, Runaround—and you will use each one of them during this course.

Dialog box tabs

	Modify

Box | Picture | Frame | Clipping | Runaround

Origin Across: `0.25"`

Origin Down: `0.25"`

Width: `1.784"`

Height: `2.25"`

Angle: `0°`

Skew: `0°`

Corner Radius: `0"`

☐ Suppress Printout

Box
Color: White ▼
Shade: `100%` ▼

Blend
Style: Solid ▼
Angle: `0°` ▼
Color: White ▼
Shade: `100%` ▼

(Apply)   (Cancel)   (**OK**)

Press ⌘+Tab⇆ (Mac) or Ctrl+Tab⇆ (Win95) to rotate among all the options. A new tab is selected every time you press the keyboard shortcut, which works anytime you see one of these multi-layered, tab-equipped dialog boxes.

Of course, you could also select a tab by simply clicking it with your mouse.

Setting the Item Origin Point

4. Choose the Box tab.

QuarkXPress always calculates the position of an object by how far its upper-left corner sits from the upper-left corner of the page.

Actually, to be precise, the calculation is from the zero point. In this case your zero point is where it normally sits, which is at the upper-left corner of the page. The zero point is the imaginary point where the zero on the horizontal ruler intersects with the zero on the vertical ruler. You can move the zero point by clicking and dragging on the intersecting dotted lines in the square located in the upper left corner of the QuarkXPress window.

The Origin Across and Origin Down amounts should be right at, or close to, .25 inches. That's because you drew the picture box by starting at the upper left margin corner and the margins were all set to .25 inches.

If your Origin settings aren't exactly .25 inches, select those fields and type in the correct amount.

Figure 2.19

The Modify dialog box, with a picture box selected.

Setting the Box Size

5. Use the Tab key to get to the **W**idth setting.

    Keep in mind that, with the Box tab chosen, you are setting attributes for the picture box, not for the graphic that's inside it.

    As with all dialog boxes you could also have used the mouse to select the Width field. In Windows 95, you could also have used the hotkey of (Alt)+(W).

6. Set the Width to 1.6 inches.

7. Tab once more to get to the Height field. Set it to 2.125 inches.

    Your Origin, Width, and Height setting should look like the ones in Figure 2.20.

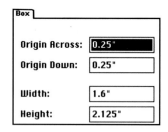

Figure 2.20

The correct Picture box Modify command settings.

Setting the Picture Size

8. (⌘)+(Tab) (Mac) or (Ctrl)+(Tab) (Win95) once to select the Picture tab.

    This layer of the Modify command dialog box allows you to work on the contents of the picture box.

9. Tab to the Scale Across setting (or use your mouse to get there) and change the setting from 100% to 50%.

Making QuarkXPress Do Arithmetic

10. Tab again to get to the Scale Down setting.

    In most QuarkXPress dialog boxes, you can have QuarkXPress do your arithmetic for you. In this case, we know that we want the picture box contents to be half the full size (50%).

    Press ↵ and notice that the blinking text insertion point acts just like it does in a word processor. Get the cursor to the end of the 100% entry, right after the percent sign. In other words, you can edit this entry.

    Add a division mark and a 2 so it looks like Figure 2.21. Dividing the 100% entry by 2—it looks just like a fraction—means cutting it in half to 50%.

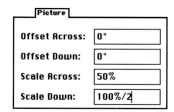

Figure 2.21

Dividing an entry in half.

11. (⬆Shift)+(Tab) to move the focus back up to Scale Across and you will see that QuarkXPress automatically does the division and changes 100% to 50%.

    You should now have 50% in both the Scale Across and Scale Down fields.

12. Press (Return) (Mac) or (↵Enter) (Win95) to OK the all of the various Modify command box and picture settings you have just completed.

    That's one of the main advantages of the Modify command. It lets you accomplish a great deal of work in one fast and easy-to-use location.

    Your results should look like Figure 2.22.

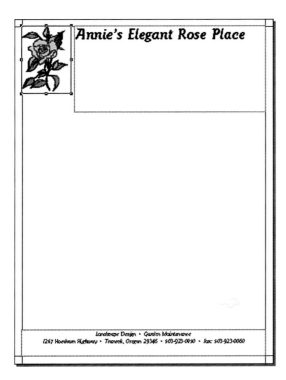

Figure 2.22

The properly sized and positioned rose picture box as it should look on the page at this stage of work.

If you need to pick up where this exercise left off to do the upcoming exercise, you can open up the file named **02BASE06.QXT** from your CD-ROM. It shows what the letterhead design should look like, including each step from all the exercises so far in this chapter.

Positioning by Eye and Ruler Guide

Many times when you are working on a design you simply won't know that you want a picture reduced by half or that its picture box should be exactly 1.6 inches wide. In those situations you do a lot of experimenting, positioning items by eye to see how they look together.

In this exercise, you'll adjust the text at the top of the page to the correct position in relation to the rose.

1. Set the view to Fit In Window, ⌘+⓪ (Mac) or Ctrl+⓪ (Win95).

Because this view gives you an overview of the entire page, it's a good magnification to use when you are first trying to position items on a page.

Sizing a Box

2. Using the Item tool, select the text box located at the top of the page.

    Move the mouse pointer over the sizing handle at the bottom center of the box. You'll know you are in the correct location when the pointer turns into a miniature hand with the index finger extended as in Figure 2.23.

    By the way, we asked you to use the Item tool here but you could also have used the Content tool to size the box.

Sizing handle   Mouse pointer hand

Figure 2.23

Using a sizing handle to adjust the size of a text box.

3. With the hand pointer activated, click the sizing handle.

    Hold down the mouse button without moving the mouse for just a moment until the text flashes slightly. When you see that flash you know you are in QuarkXPress' animation mode and that means you can see the effects of your moves in real time, before you release the mouse button.

    Experiment a bit by making the text box too short to hold all the text. Notice that if you go too far the text will disappear. There will be a little red square in its place letting you know that you have overset text, as it's called, as you see in Figure 2.24.

    Finish up by sliding the bottom edge of the text box to a point just below lowest portion edge of the letter "g" in "Elegant."

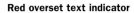
Red overset text indicator

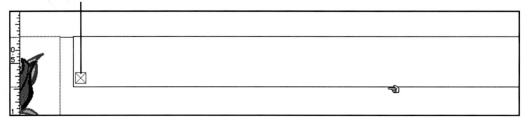

Figure 2.24

Top: Overset text, text box too short.
Bottom: Properly sized text box.

4. Still using the Item tool, click on the text box and drag it to the left and down a bit. Release the mouse button when the text box overlaps the rose.

Changing Stacking Order

5. Notice that the left edge of the text box disappears behind the rose. It's hidden behind the rose because of its stacking order.

QuarkXPress items are literally stacked in layers on the page in the order of creation, with the newest items being on the frontmost layer and the oldest ones in back.

If you remember, we created the rose picture box after the text box so the rose is in front of the text. However, you can change the stacking order.

With the text box still selected, use the **Item>** Bring To Front command and the text box will now overlap the rose. You could also use the keyboard shortcut for Bring To Front, F5.

Making Text Boxes Transparent

6. Now the text is in front of the rose but its box has obscured the rose picture as you see in the left of

Figure 2.25. You need to make the text box transparent as it is on the right side of the figure.

To make the text box transparent, you need to go back to the Modify command you used earlier in this chapter.

Double-click the text box with the Item tool to reach the Modify dialog box. If it isn't already showing, use ⌘+Tab (Mac) or Ctrl+Tab (Win95) to show the Box tab.

Change the Color to None, instead of White as in Figure 2.26, and press Return (Mac) or Enter (Win95) to OK the action.

7. From here, it's very easy to simply click and drag the text box with the Item tool to position it just where you want it.

Feel free to magnify your view for these positioning steps. It will make it easier for you to be precise.

Click and drag the text box using the Item tool and position the "A" of "Annie" so that it is centered between the two rose bud leaves you see in Figure 2.27.

Figure 2.25

Left: Text box obscures rose graphic
Right: Text box made transparent

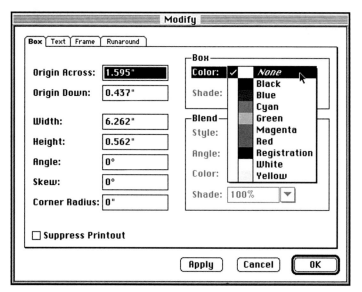

Figure 2.26

Setting a text box to be transparent.

Figure 2.27

Vertically positioning the text box.

Center between
these two leaves

Double-headed arrow pointer

Setting a Ruler Guide

8. We want to horizontally position the text box just on the right edge of those two leaves. To do so, you can use a ruler guide.

   Click and hold in the vertical ruler that runs along the left side of the QuarkXPress window. Your mouse pointer will become a double-headed arrow.

   Still holding down the mouse button, drag the mouse to the right. You will pull a line out into the main part of the window. That's a ruler guide, so named because you pull it out of one of the QuarkXPress rulers.

   Position the guide as in Figure 2.28, just touching the two leaves of the rose we used for guideposts in the last step. Release the mouse button to finalize the position of the ruler guide.

   Notice that the ruler guide goes in back of the items on the page so it won't obscure your view. That's a default setting and you can tell QuarkXPress you want ruler guides to go to the front that you can change in **Edit>Preferences>Document** dialog box.

Snapping to Ruler Guides

9. Now use the ruler guide to precisely position the left edge of the text box.

   Click and drag with the Item tool on the text box. Notice that when the left edge of the text box gets near the ruler guide it snaps to it. Release the mouse button when you have the left edge of the text box lined up with the ruler guide.

This Snap To Guides feature of QuarkXPress is normally on all the time. If you ever need to do so you can turn it off through the **View>Snap To Guides** command or by using the keyboard shortcut `◆Shift`+`F7`.

Snap To Guides works for all guides, including the margin guides. That's why you probably found that the rose picture origin point was exactly at .25 inches each way. When you drew the picture box, it snapped to the intersection of the margin guides.

The progress so far on the letterhead design has been saved as file **02BASE07.QXT** on the CD-ROM.

Using the Measurement Palette

In some ways, the Measurement palette resembles the Modify command's dialog box. You can get a lot of work done in one location. The Measurement palette has a big advantage, however, over the Modify dialog box. As we discussed in Chapter 1, palettes float over your work area. You can move them wherever you need them and, because they are so accessible, they can be a much faster tool.

In this next exercise, you will position and size the address text box.

Figure 2.28

Creating a ruler guide.

Ruler guide

1. Get to Fit In Window view, ⌘+⓪ (Mac) or Ctrl+⓪ (Win95).

2. With the Content tool, select the address text box at the bottom of the letterhead page.

Activating the Measurement Palette

3. Turn on the Measurement palette with a keyboard shortcut. Use ⌘+Option+Ⓜ (Mac) or Ctrl+Alt+Ⓜ (Win95). Notice that the first field in the palette has been automatically highlighted, ready to receive your input as in Figure 2.29.

   The other keyboard shortcut to show the Measurement palette is F9. Instead of activating the palette so you can go right to work, it just opens the palette. You could also have activated this palette by using its menu command, **V**iew>Show **M**easurements.

   One other note: the Measurement palette can look entirely different, depending on your choice of tools and items. If you had used the Item tool, only the left side of the palette would have been filled. But since you selected the Content tool, the palette is also ready to help you work with any text formatting. Also, as you would expect, the palette offers different options if, instead of a text box, you select a picture box or a line.

Scrolling with the Grabber Hand

4. You may need to move things in order to get a clear view of the text box at the bottom of the page.

If so, hold down Option (Mac) or Alt (Win95). The mouse pointer turns into a hand. Click and drag with this Grabber mouse pointer and slide the page around where you want it. Notice that using the Grabber doesn't affect your active tool and you get your chosen tool back as soon as you release the modifier key.

Moving the Measurements Palette

5. If you need to move the Measurements palette, click and drag on the gray (Mac) or blue (Win95) stripe at the left hand end of the Measurements palette.

Positioning with the Measurements Palette

6. Tab to the Y (or vertical) origin field. It's the second one down on the left end of the palette. Type in **10.25**.

   The text box won't move yet because you haven't applied your new setting. That's coming up soon.

Sizing with the Measurements Palette

7. Tab a couple more times until you are at the height field, the one that has an "H" next to it.

   Type in **.5** to correctly size the address text box.

Applying Measurements Palette Moves

8. Now apply your new settings by pressing Return (Mac) or ↵Enter (Win95).

Click and drag here to move palette   **First field activated**

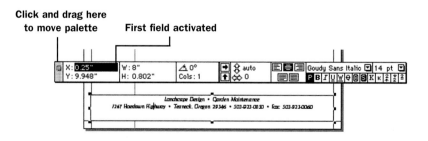

Figure 2.29

Measurement palette as it looks for a text box.

Notice that this removes the focus from the palette—deactivates it. If you have multiple moves to make in the Measurements palette it's best to wait until you have all the settings in place and apply them all at once. That is, it's best unless you need to see the effects of your moves as you go, in which case you may need to bounce back and forth between the palette and your layout several times.

Your settings for the address text box should look like the ones in Figure 2.30 and the entire letterhead (in Fit In Window view) should look like the one in Figure 2.1 at the beginning of this chapter.

9. Except for printing out a copy of your project, the letterhead is done. Save your work.

 The finished version of the letterhead has been saved on the CD-ROM in a file named **02BASE08.QXT**.

Printing out a Page

It's time to print out a proof of your letterhead project. Your instructor may need to help a bit here because there's no way we can provide instructions for all the many kinds of printer setups that exist out there in the field. However, these basic steps should work for most situations.

1. Activate the Print dialog box, **File>Print** or use the keyboard shortcuts ⌘+P (Mac) or Ctrl+P (Win95).

Choosing a Printer Description

2. This step assumes you have a printer that has PostScript built into it, the programming language that helps QuarkXPress most precisely tell the printer where to put things on the page. If your instructor says you don't have a Post-Script-capable printer you can go to the next step.

For a PostScript printer, QuarkXPress needs to know some information about your printer—what fonts it has built into it, how much memory, whether or not it has color capabilites, and so on.

⌘+Tab↹ (Mac) or Ctrl+Tab↹ (Win95) to the Setup tab in the Print dialog box, and click on the box next to the Printer Description setting as you seen in Figure 2.31.

It will probably say "Generic B&W" and you should select the name of the printer in your school's computer lab. The technical term for the special printer description file you choose in this list is the PPD, which stands for PostScript Printer Description.

3. Click the Print button, or press Return (Mac) or ↵Enter (Win95) and have a look at your completed letterhead project as it rolls out of the printer.

Figure 2.30
Correct Measurements palette settings.

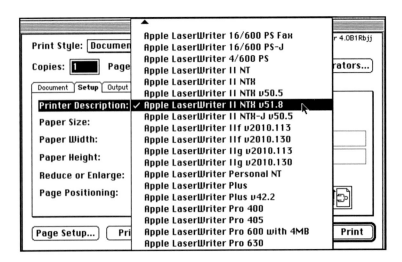

Figure 2.31
Choosing a PPD printer description in the Print dialog.

Summary

Now you have built a desktop publishing project, possibly your very first. The following questions will help you absorb all the new information you have just learned by getting you to think about this new experience in a new context.

One of the most important things you accomplished in this chapter was starting a new QuarkXPress document from scratch, setting up the page size and margins. You also performed one of the most fundamental of DTP activities, importing text and graphic elements and positioning them on your new page.

When you complete these skill check exercises, you can move on to the first of the Portfolio Builder exercises. They follow each of the five major multi-chapter sections.

Review It

As a review of what you have learned in this chapter, please answer the following questions.

1. What's the quickest way to move between fields in a QuarkXPress dialog box? To OK a dialog box action?

2. What's the number one requirement before you can put any text or graphic information on a page in QuarkXPress?

3. Some people regard this as the most powerful dialog box in QuarkXPress. Which one is it?

4. What's the measurement point on an item and the reference point on a page for locating an item?

5. If you needed to reduce a box to one-third of its size, how could you make QuarkXPress do the work for you?

6. What item will be on top in the stacking order of several items on a page?

7. What color do you use for a text box if you want it to be transparent?

8. Why should you use the ⌘+Option+M (Mac) or Ctrl+Alt+M (Win95) shortcut to call up the Measurements palette?

9. How do you apply the settings you create in the Measurements palette?

_____

_____

10. Name three main ways you can format text.

_____

_____

Check It

Multiple Choice

Please circle the correct answer for each of the following questions.

1. You can tell the difference between text and picture box tools because _____.

   a. Text box tools have the letter T for text

   b. Picture box tools contain a tiny picture

   c. Text box tools show the letter A for alphabet

   d. Picture box tools display a paintbrush

2. To prevent a tool from reverting to the Item tool after use, you _____.

   a. Press (Option) (Mac), (Alt) (Win95) when choosing the tool

   b. Press (Option) (Mac), (Alt) (Win95) when using the tool

   c. Quickly re-click the tool, within a half second

   d. All of the above

3. At low magnification views, in order to read text you may need to _____.

   a. Use the Zoom tool to go to higher magnification

   b. Use the grabber hand to draw out a marquee

   c. Turn off greeking in Document Preferences

   d. All of the above

4. To reduce the size of a picture in half you can _____.

   a. Enter 50% for Scale in the Picture section of the Modify dialog box

   b. Divide the 100% Scale by 2 in the Picture section of the Modify dialog box

   c. Enter 50% for X and Y scale in Measurements palette

   d. All of the above

5. To give your ruler guides extra positioning power you should _____.

   a. Press (F5)

   b. Turn on Snap To Guides

   c. Work at 200% view

   d. All of the above

6. To bring an object to the top of the stacking order you _____.

   a. Select it with the Item tool

   b. Drag it to the top with the Grabber hand

   c. Select it and press (F5)

   d. All of the above

7. When importing files from a CD-ROM you should always _____.

   a. Copy them to your hard drive first

   b. Check them for viruses

   c. Send the CD-ROM along with the file if you share it

   d. All of the above

8. The keyboard shortcut to style text in italics is _____.

   a. ⌘+I (Mac), Ctrl+I (Win95)

   b. ⌘+Shift+I (Mac), Ctrl+Shift+I (Win95)

   c. Alt+I (Mac), Option+I (Win95)

   d. All of the above

9. The PPD file tells QuarkXPress what _____.

   a. Details of your PostScript printer's memory and built-in fonts

   b. Your preferences settings

   c. The source of your imported CD-ROM files

   d. All of the above

10. You can start a new QuarkXPress file by _____.

   a. Using the **File>New>Document** command

   b. Pressing ⌘+N (Mac) or Ctrl+N (Win95)

   c. Opening a template file

   d. All of the above

True or False

Please circle *T* or *F* to indicate whether the statement is true or false.

T F **1.** You can temporarily switch to the Zoom tool at any time by pressing Ctrl (Mac) or Ctrl+Spacebar (Win95).

T F **2.** Get the grabber hand to scroll your view by holding down the ⌘ (Mac) or Ctrl (Win95) keys.

T F **3.** You can choose among multiple tools at any of the Tool palette locations that show a small arrowhead.

T F **4.** Move from field to field in a dialog box by pressing ⌘+Tab (Mac) or Ctrl+Tab (Win95).

T F **5.** Move from dialog box tab to dialog box tab by pressing ⌘+Tab (Mac) or Ctrl+Tab (Win95).

T F **6.** The Portrait page orientation gives you a horizontal format page.

T F **7.** You can always tell you have a box tool chosen when your pointer is in the form of a crosshair.

T F **8.** To select all the text in a text box with an active text cursor you press ⌘+A (Mac) or Ctrl+A (Win95).

T F **9.** To adopt new settings in the measurement palette just Tab to the next item.

T F **10.** The measurement palette always contains the same items, no matter what kind of item you have selected.

Design It

Explore the design possibilities of this very simple stationery layout. Move the three items on the page around into different relationships to see whether you think this is the best way to have designed the job.

■ What if you arranged things so that the name of the company and its address information were together, instead of split between the top and the bottom of the page?

■ Would you like it better if the rose was in a different position, perhaps at the right corner instead of the left one? If you move the rose, what's the best way to position and align the rest of the text?

■ Create at least three variations of this design by rearranging the items and print them out.

■ How will you decide which design is the best one? Live with the designs by tacking them up. Ask other people which they like best, and ask which they would prefer if they were paying for the design.

Illustrate Yourself

Why Portfolio Builders?

The Portfolio Builder sections in this book are all aimed at one thing—helping you get work. There's a Portfolio Builder after each of the five major multi-chapter parts of the text.

Newcomers, and many veterans, often put together a portfolio of their work to show to potential clients and employers. This portfolio can showcase their experience and abilities—sort of a visual resumé. Some people taking this course will have experience with page layout and design, and might be taking this course to learn only about QuarkXPress 4. But most of you will be new to graphic design. That means, as a student, you probably don't have much of a body of work to display. And what you do have is clearly student work done in the classroom, not real world design work.

We can't magically bulk up your experience level with paying design jobs to put in your portfolio. We can, however, help you create a beginning portfolio that will make you stand head and shoulders above the rest and will bring out the best of your talents.

In addition to our own experiences viewing portfolios in an ad agency environment, we've also interviewed a dozen design professionals to get their suggestions, which we'll be passing on to you. Each Portfolio Builder section will have two parts—an exercise for a project that you can put in your portfolio, followed by a portfolio advice section.

Exercise—Business Identity Kit

One well-known designer, when interviewed for these Portfolio Builder sections, said we should tell you this fundamental truth about portfolios: "When you put together a portfolio, you are illustrating yourself."

The point is, your portfolio ought to reflect you, not your classroom exercises—your design aesthetic, your skills, your experience, and your professionalism. It's no good for you to be one of the 20 or more new designers around town who have a rose stationery design in your portfolio. You must build something new and different that tells your story.

So, in this Portfolio Builder exercise, you quite literally illustrate yourself. You create a business identity kit for your own use. Think of it this way…what better way to illustrate yourself as a designer than by telling your own story, in graphic form, through your personally-designed stationery, business cards, resumé, and so on?

Here's a step-by-step process you might use to build a business identity kit.

■ Think first about how you want to position yourself as a designer. How would you describe your personal aesthetic to a potential employer—slick, cool, hip, avant garde, traditional, businesslike, whimsical? What two or three words would you choose to sum yourself up as a designer? That's the image that you will want to communicate in your business identity package.

■ Build on those positioning words. As a practical matter, most business identity designs are built around a single graphic element that somehow communicates to the viewer. Or, at least they spring from a central idea. So search out the graphic, typeface, line, whatever that you can use to form the core element of your business identity design.

■ Select one item from your business identity kit with which to begin. Stationery or a business card is a good place to begin, but you could also start with your resumé, some note paper, or a fax cover sheet. This will be your prototype element and will set the style for all the other elements in the kit.

■ Give some thought to how you will deal with your budget limitations. Will you need to produce these materials in small quantity through a laser printer? Can you afford to get the job run at a local quick printer shop?

■ Assuming you can't afford an expensive die cut, or scoring and folding, or color, what can you do to help this piece make a statement about your own creativity and ingenuity? Will you hand fold items? Maybe you can add a stroke of color to your pieces using water color or a felt tip pen. Do be careful to stay focused on your design goal—your positioning.

■ Keep track of your time as you work. It would be excellent if you could tell a potential employer or client how quickly you were able to conceptualize your design and then execute it to final form.

■ When you have your prototype constructed, try it out on some people whose judgment you trust. Don't just ask them if they like it. Ask them what the item makes them think about you. Are they getting your positioning words out of your design? Have you succeeded in communicating the image you wanted to convey?

■ Once you have your prototype design worked out, create the additional pieces in your business identity kit. You will want a complete set of stationery, envelope design, business card, note paper, fax cover sheet, and resumé.

■ If you can't afford to actually print all the elements of the kit, mock them up so you can include them in your portfolio. Consider just having one or two of the items printed. It makes a big impact when a student just out of school can actually show printed products in their portfolio. Wouldn't it be great to be able to leave your own business card with a potential client or employer after an interview?

At the end of this process, you will be able to show a prospective client or employer how you thought through a design from beginning to end with a design goal in mind—to convey your designer identity to prospective clients. The beauty of this approach is that it gives you a platform for expressing yourself in a job interview. You will be, in other words, illustrating yourself.

Advice—The Ideal Portfolio

For this series of Portfolio Builder exercises, we wanted to get a broad range of advice from professional designers who are out there in the field dealing with the realities of the day-to-day business world. (You can read about the backgrounds of these pros at the end of this Portfolio Builder.)

To get some input, we went online to the Compuserve Desktop Publishing Forum and threw out some questions, including, "What sorts of things do you include in your own portfolios?"

Werner Berghofer: Printed examples of "real" work I created such as business cards, ads, magazines, posters, even complete books. A lot of newspapers, too, back from the days when I used to produce infographics for a daily newspaper. Clients are impressed by work which really was printed and published, so I use "live" samples whenever possible.

Patricia Olson: I have toted portfolio pieces. However, I found that the most effective "portfolio" pieces I created were pieces which I created to market myself; meaning they were actually a live project. I depended on them to get business for me, and they did. I was able to honestly tell prospective clients, in hard numbers, how effective the pieces were.

Mike Cotterell: Just a thought but, for those items that can be viewed well as PDF files, maybe a Web-based portfolio will be the way to go in the future. I've started to generate a Web-based portfolio of some of my work on the basis that I can point anyone to it without the need to mail them anything save my Web address.

Ann Clarkson: I put most of my completed jobs in my portfolio, and shuffle them around, depending on the client's perspective. For example, if the client wants business stationery done, then those examples are at the front. If they're looking to produce a b&w news-letter, then recent issues of my regular titles are at the front. However, I still leave in other types of work, in case it gives them an idea for more work to push in my direction. Also, I should mention that shuffling the jobs in the portfolio to suit the potential client isn't always straightforward. It's very tempting to put your favorite or most technically advanced project at the front, while the client wants to see if you can lay out a page of mixed text and black and white ads. And I have two clients whose jobs *never* go into the portfolio, because their taste leans towards really bad design.

David Rozansky: My portfolio has a fully representative slice of all the work I have done. I don't shuffle, but I do know where to turn when I open it so I can dazzle the client with any unexpected desires they bring up.

Our Portfolio Builders

The professionals that provided a good deal of the raw material for these Portfolio Builder sections have our gratitude. Please allow us to introduce them.

- *Werner Berghofer* has, for 25 years, worked as a typographer and designer in Vienna, Austria. He began his career in graphics as a photographer's assistant when he was 16 years old, but says it was 1978, at a Vienna advertising agency, when he "fell in love with typography, fonts and an ancient Compugraphic Editwriter typesetting machine." For some years, in the days before personal computers took over the business, Werner worked for the world's most famous manufacturer of typesetting equipment, Linotype-Hell, teaching people how to set type. He also spent three years as a designer in the infographic department of a daily newspaper. Today he operates a well regarded design firm in Vienna.

  We should also point out that Werner created and kindly contributed the glossary of desktop publishing terms you will find on the CD-ROM accompanying this book.

- *Patricia Olson* founded Page Perspectives, a full-service graphic design and typesetting business specializing in producing catalogs and marketing materials for disability products, in 1992. Patricia is also a contributing editor for *ComputerUser* and is working on a book. Pat also volunteers on the Desktop Publishing Forum and the Professional Publishing forums on CompuServe, serving as a forum section leader.

- *Ann Clarkson* works from home in a town near Brisbane, Australia. Her main design market is newsletters, advertisements, posters, flyers, etc. for equestrian sport (mainly dressage), but referrals bring in work for other clients, including Shell Coal and petroleum industry client Santos Limited.

- *Mike Cotterell* first learned the art of lettering from his father (a signwriter who once worked for famous type designer Eric Gill). He says he never thought of developing a career using those skills until he acquired his first Mac Plus and LaserWriter. He now teaches DTP and Electronic Publishing at the University of Brighton, England and uses freelance work to ensure that he keeps abreast of developments. He says it is important that he not forget about the demands and constraints of real world publishing. Because of that, he tries to ensure that his portfolio is as varied as possible. Recent additions include a textbook for ITP, promotional literature for a games manufacturer, and a newsletter for a dog-care company.

- *Elyse Chapman* (elyse@cis.compuserve.com) is a Southern California-based graphic designer; publishing industry consultant, trainer, and speaker; contributing writer to *X-RAY Magazine* and Quark-Authorized Trainer. She has over two decades of experience in the publishing industry, from design and prepress production through press operation, bindery, and print shop management. She is a managing Sysop on CompuServe's Desktop Publishing and Professional Publishing forums.

- *David Rozansky* is a freelance writer and editor. His prior credits include Special Sections Editor for *General Aviation News & Flyer*, General Partner and Editor of *Rocky Mountain Air Traveler*, and Section Editor–USA Transportation and Government Policy for *Government Review*. Mr. Rozansky lives in Hartford, Connecticut.

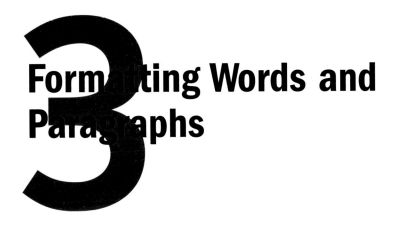

3 Formatting Words and Paragraphs

What You Will Learn

In this chapter, you will build a simple price sheet like the one you see in Figure 3.1. This simple design will provide the basis for a more sophisticated design that you will create in Chapter 4.

In the process of creating the initial price sheet design, you will:

➤ Get a better understanding of standard units for measuring type attributes—points, picas, and ems

➤ Learn how to link text boxes so your imported text falls into placeholders on your pages

➤ Gain new techniques for selecting and formatting text

➤ Learn news ways to assign typeface, size, and style (bold, italic) attributes to type

➤ Align paragraph text as centered, left-aligned, right-aligned, and justified type

➤ Use tabs to set columns of words and numbers

➤ Create paragraph indents

➤ Establish paragraph rules

Steamhouse Lighting
Spring Special Price List[1]

Specialty Items

Piano/Picture Lamp	120 volt, 40 watt	$4.99/pair
Candelabra Frosted Flame Tip	120 volt, 60 watt	$2.49/pair
Appliance	120 volt, 40 watt	$7.49
Fluorescent 18 inch	15 watt	$9.89
Motion Sensor	120 volt	$8.88
High Intensity	12V, 12 watt	$3.29/pair

Household Bulbs

Lightbulb Extra Long Life	120 volt, 60 watt	$12.49/case
Reflector Flood	120 volt, 150 watt	$7.99
Halogen Tracklight	12 volt, 20W, ESX	$23.49/case

Outdoor Bulbs

Garden Sealed Beam	12 volt	$5.99
Fixture Bayonet	12 volt	$2.99/pair

Call us toll free at 1-800-652-1067, during regular business hours, Monday through Saturday. Orders are not charged until shipped to you. [1]All prices are guaranteed until the end of the current calendar year. We are required to collect sales tax in AZ, CA, CO, CT, FL, GA, IL, IN, LA, MA, MD, MN, MO, NJ, NY, NV, OH, OK, PA, RI, TN, TX, VA, WA, DC. We charge for delivery based on the total merchandise amount per address.

Steamhouse Lighting Incorporated
1628 South Templeton Highway, Santa Susana, AZ, 85201

Figure 3.1

This simple price sheet uses only a few typefaces and some simple paragraph and tab formatting attributes.

As uncomplicated as this price sheet design is, it delivers a fair amount of visual interest, especially when you consider it is an ordinary list of data. Much of that visual interest comes from the bold statement made by the light bulb graphic and the logotype next to it.

The elements of this price list design stack up vertically on the page like a Dagwood sandwich. There's always a danger in this kind of layout that the design will become static and dull. To prevent that, some paragraph rules have been used to break up the flow of text, while visually setting off the three categories of merchandise. The paragraph rules, actually dotted lines in this case, don't run all the way across the page. Instead, they float on the right side of the page, balancing the big light bulb graphic.

Two typeface families have been used here— one of the recommended type combinations for headlines and body text in Sean Cavanaugh's book on digital type.

The typeface used for the headlines and for the company name logotype is called Opus. Although Opus is classified as a humanist sans serif, it is very different from the Goudy Sans type from that same category we used for the letterhead project. Opus, in fact, greatly resembles a more common typeface called Optima.

For the columns of information and body text, we used URW Palladio, which is a lot like the Palatino that is built into most PostScript laser printers on the market (in fact, URW Palladio was designed by the same man who created Palatino, as a more suitable substitute for desktop publishing). As Sean Cavanaugh points out, it "has a chiseled appearance, giving it a formal, slightly calligraphic look." He adds that URW Palladio not only works well as a text face but "is useful for a wide range of documents and at larger sizes as an elegant display font."

As to the man who created Palladio (and Palatino), Sean points out that he also designed Optima, the other typeface we are using in this chapter. It was none other than famous typographer Hermann Zapf. Technical Editor Phil Gaskill says he would go even further and describe Zapf as "the most famous, and greatest, living type designer in the world."

URW Palladio, by the way, is classified as an oldstyle typeface. That means it was designed to resemble the type designs from the 15th and 16th centuries when type took the place of hand lettering. Compared to other typefaces, oldstyle faces look more like the letters a calligrapher would draw—large differences between the thick and thin strokes in the letters, for example, as if the characters in the face were based on letters originally stroked with a quill pen.

Prep Notes

Copy all the files for this chapter from the CD-ROM to a work area on your hard drive. They are all in the **Steps** folder in the folder labeled **03**.

You will need the fonts Opus and URW Palladio to be installed on your computer. The typefaces used for the projects in this book can all be found on the CD-ROM that came with it. If you don't know how to install fonts, ask your instructor for help. Also, some helpful font management basics have been covered in Appendixes A and B, which you will also find on the CD-ROM.

After you finish the first exercise in this chapter, each following exercise builds on the previous one. Except where we've indicated otherwise, you should save your project at the end of each exercise so you can pick up where you left off when you begin the next exercise.

Introducing... Standard Type Measures

Picas, points, and ems are the standard measures traditionally used in typography.

You will find additional information about many of the items discussed in this—PostScript, for example— in the desktop publishing glossary included on your CD-ROM.

QuarkXPress, as you may have noticed, comes standard from the factory with its rulers set to measure inches. This is fine for measuring spatial relationships on a page. Some desktop publishers never take the time to learn about picas, points, and ems and it is possible to produce nicely designed documents using inches instead of these standard typographical measures. However, it's a fact that, as a professional in the graphic arts, you will be expected to be familiar with these traditional units of measurement.

There are 12 points to a pica, 6 picas in an inch, and a total of 72 points in an inch. You can see these relationships in Figure 3.2, showing a 3-inch by 1-inch section of the QuarkXPress vertical and horizontal rulers in three different measurement modes.

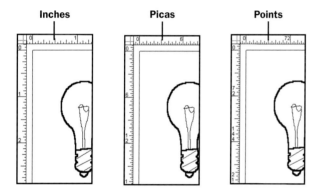

Inches   Picas   Points

Figure 3.2

QuarkXPress rulers with three different settings—inches on the left, picas in the center, and points on the right.

Traditionally, by the way, there are actually 72.27 points to an inch. This discrepancy is reputed to have been caused by the fact that type cast from molten metal would shrink slightly as it cooled. When Adobe created the PostScript programming language, the company built into the language the even number of 72 points per inch. After all, there was no need with digital typesetting to compensate for shrinking metal type.

You will find that picas, being much larger than points, are often preferred for specifying page level design elements such as margins and the size of graphics. Small details, like type and line spacing (leading), are measured in points.

In the first exercise in this chapter, when you set up this price sheet project, you will tell QuarkXPress that you want to use picas for your measurement system instead of inches. You will set that default in **E**dit> Preferences>**D**ocument, ⌘+Y (Mac) or Ctrl+Y (Win95).

"Standard" Typeface Sizes

Type used in books and newspapers usually ranges in size from 10 to 12 points, although there are plenty of dense books set in smaller type. Telephone books and dictionaries, for example, are often set in smaller type. Most computer word processors are set to create text in 12-point type, a holdover from the days when typewriters generally gave us 12-point letters.

Different typefaces, although set at the same point size, aren't visually the same size (see Figure 3.3). That's because each typeface has been designed with different typographical parameters. For example, there will be differences in the relative height of the vertical stem in relation to the round belly of letters such as "b" or "d."

Measuring with Ems

In addition to points and picas, you need to know about ems. To understand ems, you first need to understand that the characters in most typefaces take up different amounts of horizontal space. The letter *n* takes up less horizontal space than *m*, for example, and both of these characters are wider than the letter *i*. The typographer, when drawing each individual character in the typeface, decided how much space it should occupy on a line in proportion to other letters in the alphabet. For this reason, the typefaces designed in this fashion are called *proportionally spaced* type. By contrast, all the characters in *monospace* fonts, which resemble typewriter letters, occupy the same amount of space (even though the letters may vary in actual width). One common monospace typeface is Courier.

Hi, I'm 36 point Function

Hi, I'm 36 point Opus

Hi, I'm 36 point Palladio

Hi, I'm 36 point Vivaldi

Hi, I'm 36 point Savoy

Hi, I'm 36 point Goudy Sans

Figure 3.3

For any given size of type expressed in points, the apparent visual size of the characters may vary quite a lot.

When designing a typeface and its spacing, the typographer also needs a way to measure relationships among letters. For that purpose, the unit of measurement is an em. Ems are used to measure letter spacing, so the em is the basic unit of measurement for *kerning*—the adjustment of space between letters. By kerning in em units, the letter space adjustment is made in proportion to the size of the type. Ems, being relative measuring units, are consistent within a typeface but are not necessarily equal from typeface to typeface.

By the way, many people believe that an em is always the size of the letter "m" in any given typeface. That's not true. An em, by wide understanding among typographers, always equals the point size of the typeface. So 10-point type has a 10-point wide em. An en space would be half that, or 5 points, and a thin space would be one quarter of an em, or 2.5 points.

QuarkXPress Em Space Oddity

For some strange reason—no other software program in the universe does this—QuarkXPress assumes that an em is the width of two zeroes, not the width of the point size of the selected typeface.

You should never use this non-standard, bizarre setting for em space measurement. Your measurements won't match up with those used by the rest of the desktop publishing world. You may also get some pretty odd-looking text because dashes built into your typefaces

(em dashes, en dashes, and so on) will be the standard width and all the various types of fixed-width spaces (em spaces, en spaces, thin spaces) will be based on the non-standard QuarkXPress double-zero measurement.

Fortunately, Quark has made it possible to use a standard em space measure. It's a checkbox setting in Edit>Preferences>Document>Character. You will put this setting to work in the next section.

Setting Up Your Defaults

You have already learned a bit about setting defaults and preferences, but in this section you will delve much deeper into this process. You might want to re-read the section "Understanding QuarkXPress Defaults" in Chapter 1 before beginning the following steps, paying particular attention to the difference between application and document defaults. Even though we talked about these concepts in the previous chapter, this will be the first time you will really put them to work.

Getting Back to Fresh Defaults

1. Before opening up QuarkXPress, get back to the factory settings for the program, as described in Chapter 1.

   The process is the same for both Macintosh and Windows 95. Open the folder where you have installed your QuarkXPress program. Find the file named XPress Preferences and either rename it or delete it.

2. Open up QuarkXPress.

   Don't open a new document yet.

   Do, however, carefully watch the opening screen, the one with the XPress logo. The message will go by quickly but you should see a notice on the screen that QuarkXPress is creating a new preferences file.

   As you learned in Chapter 1, the menu choices you make now, with no document open, will become defaults. That means—until you change them—they will apply to all future QuarkXPress documents.

Setting Defaults for Application Preferences

3. Go to the Application Preferences dialog box, Edit>Preferences>Application. You can use a keyboard shortcut if you like, ⌘+Option+⬆Shift+Y (Mac) or Ctrl+Alt+⬆Shift+Y (Win95).

   There are myriad settings in this dialog box, but for right now we are just going to deal with a few of them.

Making XPress Do Automatic Backups

4. Click the Save dialog box tab, or you can ⌘+Tab⬏ (Mac) or Ctrl+Tab⬏ (Win95) until you have it active, as you see in Figure 3.4.

   Choose Auto Save, and set QuarkXPress to do a save every 15 minutes. (You can set this for any amount you prefer, but I find the every 5 minutes setting way too frequent, as explained in the next step.)

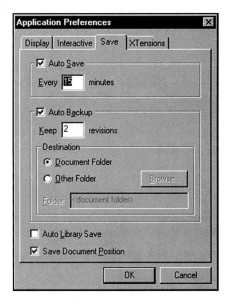

Figure 3.4
Setting program defaults for Auto Backup and Auto Save.

5. Now go to Auto Backup and click it. Tell it to Keep 2 revisions.

   It's important to understand that Auto Backup and Auto Save work together. Every 15 minutes (or however often you tell it do so) QuarkXPress will do an Auto Save to a new Auto Backup file.

   That's why I opt for moderate settings of 15 minute intervals and two revisions. Every new backup takes up space on your hard drive. If you are working on a big file—say a 60 MB file—and you leave the Auto Backup setting at five revisions, you will quickly chew up hard drive real estate with 300 MB worth of backup files!

   Notice that you can designate a specific folder for your backups. The standard is the same folder as your current QuarkXPress document. You might also decide to send the backup to a secondary hard drive in case your primary went down. Or, you could elect to save all your backups to a central folder where you would habitually clean up all the accumulated backup files on a regular basis so as to keep your hard drive from suffering from dreaded backup bloat.

6. Click OK or press Return (Mac) or Esc (Win95) to adopt these new application preferences as new program defaults.

7. Now follow the same procedures to set some program defaults for your document preferences.

   Edit>Preferences>Document takes you to Document Preferences, or use the keyboard shortcuts, ⌘+Y (Mac) or Ctrl+Y (Win95).

   Notice that the dialog box is labeled Default Document Preferences instead of just Document Preferences for the name of your document file. That's QuarkXPress' way of telling you that you will be setting a default because you don't have a document open.

Selecting a Measurement System

8. The General tab of the dialog should be active and you should set it up as you see in Figure 3.5.

Set your **H**orizontal **M**easure as Picas.

Set your **V**ertical **M**easure as Picas.

Either turn off Greek **B**elow, or set it as I usually do at 4 points.

Notice, the **P**oints/Inch setting is the digital standard, 72 points per inch.

Using Standard Ems

9. Now ⌘+Tab (Mac) or Ctrl+Tab (Win95) to the Character tab of this dialog box.

Turn on the checkbox for Stand**a**rd Em Space, as we discussed in this chapter's section on "QuarkXPress Em Space Oddities."

10. Click OK, or press Return (Mac) or ↵Enter (Win95) to adopt these defaults.

Turning Off Automatic Text Boxes

11. Use the keyboard shortcut ⌘+N (Mac) or Ctrl+N to access the New Document dialog.

Turn off the **A**utomatic Text Box option.

12. Now here's a situation where QuarkXPress doesn't set a program default quite like you might expect.

In order to get a program default of having the Automatic Text Box option turned off, you must click OK to put your choice into effect.

However, if you click OK right now, you'll get a new document and that seems to go against the grain for setting a program default—something you are supposed to do with no document open.

The resolution to this paradox is to go ahead and click OK.

This will set a program default because the New Document dialog box is "sticky." Whatever settings you use in this dialog box during a given work session will be remembered the next time you create a new document.

13. File>**E**xit from QuarkXPress.

If QuarkXPress asks whether you want to save the new document you just created, just say no.

Whatever settings you have in place, including the sticky setting for no Automatic Text Box, are automatically recorded in the XPress Preferences file. They are saved as defaults.

Next time you open QuarkXPress, the defaults you just set will be in effect for any new documents you create.

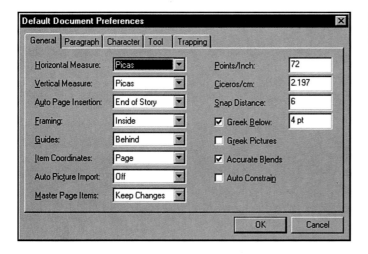

Figure 3.5

Setting the XPress measuring system.

Beginning a New Document

14. Try out your new program defaults right now. Reopen QuarkXPress.

15. Begin a new document by using the keyboard shortcut, ⌘+Ⓝ (Mac) or Ctrl+Ⓝ (Win95).

Notice that the Margin Guides, which would normally be .5 inch on each side, are set at 3 picas. That's because your new document has used your program default and is measuring in picas instead of inches.

Also, notice that the **A**utomatic Text Box option is not turned on, since you set it off as a program default.

16. Save your new document, giving it a file name of your choice, and save it to a work area on your hard drive.

● The bare new document, the foundation of your price sheet project, has been saved on the CD-ROM in a file named **03BASE01.QXT**.

We have not, however, provided you with a copy of our XPress Preferences file. There's too much danger that the internal format of the preferences file would shift as new versions of QuarkXPress are released, and using an outdated preferences file could have unexpected, undesired, results.

Linking Text Boxes

Take a look at Figure 3.1 and you'll see that this price sheet design needs several small text boxes. In fact, you need several *linked* text boxes, and that's what you will be creating by following the steps in this section.

1. If it isn't still open from your work in the last section, open the bare document you just created.

Your document should be set to use picas for measurements and to use the standard em space.

2. Set the view at Fit in Window, ⌘+Ⓞ (Mac) or Ctrl+Ⓞ (Win95).

Setting a Document Default

3. Activate the Document Preferences dialog box. You can do that by double-clicking the rectangular text box tool, the one with the letter "A" in a box. The Tool tab of the dialog box should be active.

If you need some help remembering which tool is which, you can reread the "Trying Out The Tool Palette" section in Chapter 1.

Notice that the Document Preferences dialog box title includes the name of your document, indicating that you have a document open and you will be setting a default only for this particular document.

4. Click the **M**odify button and you will get the dialog box you see in Figure 3.6, with the Box tab activated.

5. Set the box color to None and click OK twice to adopt your settings, to close the dialog boxes, and to get back to your layout.

Setting the document default box color to None means every text box you draw will be transparent, so you will be able to overlap boxes and graphics.

6. If it isn't already on-screen, open the Measurements palette. The keyboard shortcut is Ⓕ9.

Also, turn on the display of guides so your blue margin guides will show. The keyboard shortcut is F7.

● The progress so far on the price sheet has been saved on the CD-ROM in a file named **03BASE02.QXT**.

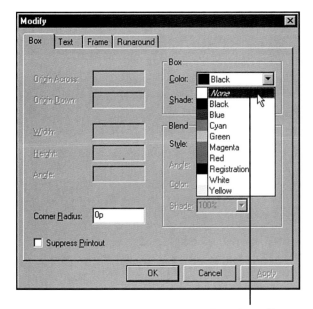

Set color to None

Figure 3.6

Setting a default for rectangular text boxes.

Review: Drawing Text Boxes

You will need four text boxes for this layout. You have already had the experience of drawing a text box in Chapter 2, so you may want to review that material before starting this exercise.

1. With the Rectangular Text Box tool selected, click the crosshair pointer on the left margin guide about 10 picas down from the top.

Drag down and to the right from the initial click point in order to draw out a text box.

Don't worry too much about precision as you first draw your text boxes because you will fine-tune measurements in an upcoming step.

As you draw the box, watch the Measurements palette. Aim for the following rough measurements:

■ X/Y coordinates of 3p and 10p, the upper-left corner of the box, its origin point.

■ Width of 45 picas, and height 8 picas and 4 points (8p4).

Fine-Tuning Text Box Measurements

2. As you know from Chapter 2, you can type measurements directly into the Measurements palette.

With the text box still selected, press ⌘+Option+M (Mac) or Ctrl+Alt+M (Win95) to activate the first field of the Measurements palette, the X coordinate.

Type in **3p**, for 3 picas, and that will precisely describe the location of the left edge of the box exactly on the left margin guide.

3. Press Tab⇄ to get to the next field, the one for the Y coordinate.

Type in **10p** for 10 picas to position the top edge of the box.

4. Tab again to the width field and type in **45p** for 45 picas.

5. Tab once more to the height field and type in **8p4**, for 8 picas and 4 points.

6. Press Return (Mac) or ↵Enter (Win95) to adopt these settings and to precisely position your text box where it belongs.

Retaining Your Tool Choice

7. You may have noticed that the tool reverted to the Item tool after you drew the first text box. To keep that from happening, hold down Option (Mac) or Alt (Win95) as you select the Rectangular Text Box tool.

8. Draw out three more text boxes and notice that your chosen tool, the Rectangular Text Box tool, stays activated after you complete each box.

As you draw each box, use the Measurements palette as an indicator that you are in roughly the right location and the box is the correct approximate size.

- X/Y coordinates of 3p and 22p6, W/H of 45p and 26p9.

- X/Y coordinates of 3p and 53p, W/H of 45p and 4p9.

- X/Y coordinates of 3p and 60p, W/H of 45p and 3p2.

9. Click the Item tool to activate it instead of the Rectangular Text Box tool.

10. Select each of the text boxes in turn and use the Measurements palette to precisely define their coordinates and measurements as listed previously and as noted in Figure 3.7.

The version of the price list as it should look so far, with the four text boxes drawn and precisely defined, has been saved on the CD-ROM in a file named **03BASE03.QXT**.

Linking Text Boxes

The ultimate goal of this exercise will be to pour the price list text, the title, and all of the numbers into the four text boxes you have just created. Before you import the text, you will want to link the text boxes so the text flows from one to the other. That way, you won't need to break up the text into pieces and conduct four different text import operations. You can import just once for all four text boxes.

Selecting the Linking Tool

1. Select the Linking tool, but instead of simply clicking it, hold down Option (Mac) or Alt (Win95).

As you learned in the last exercise, holding down these modifier keys tells QuarkXPress that you want to keep the Linking tool selected, not letting it revert to the Item tool after each use.

Figure 3.7

Four text boxes with their coordinates and measurements.

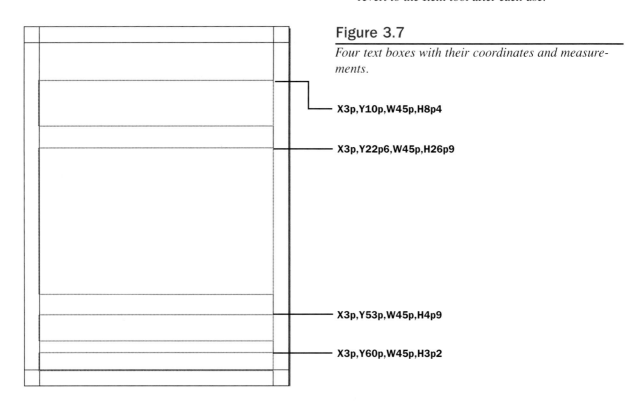

X3p,Y10p,W45p,H8p4

X3p,Y22p6,W45p,H26p9

X3p,Y53p,W45p,H4p9

X3p,Y60p,W45p,H3p2

The Linking tool is the one near the bottom of the Tool palette with the unbroken chain. The broken chain, as you might expect, is the Unlinking tool.

Beginning a Link

2. Click with the Linking tool on the top text box.

   The border of the text box will turn into a moving dotted line like the one in Figure 3.8. Some people say this dotted line looks like "marching ants."

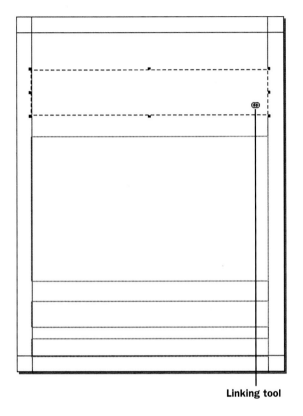

Linking tool

Figure 3.8

Beginning a text box link.

Forging a Link

3. Now forge the link to the next text box down the page, the second one.

   Click the second text box with the Linking tool.

You should see an arrow, indicating the text box link, between the lower-right corner of the first text box and the top-left corner of the second text box, as in Figure 3.9.

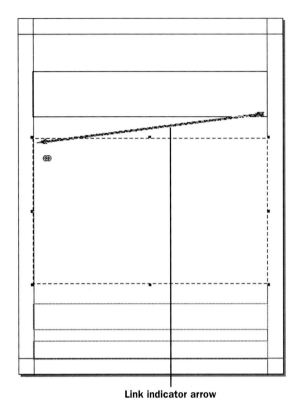

Link indicator arrow

Figure 3.9

Two linked text boxes.

4. Finish the process now. The Linking tool should still be active, since you held down Option (Mac) or Alt (Win95) when you selected it.

   With the marching ants still active on the second text box, click the third text box to establish a link from the second box.

5. Again, with the marching ants now on the third text box, click the bottom text box to complete all the links.

   When you are finished, you will have a total of three link indicator arrows, just like Figure 3.10.

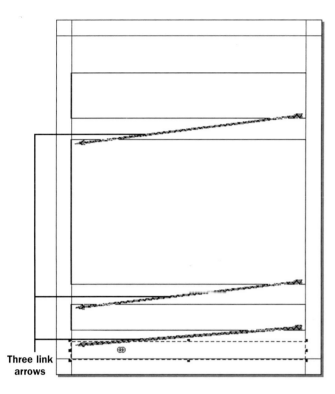

Three link arrows

Figure 3.10

All four text boxes linked.

Importing Text

6. Now import the price list text into your text boxes.

Select the Content tool, the one with the text cursor/grabber hand combination, second from the top of the Tool palette.

7. Click in the top text box with the Content tool so that a text cursor is blinking in the box.

By the way, you don't absolutely have to start with the top text box. In QuarkXPress, you can click in any one of the linked text boxes and the text will begin flowing from the beginning.

8. Press ⌘+E (Mac) or Ctrl+E (Win95), the keyboard shortcut for **File>Get Text**.

9. You will get a standard file open text box labeled Get Text.

10. Navigate to your work folder and select the file **PRICES.TXT**.

You should have already, at the beginning of the chapter, copied all the Chapter 3 files from the CD-ROM to your hard drive. This text file was one of those that came from the CD-ROM.

11. To open the file so it will be imported into your QuarkXPress document, double-click it, or press ⌐Return (Mac) or ⌐Enter (Win95).

Notice that all the text from the file PRICES.TXT spills into your linked text boxes, as shown in Figure 3.11. There's not enough text to fill all four, so right now you have text only in the top two text boxes.

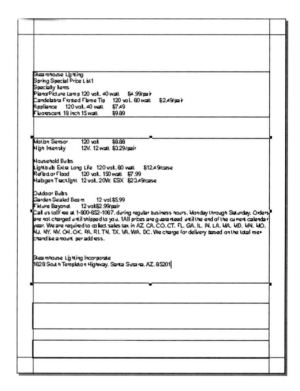

Figure 3.11

Text flows between linked text boxes.

Navigate to Top of Story

12. This entire text is called a story, even though it is spread between more than one text box. Your blinking text cursor should now be at the end of the story.

To get to the top of the story you just imported, press a keyboard shortcut, ⌘+Option+↑ (Mac) or Ctrl+Alt+↑ (Win95).

If you needed to get to the bottom of a story, you would use the same command except with the ↓ key.

Navigate to Next Paragraph

13. Move to the beginning of the next paragraph by pressing ⌘+↓ (Mac) or Ctrl+↓ (Win95).

If you wanted to move to the beginning of a paragraph, you would use the reverse of this command, ⌘+↑ (Mac) or Ctrl+↑ (Win95).

Navigate to End of Line

14. Now navigate to the end of that first line. Press ⌘+Option+→ (Mac) or End (Win95).

If you needed to get to the beginning of a line, you would use the reverse of these commands, ⌘+Option+← (Mac) or Home (Win95).

Your cursor should be blinking at the end of the second line of the story, the one that says "Spring Special Price List."

Forcing a Text Box Break

15. You need to force the text to break between boxes in order to organize it on the page. The title should be in the top box, the prices in the second box, the body copy in the third, and the address in the fourth text box.

There's a special New Text Box character for this purpose.

With your cursor at the end of the second line of the story, press ⬆Shift+↵Enter. That's the ↵Enter key in the lower-right corner of your keyboard.

(Win95) If you are a Win95 user, note that you have two Enter keys and the one you want is not the regular Enter key that you use most of the time. It's the one in the lower-right corner of your keyboard.

Notice that the text breaks to the second box. You will need to press Del to remove the empty extra line at the top of the second text box.

16. Insert a text box break at the end of the price data.

Move your text cursor to the end of the paragraph containing the words "Fixture Bayonet 12 volt $2.99/pair." That's just before the words "Call us toll free…"

You could just click your mouse at this point—sometimes a bit hard to get it just right—or you could navigate your cursor to the correct location by repeatedly hitting the next paragraph keyboard shortcut until you reach the correct paragraph, and then using the end of line shortcut.

You can check your memory on these shortcuts by looking back to steps 13 and 14 of this exercise.

17. Insert one more text box break at the end of the body text, right after the words "…amount per address."

Review…Overset Text and Sizing a Box

18. Notice that you get a red overset text marker in the bottom text box, just like the one you learned about in Chapter 2, in the section on "Sizing a Box."

The text from the third box has spilled over into the address box at the bottom of the page, shoving the address text into limbo. When all this text has been formatted, the problem will resolve itself, but this is a good chance to review a technique.

You are going to resize this text box to make room for the text. As you know, you could use either the Item tool or the Content tool to do this job, but you should already have the Content tool in use so you can stick with it.

Mouse the pointer over the bottom middle sizing handle on the third box.

When the pointer turns into a hand, click the sizing handle and hold for a beat. When you see the box flash, drag downward just enough to allow all the body text to fit in its proper box. If you waited for the flash, you will get instant feedback as the excess text flips up into the third box. Notice how text moves between these linked boxes, as if there were hollow pipes that allowed the text to leak between them.

19. Delete the extra line above the text "Steamhouse Lighting Incorporated."

When you are done, the address info will be in the fourth box and all the body text will be in the third box, as in Figure 3.12. It's now ready to be formatted, and that's what you'll do in the next exercise.

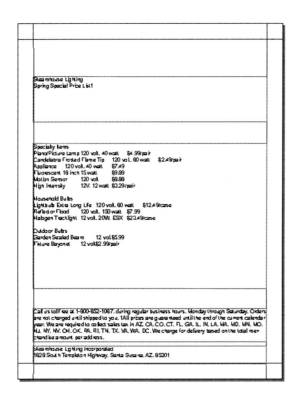

Figure 3.12

The unformatted text, organized into its correct text boxes.

The progress so far on the price list has been saved on the CD-ROM in a file named **03BASE04.QXT**.

Introducing...QuarkXPress Text Navigation

Much of this introduction, and the next exercise for selecting and formatting text, will probably seem pretty familiar to you. There aren't many people in this day and age, at your level of schooling, that have not worked before in a word processor program where you select and format text all the time. And conceptually, QuarkXPress text selection and formatting works just the same as a word processor.

QuarkXPress does not, however, always use the standard keyboard shortcuts you might expect to select or navigate through text. Still, there's logic to the way QuarkXPress helps you navigate through text. Table 3.1 shows how this all works, but here's the logic of it all. For every additional key in the shortcut, you move an even greater distance:

- If you want to move a character at a time, or one line at a time, you simply use the arrow keys.

- If you want to move a word or paragraph at a time, you add the ⌘ (Mac) or Ctrl (Win95) key to the arrow keys.

- If you want to move to the beginning or ending of a line or a story, you use add yet another key. You use ⌘+Option (Mac) or Ctrl+Alt (Win95) in combination with the arrow keys.

- If you want to select text, instead of moving the cursor to a different position, add ⬆Shift to any of the preceding keyboard shortcuts.

(Mac) Odd as it may seem, the Home and End keys don't work as you would expect them to work in the Macintosh version of QuarkXPress.

(Win95) Unlike Macintosh users, if you are working in Windows you get the use of the Home and End keys for text navigation. So, by way of example, the End key will take you to the end of a line—just like a word processor.

Table 3.1   QuarkXPress navigation and selection keyboard shortcuts in a nutshell

Move to...	Mac	Win95	Select by adding Shift...
Prior Character	←	←	
Next Character	→	→	
Line Above	↑	↑	
Line Below	↓	↓	
Prior Word	⌘+←	Ctrl+←	
Next Word	⌘+→	Ctrl+→	
Beginning of Paragraph	⌘+↑	Ctrl+↑	
Next Paragraph Beginning	⌘+↓	Ctrl+↓	
Start of Line	⌘+Option+←	Ctrl+Alt+←	or Home
End of Line	⌘+Option+→	Ctrl+Alt+→	or End
Start of Story	⌘+Option+↑	Ctrl+Alt+↑	or Ctrl+Home
End of Story	⌘+Option+↓	Ctrl+Alt+↓	or Ctrl+End

You can also select words, lines, paragraphs, and whole stories by using multiple mouse clicks, as indicated in Table 3.2. These multi-click selections also work when you make a click and drag move with the mouse. For example, if you double-click to select a word and—without releasing the mouse button—drag the mouse, you will be selecting a word at a time instead of the usual character at a time.

Table 3.2   Selecting text with multiple mouse clicks

Clicks	Selection Size
One	None, sets the insertion point, the position of the cursor in the text
Two	Word
Three	Line
Four	Paragraph
Five	Entire story

Selecting and Formatting Text

Now let's put these text navigation techniques to work. In this exercise, you will format all the plain text you've placed on your price sheet page. That will vastly improve its appearance and readability. It will also give you a nice workout using the keyboard shortcuts in Table 3.1—and a few additional text selection tricks as well.

Review: Use the Zoom Tool

1. Start by setting your magnification view to Fit In Window, ⌘+0 (Mac) or Ctrl+0 (Win95).

   Throughout this exercise, feel free to adjust the magnification to suit yourself as you work. You will probably find the Zoom tool particularly handy for selecting an area of the page that you want to magnify. When you need it, instead of selecting the Zoom tool from the Tools palette, try using the keyboard shortcut, Ctrl while you Click/Drag (Mac) or Ctrl+Spacebar while you Click/Drag (Win95).

Select All Shortcut

2. A good deal of the text needs to be formatted with the same typeface, URW Palladio. Format all the text that way to get started.

   Click with the Content tool anywhere in the text. Then select all the text using the keyboard shortcut for for **Edit>Select All**, ⌘+A (Mac) or Ctrl+A (Win95).

   As in Figure 3.13, all the text on the page has been selected. This would not have been possible without the previous exercise where you connected all four text boxes together so the text is linked in a single story.

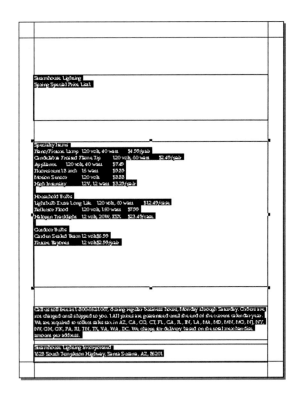

Figure 3.13

Text in linked text boxes, all selected as one story.

Review: Activating the Measurements Palette

3. If it isn't already visible, activate the palette with the keyboard shortcut, ⌘+Option+M (Mac) or Ctrl+Alt+M (Win95).

4. ⬆Shift+Tab twice to move backward through the fields in the Measurements palette, until the font name has been highlighted.

Tip

Direct Connection to Font Selection

There's another way way to get directly to font selection in the Measurements palette. It's a variation on the "M" keyboard shortcut you just used to activate the Measurements palette, except it adds the ⬆Shift key. If you press ⌘+Option+⬆Shift +M (Mac) or Ctrl+Alt+⬆Shift+M (Win95), you'll go directly to the font name in the Measurements palette.

Automatic Font Search

5. This trick will save you lots of time in the future. The alphabetical list of installed fonts has a built-in rapid access search feature.

   Begin by typing the font name, "URW Palladio," one letter at a time. Notice that the list jumps to match your typing. Probably by the time you get to "UR," the URW Palladio font will be chosen, as in Figure 3.14.

   If you have installed more than one font that begins with the letters "URW," you may have to type more letters. Just keep spelling what you want until it is automatically selected.

6. Press Return (Mac) or ↵Enter (Win95) to format all the selected type as URW Palladio.

Figure 3.14

Selecting a font in the Measurements palette.

Typeface selection

Selecting Paragraphs

7. Press ⬇ once, and your text cursor will be blinking at the very end of the selected area, the end of the story.

If your text goes into an overset condition because of the font change, expand the text box a bit to make it all fit.

Now select the last two paragraphs in the story by holding down ⬆Shift while twice pressing the keys for the up-paragraph navigation shortcut, ⌘+⬆Shift+⬆ (Mac) and Ctrl+⬆Shift+⬆ (Win 95).

Notice how you select an entire paragraph at a time when you press ⬆.

With these two paragraphs selected, you will be able to format the address at the bottom of the page in the Opus typeface, 14 points.

Mouse Operation of Measurements Palette

8. So far, you have operated the Measurements palette from the keyboard. But you can, of course, operate it with the mouse. I prefer the keyboard because I believe that's usually a faster technique.

Click your mouse on the arrow next to the type size field, the one at the extreme right end of the palette. You will get a list of "standard" type sizes, as in Figure 3.15.

Review: Menu Text Formatting

9. As you know from Chapter 2, you can use the QuarkXPress menu system to format type, although it is often more convenient to perform these functions from the Measurements palette.

Use Style>Font and select the Opus font from the list, as in Figure 3.16.

Multi-Click Text Selection

10. Quadruple-click with the Content tool on the paragraph that begins "Call us toll free...," the one right above the address. As you know from Table 3.2, a quadruple click selects an entire paragraph.

You may find it difficult to click four times in such rapid succession. As you are trying this, you will probably inadvertently select a word (double-click) or line (triple-click). In fact, the double- or triple-click moves are more useful and it's almost easier to use a keyboard shortcut to select a paragraph.

11. This paragraph has already been formatted in URW Palladio but it needs to be sized to 11.5 points.

Activate the Measurements palette, ⌘+Option +M (Mac) or Ctrl+Alt+M (Win95), and ⬆Shift+Tab⬄ once to get to the type size field.

Type in **11.5** and press Return (Mac) or ⏎Enter (Win95).

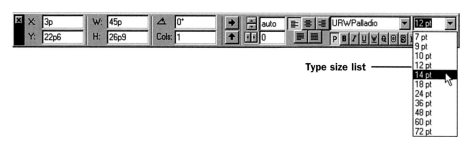

Type size list

Figure 3.15

Selecting a type size in the Measurements palette.

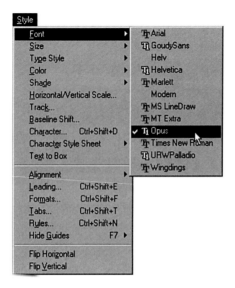

Figure 3.16

Menu selection of a font.

Multi-Click Drag Selection

12. You need to select the large block of text in the middle of the page, the pricing information, so you can format it.

Triple-click the last line of the text, and hold the mouse button down on the last click. If you selected the line, you will now be in a line selection mode. Dragging the mouse will select a line at a time instead of the usual character at a time.

Drag up until all of the text in this text box has been selected, including the line that says "Specialty Items."

Type Size Shortcut

13. Use a keyboard shortcut to set the type size. If you look in the Measurement palette, you will be able to see the present size of the type, probably 12 points.

Increase the type size to 14 points by using a keyboard shortcut based on the "greater than" key, ⌘+⬆Shift+> (Mac) or Ctrl+⬆Shift+> (Win95).

The type will be boosted up to the next "standard" increment of type size, which is 14 points. The standard sizes are the ones listed in the size list under the Style menu or in the pop-up menu in the Measurements palette.

You can also change the type size one point at a time by adding the Option or Alt key to the shortcut, ⌘+Option+⬆Shift+> (Mac) or Ctrl+Alt+⬆Shift+> (Win95).

You can go the opposite direction and reduce the size of your type by using the "less than" key, ⌘+⬆Shift+< (Mac) or Ctrl+⬆Shift+<.

14. Next, use the keyboard shortcuts to maneuver to and select one of the price headlines, "Outdoor Bulbs."

Use ⌘+⬆ or ⌘+⬇ (Mac), or Ctrl+⬆ or Ctrl+⬇ (Win95), to get to the correct line. Then add ⬆Shift to the key combination to select the paragraph.

15. Increase the size of this headline by two points to 16 points, ⌘+Option+⬆Shift+> (Mac) or Ctrl+Alt+⬆Shift+> (Win95), applying the keyboard shortcut twice since each press increases the size by one point.

16. Use the paragraph navigation and selection shortcuts to locate and select each of the other two price headlines in turn, formatting them as you go, "Household Bulbs," and "Specialty Items." If you need to refresh your memory on how this works, read back through the steps you have completed. You have already learned all of the techniques you need to accomplish this formatting and this will help you review them.

Adjust each headline's type size to 16 points, either using the keyboard shortcut you used in step 16, or by using the Measurements palette.

Select the Opus typeface for each of the headlines while you have them selected.

17. Now format the title paragraphs, again using the techniques you have already learned.

The subtitle, "Spring Special Price List," should be Opus, 32 points.

The main title at the very top of the page, "Steamhouse Lighting," should be Opus, 50 points.

When you have reached this point, your price sheet should look like the one in Figure 3.17.

We'll take a break from formatting the text on the price sheet now so we can have a talk about styling type. The progress so far on the price sheet has been saved on the CD-ROM in a file named **03BASE05.QXT**.

Introducing...Type Styles

In Chapter 2, you used the **S**tyle>**Ty**pe Style menu to make some type bold. You can also style type from the Measurements palette and by using keyboard shortcuts. Figure 3.18 shows you all the options.

(Win95) The menu in Figure 3.18 shows how each of the type style options looks—bold, italic, strikethrough, and so on. Although your menu in the Windows 95 version of QuarkXPress has all the same items, exactly the same power, you don't get the same visual display of the effects.

Plain means no styling. This is a quick way to remove any styling from selected text. Keyboard Shortcuts: ⌘+⬆Shift+P (Mac) or Ctrl+⬆Shift+P (Win95).

Bold means bold, selecting the heavier form of the typeface if it exists. If it doesn't exist, QuarkXPress will try to make the plain style heavier. The technical name for this is smearing and it looks about as bad as it sounds. It is also possible, if the bold type isn't actually installed, that you won't get even this smearing effect when you print your file. Keyboard Shortcuts: ⌘+⬆Shift+B (Mac) or Ctrl+⬆Shift+B (Win95).

Italic gives you the italic form of the typeface if it exists. Like the bold style, QuarkXPress will try to make the type look italic if the italic form of the typeface has not been installed. Fake italics are said to be obliqued, leaned over to the side. Fake italic type may or may not work when you print the file. Keyboard Shortcuts: ⌘+⬆Shift+I (Mac) or Ctrl+⬆Shift+I (Win95).

Underline results in an underline beneath all the selected characters.

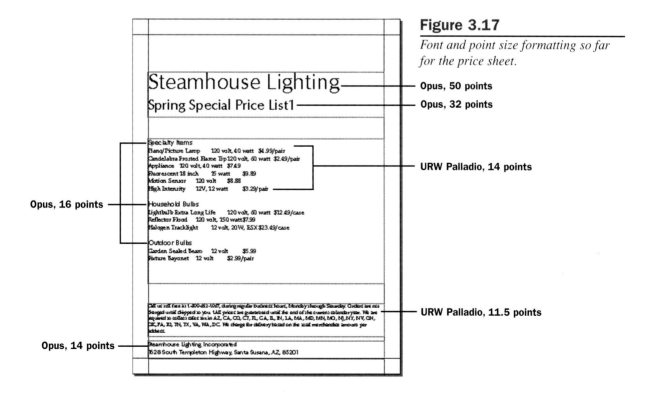

Figure 3.17
Font and point size formatting so far for the price sheet.

— Opus, 50 points
— Opus, 32 points

— URW Palladio, 14 points

Opus, 16 points —

Opus, 14 points —

— URW Palladio, 11.5 points

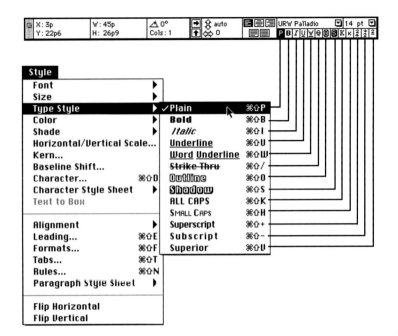

Figure 3.18

QuarkXPress type styles from the menu and Measurements palette, along with all their keyboard shortcuts.

Word underline skips the underline for any space characters.

Strike thru draws a line through the middle of selected letters. You might use strike thru if you were noting wording changes in a contract, although I'm not sure why you'd ever write a contract in QuarkXPress instead of a word processor.

Outline makes the letter forms look hollow. This artifact from the early days of desktop publishing tends to identify your work as being done by an amateur. Instead, find a typeface that will give you a true outline effect.

Shadow outlines your type and puts a shadow behind it. Aside from being an ugly form of shadowing like outline, this type style will brand you as an amateur.

All caps makes all your letters capital letters through formatting, as opposed to retyping them.

Small caps gives you upper and lower case, but all in capital letters. Any letters that were originally typed as capital letters don't change. Any letters that we typed as lowercase are formatted as small capital letters.

Superscript and **Subscript** raise or lower your type in relation to the rest of the type on the line.

Superior not only raises the selected type, but also makes it smaller, more like a footnote reference number would look in text.

The last four of these styles can be customized to your taste in the **E**dit>**P**references>**D**ocument>**C**haracter command, shown in Figure 3.19.

Notice that you can adjust the vertical and horizontal size (VScale/HScale) of the characters as well as how high or low they ride on the line of text (offset). All the settings are in percentages so they are relative, depending on the size of the selected type.

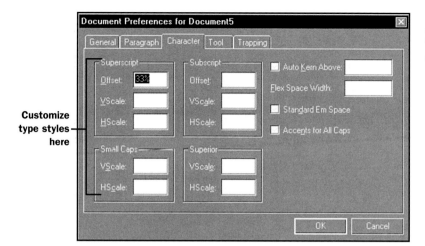

Figure 3.19

Customizing superscript, subscript, small caps, and superior type styles.

Customize
type styles
here

Styling Type from the Keyboard

In this exercise, you will be styling the type for this price sheet. We will be emphasizing keyboard shortcuts to do this work, usually the fastest way to get things done. Of course, as we've just discussed, it's possible to do all of these things using menu commands or the Measurements palette.

We've already talked about all the navigation and text selection keyboard shortcuts you will need. You have used many of them, so feel free to review Table 3.1 if you need to do so at any time.

1. We will work from the top down on the price sheet.

   Click anywhere in the price sheet text with the Content tool and go to the top of the story, ⌘+Option+↑ (Mac) or Ctrl+Alt+↑ (Win95).

   Select the first three paragraphs, the main title, the subtitle, and the first price headline. Use the keyboard shortcut to do this, ⌘+Shift+↓ (Mac) or Ctrl+Shift+↓ (Win95).

Bold

2. Make each of these title and headline items bold by pressing ⌘+Shift+B (Mac) or Ctrl+Shift+B (Win95).

Italic

3. Make the subtitle italic, as well.

   Use the paragraph navigation and selection keyboard shortcuts (the ones you just used) to select the subtitle.

   Press ⌘+Shift+I (Mac) or Ctrl+Shift+I (Win95) to italicize the selected text.

Superior

4. There's a footnote reference at the end of this line and it needs to be formatted as superior.

   Press ← once to unselect the text and then go to the end of the line, ⌘+Option+→ (Mac) or End (Win95).

   Select just the character "1" by pressing Shift+←.

   Format the character as superior by using the keyboard shortcut, ⌘+Shift+V (Mac) or Ctrl+Shift+V (Win95).

5. Four more paragraphs need to be formatted as bold.

   The four paragraphs are the two price headlines, "Household Bulbs" and "Outdoor Bulbs," and the two paragraphs in the address at the bottom of the page.

   Use the paragraph navigation and selection shortcuts to highlight them and then use the shortcut for bold to format them, ⌘+Shift+B (Mac) or Ctrl+Shift+B (Win95).

6. Select the footnote number in the body copy text. It's the character "1" before the words "All prices are guaranteed…"

In order to get to that location, you may find it handy to use the keyboard shortcut for navigating a word at a time, ⌘+← or ⌘+→ (Mac), or Ctrl+← or Ctrl+→ (Win95).

Again, use the keyboard shortcut to format it in the superior style, ⌘+⬆Shift+V (Mac) or Ctrl+⬆Shift+V (Win95).

Notice that the character is raised up and reduced in size just like the footnote reference in the subtitle. However, because the amounts of these adjustments are expressed in percentages in the preferences dialog box you saw in Figure 3.19, the actual size and offset of the type are relative to the type's overall point size.

Figure 3.20 shows how the price sheet ought to look so far and the document has been saved as a file on the CD-ROM named **03BASE06.QXT**.

Introducing…Paragraph Alignment

Maybe the most important thing to remember about alignment is that it is a paragraph attribute. That means you do not need to highlight an entire paragraph to apply it. Just click anywhere in a paragraph or select any piece of a paragraph and it will be selected well enough to take on the alignment formatting when you apply it.

QuarkXPress offers five ways for you to automatically align your text—left, right, centered, justified, and force-justified. You can see an example of each of these in Figure 3.21.

Each of these alignments has a keyboard shortcut, as you see in Figure 3.22, which shows both the Style>Alignment menu (with the keyboard shortcuts shown on the menu) and the Measurements palette alignment buttons.

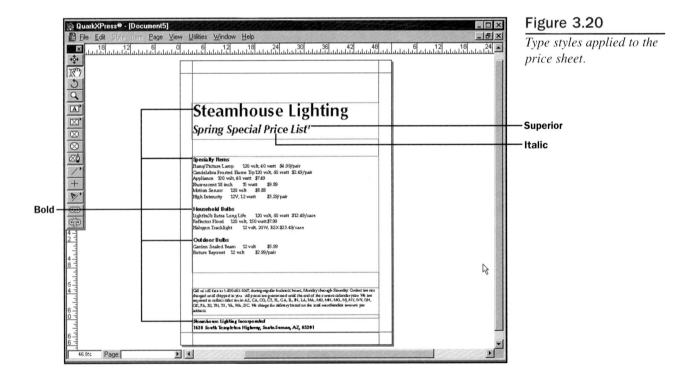

Figure 3.20
Type styles applied to the price sheet.

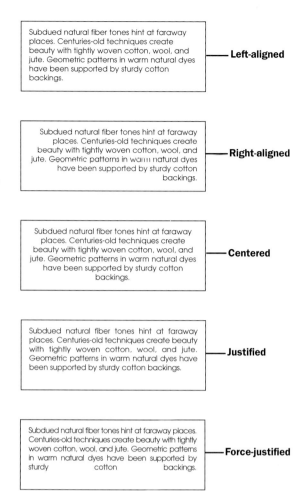

Left-aligned

Right-aligned

Centered

Justified

Force-justified

Figure 3.21

QuarkXPress five text alignment options.

Aligning Paragraph Text

It takes less time to align text than it does to talk about it, as you'll see in this exercise.

Review: Adding a Picture

1. Begin by adding the light bulb sketch to this page, since that's the reason you will be applying right alignment to the title and subtitle during this exercise.

   If any of the following commands seem hazy to you, take a moment to review Chapter 2. You performed all these tasks in those exercises.

   Select the Rectangle Picture Box tool and draw a picture box out from the upper-left corner where the top and left margins intersect. The crosshair pointer should start at 3 picas for both the X and Y coordinates in your Measurements palette. Make the box roughly 8p5 wide and 14p5 high.

2. Notice that the box has pushed the type out of the way. With the picture box still selected, use the Item>Send To Back command to change the stacking order so the picture will ride behind the text box.

Figure 3.22

Menu and Measurements palette access to text alignment.

Menu

Palette

Style	
Font	►
Size	►
Type Style	►
Color	►
Shade	►
Horizontal/Vertical Scale...	
Kern...	
Baseline Shift...	
Character...	Ctrl+Shift+D
Character Style Sheet	►
Text to Box	
Alignment	►
Leading...	Ctrl+Shift+E
Formats...	Ctrl+Shift+F
Tabs...	Ctrl+Shift+T
Rules...	Ctrl+Shift+N
Paragraph Style Sheet	►
Flip Horizontal	
Flip Vertical	

✓ Left	Ctrl+Shift+L
Centered	Ctrl+Shift+C
Right	Ctrl+Shift+R
Justified	Ctrl+Shift+J
Forced	Ctrl+Alt+Shift+J

X: 3p   W: 45p   △ 0°   auto   Opus   50 pt
Y: 10p   H: 8p4   Cols: 1

This works because we set a default for text boxes to have a color of None.

3. With the picture box still selected, activate the Measurements palette, ⌘+Option+M (Mac) or Ctrl+Alt+M (Win95).

If they are not already correct, type in the X/Y and W/H numbers for the picture box:

X/Y = **3p, 3p**

W/H = **8p5, 14p5**

4. Get the picture from your CD-ROM, ⌘+E (Mac) or Ctrl+E. It is the file named **LightBulb.EPS**.

As always, copy it from your CD-ROM to your hard drive first. Never, except in very unusual circumstances, import a file from removable media such as a CD, a floppy, or a Zip drive.

Right-Aligning Text

5. With that out of the way, you can right-align both the title and subtitle paragraphs.

Click and drag the Content tool through at least a little bit of both paragraphs.

Use the keyboard shortcut for right alignment, ⌘+Shift+R (Mac) or Ctrl+Shift+R (Win95).

Notice that most of the text on this page has already been aligned correctly by default, including the main group of text in the middle, the pricing data.

Justifying Text

6. Click anywhere in the body copy text that begins "Call us toll free…" and set it to be justified, ⌘+Shift+J (Mac) or Ctrl+Shift+J (Win95).

Centering Text

7. Center the address paragraphs. Select both of them with the Content tool and press ⌘+Shift+C (Mac) or Ctrl+Shift+C (Win95).

The progress so far on the price sheet has been saved on the CD-ROM in a file named **03BASE07.QXT**. You can see what it should look like in Figure 3.23.

Figure 3.23

The price sheet with paragraphs correctly aligned.

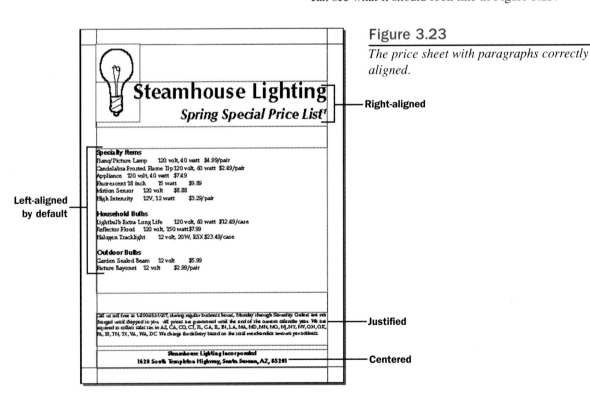

Setting Tabs and Indents

Another way we align text is to set tabs and indents.

For this project, the pricing information needs to be organized into columns of data. In addition, we want to slightly indent the pricing data underneath the headlines.

By the way, tabs and indents are paragraph attributes just like paragraph alignment. It isn't necessary to highlight an entire paragraph in order to apply these attributes, although it is often convenient to set tabs or indents by selecting a number of paragraphs at the same time.

1. Begin by selecting all the pricing data paragraphs.

    Go ahead and include the category headlines in the selection. That will make it easy to apply tabs to all the pricing data in one move and will have no effect on the formatting of the text since there are no tabs in the headlines.

Panning the Page

2. Hold down Option (Mac) or Alt (Win95), then click and drag the page to the right as far as you can and still see the text. That will leave room for the tab dialog so you can see your formatting take effect.

    This page panning technique will save you tons of time during your design work. Notice that you were able to move the view around even though you had something selected.

Tab Dialog Box and Tab Ruler

3. Open the Paragraph Attributes dialog with the Tab mode selected, **Style>T**abs or use the keyboard shortcuts, ⌘+⬆Shift+T (Mac) or Ctrl+⬆Shift+T (Win95).

    Click and drag the title bar of the dialog to shift it to the left. The idea is to be able to simultaneously see the tab dialog and your text as much as possible in your available screen space.

Notice that a special tab ruler has opened along the top edge of the text box where you selected your text.

Setting a Centering Tab

4. In order to center all the voltage and wattage entries on one another, you need a centering tab.

    Select a centering tab by clicking it in the dialog box.

5. Now click in the empty space inside the tab ruler at 24 picas. A centering tab marker will be placed in the ruler.

    You may need to directly type in the 24p position in the dialog box. It's not always easy to get the position just right with the mouse.

6. Click the Apply button to see the effect of your tab. It should look something like Figure 3.24, with all the voltage and wattage items centered on the 24 pica mark.

Setting a Decimal Tab

7. Perform the same operation again, except this time select a decimal tab and click it onto the tab ruler at the 40-pica mark.

8. Press Return (Mac) or ⬏Enter (Win95) to finalize the tab setting and close the dialog box.

Indenting Paragraphs

9. Select the first set of items that need to be indented, the first group of price data. You want the items beginning with "Piano/Picture Lamp" through "High Intensity," but don't include the headline.

10. Use the **Style>Form**ats command, ⌘+⬆Shift+F (Mac) or Ctrl+⬆Shift+F (Win95), to open up the Paragraph Attributes dialog box. It's the same dialog that has the tab section but this time in a different mode.

11. The Left Indent field should already be highlighted. Just type in **1p3** and click OK or press Return (Mac) or ⬏Enter (Win95).

Tab alignment selections

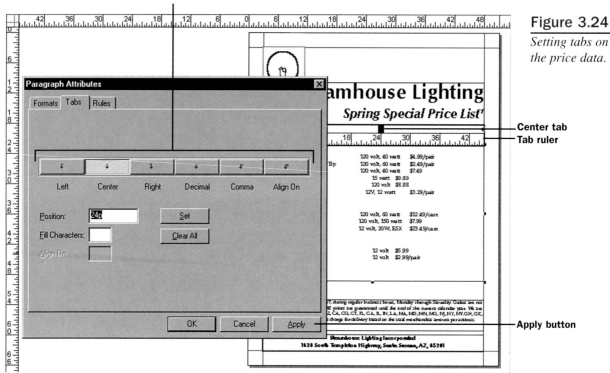

Figure 3.24
Setting tabs on the price data.

Center tab
Tab ruler

Apply button

12. Use this same technique to indent the other two groups of pricing data—being sure not to indent the headlines. Go back through the steps to refresh your memory, if you need to do so.

Select at least some part of each paragraph in the group. Open up the paragraph formats dialog box using the keyboard shortcut. Set the left indent at 1p3.

Your price sheet is almost done and it should look like the one we have saved for you on the CD-ROM under the name **03BASE08.QXT**. It also should look like the one in Figure 3.25.

Establishing Paragraph Rules

Usually people think of drawing lines, but QuarkXPress has yet another paragraph attribute to add to the ones you have already learn in this chapter. It will automatically draw lines for you, lines called paragraph rules. In this exercise, you will set up some dotted paragraph rules to visually break up the three groups of price data.

1. With the Content tool, click the first price headline, "Specialty Items."

2. There's only one place you can set a paragraph rule in QuarkXPress and that's back in Paragraph Attributes.

Tip

Copy Paragraph Formatting

If we hadn't wanted you to get the experience of performing this formatting, we could have saved you some time. You can save yourself some time in the future by "pasting" formatting from one paragraph to another. Click in or select any part of the paragraph or paragraphs that you want to receive the new formatting. Then Option + ⬆Shift + click (Mac) or Alt + ⬆Shift + click (Win95) on the paragraph that has the formatting you want to copy.

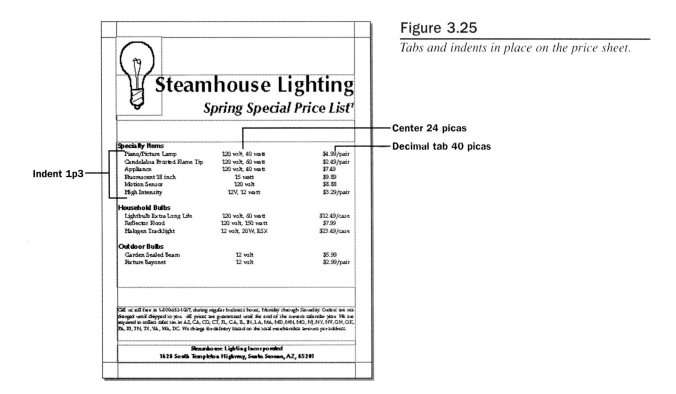

Figure 3.25

Tabs and indents in place on the price sheet.

Center 24 picas
Decimal tab 40 picas
Indent 1p3

Go there now, either by using the menu command of **St**yle>**Ru**les, or through the keyboard shortcut, ⌘+⬆Shift+N (Mac) or Ctrl+⬆Shift+N (Win95).

3. Set up your paragraph rule as you see in Figure 3.26.

Turn on the rule above checkbox. That means the rule will be above the type in the paragraph you have selected.

Set a left indent of 19p6 so the rule will be well clear of the headline text.

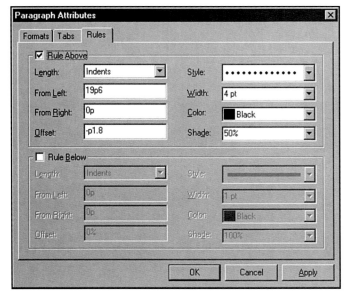

Figure 3.26

Setting up paragraph rules.

Offset the rule a minus 1.8 points so the line will ride down into the line and will be more or less vertically centered on the headline.

Select the "All Dots" style of line.

Make its width 4 points.

Shade it 50% so we will have a gray dotted line, not a 100% black one.

Click OK to accept all the settings and you will see that QuarkXPress has automatically drawn a gray dotted line, a paragraph rule.

4. Duplicate the paragraph rule settings for the other two price data headlines, using the same settings as in step 3.

Tip

Use Paragraph and Character Styles

In Chapter 7, you will learn about paragraph and character stylesheets. You will especially love styles if you keep in mind how tedious it has been to do all the repetitive formatting in this chapter. One of the great benefits of styles is their ability to apply many formatting attributes in a single click of the mouse.

That's it. You've created the price sheet, which should look like the one in Figure 3.1. We've saved the final version on the CD-ROM for you as the file named **03BASE09.QXT**.

Checking Your Skills

You've picked up some important concepts in this chapter, very basic to almost anything you will want to do in QuarkXPress. Knowing about basic type measurements, linking text boxes, how to navigate through and select text—all these things are as important to someone in the graphics arts as it is for an accountant to know how to add. They are, in fact, the foundations for moving on to the next chapter where you will learn some of the aspects of fine typography.

Review It

As a review of what you learned in this chapter, please answer the following questions.

1. What is the default size of an em space in QuarkXPress when it comes fresh from the factory?

2. What is the standard size of an em space in other desktop publishing programs?

3. How many picas are there in an inch? Points in a pica?

4. What happens every time QuarkXPress does an Autosave?

5. How many kinds of text alignment does QuarkXPress have? What are they?

_____

_____

6. What feature enables QuarkXPress to automatically draw lines?

_____

_____

7. What tool allows you to flow text from text box to text box?

_____

_____

8. What does the keyboard shortcut ⌘+Ⓐ (Mac) or Ctrl+Ⓐ (Win95) do if you have an active text insertion point?

_____

_____

9. What's the logic behind XPress text navigation keyboard shortcuts?

_____

_____

10. What's the keyboard shortcut to move backwards through the Measurements palette fields?

_____

_____

Check It

Multiple Choice

Please circle the correct answer for each of the following questions.

1. It would have been easier to perform the formatting of the price sheet if you had _____

    a.   used menu commands

    b.   used keyboard shortcuts

    c.   used stylesheets

    d.   all of the above

2. To align paragraph text, you _____

    a.   click on Measurements palette buttons

    b.   use keyboard shortcuts

    c.   choose from menu commands

    d.   all of the above

3. In order to make QuarkXPress measure ems in the standard way, you must _____

    a.   change a setting in Document Preferences

    b.   change Application Preferences

    c.   send away for a software patch

    d.   type it explicitly in the Measurements palette

4. To precisely set the origin point and size of a box, you can use _____

    a.   modify command or Measurements palette

    b.   click and drag while monitoring the Measurements palette

    c.   watch the marks on the rulers

    d.   all of the above

5. In order to style type as bold, you can use _____.

   a. keyboard shortcuts

   b. Measurements palette

   c. type style menu command

   d. all of the above

6. The difference between the superior type style and the superscript/subscript typestyles is _____.

   a. superior changes the alignment of the type

   b. superior reduces size

   c. superior can be set in preferences

   d. all of the above

7. You can precisely set the position of a tab by _____.

   a. sliding the marker with a click-and-drag move

   b. nudging it with the arrow keys

   c. explicitly typing it into the dialog box

   d. all of the above

8. Which paragraph attributes can be set through the Style>Formats dialog box?

   a. Tabs, borders, indents

   b. Tabs, rules, indents

   c. Tabs, alignment, superscript

   d. All of the above

9. The keyboard shortcut for centering text is _____

   a. ⌘+Alt+C (Mac) or Ctrl+Alt+C (Win95)

   b. ⌘+Shift+E (Mac) or Ctrl+Shift+E (Win95)

   c. ⌘+Shift+C (Mac) or Ctrl+Shift+C (Win95)

   d. None of the above

10. Some type styles are considered amateurish, such as _____.

   a. rotated and skewed

   b. shadow and outline

   c. italic and superscript

   d. all of the above

True or False

Please circle _T_ or _F_ to indicate whether the statement is true or false.

T F **1.** It's easy to increase the size of type by pressing the keyboard shortcuts ⌘+Shift+> (Mac) or Ctrl+Shift+> (Win95).

T F **2.** You can find a font in a QuarkXPress Measurements palette list by typing its first few letters.

T F **3.** To select an entire story, you quadruple-click it.

T F **4.** To force text into the next linked text box, press Shift+Enter.

T F **5.** Move backward through text one word at a time by pressing ⌘+← (Mac) or Ctrl+← (Win95).

T F **6.** In order to keep your tool in place after using it, so it won't flip back to the Item or Content tool, hold down ⌘ (Mac) or Ctrl (Win95) while selecting it.

T F **7.** In order to set a default for all future documents, you make the setting with no document open.

T F **8.** To pan your page view, hold down the Option (Mac) or Alt (Win95) key while clicking and dragging.

T F **9.** To set a paragraph rule, indent or tab, you must first select the entire paragraph.

T F **10.** You adjust the height of small caps in the Measurements palette.

Design It

Setting up tables of information can be a deceptively easy task in desktop publishing. Deceptively easy because as simple as the formatting steps are, it can be quite difficult to make good-looking, easy-to-read tables.

- Spend some time experimenting with the headline formatting in the price sheet you have just completed. Would it have been better to have the headlines categorizing groups of data formatted in Opus?

- How would the bulb descriptions have looked if they were left tabs instead of center tabs?

- How might you change the paragraph rules in order to serve up the data in a more readable way? What if they were solid lines? If they were solid lines, how thick would they need to be?

Spacing Type: Part One

Giving the Price List a New Look

What You Will Learn

When you look at a page of type, it may seem as if the thin lines of ink that form the letters are pretty much the only important thing on that page. However, that entire page of type simply would not exist if not for the *space* between those thin lines. The space between letters and words—the visual space that separates the thin lines of ink—literally makes it possible for us to read what's on the page.

The amount of space you, as the designer, decide to allow between letters and words and lines can have an enormous impact on the readability and the visual appeal of a page of text. If you think about it, this makes a lot of sense. After all, the ink forming letters on the page may cover only 20% or 30% of the actual surface area of the page—with the rest being the space between the ink marks.

This chapter is the first of two that cover almost every aspect of how you create space when you set type. In this chapter, you will learn about:

➤ Adjusting the spacing between specific pairs of letters using kerning

➤ Taking advantage of built-in kerning with the autokerning feature

➤ Setting type tracking—making overall adjustments of spacing between many letters at a time

➤ Managing letter spacing, word spacing, and hyphenation parameters for justified text

➤ Setting leading, the spacing between lines of type

Steamhouse Lighting
1628 South Templeton Highway
Santa Susana, AZ 85201

See Our New Line Of Table Lamps!
We have listed here only a few of the lighting possibilities opened up by our new line of table lamps. They have been hand-crafted using fine materials flown in to our Arizona workshop—rich green marble and warm mahogany wood, set off by shades of linen and bamboo.

Lamp Bases
Marble $99.95
Granite , , ...$119.95

Lamp Shades
Linen.....................................$29.99
Canvas $39.99
Split Bamboo.........................$49.99
Woven Reed $64.99

Household Bulbs
Long Life ....120 volt, 60 watt................$12.49/case
Reflector Flood ....120 volt, 150 watt................$7.99
Halogen Track ....12 volt, 20W, ESX.............$23.49/case

Outdoor Bulbs
Sealed Beam ....12 volt.............................$5.99
Fixture Bayonet................12 volt.............................$2.99/pair
No Bug Orange................120 volts, 60 watt ....$1.49 each

Specialty Items
Piano/Picture...................120 volt, 40 watt.................$4.99/pair
Candelabra ....   120 volt, 60 watt.................$2.49/pair
Refrigerator ....120 volt, 40 watt.................$7.49
Oven.................................120 volt, 40 watt.................$7.99
Fluorescent ....15 watt, 18 inch $9.89
High Intensity.................12V, 12 watt.......................$3.29/pair
Motion Sensor ....120 volt..............................$8.88

Call us toll free at 1-800-652-1067, during regular business hours, Monday through Saturday. Orders are not charged until shipped to you. All prices are guaranteed until the end of the current calendar year. We are required to collect sales tax in AZ, CA, CO, CT, FL, GA, IL, IN, LA, MA, MD, MN, MO, NJ, NY, NV, OH, OK, PA, RI, TN, TX, VA, WA, DC. We charge for delivery based on the total merchandise amount per address.

Spring Sale Specials!

Figure 4.1

This new version of the price list you built in the last chapter has been spun around into a horizontal format.

Design Notes

You will find many occasions in your design career where an existing design must be revamped to accommodate some new circumstance. That's what you'll be doing in this chapter, redesigning the price sheet design you created in Chapter 3. In this case, our hypothetical lighting company has been growing. By adding a new line of goods, table lamps, they outgrew their old price sheet design. They needed to fit more information on a page and also, like a lot of clients, they told us they "just want a new look."

The solution to this design challenge, as you see in Figure 4.1, was to turn the price sheet on its side and set the pricing information in two columns, a more economical use of space that permitted us to fit more items into the price list. Some other changes were also made—adding the information about the new line of table lamps and some copy editing of descriptions, as well as making the type a bit smaller. In addition, the light bulb graphic has been made much larger and some new graphic elements have been added.

Prep Notes

Copy all the files for this chapter from the CD-ROM to a work area on your hard drive. They are all in the **Steps** folder in the folder labeled **04**.

You will need the same fonts you used in Chapter 3 to be installed on your computer system, Opus and URW Palladio.

After you finish the first exercise in this chapter, each following exercise builds on the previous one. Except where we've indicated otherwise, you should save your price list design project at the end of each exercise so you can pick up where you left off at the beginning of the next exercise.

Getting Set Up...Mostly Review

In this section, you will literally turn the price sheet you constructed in Chapter 3 on its side, converting it from a vertical design into a horizontal one. In the process, you will learn a few new skills but primarily you will get some practice—as well as gain more confidence—with some of the skills you learned in the first three chapters of this book.

Changing Page Orientation

It should be the simplest thing in the world to tell QuarkXPress to turn this page on its side. In fact, it is quite simple, except for a QuarkXPress idiosyncrasy you are about to encounter. As a solution, you will use the QuarkXPress pasteboard feature for the first time in this course.

1. Begin by opening a copy of the vertical version of the price sheet.

   For best results, you should copy the file you built as it was at the end of Chapter 3. A few of the upcoming steps dealing with picture usage will work best that way.

   However, if you prefer, we have included the Chapter 3 version of the price sheet as the first of the Chapter 4 step files on the CD-ROM. Its new

name is **04BASE01.QXT**. If you decide to use the CD-ROM file instead of copy the last chapter's file, some of the following steps won't work quite right. Those will be the ones having to do with picture usage.

Whichever approach you choose, copying the file from Chapter 3 or using the one on the CD, save the new file under a name of your choice in your working folder.

Exploring Pasteboard Limits

2. You should now try to change the orientation of the page from vertical to horizontal. (You'll see that it won't work but that's okay, it's just part of this learning exercise.)

   Use **File>Document Setup**, ⌘+Option+⬆Shift+P (Mac) or Ctrl+Alt+⬆Shift+P (Win95), to reach the Document Setup dialog box in Figure 4.2.

Figure 4.2

Document Setup dialog box with horizontal or landscape orientation selected.

(Win95) The Windows 95 version of the Document Setup dialog box has buttons instead of icons for Portrait (vertical) and Landscape (horizontal) views.

3. Select landscape orientation, the horizontal view, and click OK, or press Return (Mac) or ⏎Enter (Win95).

4. You will get the dialog box in Figure 4.3, telling you that you can't change the page orientation because some of the objects just won't fit.

The explanation for this difficulty can be seen in Figure 4.4.

When you try to cram a vertical format document into the 52-pica-tall horizontal layout space window, you run out of space; then QuarkXPress just doesn't know what to do with the items that fall out of bounds of its available layout space.

The wide area to the sides of the page, and the small space above and below the page, are the Pasteboard. The main purpose of the Pasteboard is temporary storage as you work on a layout. You can drag items there to hold them off the page while you work with other elements.

However, as useful as it is, the QuarkXPress Pasteboard has a downside. It's much smaller above and below the page than it is to the left and right of the page. You might say, so what? Who cares how big the Pasteboard is?

But that is the crux of the QuarkXPress idiosyncrasy we mentioned because QuarkXPress insists that there be enough room above and below the page to make room for all the objects on the page

as they rotate. If the Pasteboard space above and below the page is too small to make room for the items to swing through, QuarkXPress will deny you permission to change the page orientation.

5. The solution in this particular case is to eliminate some of the material on the page so everything can fit in the new, shorter vertical layout space available in the horizontal orientation. That's okay because we have some copy edits to complete as part of this redesign job.

Close out of the message and dialog boxes and we will get to work on the copy edit. And, if your Tool palette isn't showing, activate it by pressing F8.

Choose the Content tool to get ready for editing this text.

6. Select the order information paragraph, the one beginning with the words "Call us toll free,,,," You can select the text by clicking and dragging the selection pointer over the text, or by one of the other text selection methods you studied in the "Introducing...QuarkXPress Text Navigation" section of Chapter 3.

Figure 4.3

QuarkXPress denying permission to rotate the page orientation.

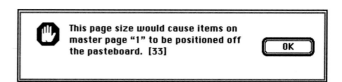

Figure 4.4

Stacked views of the QuarkXPress layout space, horizontal page (top) and vertical page (bottom).

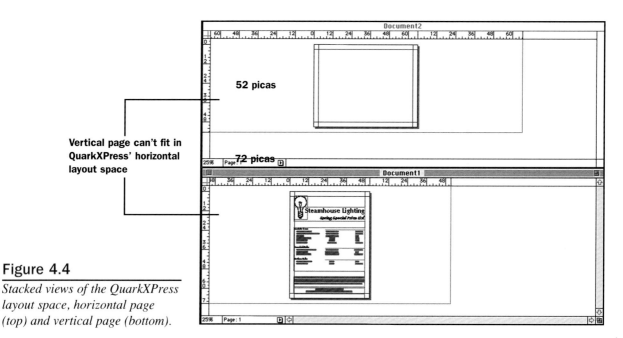

Cutting Text

7. With the paragraph selected, use the shortcut for the **Edit>Cut** command, ⌘+X (Mac) or Ctrl+X (Win95), to get the text onto your Clipboard memory.

Storing Text on the Pasteboard

8. Select the Rectangular Text Box tool and draw out a text box on the Pasteboard to the right of the page.

Pasting Text

9. Paste the text into the new text box using the shortcut for the **Edit>Paste** command, ⌘+V (Mac) or Ctrl+V (Win95).

Deleting Text

10. Get the ordering information text ready by editing out two items.

Drag out the box so you can see the entire paragraph of text.

Navigate your text cursor to just after the subscript number, located before the words, "All prices are guaranteed." Use the Del (Mac) or ◄Backspace (Win95) key to wipe out the number.

Also, delete the new box character, the red square after the words "merchandise amount per address" at the end of the paragraph. It's at the absolute end of the text box so you'll need to navigate to the point just before it and press Del (Mac) or Del (Win95).

Your document should look like the one in Figure 4.5.

11. Select and delete all the text between the title and the address, including the paragraph, "Spring Special Price List" through the company name in the address text box.

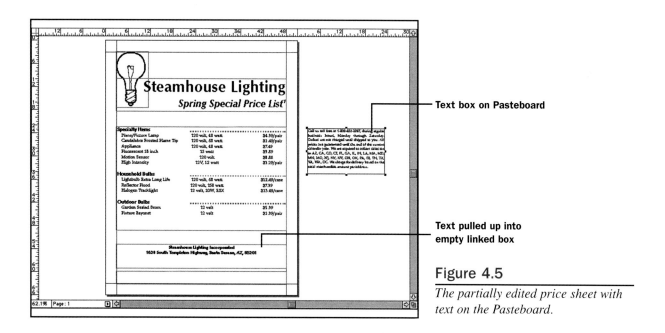

Text box on Pasteboard

Text pulled up into empty linked box

Figure 4.5

The partially edited price sheet with text on the Pasteboard.

Because the text boxes are linked, the address paragraph should snap up into the title text box, right below "Steamhouse Lighting."

12. Remove the empty text boxes from the page.

With the Item tool selected, click the bottom text box.

⟨⬆Shift⟩+Click the other two empty text boxes.

Press ⟨Del⟩ (Mac) or ⟨⬅Backspace⟩ (Win95) and you will get a warning dialog box that these are linked text boxes. Say OK to the warning in order to finish the text edits. Your publication should now look something like Figure 4.6.

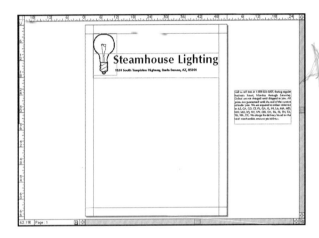

Figure 4.6

The final edited text.

Changing Document Orientation

13. This time, the document orientation should work just fine since we've removed from the page the items that were causing it to be too tall to rotate.

Use **File>Document Setup**, ⟨⌘⟩+⟨Option⟩+⟨⬆Shift⟩+⟨P⟩ (Mac) or ⟨Ctrl⟩+⟨Alt⟩+⟨⬆Shift⟩+⟨P⟩ (Win95), and choose the landscape orientation, just as you did once before at the beginning of this section.

The result should look like Figure 4.7.

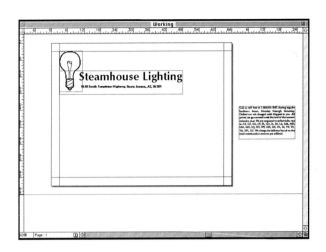

Figure 4.7

The beginnings of the new horizontal layout.

Setting Ruler Guides

14. To speed this layout process along, we've figured out ahead of time where you will need guides. That will make it easier to position text boxes and other items on the page so we can focus on the main point of this chapter—spacing text.

If the Measurements palette isn't showing, activate it now by pressing ⟨F9⟩. If Show Guides isn't turned on, press ⟨F7⟩.

It can be easier to accurately set guides at a higher magnification so you may want to be at Actual Size or 200% view.

Make sure Snap to Guides is on, **View>Snap to Guides**, ⟨⬆Shift⟩+⟨F7⟩.

15. Set the vertical guides.

Pull a ruler guide out from the vertical ruler at the left side of the QuarkXPress window and position it so the X coordinate on the Measurements palette reads 15 picas. Repeat this operation until you have ruler guides with X coordinates at 16 picas, 32 picas, 34 picas, and 35 picas.

16. Set the horizontal guides.

Pull a ruler guide out from the horizontal ruler at the top of the QuarkXPress window and position it so the Y coordinate on the Measurements palette reads 9 picas. Repeat this operation until you have three more ruler guides at the Y coordinates of 14 picas, 39 picas, and 46 picas.

Take note that you already have margin guides set at 3 picas around the page.

All the guides have been noted in Figure 4.9 at the end of this section.

Checking Picture Usage

17. Working on an old version of a file can be treacherous. How do you know, for instance, that the light bulb graphic is the latest one? And how do you know that the graphic in this publication is the one from folder 04, as opposed to the old project folder 03?

Use the Utilities>Usage command and click the Picture tab in the dialog box to check your graphic. Click on the name of the graphic in the dialog box to select it, and click the **M**ore Information option so the dialog box looks like the one in Figure 4.8.

Notice where the actual linked graphic is located. Chances are, since this was a copied file from the last chapter, it will not be in your current working folder.

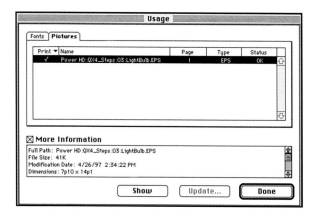

Figure 4.8

Checking picture usage.

Updating a Picture

18. Select the light bulb graphic with either the Content or Item tool and Get Picture, ⌘+E (Mac) or Ctrl+E (Win95).

In the file selection dialog box, choose the **LIGHTBULB.EPS** file you copied for this chapter from the CD-ROM.

It will automatically replace the old graphic. If you went to Usage now, it would show that the graphic was located in your working folder.

Sizing and Positioning a Graphic

19. You need to increase the size of the light bulb graphic for this new design.

Select the light bulb graphic with the Item tool.

In the Measurements palette (or you could do this using the Modify command if you prefer), edit the X% and Y% scale of the light bulb to 150%.

20. Drag out the picture box around the bulb so it is completely visible.

Snap the width of the box to the ruler guide at 12 picas. Pull the box down so it's 21 picas deep or more.

Positioning and Sizing Text Boxes

21. Slide the title text box into position so the base of the letters in the company name align with the filament of the light bulb. The left edge of the letter "S" should line up with the 16-pica vertical guide. You can check Figure 4.9 to get an idea of the vertical and horizontal positioning you are trying to achieve.

Using the Item tool, click and drag the title text box until the letters rest on the 9-pica horizontal ruler guide.

22. Format the title text.

Select the Content tool by using the ⌘+Tab⇥ (Mac) or Ctrl+Alt+Tab⇥ (Win95) keyboard shortcut to switch down from the Item tool.

With the text box still selected, select all the text inside it, ⌘+A (Mac) or Ctrl+A (Win95).

Left align the text, ⌘+⇧Shift+L (Mac) or Ctrl+⇧Shift+L (Win95).

Select all of the type in the address paragraph and use the Measurements palette to set this type at 22 points. At this size, the text may overflow the box so you may need to tweak the size up a bit.

Navigate to the point following the word "Highway," then delete the comma and its following space. Press Return (Mac) or ↵Enter (Win95) to put the city, state, and ZIP code in a new paragraph.

If necessary, resize the title text box by dragging down its bottom sizing handle to make all its text visible.

Edit out the comma following the state abbreviation, "AZ."

23. Using the Item tool, click and drag the ordering instructions, sliding this text box from the Pasteboard where you stored it earlier into the lower-right corner of the layout.

At this point, your layout should look like Figure 4.9.

The progress so far on the horizontal version of the price sheet has been saved on the CD-ROM in a file named **04BASE02.QXT**.

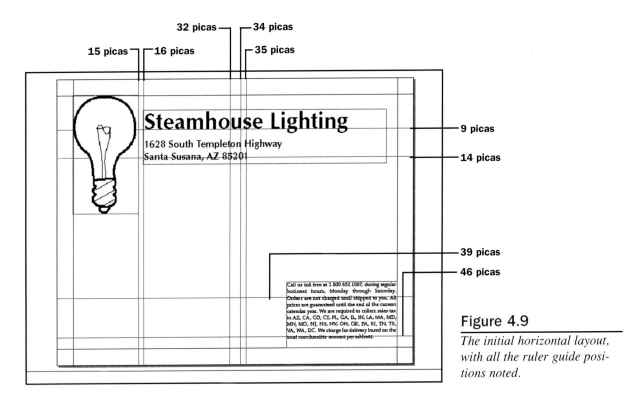

Figure 4.9

The initial horizontal layout, with all the ruler guide positions noted.

Introducing...Kerning, Autokerning, Tracking

All three of these typesetting techniques—kerning, autokerning, and tracking—allow you to take control of the space between letters.

A little printing history will help you understand the concept of kerning, and once you understand kerning, it'll be easy to grasp autokerning and tracking.

Most historians believe that Johannes Gutenberg was the first person to print a large book using movable type. That book was the Gutenberg Bible of 1456. In virtually all the years since then—roughly five centuries until we reached the modern ages of phototypesetting and digital typesetting—typesetters had only one way to reduce or increase the space between letters of type. They had to actually remove or add metal on each side of a piece of type.

In order to reduce the space between two letters, they would use a knife to shave bits of lead from the sides of the letters. The resulting overhang was called a kern and thus we got the term kerning.

Kerning

Today, the original meaning of the word kern has been somewhat distorted to mean both the subtraction and addition of space between letters. Not only that, we've turned the word into a verb. So, we use the word kerning to describe the removal—or the insertion—of space between two letters. That's really important to understand. Kerning is the adjustment of space between a pair of letters.

Generally, we kern letters to make subtle changes so type looks better or is more readable, as in Figure 4.10.

In Figure 4.11, some not so subtle kerning has been used to easily achieve special effects that would have been nearly impossible to achieve with the old metal type.

Figure 4.10

The top example has been kerned too closely and the middle has no kerning applied at all. In the bottom example, the left edge of the letter "O" has been tucked beneath the right edge of the letter "T."

Figure 4.11

Using QuarkXPress kerning, you can even overlap letters, as in these special effects.

Autokerning

Certain pairs of letters seem to always require adjustment. For example, capital T, V, W, and Y almost always need kerning when they are preceded or followed by A, a, e, or o. Kerning instructions for these commonly adjusted pairs of letters, called kerning pairs, can be built into a font by the designer. Some programs, QuarkXPress being one of them, can interpret those instructions and automatically apply kerning to these standard kerning pairs—autokerning.

Tracking

Tracking makes automatic spacing adjustments on large spans of type, not pairs of letters. It is used to compensate for the spacing aberrations caused when you make type much bigger or smaller. Most typefaces have been designed for use as body text at 10- to 12-point size, so spacing compensation is needed when you radiaclly diverge from the original design size. Large type often needs to be tightened and small type sometimes needs to be loosened, as you can see in Figure 4.12.

Tracking set very loose on 12 point type

Tracking set normal on 12 point type

Tracking set tight on 12 point type

Tracking set very loose on 9 point type

Tracking set normal on 9 point type

Tracking set tight on 9 point type

Figure 4.12

Tracking reduces or expands spacing between letters to aid readability of different size settings of the same typeface.

Range Kerning

Now here's where things may get a bit confusing. Range kerning is where you select a range of text and apply a kerning adjustment. In other words, you apply kerning to more than a pair of letters. But, and this is a very big and confusing but, QuarkXPress uses the term tracking to refer to range kerning. In other words, QuarkXPress actually has two tracking commands. We will come back to this subject near the end of Chapter 5 and make sure you can keep them straight.

H&J Letterspacing

One last thing before we move ahead. Just to make sure you have the big picture, there's one more way that letter spacing gets adjusted in QuarkXPress. If you are working with justified type, you can allow QuarkXPress to make adjustments between letters in order to make lines of type come out even along both the left and right sides of a column. This letter spacing is one aspect of your H&J (hyphenation and justification) settings. We'll be setting H&Js in this chapter as well.

Kerning Type

In this section, you will kern the letters in the price list title. You'll need the keyboard shortcuts listed in Table 4.1 in order to complete the upcoming steps.

Keyboard Commands for Kerning

Table 4.1   QuarkXPress kerning keyboard shortcuts

Kern Amount (in 1/200 em units)	Mac	Win95
Increase 1 unit	⌘+Shift+Option+]	Ctrl+Shift+Alt+]
Decrease 1 unit	⌘+Shift+Option+[	Ctrl+Shift+Alt+[
Increase 10 units	⌘+Shift+]	Ctrl+Shift+]
Decrease 10 units	⌘+Shift+[	Ctrl+Shift+[

1. Magnify your view by dragging out a marquee around the company name "Steamhouse Lighting" with the Zoom tool, Ctrl+Click & Drag (Mac) or Ctrl+Spacebar+Click & Drag (Win95).

2. Turn on the Measurements palette if it isn't already showing, F9.

3. Use the kerning shortcuts in Table 4.1 to close up the letters in the title.

   Navigate your text editing cursor to the first pair of letters and narrow the space between them until it seems too crowded and then back off a bit.

   Notice how you can see the kerning amount change as you work by observing the kerning field in the Measurements palette, just to the right of center.

   You will probably find yourself working with the smallest kerning increments, one unit at a time, rather than the big kerning movements of ten units at a time. In QuarkXPress, each unit of kerning registered in the Measurements palette is 1/200 of an em.

4. When the visual space between the first pair of letters seems about right, move to the next pair of letters.

   Notice the use of the words "visual space." Each pair of letters will need a different kerning amount, but your goal is to have the letters look evenly spaced.

5. Once you have done all the kerning you feel is needed, have a look at your work at a lower magnification to evaluate the overall look of the job.

   If any of the spacing looks uneven, make further adjustments.

6. When you are all done, have a look at Figure 4.13.

   You don't need to do this on your own page, but we have stacked before and after versions of the title in Figure 4.13 so you can see the visual changes between unkerned and kerned type.

Your letters should look more closed up than the unkerned version, yet they should look quite evenly spaced.

Move your text editor cursor through the letters and examine the amount of kerning between each one, compared to the amounts in Figure 4.13.

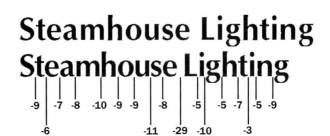

Figure 4.13
Before and after kerning versions of the price list title.

7. Perform the same kerning operations on the address.

   Notice with the smaller size of type used in the address, you may not need quite as much kerning in order to achieve the same degree of tightness of the letters.

   Do take care to tighten up the address so it will fit in the space between the initial letter "S" in "Steamhouse," and the "g" in "Lighting." That spacing will become important in a later step in this chapter. The address will actually be pulled up into this space when we adjust the leading, the vertical spacing, of these lines.

   Take special note of how certain combinations seem to nestle closer together, such as the "62" combination in "1628," or the "Te" combination in "Templeton."

8. Compare your final results to our finished kerning job shown in Figure 4.14.

   Bear in mind that these kerning adjustments are subjective judgments and there's no perfect answer here. Your adjustments may vary from ours.

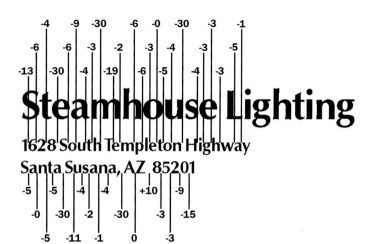

Steamhouse Lighting

1628 South Templeton Highway

Santa Susana, AZ 85201

Figure 4.14

The completed kerning job on the title text block.

Autokerning is controlled in **E**dit>Preferences> Document, ⌘+Ⓨ (Mac) or Ctrl+Ⓨ (Win95), in the Character tab of the Document Preferences dialog box.

The default setting you see in Figure 4.15 means that QuarkXPress will use a font's built-in kerning pair information for any type set in a size above 4 points.

Remember that the power of Autokerning depends on the designer of the font. Some fonts have many hundreds of kerning pairs built into them, and others have only a few.

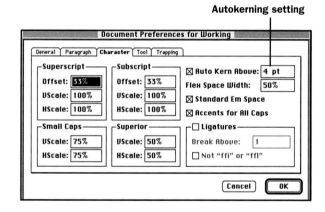

Figure 4.15

Checking to see that Autokerning is turned on.

Tip

Print Proofs to Evaluate Kerning on the Page Instead of the Screen

A screen representation of type can be only so accurate. For reliable proofing of critical letter spacing, including manual kerning, you'll need to evaluate actual printouts. Do use caution, though, in evaluating letter spacing for type below 16 points or so if you are proofing on a printer with a resolution of less than 600 dpi. The results at such low resolution may not match the results you get when you go to a high resolution imagesetter for final output to give your commercial printer.

Setting Autokerning

It would be totally impractical to kern large amounts of text as meticulously as you've just kerned the title of this price sheet. Imagine the time it would take to kern all the 10- or 11-point body copy in a 600-page book.

That's where Autokerning comes in.

By default, QuarkXPress has Autokerning turned on. That's good because it really helps the look of your type and there aren't many situations where you wouldn't want it.

Tip

Create Your Own Kerning Pairs

As you gain in typographical sophistication, you may find yourself always kerning certain letter pairs in your favorite fonts. You can create your own kerning pairs by using Utilities>Kerning Table Edit. Of course, these kerning pairs only apply in QuarkXPress and won't have any effect in other programs such as Adobe Illustrator or another page layout program such as PageMaker.

- The current price sheet, as in Figure 4.16, has been saved on the CD-ROM in a file named **04BASE03.QXT**.

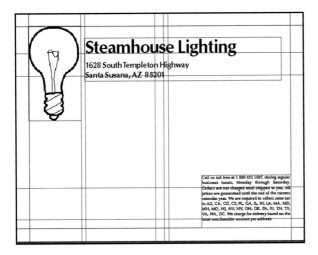

Figure 4.16

Progress to this point on the price sheet.

Introducing...Leading

The term *leading* comes from the old days when typesetters set type by hand. Line spacing was achieved with strips of metal (actually lead or brass) that fit between the lines of type. In those days, adding two points of leading to a section of type meant inserting a two-point-thick shim of metal to open up an extra two points of space between a pair of lines of type.

DTP Leading

In the DTP (Desktop Publishing) world, leading has generally come to mean something slightly different than the traditional definition. Leading these days means the total space occupied by the entire line of type—the point size of the type as well as any negative or positive vertical line spacing adjustments you make in QuarkXPress.

Using QuarkXPress, a typographer might say that type has been set "11 on 13," meaning 11-point type in 13-point leading (11 points of type plus 2 points of old-fashioned leading).

You may understand this point more easily by looking at Figure 4.17, which shows a variety of leading amounts on some sample type. (As you may surmise from the illustration, sometimes the total height of a line is called a *slug*. The term slug comes from the days of hot metal typesetting with a Linotype, where the type was cast in strips, called slugs.)

When the typesetter punched out this slug, he was slugged by the editor. This was no surprise, since the typesetter had made the type **14 points on 14** points leading.

When the typesetter punched out this slug, he was slugged by the editor. This was no surprise, since the typesetter had made the type **14 points on 16** points leading.

When the typesetter punched out this slug, he was slugged by the editor. This was no surprise, since the typesetter had made the type **14 points on 20** points leading.

When the typesetter punched out this slug, he was slugged by the editor. This was no surprise, since the typesetter had made the type **14 points on 24** points leading.

Figure 4.17

A variety of leading amounts, all shown on 14-point type.

Three QuarkXPress Leading Techniques

In QuarkXPress, leading is a paragraph attribute. You can't set 14-point leading on a paragraph and then apply 20-point leading to just one word in the paragraph.

You have three ways to set the amount of leading.

You can set leading from the menu with Style>Leading, ⌘+◆Shift+E (Mac) or Ctrl+◆Shift+E (Win95). That takes you to the Formats tab of the Paragraph Attributes dialog box in Figure 4.18.

You can also set leading right in the Measurements palette by typing in an amount, or by clicking the increase/decrease arrows just above the setting for kerning, as in Figure 4.19.

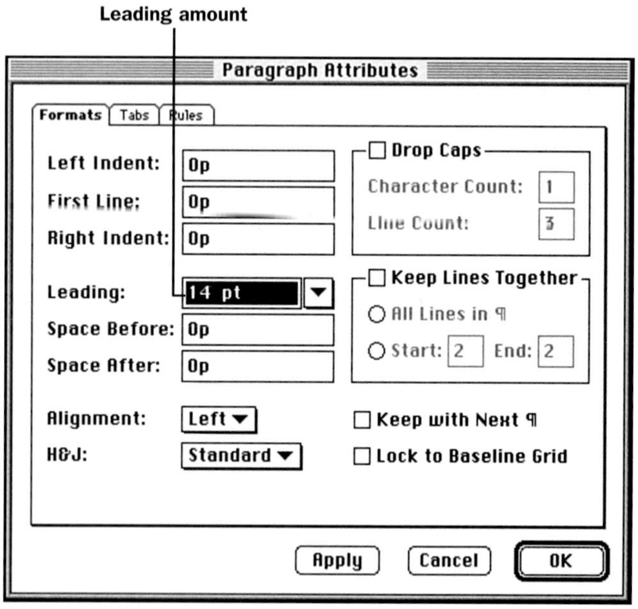

Leading amount

Figure 4.18

Setting leading from the menu.

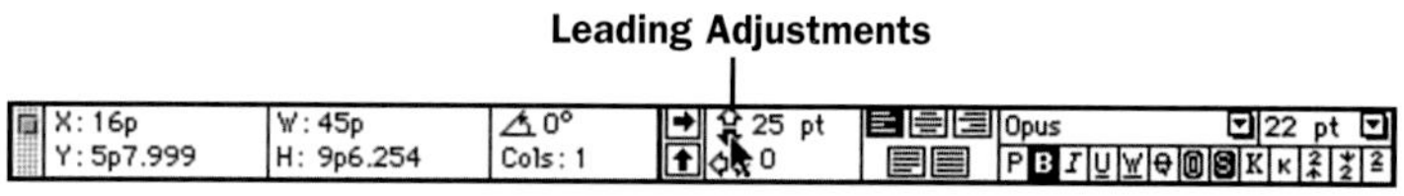

Leading Adjustments

Figure 4.19

Setting leading from the Measurements palette.

Finally, and conveniently, you can set leading from the keyboard, as in Table 4.2.

Table 4.2 QuarkXPress leading keyboard shortcuts

Leading Amount	Mac	Win95
Increase 1 point	⌘+◆Shift+"	Ctrl+◆Shift+"
Decrease 1 point	⌘+◆Shift+:	Ctrl+◆Shift+:
Increase $\frac{1}{10}$ point	⌘+◆Shift+Option+"	Ctrl+◆Shift+Alt+"
Decrease $\frac{1}{10}$ point	⌘+◆Shift+Option+:	Ctrl+◆Shift+Alt+:

Leading Mode

You have a choice of two types of leading in QuarkXPress—Word Processing and Typesetting. You make your choice in **E**dit>Preferences>**D**ocument, in the Paragraph tab of the Document Preferences dialog box.

The default setting is Typesetting mode. Typesetting leading mode always measures the leading up from the baseline of a line of type—simple, straightforward, consistent. Good.

It's a good thing that Word Processor leading mode isn't the default because you should never use it. It measures the leading from the top of a capital letter on one line to the top of a capital letter on the next line. That means with all the variations in typeface design, you will never be able to tell exactly where your type will float within the slug. Nasty.

The baseline of your text runs along the bottom of the letters (except where their descenders, their "tails," fall below the baseline, as in the letters j, p, y, and g).

Controlling the Amount of Leading

Another type of leading you probably shouldn't ever use is autoleading. Autoleading notes the size of the tallest letter in a line and automatically calculates an extra amount of leading to make sure it has enough space on the line, and then applies that leading to the entire paragraph. The QuarkXPress default is to add 20% to the point size. So 12-point type would have 14.4 points of leading.

You can turn on autoleading in any paragraph using two of the three methods of leading technique we've already discussed in this section—menu and Measurements palette.

You can set the percentage amount of the autoleading in the same place as you set leading mode, the Paragraph tab of the Document Preferences dialog box.

Autoleading is convenient and easy, but you almost always should use fixed leading. For one thing, you usu-ally want to have all the lines in a paragraph evenly spaced and you want the spacing to be consistent from paragraph to paragraph. Check Figure 4.20 to see what happens when you put a bit of large type into a paragraph formatted with autoleading rather than fixed leading.

For another thing, who says that 120% leading is the right thing for your publication? Leading is a design decision and a big part of your control over how your type looks. So, the best thing is to control it with a specific amount of fixed leading.

Even now, the lurking aardvark crept forward across the desert sands. Its belly scraped along on the cool grit, providing an unnecessary reminder that hunger gnawed at the edges of its dim existence.

Even now, the lurking aardvark crept forward across the desert sands. Its belly scraped along on the cool grit, providing an unnecessary reminder that hunger gnawed at the edges of its dim existence.

Fig. 4.20

The unevenly spaced paragraph on the top is set with autoleading but the bottom has fixed leading.

Setting Leading

You may have noticed in the Measurements palette that all your type so far on this project is set with autoleading. It's time to remedy that. In this exercise, you'll try out all three leading techniques.

Setting Leading from the Menu

1. Using the Content tool, click a text insertion point anywhere in the title paragraph—the name of the company.

   Access the leading command with the keyboard shortcut, ⌘+⬆Shift+E (Mac) or Ctrl+⬆Shift+E (Win95).

   This type is 50 points and you should set it 50/55, that is 50-point type set in 55-point leading.

   Type **55** into the leading field of the dialog box, just like the one you saw in the "Introducing…Leading" section.

   Press Return (Mac) or ↵Enter (Win95) to put your leading setting into effect.

   Notice that this change doesn't seem to have much effect. That's because it's the first line in the text box. This is a general rule in QuarkXPress, that paragraph spacing settings such as leading and space above don't affect the position of the first line's baseline.

Setting Leading in the Measurements Palette

2. ⬇ to the first address paragraph, the one beginning "1628."

In the Measurements palette, click where it says "auto." Delete the word and replace it with fixed leading.

This is 22-point type and should be set 22/22. Type in **22** to replace auto in the Measurements palette and press `Return` (Mac) or `↵Enter` (Win95).

Notice how this fine leading adjustment capability has enabled us to snug the address line up under the name of the company, riding between the beginning of the line and the "g" in "Steamhouse Lighting."

Setting Leading from the Keyboard

3. ⬇ again to the second address paragraph, the one beginning "Santa Susana."

Use keyboard shortcuts to set this paragraph 22/22.

⌘+`⬆Shift`+`:` (Mac) or `Ctrl`+`⬆Shift`+`:` (Win95) several times until you see that the leading is set for 22 points in the Measurements palette.

4. Reduce the height of the text box by clicking and dragging up the bottom sizing handle until it is above the 14-pica horizontal guide line. You might want to zoom in for a closer view to help you make this adjustment.

5. Set the ordering information paragraph in the lower-right corner of the page at 11.5/16.

The type has already been set to 11.5 point size so use your favorite of the three leading techniques to adjust leading from auto to 16.

Whichever technique you use for this paragraph, you will probably need to adjust the text box so all the text is showing once you've set your leading.

Drag the left side sizing handle out to the left, well past the 32-pica vertical guide, until all the text is showing. You will come back and finish fine-tuning this text box later in this chapter.

When you are done, your layout should look like the one in Figure 4.21. This version of the layout has been saved on the CD-ROM in a file named **04BASE04. QXT**. You will want to start again with this file at the beginning of Chapter 5.

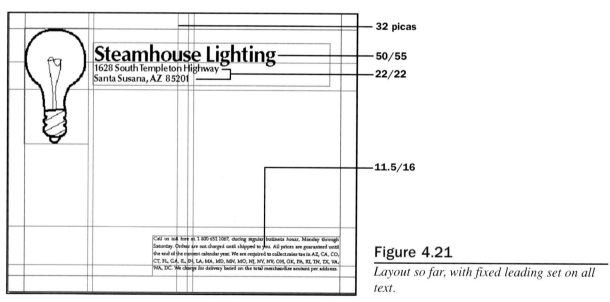

Figure 4.21

Layout so far, with fixed leading set on all text.

Summary

This chapter and the next one are one of those nine times eight makes seventy-two chapters. If you somehow missed out on that part of the multiplication tables in first grade, you probably had trouble with that bit of math for the rest of your life. The same is true here. These two chapters are the most fundamental ones in the book to your capabilities as a typesetter and, in truth, setting type is what you will be doing most of the time you are working in QuarkXPress. Spend extra time on this chapter and the next one if you need to do so in order to have these typesetting skills at your complete command.

Review It

As a review of what you have learned in this chapter, please answer the following questions.

1. What does it mean if a typographer specifies type as Times 10.5/14?

   _____

   _____

2. Describe the width of an em space for typographers and for the default QuarkXPress em space.

   _____

   _____

3. What's the difference between kerning and range kerning?

   _____

   _____

4. How would you use the Pasteboard during a layout job?

   _____

   _____

5. Give the key command for Select All, for reaching the Paragraph Attributes dialog box, and for Character Attributes.

   _____

   _____

6. What three methods do you have for setting leading?

   _____

   _____

7. Describe the main similarity and the main difference between kerning and autokerning.

   _____

   _____

8. What are the two QuarkXPress leading modes and how are they different?

   _____

   _____

9. What are the two leading methods that you should generally not use and why shouldn't you use them?

_____

_____

10. What are the basic keys (leaving off any modifier keys such as ⌘ or Ctrl), that form the heart of the shortcuts to adjust kerning and leading from the keyboard?

_____

_____

Check It

Multiple Choice

Please circle the correct answer for each of the following questions.

1. How can you set the leading on a paragraph?

   a. Keyboard shortcut

   b. Menu

   c. Measurements palette

   d. All of the above

2. Some of the QuarkXPress kerning reduction shortcuts are _____.

   a. Option+→ (Mac) or Alt+→ (Win95)

   b. ⌘+Shift+← (Mac) or Ctrl+Shift+← (Win95)

   c. ⌘+Shift+[(Mac) or Ctrl+Shift+[(Win95)

   d. All of the above

3. Which of the following leading modes is best?

   a. Word processing

   b. Typesetting

   c. Range length

   d. Enhanced

4. Autokerning settings are controlled by _____.

   a. Document Preferences setting

   b. Kerning pairs built into type

   c. Your own Kerning Table edits

   d. All of the above

5. The units of measurement for kerning are _____.

   a. $\frac{1}{200}$ of an em

   b. $\frac{1}{200}$ of a point

   c. $\frac{1}{20}$ of an em

   d. $\frac{1}{20}$ of a point

6. Typesetting leading mode measures the height of a line _____.

   a. From capital to capital

   b. By multiplying point size by 120%

   c. From baseline to baseline

   d. None of the above

7. A keyboard shortcut for reducing leading is _____.

   a. ⌘+Shift+: (Mac) or Ctrl+Shift+: (Win95)

   b. ⌘+↓ (Mac) or Ctrl+↓ (Win95)

   c. ⌘+- (Mac) or Ctrl+- (Win95)

   d. None of the above

8. To make a ruler guide, you _____.

   a. Type a location into the Measurements palette

   b. Use **Edit>Guide**

   c. Click and drag out from a ruler

   d. All of the above

9. When a document has been moved from one hard disk location to another, it's a good idea to _____.

   a. Always update all picture links

   b. Check picture usage with the Utilities>Usage command

   c. Examine the document for flaws

   d. All of the above

10. A slug of type is _____.

    a. The height of a line of type

    b. Equal to the leading amount

    c. The point size plus the extra space added by leading

    d. All of the above

True or False

Please circle *T* or *F* to indicate whether the statement is true or false.

T F **1.** Kerning is done in units, each one being $^1\!/_{200}$ of an em wide.

T F **2.** You can increase leading with the short-cut ⌘+⬆Shift+' (Mac) or Ctrl+⬆Shift+' (Win95).

T F **3.** The Pasteboard height can prevent you from rotating a page's orientation from horizontal to vertical.

T F **4.** One way to update pictures is to ⌘+ Click (Mac) or Ctrl+ Click (Win95) on them.

T F **5.** You should always turn on word processor mode leading.

T F **6.** Autoleading is generally the wrong choice for setting leading.

T F **7.** The Pasteboard is used for storing items during layout.

T F **8.** For best final proofing of kerning, use a high magnification view.

T F **9.** Leading is a paragraph level attribute.

T F **10.** You can change the size of a flex space without affecting the existing line breaks in your document.

Design It

We can't emphasize enough the importance of having a total grasp of the fundamentals in this chapter and the next one. Spend some time making kerning and leading adjustments on this document before moving on to the next chapter.

■ How would the headline on the price sheet look if it were kerned much more tightly or more loosely?

■ What would be the best way to adjust the kerning in the headline? Would you use range kerning to do that, or should you use pair-by-pair kerning adjustment?

■ Experiment with how tight the leading can be in the pricing data lines before interfering with their readability.

■ How does it affect readability if you give the pricing data lines very wide leading?

■ Experiment with how tighter or looser leading affects the look and readability of the paragraphs of prose on the price sheet.

5

Spacing Type: Part Two

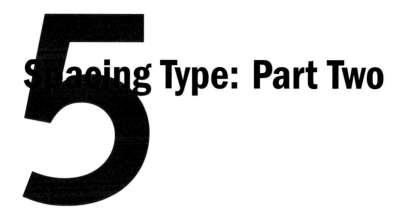

What You Will Learn

In this chapter, you continue work on the price list design from
Chapter 4, learning more about how to space type. In addition to
vertical spacing of paragraphs, you will work on shaping the
space the type occupies on the page by setting lines into
columns and indents.

In this chapter, you will learn about:

➤ Opening up space before and after paragraphs

➤ Creating columns of type

➤ Advanced tabbing techniques, including setting dot leaders

➤ Setting reversed-out type, white or any other light-colored
type set against black or some other dark background

Steamhouse Lighting
1628 South Templeton Highway
Santa Susana, AZ 85201

See Our New Line Of Table Lamps!
We have listed here only a few of the lighting possibilities opened up by our new line of table lamps. They have been hand-crafted using fine materials flown in to our Arizona workshop—rich green marble and warm mahogany wood, set off by shades of linen and bamboo.

Lamp Bases
Marble $99.95
Granite $119.95

Lamp Shades
Linen......................................$29.99
Canvas $39.99
Split Bamboo.........................$49.99
Woven Reed $64.99

Household Bulbs
Long Life ....120 volt, 60 watt $12.49/case
Reflector Flood ....120 volt, 150 watt $7.99
Halogen Track ....12 volt, 20W, ESX.............$23.49/case

Outdoor Bulbs
Sealed Beam ....12 volt...............................$5.99
Fixture Bayonet................12 volt...............................$2.99/pair
No Bug Orange.................120 volts, 60 watt ....$1.49 each

Specialty Items
Piano/Picture...................120 volt, 40 watt..................$4.99/pair
Candelabra ....120 volt, 60 watt..................$2.49/pair
Refrigerator ....120 volt, 40 watt..................$7.49
Oven ....120 volt, 40 watt..................$7.99
Fluorescent ....15 watt, 18 inch...................$9.89
High Intensity..................12V, 12 watt.........................$3.29/pair
Motion Sensor ....120 volt...............................$8.88

Call us toll free at 1-800-652-1067, during regular business hours, Monday through Saturday. Orders are not charged until shipped to you. All prices are guaranteed until the end of the current calendar year. We are required to collect sales tax in AZ, CA, CO, CT, FL, GA, IL, IN, LA, MA, MD, MN, MO, NJ, NY, NV, OH, OK, PA, RI, TN, TX, VA, WA, DC. We charge for delivery based on the total merchandise amount per address.

Spring Sale Specials!

Figure 5.1

In this chapter, you will complete the layout of this price list, the one you began in Chapter 4.

Design Notes

Have a look at Figure 5.1 and think about how the use of type spacing in a design can shape and organize information on a page. For example, the pricing data is much easier to read on this page because it has been organized into groups that are set off with extra space between them.

The use of dot leaders to organize lines of data accentuates the price data groupings as well.

The leaders give the groups of text an overall "color" that makes them look even more like blocks of collected information.

Have a look, also, at the two-column prose text box in the lower-right corner of the page. Designing this information to occupy two columns where all the other information on this page is set single-column helps to set it off.

Prep Notes

Copy all the files for this chapter from the CD-ROM to a work area on your hard drive. They are all in the **Steps** folder in the folder labeled **05**.

You will need the same fonts you used in Chapter 4 to be installed on your computer system, Opus and URW Palladio.

After you finish the first exercise in this chapter, each following exercise builds on the previous one. Except where we've indicated otherwise, you should save your price list design project at the end of each exercise so you can pick up where you left off at the beginning of the next exercise.

You will begin working in this chapter with the same file that ended Chapter 4. We have included the Chapter 4 version of the price sheet on the CD-ROM and its name is **04BASE04.QXT**.

Setting Columns, Advanced Tabs, and Indents

For this redesigned price sheet project, one of the challenges was to fit more information onto the page. To achieve that goal, we decided to use columns—like the parallel columns of text in newspaper stories.

In this section, you will create a new text box with two columns. You will also learn to fake uneven columns using indents, and to set dot leaders for your tabs.

1. Open file **04BASE04.QXT**, the one you copied from the **05** folder on your CD-ROM.

   Draw out a text box in the large open area in the center of the page.

   Using the Rectangular Text Box tool, draw the box from the left margin intersection with the 14-pica horizontal ruler guide (top-left corner of the text box) down to the right margin intersection with the 39-pica horizontal ruler guide.

2. You should still have **View>Snap To Guides** turned on so the crosshair pointer of the tool ought to snap right to these intersections, making for a very accurately positioned text box.

Check the box position through the Modify command, ⌘+M (Mac) or Ctrl+M (Win95). (You could also check through the Measurements palette, but you'll need the Modify dialog box for the next step anyway.)

The origin points should be 3 picas across and 14 picas down and the box should be 60 picas wide by 25 picas high. If necessary, adjust the settings to these specifications.

Setting Columns in a Text Box

3. Set two columns in this text box.

   With the Modify dialog box still open, get to the Text tab either by clicking it or by pressing ⌘+Tab⇥ (Mac) or Ctrl+Tab⇥ (Win95).

   As in Figure 5.2, set this dialog box to have two columns with a gutter of 2 picas. The gutter is the spacing that QuarkXPress will maintain between the two columns.

   Press Return (Mac) or ↵Enter (Win95) to put these column and gutter settings into effect.

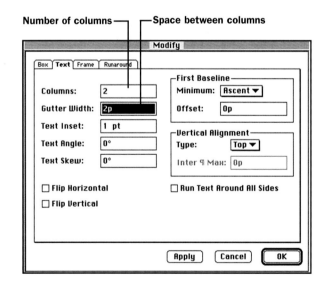

Figure 5.2

Using Modify to set up columns.

Flowing Text into Columns

4. Getting the text organized into columns, now that the text box has been set up, really isn't different from any other text-import operation.

    Select the Content tool and go to **File>Get Text**, ⌘+E (Mac) or Ctrl+E (Win95).

    Open the file **PRICES.DOC** by double-clicking it.

    The text will flow into the text box but, as you see in Figure 5.3, it will be channeled into two columns within the text box, just as you set it up in the last step.

    Don't worry right now that the text has collided with the light bulb graphic. We'll fix that shortly.

    Also, although much of the text formatting was already done in this imported word processor text, we need to set leading, indents, and dot leader tabs.

Forcing Column Breaks

5. All the lamp information should go in the left column and all the light bulb information belongs on the right.

    You can force a column break the same way you forced text to break to the next linked text box in Chapter 3.

    Navigate to the end of the "Woven Reed" price information line.

    Press ↵Enter in the lower-right corner of your keyboard.

    (Win95) There are, as you know from Chapter 3, two Enter keys on a Windows keyboard. For this job, you want the one below the numeric keypad.

    Delete any extra lines (carriage return characters) at the top of the right column.

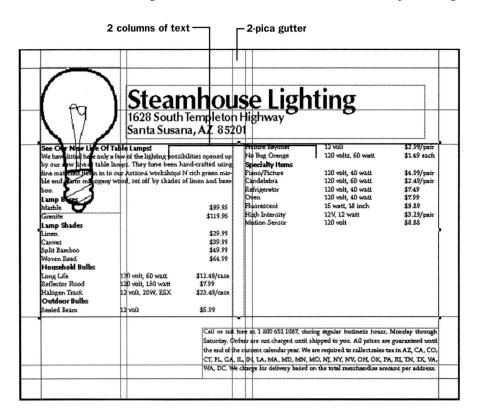

Figure 5.3

Imported text organized into columns.

6. Set the leading on this new price information text.

Select All, ⌘+Ⓐ (Mac) or Ctrl+Ⓐ (Win95). Notice that all the text in this story has been selected, even though it is in two columns.

In the Measurements palette, double-click the "auto" leading setting to select it. Type **16** right on top of the selected text to replace it.

Press Return (Mac) or ↵Enter (Win95) to put the leading into effect.

Setting Fake Unequal Columns

7. One problem with QuarkXPress is the fact that text box columns must be equal. They share exactly the available space in the text box.

That means you can't set a narrow column on the left in this text box in order to avoid the light bulb graphic. The solution is to set a very deep indent on the text in the left column.

Select the paragraphs on the left by clicking and dragging through them. Remember that indents are a paragraph attribute so you don't need to select all of the paragraph text; any part will do.

8. Open up Paragraph Attributes, ⌘+⬆Shift+Ⓕ (Mac) or Ctrl+⬆Shift+Ⓕ (Win95), in order to get to the indent settings.

Type in a **13** pica left indent, as in Figure 5.4.

Left indent 13 picas

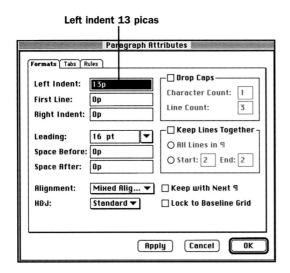

Figure 5.4

Set several kinds of indents in Paragraph Attributes.

Fine-Tuning Indents

9. Each of the headlines needs a slightly smaller indent, however.

Navigate your text insertion point to the first headline, beginning with the words "See Our New."

Open Paragraph Attributes again, ⌘+⬆Shift+Ⓕ (Mac) or Ctrl+⬆Shift+Ⓕ (Win95) and change the left indent to 12 picas.

Repeat this operation for the other two headlines in the left column, "Lamp Bases" and "Lamp Shades."

10. Set left indents on all the pricing information paragraphs in the right column using the same technique as you have used in the last two steps.

The headlines in the right column do not get an indent since they are already set automatically to the left edge of the column gutter.

The pricing items should have an indent of 1 pica.

When you have the indents set, they should look like Figure 5.5.

Setting Dot Leader Tabs

11. You may have noticed in Figure 5.1 that all the pricing information lines have a series of periods connecting them.

You don't set these by typing a bunch of periods. You automate the process by giving your tab settings a special attribute...called dot leaders. Actually, you can have pretty much any character you want as a leader but dots or periods are the most common.

Select a group of pricing information. Start with the prices for lamp bases in the left column.

Open up the Tab section of the Paragraph Attributes dialog, ⌘+⬆Shift+Ⓣ (Mac) or Ctrl+⬆Shift+Ⓣ (Win95).

12. Click the tab at 27 picas, being careful not to jostle it out of position. You just want to select, not move it.

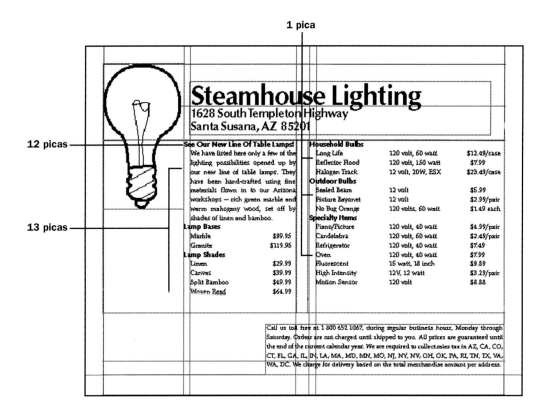

1 pica

12 picas

13 picas

Figure 5.5

The indents as they should look in your price list.

As you see in Figure 5.6, type a space and a period in the space where it says Fill Characters.

When you press [Return] (Mac) or [↵Enter] (Win95), you will see that your selected price group has a dot leader added to it.

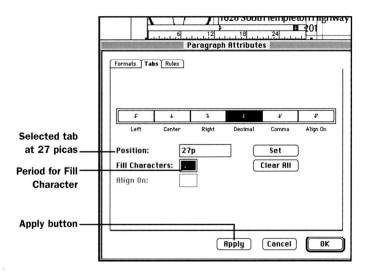

Selected tab at 27 picas

Period for Fill Character

Apply button

Figure 5.6

Setting a dot leader.

Using the Apply Button

13. Select each of the pricing information groups in turn, leaving out the headlines, and add dot leaders to each of the tab settings. Use the same technique you used in the last step.

    In the right column, don't forget to get both tabs in the right column, at both 12 picas and 25 picas. To save some time, use the Apply button for the first tab and then OK the dialog box after you set the dot leader for the second tab.

● The progress so far on the price sheet—showing the dot leaders, indents, and columns—has been saved on the CD-ROM in a file named **05BASE01.QXT**. It should look like Figure 5.7.

Introducing...Paragraph Spacing

Use paragraph spacing settings, Space Before and Space After. Don't even think about just hitting the ↵Enter/↵Enter key a couple of times to put extra lines above a paragraph to space it out.

Why? Several reasons.

■ It's inflexible because it will only allow you to insert space above a paragraph in the amount of that paragraph's leading. If you have set the paragraph at 16 points leading, you won't be able to put 14 points of space above a paragraph using the double ↵Enter/↵Enter approach. You'll only be able to insert multiples of 16—16, 32, or 48 points and so on.

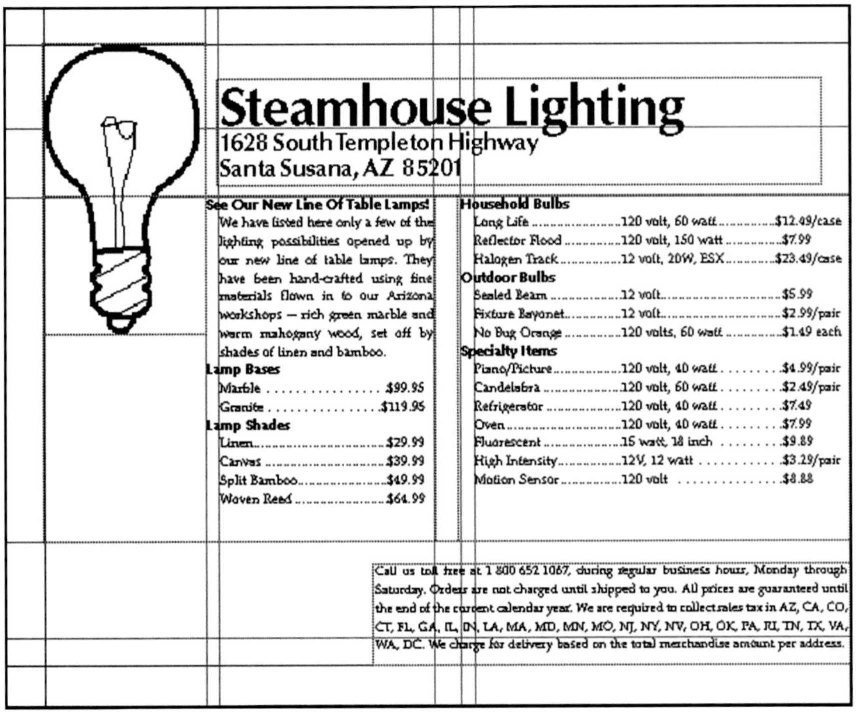

Figure 5.7

Completed dot leaders.

■ If your extra space happens to fall at the top of a column, the tops of your columns won't line up because the extra return characters are pushing one of the columns down from the top. Space Before knows enough to shut itself off if it's in a paragraph at the top of a text box column.

■ It's unprofessional. It will brand your work as that of someone who doesn't know the first thing about typesetting...not good for your chances in the graphic design job market.

Instead, use paragraph spacing, the Space Before and Space After settings located just below the leading setting in the familiar Paragraph Attributes dialog box, ⌘+⬆Shift+F (Mac) or Ctrl+⬆Shift+F (Win95), as in Figure 5.8.

Paragraph spacing settings ────

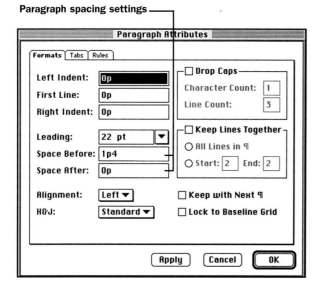

Figure 5.8

The Paragraph Attributes dialog box, the place to set paragraph spacing.

Setting Paragraph Spacing

Each of the headlines in the body of the pricing information need to have some space opened up above them. You will use paragraph spacing—in this case, the Space Before attribute—to accomplish that job in this exercise.

1. With the Content tool active, position the text insertion point in the first headline, the one beginning with the words "See Our New Line."

2. Try to add some space above this paragraph. Note that it's the first paragraph in its column, sitting at the top of the text box.

   Use ⌘+⬆Shift+F (Mac) or Ctrl+⬆Shift+F (Win95) to open the Paragraph Attributes dialog box.

   Click and drag the title bar at the top of the dialog box, moving it so you can see the headline while you operate the dialog box in the next step.

3. Type **16 pt** into the Space Before field and click the Apply button.

   Notice that nothing happens. QuarkXPress will not add space at the top of a column, a key advantage over the double carriage return approach to spacing out paragraphs.

   Set the Space Before field back to 0 and click the OK button.

4. Add Space Before to the next headline down, the one that says "Lamp Bases."

   ⌘+↓ (Mac) or Ctrl+↓ (Win95) to the headline, open the Paragraph Attributes box with the keyboard shortcut or with the Style>Formats menu command.

   Type **1p4** into the Space Before field. That's the same as 16 points (1 pica equals 12 points, 1p4 equals 12 points plus 4 points).

   Press Return (Mac) or ⏎Enter (Win95) to accept the setting and close the dialog box.

   Notice that a space has been opened up above the headline.

5. Work your way through the rest of the headlines, except for the top of text box headline in the right column, and add 16 points Space Above to each one using the same procedure you followed in the previous step.

   You'll need to drag down the bottom of the text box to resize it to make room for the spaced-out text.

● The progress so far on the price sheet has been saved on the CD-ROM in a file named **05BASE02.QXT**. You can see how your layout should look at this point in Figure 5.9.

Introducing...H&J Settings

H&J stands for hyphenation and justification. The H&Js feature of QuarkXPress covers a rich set of features that ultimately have a major impact on the look of your type—and we don't just mean justified type.

You've probably worked with a word processor and are familiar with the way it wraps lines of text. The word processor software uses the computer to work through each paragraph of text line by line, calculating where to break off and send the rest of the text down to the next line. The word processor tries to fit as many words as possible on a single line of text.

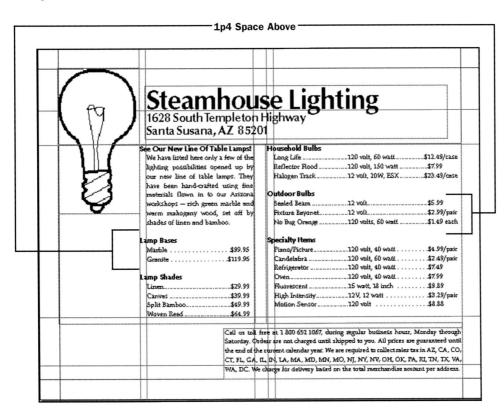

Figure 5.9

The layout so far, with Space Above settings in place.

QuarkXPress does the same thing, except it has a lot more power than a word processor when it comes to composing a line of text. Your word processor does a few simple background calculations to figure out a line. QuarkXPress may do hundreds of calculations to optimize the fit of each line. QuarkXPress, in other words, has true typographical power. And it really gets supercharged when it is working on a justified paragraph where all the line endings must come out even to the right side of the column.

The net result of this typographical power for your design work in QuarkXPress—as opposed to working in a word processor—is the amount of control you can have over the space between words and the space between letters. In addition to the things that you have already learned kerning, autokerning, and tracking—you also have at your disposal the items you control through the H&J settings—word spacing, letter spacing, and hyphenation.

Two-Step Process

Setting up H&Js in QuarkXPress is a two-step process.

■ You must first define a group of hyphenation and justification settings by adjusting the Standard settings, or by creating and naming as many new settings as you like.

You set up H&J settings through the Edit>H&Js command, ⌘+Option+H (Mac) or Ctrl+Shift+F11 (Win95), in the H&Js dialog box shown in Figure 5.10.

■ Once you have defined one or more H&J settings, you can apply those settings to individual paragraphs in the Paragraph Attributes dialog box.

Like leading, indents, and paragraph spacing, H&Js are paragraph-level formatting attributes in QuarkXPress. You have probably memorized the Paragraph Attributes dialog box by now, since you have been spending so much time with it in this chapter.

Click here to edit settings

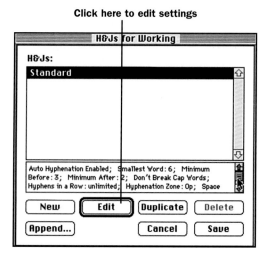

Figure 5.10

Create new groups of H&J settings here.

Minimum, Optimum, Maximum

QuarkXPress needs you to give it directions for how much space to allow between words and letters when composing a line of type. In justifying a line, however, it wouldn't work to tell QuarkXPress to apply a fixed amount of space as you do when kerning. The program needs a range in which to work.

You express this range by providing QuarkXPress with minimum, optimum, and maximum percentages. It then applies those percentages to expand or reduce whatever space already exists between words and letters.

As you can see in Figure 5.11, QuarkXPress' Standard H&J setting comes with certain values by default, values that you may want to adjust.

■ Space between words in the default settings can be adjusted in a range of 85% to 250% with the optimum word spacing set by default at 110%.

■ Character spacing is limited, with the default standard settings, to a range of 0% to 4%.

Name of H&J setting

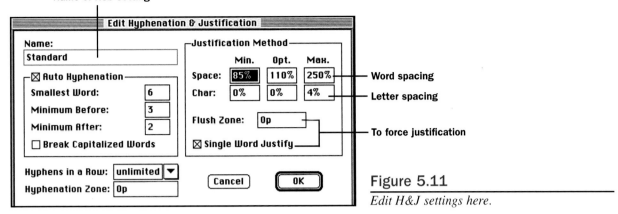

Figure 5.11
Edit H&J settings here.

Avoid Letter Spacing

Many highly respected typography experts strongly oppose using letter spacing to achieve justified lines. They believe that anything other than 0% in the minimum, optimum, and maximum character spacing settings is a violation of the type designer's work. The type designer, they say, worked hard to create an overall look for the typeface, building into each of the letters a particular amount of space—called side bearings.

Don't Automatically Accept 110% Default Word Spacing

QuarkXPress set, as we mentioned previously, a default word spacing value of 110% (the optimum setting). It's hard to understand why QuarkXPress would have done this because the typeface designer probably spent a great deal of time figuring out how wide an optimum space should be for any particular typeface. This is like QuarkXPress saying that all type designers set their word spacing too wide by 10%. So, if you want to go with the typographer's original design, at least to start, go with 100% optimum word spacing.

Forcing Justification

We have been talking about regular justification in this section, but there's also forced justification. You saw a picture of what it looks like in Chapter 3 in Figure 3.21.

Two settings in the Justification Method section of the Edit Hyphenation & Justification can impose forced justification on certain lines of a regular justified paragraph.

■ The Flush Zone determines where, in the last line of a paragraph, QuarkXPress forces the last line to spread across the entire column. A setting of 0p, the default, for all practical purposes turns this setting off.

A wide Flush Zone may cause QuarkXPress to spread two or three words across a single line, creating an ugly gap between the words.

■ Single Word Justify tells QuarkXPress to spread a single word across the entire line if it is the only word on that line. You might, for example, have narrow columns and a compound word that takes up most of the line. If you have this setting turned on, you'll get an even right edge on the column. If you have it turned off, you may get one line that doesn't meet the right edge. In general, don't use this option because it has a tendency to spread a single word across an entire line of type, which looks pretty silly.

Controlling Automatic Hyphenation

We always say H&J as if hyphenation and justification are inseparable. Most of the time you set them together, and hyphenation clearly has a major influence over how a line gets justified. But the hyphenation settings apply to non-justified text as well.

You control QuarkXPress hyphenation in two locations. One is the H&J command about which we have been speaking. You also have one hyphenation setting in the paragraph section of the Document Preferences dialog box.

Here are the basics on what each of the items in the hyphenation section of the H&J commands, if you will follow along in Figure 5.12.

■ Auto Hyphenation is the main on/off switch for QuarkXPress hyphenation. If you want hyphenation, make sure this check box has been turned on.

■ Smallest Word tells QuarkXPress of your hyphenation tolerance level. If you think it makes no sense to hyphenate any word unless it is six characters or longer, then let the default in this setting remain at 6.

■ Minimum Before/After determine how many letters are required before and after an automatic hyphen. You might think, and many would agree with you, that it looks silly to have two letters like "ly" or "py" sitting all alone at the beginning of a line. We usually set both these settings at 3.

There is a school of thought that argues in favor of 2 for Minimum Before and 3 for Minimum After. These folks say that it's just fine to hyphenate two-letter prefixes.

■ Break Capitalized Words, usually off by default, lets QuarkXPress know whether you think it's okay to hyphenate proper nouns (and the first word of a sentence).

■ Hyphens in a Row is, unfortunately, set to unlimited by default. That means you could theoretically have a paragraph of text where there was a ladder of hyphens, a hyphen at the end of every line. We usually set this to 2, a generally accepted standard in the industry.

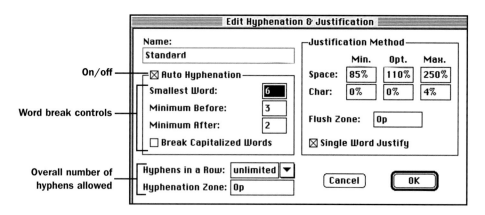

Figure 5.12

You set most QuarkXPress hyphenation controls in this dialog box.

- Hyphenation Zone creates a strip of territory at the right side of your column where QuarkXPress makes its hyphenation decisions. It looks at a word, and figures out whether the word can fit on the line before it ends within the hyphenation zone. If it does, QuarkXPress won't try to hyphenate that word but will just move it to the next line. In general, the bigger the zone, the fewer hyphens you will have.

  Keep in mind that the Hyphenation Zone setting only applies to unjustified text, so it's automatically null and void when you are working with justified text.

Controlling Hyphenation Method

There's one more hyphenation setting in QuarkXPress and, oddly enough, it's in a completely different location from the hyphenation and justification settings. That's a bit inconvenient but this setting may be the most important one of all.

You can control the hyphenation method QuarkXPress uses by going to **E**dit>**P**references>**D**ocument and selecting the Paragraph tab where you will see the Hyphenation Method setting as shown in Figure 5.13.

You have three choices for hyphenation method. They are like an archeological dig down through QuarkXPress time since each one of them has advanced the program's ability to perform accurate hyphenation.

- Standard hyphenation should be used only when you are working on an old QuarkXPress document composed with this setting in place. That will help avoid triggering any new line breaks because the program might find different and better hyphenation points with the other two methods.

- Enhanced hyphenation works the same way as Standard, but it does a better job. Still, as with Standard mode, you should use Enhanced only if you are working in an old document that was composed with that specific hyphenation method.

  The problem is that both Standard and Enhanced hyphenation rely on software code—an algorithm—to take a best guess at where to split a word. For example, if the Standard or Enhanced methods see a double-p, they'll assume it's okay to split a word there. That works out fine most of the time, but there are plenty of really dumb hyphenation guesses that QuarkXPress makes when in Standard or Enhanced hyphenation mode.

- Expanded hyphenation, on the other hand, actually goes into a dictionary to find where a word should be broken for hyphenation. This is new with version 4 of QuarkXPress, a hyphenation dictionary that overrides the old QuarkXPress Standard and Enhanced methods—much more accurate and reliable.

  Unless you are working on an old document, always use Expanded hyphenation mode. It's the best.

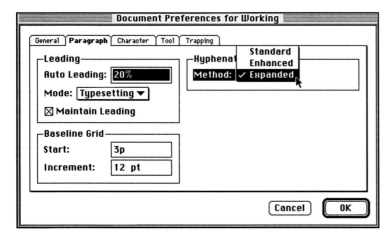

Figure 5.13

Setting the hyphenation method to Expanded.

Setting H&Js

As with many typographical activities, the "correct" settings for word and letter spacing are the subject of endless debate. The trends ebb and flow, some designers favoring very tight settings and others opting for a loose look.

For our purposes, we've created a routine that helps us decide on the right settings for pretty much any given typographic circumstance. In this exercise, you can try it out for yourself and, if you like it, you can adopt it into your own workflow.

Setting Hyphenation Mode

1. Before getting started with the main part of the exercise, take the advice we discussed in the previous section on hyphenation. Turn on Expanded hyphenation mode.

With the keyboard shortcut ⌘+Y (Mac) or Ctrl+Y (Win95), access the Document Preferences dialog box and select the Paragraph tab.

Click the Hyphenation Method pulldown list and select Expanded.

Press Return (Mac) or ↵Enter (Win95) to put the new hyphenation mode into force.

Defining a New H&J Setting

2. Create a new H&J setting in addition to the Standard H&J setting that QuarkXPress sets as a default. You will use this and some additional settings to experiment until you have the right spacing settings for your justified text.

Use the keyboard shortcut ⌘+Option+H (Mac) or Ctrl+⬆Shift+F11 (Win95) to open up the H&J dialog box.

3. Click the New button to begin creating the new H&J setting.

Creating a Neutral H&J Setting

4. You need to see what your text would look like with no word and letter spacing and no hyphenation. So you are going to create a neutral H&J setting.

Type in a new name for the new setting, **Neutral**.

5. Now turn off hyphenation and set up neutral word and letter spacing.

Click off Auto **H**yphenation.

Tab to the Justification Method section and set all the Space (word spacing) settings to 100%.

Do the same for Character (letter spacing), setting Minimum, Optimum, and Maximum to 0%.

Press Return (Mac) or ↵Enter (Win95) to accept those settings.

Click Save to complete the process of defining your Neutral H&J setting.

Applying H&J Settings

6. Even though you've created a new setting, none of your text has yet been affected by it. The H&J setting is a paragraph level attribute and you must explicitly apply your newly defined setting to some text in order to put it to use.

Click with the Content tool in the ordering information text box. It's in the lower-right corner of the price list page, the paragraph that begins "Call us toll free…."

7. Open up the familiar Paragraph Attributes dialog, ⌘+⬆Shift+F (Mac) or Ctrl+⬆Shift+F (Win95) and go to the lower-left corner of the dialog box.

Select your new **H**&J setting—Neutral—from the pulldown list as you see in Figure 5.14.

Click OK to accept the new setting.

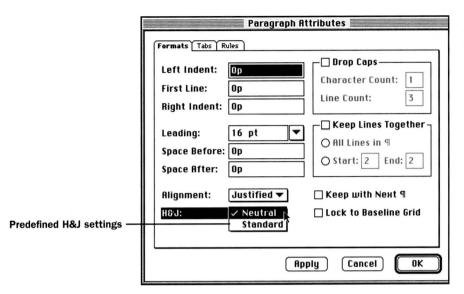

Figure 5.14

Selecting an H&J setting.

Tip

Guideline: Try a 2 ½ Alphabet Measure

When it comes to composing a justified line and deciding which H&J settings you should use, everything has to do with how long you want that justified line to be. That's called the measure—the width of the column of type.

Here's a rough guideline. Begin determining your measure by formatting your type as you wish, then try a column width equal to 2 ½ alphabets. When we say 2 ½ alphabets in this case, we don't literally mean 65 letters. It should also include a mix of letters, spaces, and punctuation.

Using a Line-Length Yardstick

8. As we suggest in the tip, consider setting this paragraph to a width of 2 ½ alphabets, a starting point guideline for a line-length yardstick. In the case of this paragraph, that means we'd like to see how wide our measure would be if it were 2 ½ alphabets wide with the text set in URW Palladio at 11.5/16 (11.5 point size, on 16 points leading).

Navigate your text insertion point to the beginning of the paragraph, ⌘+↑ (Mac) or Ctrl+↑ (Win95).

9. One of the files you copied from your CD-ROM for this chapter was called **ALPHABET.TXT**.

Get Text, ⌘+E (Mac) or Ctrl+E (Win95), and import that text now.

If you positioned your text insertion point correctly, it should slip right in at the front of this paragraph.

Notice that the text consists of two alphabets with spaces and punctuation added to bring it out to roughly 65 characters long.

10. Highlight the alphabet text and set it to 11.5 point URW Palladio on 16 points leading. To format the text, use the Measurements palette or any of the other techniques you have learned in previous chapters.

(It may already be formatted correctly since QuarkXPress tries to format inserted imported text to match the existing text.)

Setting Line Length (Measure)

11. Now you have an alphabet yardstick for adjusting your measure.

Click and drag the left-side sizing handle for the ordering information text box, holding for a beat or two before you drag.

As you make the box narrower and wider, observe how the alphabet line wraps to the second line, as you see in the top of Figure 5.15.

Stretched out wide, the alphabet text won't fill the first line of the text box.

As you narrow the box, the alphabet text is squeezed together as QuarkXPress tries to justify the letters and fit them onto one line.

At some point, past the 35 pica vertical guide as you narrow the text box even further, some of the text from the alphabet will wrap down to the second line, the middle view in Figure 5.15.

You want to finish up with the measure (the width of the text box) set at the length of the alphabet text, at the 34-pica vertical guide. The alphabet should be taking up the entire first line, as in the bottom view shown in Figure 5.15.

Too wide

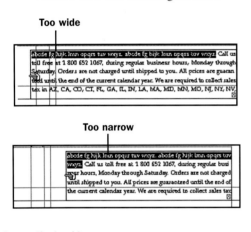

Too narrow

34-pica vertical guide

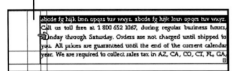

Figure 5.15

Setting the text box to a 2 ¹/₂ alphabets measure.

During a regular design process, when you are working on your own and not in a learning exercise, you will want to conduct this alphabet yardstick exercise early in your design process. You will do this when you are first specifying type size and deciding on your column widths.

Remember, this alphabet approach is just a guideline. In a real life situation, you would feel free to tune your measure width from here. In fact, as you may have noticed, there is some justified text in the first column of the pricing information that is set on a measure quite a bit narrower than 2 ¹/₂ alphabets.

12. Delete the alphabet text from the ordering information text box, now that you don't need your yardstick any longer.

Resize the height of the text box, if necessary, so that all the text is showing.

Tip

Maintain a Set of H&Js

Rather than build a new set of H&Js every time you build a new document, keep some standard ones on file. As you will see in the next step, QuarkXPress can import H&Js so you can store a range of H&J settings in a document. Keep that document in a handy place!

Importing/Appending H&J Settings

13. Go to Edit>H&Js again, ⌘+Option+H (Mac) or Ctrl+Shift+F11 (Win95). You will be appending some ready-made H&J settings that we have provided for you on one of the files you copied from the CD-ROM.

Click the Append button and double-click the file **H&JAPPEND.QXT**.

14. You will get a dialog box like the one in Figure 5.16, allowing you to choose from among the H&J settings contained in the file you just opened.

Click the right-facing arrow until all the H&J settings, except Standard, have been copied from the source window labeled "Available" to the right-hand window, the destination window labeled "Including."

You can copy all the settings at once by clicking on the first one and then Shift+ clicking on the last one. This will select all of them and then you can click just once on the right-facing arrow.

Click OK in the Append H&Js dialog box.

Click Save in the H&J dialog box.

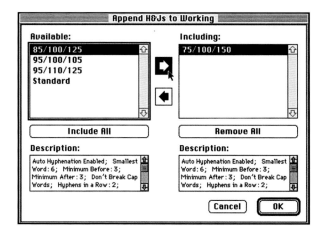

Figure 5.16

Appending ready-made H&J settings.

All of these newly appended H&J settings are the same, except for the minimum, optimum, and maximum word space settings.

They all have Auto Hyphenation enabled, smallest word set at 6 with minimum before and after at 3. Hyphens in a row is set at 2. Letter spacing has been completely neutralized at 0% for minimum, optimum, and maximum.

Experimenting with H&J Settings

15. With your text insertion point still active in the order information paragraph, experiment with each of the four new settings you have appended.

Open Paragraph Attributes, ⌘+⬆Shift+F (Mac) or Ctrl+⬆Shift+F (Win95) and use the Apply button to try out each one in turn, observing the effect on the text.

If you are like us, you probably won't see much difference between the 75/100/150 setting and the 85/100/125 setting. That's an indication that this text width, this measure, pretty well fits the spacing the designer of URW Palladio intended.

The 95/110/125 setting gives roughly the same look as the first two, except it tightens up the text passage with all those two-letter state abbreviations in it.

The tightest setting of all, 95/100/105 tightens up the text enough to leave only a single word on the last line of the paragraph.

After experimenting with the effects of each one of them, make a choice among these H&J settings and click OK to adopt your decision. (You can use your own judgment about which one looks better, but we're partial to 95/110/125 for this paragraph of text.)

Adjusting for a Better Look

16. It's important, when developing a design, to re-examine earlier decisions and make adjustments when they aren't working. This willingness to tinker doesn't have anything in particular to do with how to operate QuarkXPress, but it has a lot to do with achieving a professional look in your typesetting work.

Have a close look at the lamp text with strong magnification. Drag out a marquee with the Zoom tool, ⌘+ Click/Drag (Mac) or Ctrl+Spacebar+ Click/Drag (Win95).

In Figure 5.17, you can see that the spacing between words is uneven from line to line, even to the point where there are even some unsightly large gaps as QuarkXPress struggles to justify these lines into this narrow measure.

17. Try these steps to fix this paragraph.

Go to Paragraph Attributes, ⌘+⬆Shift+F (Mac) or Ctrl+⬆Shift+F (Win95) and change the Left **Indent** from 13 picas to 12 picas, widening the measure by 1 pica.

Use the **Apply** button to see the results of this change. You should notice that the spacing is more even, although there's still a fair amount of word spacing happening in these lines.

18. With Paragraph Attributes still open, try some different word spacing. Try several of the H&J settings you appended earlier. Click the **Apply** button to try out each setting.

You will end up with the 95/100/105 H&J setting. It pulls the word spacing within a narrow range and ends up tightening this paragraph while maintaining even spacing within the new wider measure. Our result looked like Figure 5.18.

Figure 5.17

Checking for unsightly justification problems.

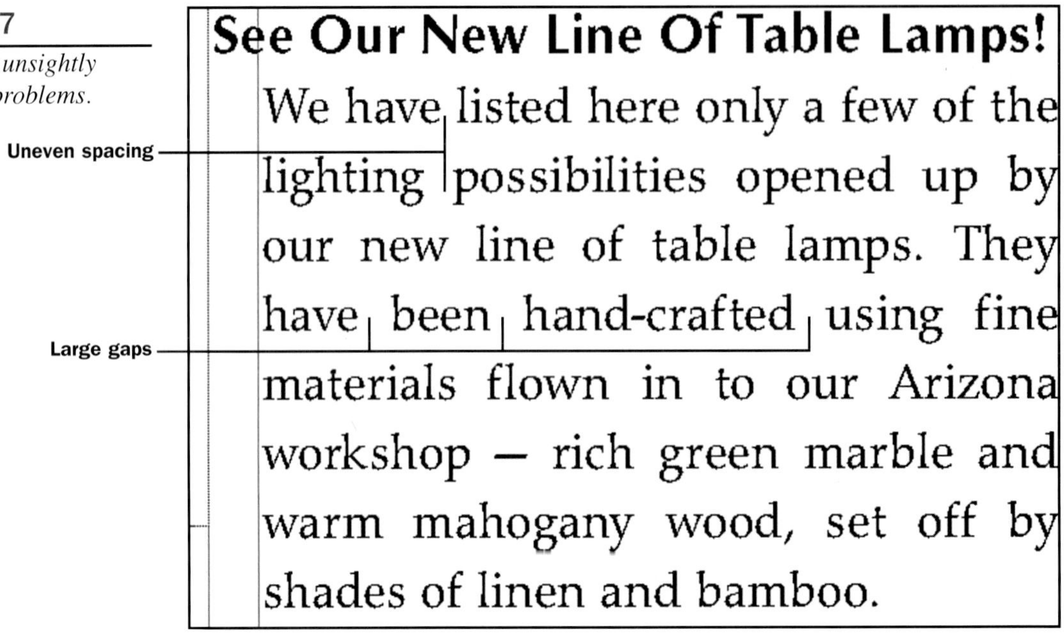

Uneven spacing ⟶

Large gaps ⟶

See Our New Line Of Table Lamps!
We have listed here only a few of the lighting possibilities opened up by our new line of table lamps. They have been hand-crafted using fine materials flown in to our Arizona workshop — rich green marble and warm mahogany wood, set off by shades of linen and bamboo.

Figure 5.18

Better looking type with the adjustment completed.

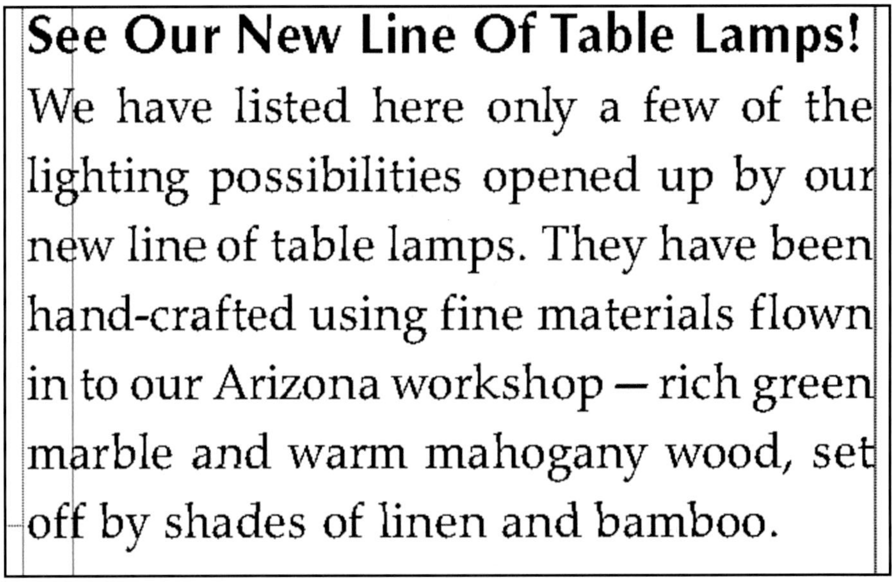

See Our New Line Of Table Lamps!
We have listed here only a few of the lighting possibilities opened up by our new line of table lamps. They have been hand-crafted using fine materials flown in to our Arizona workshop — rich green marble and warm mahogany wood, set off by shades of linen and bamboo.

Click OK when you are done with the H&J adjustment, or press (Return) (Mac) or (↵Enter) (Win95).

Notice that this setting also has the advantage of shortening the paragraph by one line and evening up the columns so they end at the same vertical point on the page. That's good, too.

19. Resize the bottom of the pricing information text box, pulling it up to the 39-pica horizontal guide line.

The progress so far on the price sheet has been saved on the CD-ROM in a file named **05BASE03.QXT**. You can see what it should look like in Figure 5.19.

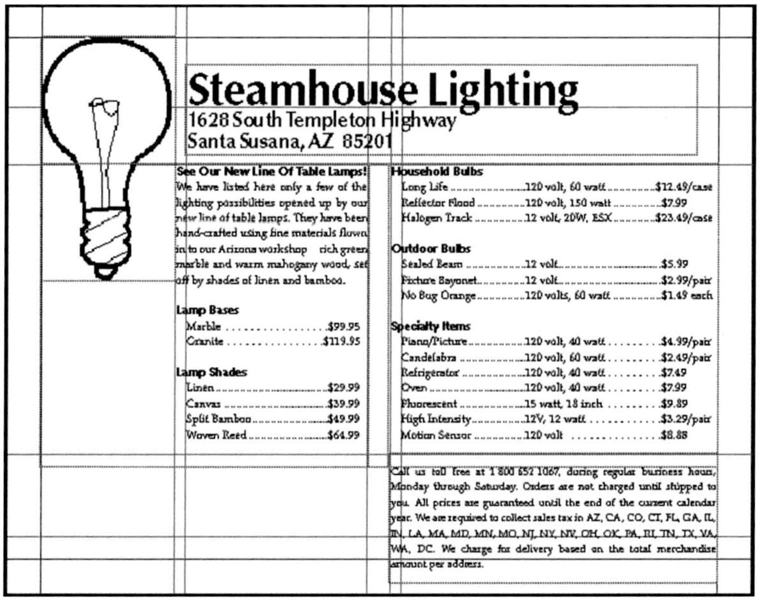

Figure 5.19

The layout so far with all H&J adjustments in place.

Introducing...Spacing and Line Adjustment Characters

If H&Js and kerning are the sandpaper and planing tools to make your type look smooth and even, then the special characters we'll talk about in this section are the chisels and saws. As such, you'll be using them through the proceeding chapters, and now's a good time to introduce them to you. They have to do with spacing letters, words, and lines of type.

We've listed in Table 4.3 the special characters you can use when you are chiseling and sawing away on lines of type, fine-tuning spacing and line breaks—specialized space characters, forced line break characters, manual hyphenation characters, and so on.

Table 4.3 Special spacing and line break control characters

Character	Mac	Win95
Nonbreaking Space	⌘+Spacebar	Ctrl+Spacebar
Thin Space	Shift+Spacebar	Shift+Spacebar or Ctrl+6
Nonbreaking Thin Space	⌘+Shift+Spacebar	Ctrl+Shift+Spacebar or Ctrl+Alt+6
En Space	Option+Spacebar	Ctrl+Shift+6
Nonbreaking En Space	⌘+Option+Spacebar	Ctrl+Alt+Shift+6
Flex Space	Option+Shift+Spacebar	Ctrl+Shift+5
Nonbreaking Flex Space	⌘+Option+Shift+Spacebar	Ctrl+Alt+Shift+5
Soft Hyphen	⌘+-	Ctrl+-
Nonbreaking Hyphen	⌘+=	Ctrl+Shift+-
New Line	Shift+Return	Shift+Enter
Soft New Line	⌘+Return	Ctrl+Enter
Indent Here	⌘+\	Ctrl+\

Nonbreaking Characters

Many of the items you see in Table 4.3 have the term "nonbreaking" in their names. That means they glue together the two characters on either side of them. If you type a nonbreaking space in the middle of someone's first and last name, that will keep the name from breaking at the end of a line. The entire name will be forced onto a single line (unless, of course, you have turned on the Break Capitalized Words option in your H&J settings for that paragraph).

Special Width Spaces

You can have thin spaces, en spaces, and flex spaces.

An en space is one en wide, half an em.

Thin spaces are sometimes called punctuation spaces. They are just what they sound like, very narrow spaces. Their actual width depends on the designer of the typeface you are using, but they are often ¼ of an em wide or about the width of a punctuation mark like a comma.

You get to decide the width of a flex space. You set it in the Character section of the Document Preferences dialog box, ⌘+Y (Mac) or Ctrl+Y (Win95). Set the width of a flex space as a percentage of an en space and QuarkXPress defaults the flex space setting to 50%, meaning ¼ of an em.

QuarkXPress doesn't have an em space, which is about as weird as saying an em space is always equal to the width of two zeroes, as we discussed in Chapter 3. Some people set their flex space to always equal an em space, 200% of an en space. Others just type two en spaces and save the flex space for another purpose.

Indent Here

Wherever this character falls on a line, all the rest of the lines below it in that same paragraph will be indented to that point. WordPerfect and Microsoft Word have indent characters that work in a very similar manner. Some people like to use this character instead of setting up hanging indents, which you will learn more about in Chapter 9. You use hanging indents to set up numbered or bulleted lists where the number or bullet hangs in an empty space to the left of the main text.

New Line

Sometimes you want to force QuarkXPress to break a line. Maybe you want to create a two-line headline, for example. For that, you use a new line character. By jumping down to the next line, you keep all the paragraph formatting such as leading, tabs, and indents. But you do not trigger paragraph space before or space after when you use a new line character.

Manual Hyphenation

Sometimes you need to take hyphenation into your own hands instead of letting QuarkXPress handle it for you. You can perform word-by-word manual hyphenation by inserting soft hyphens in text. They are sometimes called discretionary hyphens.

If you manually hyphenate a word, you don't want to type a hyphen character. You want a soft hyphen. If you edit the text or change the width of a measure, that could cause the line breaks to change down below the edited location. If you used a regular hard hyphen somewhere in text, you might end up with a hyphenated word being pulled into the middle of a line. A soft hyphen, however, is smart enough to show some discretion. If the edited text shifts the word with a soft hyphen into mid-line, the soft hyphen simply disappears from view.

You can also use a soft hyphen to tell QuarkXPress to never hyphenate a particular instance in the text of a particular word. Just insert a soft hyphen directly in front of the word instead of inserting it inside the word to form a break.

Final Touches

It's time to put finishing touches on your price sheet. In this exercise, you will create white-on-black text and draw a dotted line. You will also use a few of the special spacing and line control characters you just learned and apply tracking (actually, range kerning) to some text.

1. Draw out a text box, using the Rectangular Text Box tool.

Reversing Out Text (White on Black)

2. Position, size, and fill in the box with black so you can reverse out some type against it.

   Open the Modify command and set the box with origin points of 3 picas across and 43 picas down. (You will fine-tune this setting later.)

   Size the box as 29 picas wide and 4 picas and 3 points tall.

   Set the color as Black and shade it at 80%.

   So far, your Modify dialog box should look like the one in Figure 5.20.

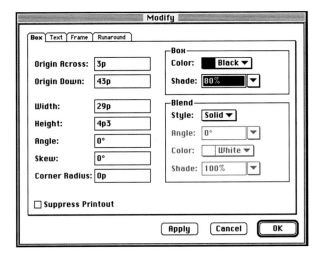

Figure 5.20
Setting up a text box for reversed-out text.

Text Box Inset

3. When setting reversed-out text, it's good to inset the text a bit so it doesn't run too close the edges. You want the black part of the box to frame the text.

   Choose the text section of the Modify dialog box and set the text inset to 3 points.

   Click OK to adopt all your text box settings.

Formatting Reversed-Out Text

4. You need to set up the formatting for your text or you won't be able to see what you are typing in the next step.

   Click the content tool in the text box so you have an active text insertion point.

   Open the Character Attributes dialog box, Style>Character. You can also use the keyboard shortcut, ⌘+⬆Shift+D (Mac) or Ctrl+⬆Shift+D (Win95).

   Use this dialog box to set the text as Opus, 33 points, Bold.

   And here's the trick of reversing text. For this 80% black text box, set the text color to white. Your Character Attributes dialog box should look like the one in Figure 5.21.

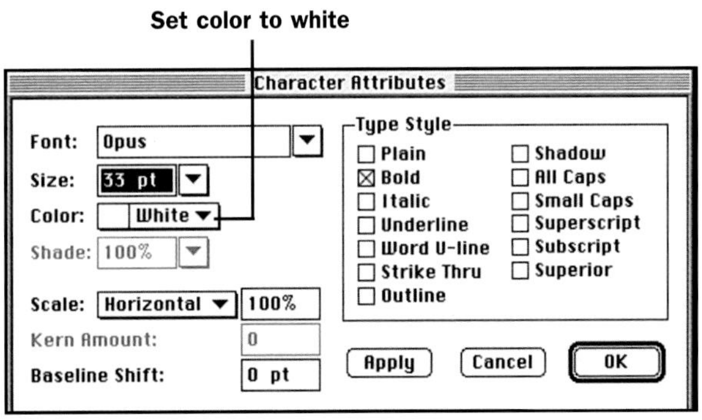

Figure 5.21
Formatting text so it will reverse out of a black box.

5. Now type in your text.

   Type **Spring Sale Specials!** and be sure to include the exclamation mark.

   It's magic! You've created reversed-out text.

Centering Text in a Box

6. This text would look better if it were centered in the box.

Center it horizontally by using paragraph alignment, ⌘+Shift+C (Mac) or Ctrl+Shift+C (Win95).

You can also center it vertically by going back to the text tab of the Modify command, ⌘+M (Mac) or Ctrl+M (Win95).

Set the Vertical Alignment Type to centered and click OK.

Applying Tracking (Range Kerning)

7. In general, range kerning is a pretty crude typographical technique. You apply letter spacing to many characters at a time, disregarding their case-by-case needs. However, there are a few situations where tracking makes sense. One of them is when you are reversing text. Opening up the lettering helps make the text more readable.

Open up the Measurements palette, if it isn't already showing, and select all the text, ⌘+A (Mac) or Ctrl+A (Win95).

Use the regular kerning keyboard shortcuts to open up this text, then watch what happens in the Measurements palette. Apply 11 units of range kerning.

The kerning shortcuts are in Table 4.1, if you need to refresh your memory.

8. QuarkXPress actually calls this range kerning "tracking." If you go to Style>Track, you will see that the menu command has a check next to it, indicating that it is in use.

The menu command actually opens up Character Attributes. You will see that your text has a Track Amount of 11 units, just as indicated in the Measurements palette.

However, QuarkXPress doesn't show you this range kerning unless you actually select some text.

→ or ← so you have a text insertion point and your Measurements palette will indicate zero kerning.

Shift+→ or Shift+←, depending on where you find yourself after the previous step, so you have at least one letter selected. The Measurements palette will indicate your 11 units of range kerning or tracking again.

The most important lesson from this experiment is that range kerning and pair kerning add to each other. If you now did some pair kerning, you could reduce or increase the amount of letter spacing in effect on your text. But your Measurements palette kerning indicator doesn't add them up for you. You must add them up in your head to find out the total amount of kerning in text where range kerning has been applied.

Tip

Use True Tracking for Large Document Projects

If you are working on a large document where you have many situations requiring you to track text, use QuarkXPress' real tracking command, Utilities>Tracking Edit. This command allows you to set up letter spacing for specific typefaces, varying the letter spacing depending on the size of the type. Because it automates and standardizes the process, this is a lot faster than range kerning as you work through your text. Be careful, though, because this true form of tracking is always on for all instances of the typeface throughout a QuarkXPress document. That's not good if you want large headlines to be tightened and large reversed-out type to be widened.

Aligning Two Text Boxes

9. It would be good to visually align the reversed-out text box with the ordering information text.

They should be visually aligned. In other words, the bottom of the reversed text box should be aligned with the baseline of the last line of ordering information text.

Use the Zoom tool to draw out a marquee and magnify the bottom area of the page containing the two text boxes.

Arrow Key Nudging

10. Use the Item tool to select the ordering information box.

⬇ until the base of the last line of text rests right on the bottom margin guide. You can use arrow keys to nudge an item into position in any direction, as long as the item has been selected with the Item tool.

11. Select the reversed text box and use arrow key nudging to set the bottom of the 80% black box right on the bottom margin.

12. Zoom in even closer, as in Figure 5.22, and check the alignment.

If the visual alignment has worked out just right, the baselines of the text in both boxes will be aligned. Click and drag the 46-pica horizontal guide to see if that's right.

Panning Your View

13. Staying at this magnification, pan your view. Panning is a great time-saving feature, much faster than using the scroll bars at the bottom and right of your window.

Click and drag while holding down (Option) (Mac) or (Alt) (Win95). Drag the screen to the right so you get the "i" in the word "Spring" centered in your screen.

14. Create a guide that you will use in the next several steps for aligning elements.

Pull out a vertical guide from the ruler and center it on the dot of the letter "i." On our page, this guide rested just about exactly at 8p6 on the horizontal ruler.

Drawing a Dotted Line

15. Back off from your view so you are able to see both the reversed text block and the base of the light bulb. You might try Actual Size view, ⌘+①(Mac) or Ctrl+① (Win95), and then pan to get the objects onto your screen.

16. Choose the Orthogonal Line Tool. It's the one that looks like a plus sign, fourth up from the bottom in the Tool palette.

It may be easier to think of this as the straight line tool because that's what orthogonal means and that's what it draws—straight vertical or horizontal lines.

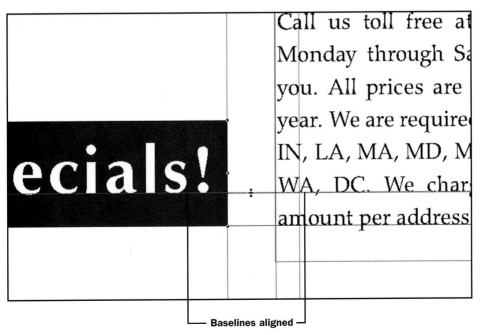

Figure 5.22

Achieving visual alignment of the text boxes and text.

Baselines aligned

17. Click the line tool just above the dot in the "i"—right on top of the vertical guide you just pulled out—and drag up to draw out a line. It should be around 20 picas long, depending on how closely your layout matches ours. You can check Figure 5.23 to get your bearings on where the line goes.

In the Modify dialog box, select the line style All Dots and make it 6 points wide so it will echo the dot of the "i."

It should be 80% black to match the reversed-out text box.

When you are through, your dialog box should look like the one in Figure 5.23.

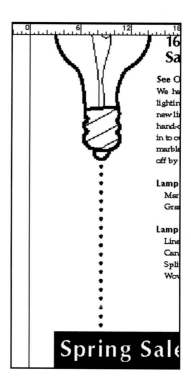

Figure 5.24
Final positioning of bulb, line, and reversed text.

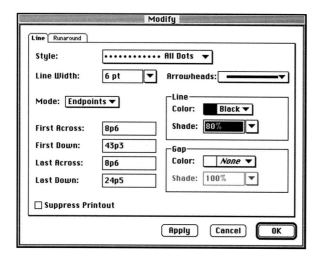

Figure 5.23
Setting line attributes.

Adjusting Picture Position

18. Click the light bulb with the Item tool to select it, then → or ← nudge the graphic so the base of the bulb has been centered on the line.

If you need to do so, zoom back out to a wider view so you can see the light bulb.

When everything is in position, it should look like Figure 5.24.

Setting an Em Dash

19. Draw out a Zoom tool marquee around the paragraph about the new line of table lamps text. Have a close look at the text, as in Figure 5.25.

In the United States, the em dash is often set with no space on either side of it. You type an em dash (or long dash, almost always one em in width) with Option+◆Shift+- (Mac) or Ctrl+◆Shift+= (Win95).

Problem is, with no space around it, the em dash often crashes into the adjacent letters or otherwise looks just plain ungainly.

So, as in Figure 5.25, many people put a regular space either side of the em dash which opens up the space. It probably provides way too much space, in most cases. But there's a better way to go.

Four alternative choices for space around an em dash are:

- Use the Character Attribute horizontal width setting to narrow the spaces, and sometimes the dash as well, to 75% or another setting that suits your taste.

- Laboriously kern all the em dash spacing in the text.

- Set thin (or punctuation) spaces either side of the em dash.

- Define the flex space as an especially thin space for this special purpose.

In the next step, you'll try out the flex space approach.

Defining and Inserting Flex Space

20. Edit the spaces around the em dash.

    Delete the regular spaces and replace them with flex spaces, Option+⇧Shift+Spacebar (Mac) or Ctrl+⇧Shift+5 (Win95).

This won't make much difference in the spacing, until you set up a narrower width for your flex spaces.

Remember, you can adjust your flex space definition at any time, but you must keep in mind—as you will see in the next step—the change is retroactive for all existing flex spaces. In a large passage of text, where you have many flex spaces, this could trigger massive changes in line endings.

That's a very important point. You can have only one value for all the flex spaces in your document.

21. Set a narrow flex space width.

    Go to Edit>Preferences>Document to the Character tab.

    Set Flex Space Width to 15% (15% of the width of an en space) and click OK to put the change into effect.

    Notice how the width of the space changes and pulls the two words either side of the em dash in much closer. However, because the space is there to fend it off, there's no chance of a crash between the dash and its companions.

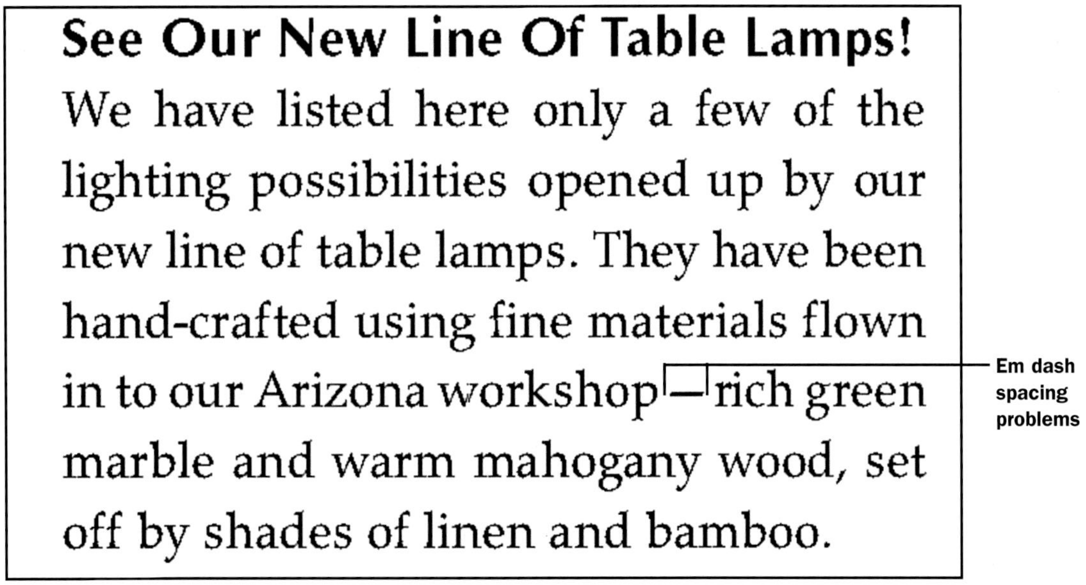

See Our New Line Of Table Lamps!
We have listed here only a few of the lighting possibilities opened up by our new line of table lamps. They have been hand-crafted using fine materials flown in to our Arizona workshop—rich green marble and warm mahogany wood, set off by shades of linen and bamboo.

— Em dash spacing problems

Figure 5.25

Checking for spacing problems.

Setting an En Space

22. The space between the state and the postal code in an address often needs special attention. Generally, I use a fixed space of some kind, an en space or an em space, to emphatically create separation.

Replace the regular space before the ZIP Code with an en space, ⌥Option+Spacebar (Mac) or Ctrl+⬆Shift+6 (Win95).

Temporary Item Tool

23. One last fine-tuning touch is to move the title over to match the indent on the first headline and paragraph in the price information.

You need the Item tool to do this, but there's a quick way to temporarily bring up the tool for a quick move.

Hold down the ⌘ (Mac) or Ctrl (Win95) key and you will see that the pointer turns into the familiar four-arrow Item tool. Add the ⬆Shift and you will constrain the pointer so it only moves orthogonally, meaning in straight lines.

Click and drag to the right the title text box until it snaps to the 12-pica vertical guide, keeping the baseline of the text riding on the 9-pica horizontal guide.

Go to Fit To Window view to have a look at your results, which should look like Figure 5.26.

The final layout of the redesigned price sheet has been saved on the CD-ROM in a file named **05BASE04.QXT**.

Summary

If you have absorbed all the material in the last two chapters, you now possess a basic knowledge of some of the most important aspects of fine typography—the techniques for spacing letters, words, lines, and paragraphs of type. In addition, you have learned techniques for giving type shape and form on the page by using columns and indents.

Be sure to go back over any of the reading or the exercises you are hazy on, as revealed by the following skills check. As we explained in the last chapter, these are probably the two most crucially important chapters in this entire book, containing essential basic concepts about QuarkXPress and desktop publishing.

Figure 5.26

Completed price list design.

Review It

As a review of what you have learned in this chapter, please answer the following questions.

1. Describe the two basic steps in setting H&Js.

2. What's the difference between paragraph spacing and leading?

3. Where can you tell QuarkXPress how many columns you want in a text box?

4. What's the advantage of the Apply button in the QuarkXPress formatting dialog boxes?

5. Describe the difference between the Hyphenation Zone and Flush Zone hyphenation settings.

6. Why shouldn't you type extra carriage returns to space out paragraphs?

7. How do you turn hyphenation off and on? What are the three main settings that control the length of letters divided by hyphenation?

8. What is the special character you use for forcing line breaks manually? The tool for manual hyphenation? How do you type them on the keyboard?

9. Describe the width of the following spaces in ems: flex, en, em, thin.

10. What are the two techniques for centering some text vertically and horizontally in a text box?

Check It

Multiple Choice

Please circle the correct answer for each of the following questions.

1. What's the easiest way to set up a bunch of H&Js?

   a. Append in H&J dialog

   b. Copy and edit existing ones

   c. Type in parameters

   d. All of the above

2. Which of the following hyphenation modes is best?

   a. Standard

   b. Expanded

   c. Enhanced

   d. Zone

3. To nudge an item into position, you can _____.

   a. Select its content and perform a Click and Drag with the Option (Mac) or Alt (Win95) key held down

   b. Select it with Item tool and use ◆Shift+→ to nudge

   c. Select with Item tool and nudge with Arrow keys

   d. Click and drag a marquee around it and nudge with Arrow keys

4. The gutter is _____.

   a. Another name for a slug of type

   b. Space opened up between paragraphs

   c. Distance between columns

   d. Shim used in old typesetting to space lines

5. To get the Item tool temporarily, you can...

   a. Hold down ◆Shift+Option (Mac) or ◆Shift+Alt (Win95)

   b. Click and drag while holding down ⌘ (Mac) or Ctrl (Win95)

   c. Hold down ⌘ (Mac) or Ctrl+◆Shift (Win95)

   d. Hold ⌘ (Mac) or Ctrl (Win95)

6. One technique to achieve uneven columns in a text box is _____.

   a. Tab each line in to the column edge

   b. Indent the text using Paragraph Attributes

   c. Insert em spaces where needed

   d. Use Indent Here character

7. Autokerning settings are controlled by _____.

   a. Document Preferences setting

   b. Kerning pairs built into type

   c. Your own Kerning Table edits

   d. All of the above

8. One H&J word spacing setting that applies even in unjustified text is _____.

   a. Minimum

   b. Optimum

   c. Maximum

   d. All of the above

9. When setting a tab leader, you can use _____.

   a. Period

   b. Space

   c. Underline character

   d. Any of the above

10. To constrain a move—such as an Item tool move or drawing a line—hold down _____.

    a. ⌘ (Mac) or Ctrl (Win95)

    b. Option (Mac) or Alt (Win95)

    c. ◆Shift

    d. None of the above

True or False

Please circle *T* or *F* to indicate whether the statement is true or false.

T   F   **1.** Always use Space Before and Space After instead of a carriage return to open space between paragraphs.

T   F   **2.** Always use Enhanced mode hyphenation.

T   F   **3.** You can create dot leader tabs by selecting the tab and typing a period into one of the blanks in the Paragraph Attributes dialog.

T   F   **4.** Autoleading works well because it provides consistent leading amounts.

T   F   **5.** The H&J word and letter space settings only affect justified text.

T   F   **6.** Space Before a paragraph will shove it down from the top of a column or text box.

T   F   **7.** Both reversed-out type and large type should be set as loosely as possible to make them more readable.

T   F   **8.** Use Centered paragraph alignment along with the Modify command vertical alignment setting to center type in a box.

T   F   **9.** A nonbreaking space works to hold together words, as if they were glued together.

T   F   **10.** The fastest way to set a bit of space around all the em dashes in a book would be to kern them.

Design It

Now that you have gained a pretty complete set of knowledge about all the different kinds of horizontal and vertical spacing of type, have a long hard look at the pricing sheet. What would you change, or at least experiment with changing, to see if you can make it better?

■ What different kind of dot leader might be attractive for this pricing data information? What about a different character? What if there were two spaces between each dot?

■ Have a close look at how the lines of pricing data have been set off and organized with paragraph spacing. Try some different spacing. How close could the groups be and still maintain this effect?

■ The effect of spacing out the groups works because of the contrast between the line spacing (leading) and the paragraph spacing. Experiment with the leading to see how close together the lines of price data need to be to provide adequate contrast with the paragraph spacing. How might that influence your choice of paragraph spacing?

6 Copy Editing

What You Will Learn

QuarkXPress really isn't designed as a word processor. Instead, you will generally use it as a page composition program at the final stage in the layout process. With QuarkXPress, you electronically paste up pages of words and pictures created by word processors, scanners, and drawing programs.

Nonetheless, you will inevitably end up doing quite a lot of copy editing in QuarkXPress. You will deal with last-minute client requests for changes and corrections, for example. And sometimes, for small documents, you will just type text directly into QuarkXPress.

No problem. QuarkXPress has that complete set of navigation and editing tools that you learned about in Chapter 3. It even has search-and-replace capability and a spelling checker. All these copy editing tasks are the focus of this chapter. You'll learn how to:

➤ Edit text with the Find/Change command

➤ Set up your QuarkXPress screen to display the invisible characters in your publication

➤ Find and change special characters such as tabs and en spaces

➤ Use the Find/Change command to format text

➤ Run spelling checks

➤ Add words to a personal auxiliary spelling dictionary

Just Plain Cafe

Hamburgers

Classic – *tomato, sweet onion*	4.00
Deluxe – *bacon, cheddar*	4.00
Mexican – *napoles, jalapeno*	4.00
Salmon – *mayonnaise, capers*	4.00
Soy – *roasted eggplant, scallions*	3.00

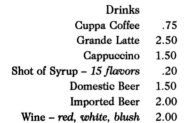

Chicken

Southern – *dipped and fried*	4.50
Barbecue – *howlin' hot sauce*	4.50
Date Night – *roasted with garlic*	4.50
Caesar – *chopped, tossed, romaine*	4.50
Mediterranean – *tomatoes, basil*	4.50

Drinks

Cuppa Coffee	.75
Grande Latte	2.50
Cappuccino	1.50
Shot of Syrup – *15 flavors*	.20
Domestic Beer	1.50
Imported Beer	2.00
Wine – *red, white, blush*	2.00

Desserts

Pie – *fresh three times a day*	2.50
Ice Cream – *new flavors daily*	2.25
Croissant, Sweet Rolls, Brioche	2.00
Chocolate Sin	3.00

111 Timberline Road, Wenatchee, (514) 876-3001

Figure 6.1

The project for this chapter builds a menu using woodcut-style clip art images.

The menu for the "Just Plain Cafe" resembles its name, just a straightforward composition of text and graphics.

You may have noticed that this menu page layout has an underlying structure. The elements are arranged in a sort of checkerboard pattern. In fact, the art items have been aligned into two vertical "stacks," providing informal columns for organizing the information on the page. (You'll learn more about design grids in Chapter 9, "Using a Design Grid.")

The font used for the menu is Caslon. In Sean Cavanaugh's *Digital Type Design Guide*, he suggests that you use Caslon for all-purpose text such as books, magazines, journals, and correspondence. He continues...

Designed by William Caslon in 1725, this face's classic lines, sturdiness, and legibility have made it one of the most popular text faces of all time. Suitable for long text passages as well as headlines and titles, Caslon's versatility leads to an adage among designers and typographers that says "when in doubt, set in Caslon."

Prep Notes

Getting Set Up

Copy all the files for this chapter from the CD-ROM to a work area on your hard drive. They are all in the **Steps** folder in the folder labeled **06**.

You will need to have the Caslon font installed on your computer for this chapter.

The menu that needs updating has been stored in its initial form as file **06BASE01.QXT** on the CD-ROM. In this chapter, you will make changes to this beginning version of the design until it matches the version shown in Figure 6.1.

Introducing...the Find/Change Command

The Find/Change command—search and replace operations—can save you enormous amounts of time when trying to edit or format anything more than a small amount of text. Also, and perhaps more important, using search-and-replace techniques can vastly improve your accuracy when making editing changes.

Scanning every line of a 300-page manuscript looking for every instance of a certain word could take you a couple of days—and you still might miss a few. But QuarkXPress can do it for you in a few minutes, maybe even seconds.

Think about specifying a search-and-replace operation as a series of steps. Like a camera with a range of increasingly powerful and narrow lenses, each additional step focuses in closer on the object of your search. The three basic steps are to: specify the search area, set search filters, and define the search target.

Have a look at Figure 6.2 so you can follow along in the QuarkXPress Find/Change command dialog box as we walk through each of these three steps.

By the way, later in this chapter we'll be talking about spell checking. You might want to keep in mind as we go through the steps of constructing a search that the QuarkXPress spelling checker uses a similar sort of conceptual process.

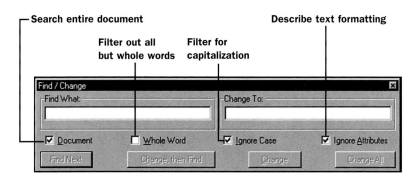

Figure 6.2

QuarkXPress' Find/Change dialog box.

Specify Search Area

Think of the process of constructing a search as being similar to looking for a lost item.

Looked at that way, specifying the search area would be comparable to the geographic description—the size of the location area where you want to look for the item. For example, if you click **Document** in the dialog box in Figure 6.2, QuarkXPress will search the entire document.

You might begin looking for a lost item right in your immediate vicinity. In QuarkXPress, a lot depends on where you are in your document just before you call up the Find/Change dialog box.

If you select some text before going to the Find/Change command, QuarkXPress will limit its search to the selected text unless you tell it to search the entire document.

If you are on a master page (something you will learn more about in Chapters 8 and 9), then you will have a **M**asters feature instead of a **D**ocument feature and the search will be limited to your master pages.

Set Search Filters

If your lost item was a shirt, you might, as you look for it, filter out certain kinds of items. If you knew, for example, that it was a T-shirt, you would be able to search more quickly and precisely by blocking out of your mind all the other kinds of shirts you might run across during your search.

In QuarkXPress, you can narrow your search to whole words only. If you, for example, told QuarkXPress you wanted to search for the letters "c-a-t" and you filtered for whole words, the program would skip over the words "catch" and "scat" but it would find the whole word "cat."

You can also filter out all items whose capital letters don't match your search terms. If you turn off **Ignore Case** and search for "Cat" with a capital "C" the search will skip over "cat" with a lowercase "c."

Define Search Target

Finally, you precisely describe the item you are seeking.

This could be a sequence of letters, or it could be some text characteristic such as bold or italic formatting. If you click off the Ignore **A**ttributes feature, you get a much more detailed dialog box like the one in Figure 6.3.

Changing

Once you have completely constructed your search, you have the option of changing whatever you find into something else. You could exchange found letters or words for other letters or words. You can even change the formatting of the found text, within the limits of the Find/Change dialog box. Unfortunately, for example, the Find/Change command can't search for or change certain text formatting attributes, such as leading or alignment. It can't find any paragraph attributes, in fact, except for styles.

Now that you have a handle on the concepts behind conducting search-and-replace operations, it's time to put the Find/Change command to work yourself.

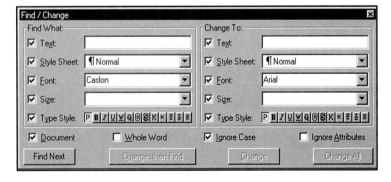

Figure 6.3

Find/Change expanded to enable searching for text attributes.

Defining a Simple Find Operation

This section constructs an example search using the three fundamental steps: specifying the search area, setting search filters, and defining the search target.

1. In this exercise, we are going keep it extremely simple. You are going to search for a particular word in the menu text, "tomato."

   Begin by opening the beginning file for this chapter, which you should already have copied to a working folder on your hard drive, **06BASE01.QXT**. Save the opened file from this template in a name of your choice.

2. Set your view magnification up high enough that you can easily read the text on your screen. You will want to be able to read what you find.

Specify Search Area

3. Begin specifying your search area first. In this case, that is extremely simple to do because you are working on a one-page document.

   Click the Content tool in the main story on the page, anywhere in one of the four threaded text boxes in the main portion of the page containing the menu items and prices.

4. QuarkXpress will begin its search from wherever your cursor sits in the story. That means you can further specify your search area by navigating to the very top of the story, ⌘+Option+↑ (Mac) or Ctrl+Alt+↑ (Win95).

Activating Find/Change

5. Use the Edit>Find/Change command—⌘+F (Mac) or Ctrl+F (Win95)—to open the Find/Change dialog box in Figure 6.2.

Notice that the search and the replace operations are combined into a single command. Many programs have two different commands for Find (searching) and Change (replacing) but the Change command is just an expanded version of the Find command. It makes a lot of sense to simplify things by combining them into a single command. You, as the user, don't need to bother with the Change part of the dialog box if you don't need it for a particular job.

Search Current Story

6. You've already specified the search area to a great extent by getting your cursor to the top of the current story before opening the Find/Change command. But there's one last step.

   Click off the **Document** checkbox to limit the search to the currently selected story.

Setting Search Filters

7. Set your search filter settings.

   Leave **I**gnore Case turned on and turn on **W**hole Word.

Defining the Search Target

8. Check on the Text checkbox. That will make it possible for you to specify your exact text search target. Type **tomato** in the Find What box.

Find Next

9. Click Find First, or press Return (Mac) or ↵Enter (Win95) to launch the search operation.

   The word "tomato" will be selected as in Figure 6.4.

   You might need to move the Find/Change dialog box to see the text behind it. You can click and drag the title bar across the top of the dialog box. The spelling checker works the same way.

Figure 6.4

Find/Change with the Whole Word filter turned on.

10. Click Find Next again and your machine will beep at you.

That's the signal that no further instances were found that matched your search parameters.

11. However, we know that the letters "tomato" occur in the text at least one more time.

Try again, but this time click off **W**hole Word.

Find First

12. Hold down Option (Mac) or Alt (Win95) and the Find Next button will change to Find First.

Click Find First and you will find the whole word "tomato" again.

13. Release the modifier key to change the button back to Find Next and click it.

This time, when you click Find Next, you will get an additional search hit, the front portion of the word "tomatoes" as in Figure 6.5.

14. Click any item on the page behind the Find/Change dialog box and notice that you get your active cursor back.

The Find/Change dialog box acts like a palette in that it is *non-modal*. That means you can keep it open while you perform other work.

Leave the Find/Change dialog box open now as you move on to the next exercise.

Editing with Find/Change

That simple search exercise was good for showing you some concepts but the real power of the Find/Change command is the second half of its name—Change. It enables you to make massive changes to your text very quickly.

For example, we need to strip out all the dollar signs on this menu. There are probably a couple dozen of them, which would take a lot of editing if we did them one at a time. Instead, we'll use Find/Change.

By the way, from a design point of view, there's a good reason to get rid of the dollar signs. They are a visual irritation because their repetition is distracting.

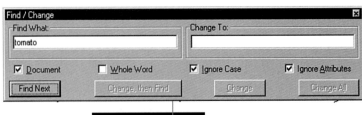

Figure 6.5

Find/Change with the Whole Word filter turned off.

Also, they don't really add any information. There's no doubt from the layout that the prices are money amounts and there's no question about the type of currency since the Just Plain Cafe is located in Oregon.

1. With the Find/Change dialog still open and with a text cursor still active, get to the top of the story with ⌘+Option+↑ (Mac) or Ctrl+Alt+↑ (Win95).

Searching for Symbols

2. Specify your search.

Leave the **D**ocument checkbox turned off.

Since the dollar sign is a symbol, similar to punctuation, the **W**hole Word and **I**gnore Case checkboxes don't matter for this search.

3. Type a dollar sign (**$**) in the Find What section of the Find/Change dialog box.

Specifying a Change

4. Leave the Change To box empty. That will replace the dollar sign with nothing.

But hold on, all of the change buttons are grayed out and unavailable: **Ch**ange then Find; **C**hange; and Change All.

Deleting Text with Change

5. QuarkXPress insists on a step at this point if you want to change even simple text. Change doesn't work until you have found your first text. This is probably different than you are used to in a word processor.

Click off the Ignore **A**ttributes checkbox to expand the Find/Change dialog box to its full power state.

On the Change To half of the dialog box, make sure the Text Style checkbox is turned on. That should activate all the change buttons.

6. Do a Find First operation to get to the first occurrence of the search item in the story. As before, hold down Option (Mac) or Alt (Win95) and click the Find First button.

7. Click Change Then Find.

Notice that the first dollar sign will be edited out and the next one highlighted.

Use this Change Then Find technique to work through text when you aren't positive you've got the Find/Change operation set up perfectly. It lets you evaluate each find and decide whether to change it before moving on to the next one.

8. Click Change.

Notice that the change buttons go gray again and there's no highlighted text, but the next dollar sign was deleted.

In order to reactivate the change buttons, click Find Next.

9. Now finish up this editing job by clicking Change All. Like lightning, every dollar sign will be removed.

10. You will get an alert box telling you how many instances of the dollar sign were changed.

Click OK to get out of this report dialog box and return to the Find/Change dialog box.

Close Find/Change by clicking the close box in the upper-left corner (Mac) or the upper-right corner (Win95).

As you can see, using the Change command was a lot faster than manually editing out each of the dollar signs one by one. The menu version as it should appear to this point has been saved as **06BASE02.QXT**.

> **Tip**
>
> **Revert to Saved When the Change Command Goes Wrong**
>
> Unlike many word processors, the Edit>Undo command in QuarkXPress doesn't work after you make a Change move. A big Change All operation, if you somehow set it up wrong, could ruin your day. That's why you should always save your file right before using the Change command. Then you can revert to the last saved version using the File>Revert To Saved command.

Find/Change Invisible Characters

QuarkXPress makes powerful use of a number of what it calls invisible characters. In fact, you have already made some powerful use of them yourself—tab characters, paragraph endings, new box and new column characters, forced line breaks, and so on.

As it happens, you can search and replace the invisible characters, which makes them very powerful tools indeed. To do so, however, you can't simply type those characters into the Find/Change dialog box as you can the regular alphabet. You must use special codes in the Find What and Change To boxes. Before beginning this exercise, where you make use of some of these codes, have a look at the full list of them in Table 6.1.

(Mac) As you can see in Table 6.1, Macintosh users have an additional way to enter many of these special search and replace codes. In most cases, you can type ⌘ plus the item you desire.

In this exercise, you will remove all the parentheses in the menu and insert en dashes and thin spaces to set off the dishes from their descriptions.

Show Invisibles

1. Go to **View>Show Invisibles**, ⌘+I (Mac) or Ctrl+I (Win95) in order to make the special characters visible on your screen.

   As you can see in Figure 6.6, you have tab characters and paragraph ending carriage returns scattered all through your text.

Table 6.1 The special Find/Change codes for QuarkXPress invisible characters

To Find/Change...	Win95 & Mac	Mac Only
Paragraph End	\\+P	⌘+Return
New Line	\\+n	⌘+Shift+Return
New Column	\\+c	⌘+Return
New Box	\\+b	⌘+Shift+Return
Tab	\\+t	⌘+Tab
Any Single Character (Wildcard)	\\+?	⌘+?
Backslash	\\+\\	⌘+\\
Thin Space (Punctuation Space)	\\+.	
Flex Space	\\+F	
Automatic Page Numbers		
Current Text Box	\\+3	⌘+3
Previous Linked Box	\\+2	⌘+2
Next Linked Box	\\+4	⌘+4

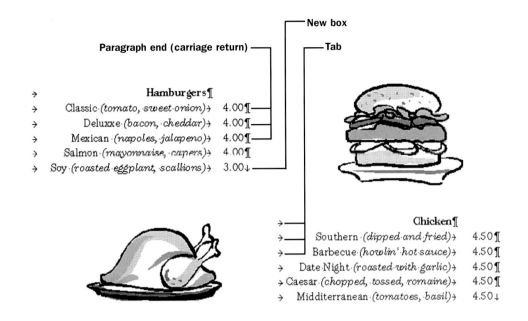

Figure 6.6

Show Invisibles has been turned on.

Changing All...Review

2. Do a Save before moving ahead so you can revert if you need to do so.

3. Do a Change All operation to remove all the closing parentheses.

   Click the Content tool in the menu item and prices story.

   Open the Find/Change dialog box, ⌘+F (Mac) or Ctrl+F (Win95).

4. Specify your search and replace.

   Type a closing parenthesis, ")", in Find What and leave Change To empty.

   Make sure **Document** is checked off so you only search in the current story. You don't want to remove the parenthesis mark at the end of the phone area code.

5. Conduct the search and replace operation.

   Hold down Option (Mac) or Alt (Win95) and click Find First.

   Click Change All to delete the closing parentheses.

Changing to Invisibles

6. The next task is to replace the open parentheses and their preceding spaces with two thin spaces and an en dash.

   Type a space followed by an open parenthesis "(" in the Find What box.

7. In the Change To box type a "\" followed by the en dash, Option+- (Mac) or Alt+Keypad 0150 (Win95).

   Add the second thin space after the en dash, another backward slash, and a period.

   Your Find/Change dialog box should look like the one in Figure 6.7.

8. OK the advisory dialog box on how many instances were changed.

   Close the Find/Change dialog box with the close box.

   Your menu should now have en dashes instead of parentheses and the menu item text should look like Figure 6.8.

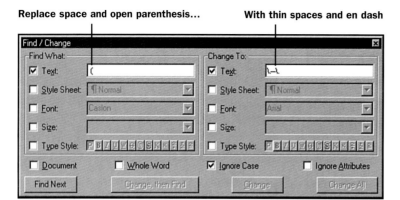

Figure 6.7

Find/Change set up to change to thin spaces and en dash.

Thin spaces surrounding en dashes

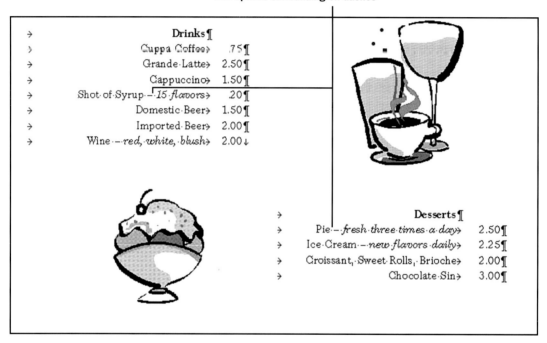

Figure 6.8

The menu so far.

The progress so far on the revised menu has been saved on the CD-ROM in a file named **06BASE03.QXT**. You have a close-up view of what your menu item text should look like in Figure 6.8.

Formatting Text with Find/Change

You can do a lot more than change text characters using the Find/Change command. You can find—and change—many text attributes. (You can also conduct Find/Change operations for styles, the subject of the next chapter.) In this way, the Find/Change command has the power to help you as a formatting tool in addition to its text-editing capabilities.

In this set of exercises, you will quickly make a small increase in the type size of the menu category headline.

Sticky Find/Change Command

1. Open the Find/Change command, ⌘+F (Mac) or Ctrl+F (Win95).

    If you kept QuarkXPress open from the last exercise, notice that all your settings from the last task are still there. That means QuarkXPress has a "sticky" Find/Change command. It tries to help you by remembering what you did last time you used the command.

    On the other hand, Find/Change is sticky only for the current work session. If you closed down QuarkXPress between exercises, you will discover the Find/Change dialog box has snapped back to its default, in its slimmed down version with Ignore Attributes checked on.

2. You need the full Find/Change dialog so click off Ignore Attributes, expanding the dialog box to its most powerful form.

    Click somewhere in the menu items story with the Content tool.

Finding/Changing No Text

3. Click off the Text checkboxes.

    Notice that you don't need to clear the old search text from the text fields, just turn off the text checkboxes.

Setting Find/Change Type Style

4. We know that the category headlines are the only text items in the menu items story that have been formatted bold so we can use that attribute for the Find What search parameter.

    Click the Find What checkbox for Type Style.

5. Notice that the row of type style buttons looks a lot like the ones that perform the same service on the Measurements palette.

Click the Bold icon several times in the Type Style area. Notice that the type style buttons have three states and you can rotate through the states by clicking on them repeatedly.

You want the icon to be fully activated, not just gray.

Button Activation System

Deactivated means you do not want to find text that has this style (Find What) or you don't want to change the text to this style (Change To).

Activated means you want to find text with that style (Find What) or you do want to change the found text to this style (Change To).

Gray means you don't care one way or the other.

(Win95) In Windows 95, the Type Style buttons have a 3-D effect. The buttons, when activated, will actually look like they have been pushed in, like push buttons.

(Mac) The Macintosh Type Style buttons are not 3-D. They are either black (activated), white (deactivated), or gray.

6. Now that the Find What part of the dialog box has been set, we need to specify the Change To side. We want to bump up the boldface type in the menu category headlines one point, from 12 points to 13 points.

    In the Change To section, click Size and enter the new size, which is 13 points.

7. Make sure you turn off the Document checkbox. You don't want to change the boldfacing in the entire document, just in the story you have selected.

Formatting with Find/Change

8. Find the first instance by holding down Option (Mac) or Alt (Win95) and clicking Find First.

9. Your change buttons should now be available so click Change All.

    In a split second, the four headlines will automatically be transformed from 12-point type to 13-point type.

10. Close Find/Change.

11. Turn off Show Invisibles, ⌘+I (Mac) or Ctrl+I (Win95) and (if they are on) turn off guides, F7.

Have a look at your menu after all the Find/Change operations have been completed. It should look like Figure 6.9.

Figure 6.9

The menu so far, after all Find/Change operations.

● The menu project, as it looks after all the exercises so far in this chapter, has been saved as **06BASE04.QXT** on your CD-ROM.

Checking Spelling

If you have experience with a word processor, you have a general idea about how QuarkXPress spell checking works. You open up a dialog box where you set a few parameters. QuarkXPress checks each word in the search area against its spelling dictionary. Then you scan through your spelling check search area as the program shows you the suspect words that it believes might be misspelled.

Like most spelling checkers, you can set up one or more custom dictionaries—called auxiliary dictionaries in QuarkXPress—to add your own sets of words to the QuarkXPress spelling checker capability, although you can have only one of these dictionaries active at any one time.

As you may have already noticed (hope you didn't correct them already), the menu project has been set up with some misspelled words so you can try out the QuarkXPress Spelling command for yourself.

Specifying Spelling Check Area

1. Go to the **U**tilities>Check Spelling command.

You may remember earlier in the chapter we said the spelling checker operated on similar concepts to the Find/Change command. You will see as we move forward how similar they are.

(Mac) The keyboard shortcuts for the Macintosh spellng checker are based on the letter L, and the size of the spelling check search area grows as you use more keys. So the shortcut for Word is ⌘+L. Story is ⌘+Option+L. Document is ⌘+Option+⬆Shift+L.

(Win95) The keyboard shortcuts for the Win95 spelling checker are based on the letter W and, like the Mac, the size of the spelling check search area grows as you use more keys. So the shortcut for Word is Ctrl+W. Story is Ctrl+Alt+W. Document is Ctrl+Alt+⬆Shift+W

2. Choose **D**ocument from the menu.

Word Count

3. You will get an advisory Word Count alert box that tells you how many words are in the area you are spell checking, the number of those words that are unique, and the number of words that QuarkXPress suspects may be misspelled. It looks like the alert box you see in Figure 6.10.

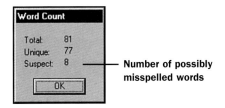

Number of possibly misspelled words

Figure 6.10

The Word Count alert box.

4. OK the Word Count box and you will reach the actual spelling checker you see in Figure 6.11.

Notice that the title of the dialog box automatically adjusts to reflect your spelling check search area, so it is called Check Document.

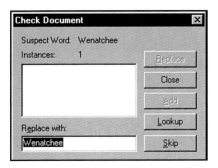

Figure 6.11

The QuarkXPress spelling checker dialog box. (The Macintosh version looks a bit different cosmetically but has all the same functions.)

Suspect Words

5. The spelling checker will jump immediately to the first questionable word.

If your spelling check turns up the words in a different order than shown in these steps, read through the entire exercise and then go back through the exercise in your own order, matching your own spelling check search. The order doesn't matter in this case.

When we ran our check, the first word was the name of the city, Wenatchee. That's only natural because you wouldn't expect such an unusual name to be in the QuarkXPress spelling dictionary.

In the next exercise, you will add this word to your personal QuarkXPress auxiliary dictionary.

Skipping Words

6. Skip Wenatchee to move on to the next questionable word.

You can either click the Skip button or you can use the keyboard shortcut command, ⌘+⑤ (Mac) or Alt+⑤ (Win95).

Replacing Words

7. The next word in our check was "Deluxxe."

It's obviously misspelled but as yet QuarkXPress is not offering you any suggested correction.

Click on the Lookup button or use the keyboard shortcut, ⌘+ⓛ (Mac) or Alt+ⓛ (Win95).

8. The QuarkXPress spelling dictionary offers only one alternative suggestion. It's the right one, of course, so click it to select it.

The dialog box will shift to show a Replace With box with the new spelling inside it.

9. Now make the spelling correction.

Click Replace or press Return (Mac) or Alt+Ⓡ (Win95).

We are emphasizing the keyboard shortcuts in this section because, when you are spell checking a large volume of text, you will want to work quickly. It's faster to keep your hands on the keyboard instead of repeatedly switching between the keyboard and the mouse.

Tip

Keyboard Selection of Suggested Words

You can even select individual suggested words from the keyboard. On the Macintosh, use ⬆ or ⬇. In Win95, you'll need to Tab⇆ until you are in the suggested word area (with the border highlighted) and then you can select a word with ⬆ or ⬇.

Drastic Effects of Skip and Return

10. Work your way through some more of this spelling check. You will come across some correct but unusual words like "nopales" and the slang word "howlin." These will not appear in the dictionary but you can go ahead and skip them.

Take careful note, skip really does mean skip. If you choose to skip a questionable word at any point in a spelling check run, QuarkXPress won't show it to you for correction again during that spelling check session—even if there are 20 or 30 more instances of the word in the text.

That applies to Replace as well. If you replace a questionable word with a new spelling, then QuarkXPress will carry on through the rest of the session changing the spelling in absolutely every other instance of the word.

This all-or-nothing approach can lead to some unexpected results and you should be very alert when using it.

Word Not Found

11. Eventually you will hit a seriously misspelled word, "Midditerranean."

The Lookup feature won't find a suggested replacement for this one. It's just too far off for QuarkXPress to find it in the dictionary.

All you can do in a situation like this is consult your own dictionary and type the correction in the space provided in the dialog box.

(It would be nice if QuarkXPress would let you experiment with the spelling and try a couple of lookups to see if you could get it right, but the Lookup button is grayed out after your first look.)

Type in the correct spelling, which is "Mediterranean." When you have it right, Replace it, (Return) (Mac) or (Alt)+(R) (Win95).

12. Finish the spelling check, accepting the slang spelling for "Cuppa" and the foreign language words "Grande" and "Latte."

The spelling checker will automatically close when it runs out of suspected words.

Managing an Auxiliary Dictionary

Repeatedly running through all the unusual words in this menu could be a pain if you had to update it frequently. It would be nice to be able to add these words to a personal dictionary so they wouldn't be slowing you down, but at the same time you would have a way to check that they are spelled as you want them to be spelled.

This exercise will help you do just that.

1. You must first establish an auxiliary dictionary.

Go to the **Utilities>Auxiliary** Dictionary command.

2. In the resulting dialog box, you will get a standard file dialog box just like you would see in this and other Mac and Windows software programs.

It will look a bit different depending on whether you are on a Macintosh or in Windows 95. How-ever, both dialog boxes will have a button labeled New.

Navigate to your working folder if the dialog box isn't already focused there and create a new file, an empty auxiliary dictionary called MENU.

(Mac) In the Macintosh operating system, this operation requires two dialog boxes. However, they should be familiar to you since they are a basic part of the operating system. You will click New and get a second dialog box where you can enter the name of the dictionary. Click the Create button to finish up.

(Win95) In the Windows 95 operating system, this is all done in one dialog box. You type in the name for your new dictionary and then click on the New button.

3. Now you must open the auxiliary dictionary.

To do that, go back to **Utilities>Auxiliary** Dictionary.

Double-click the new dictionary named MENU to open it. (On a Windows 95 machine, the file will be named **MENU.QDT**.)

4. Run the document-wide spelling check again.

5. There's a difference in the spelling check dialog box this time. The **A**dd button is now active and not grayed out.

As you run through the check, and when you get to the possibly misspelled words that you know are unusual but nevertheless spelled the way you want them, click the Add button, ⌘+Ⓐ (Mac) or Alt+Ⓐ (Win95).

Go through the menu and **A**dd "Wenatchee," "Napoles," "Howlin," "Cuppa," "Grande," and "Latte."

6. Now run the spelling check again.

You will find that the Word Count dialog box shows zero suspect words and, when you OK it, your spelling check will end without ever getting to the spelling check dialog box.

7. You can edit this auxiliary dictionary.

Use the **U**tilities>**E**dit Auxiliary command to open it up and you will see the dialog box in Figure 6.12.

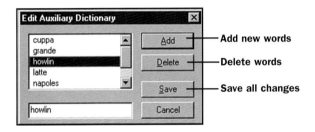

Figure 6.12

Editing the auxiliary dictionary.

8. On second thought, maybe it wasn't such a good idea to put the word "howlin" in the auxiliary dictionary.

Select it in the scrolling box and click the **D**elete button.

Click the **S**ave button to preserve your edits to the dictionary and close the dialog box.

9. Save your menu file, ⌘+Ⓢ (Mac) or Ctrl+Ⓢ (Win95).

Now, whenever you open this file, the existence of the auxiliary dictionary is recorded in the file. As long as it is in the folder with the publication, the dictionary will open automatically and you won't need to go through the process of using a special command to open it.

The final version of the menu has been saved on the CD-ROM in a file named **06BASE05.QXT**.

Summary

In this chapter, you have explored two of the key ways that QuarkXPress resembles a word processor—the ability to conduct search-and-replace operations and the ability to run spelling checks. In each case, these facilities aren't as powerful as one of the major word processors. Nevertheless, they can be very helpful during production in making you fast and accurate as you accommodate the inevitable last-minute changes to the content of a document.

Review It

As a review of what you have learned in this chapter, please answer the following questions.

1. What are the three basic steps in constructing a search?

_____

_____

2. Name at least three of the four levels of search area available in QuarkXPress.

_____

_____

3. Why would you use Find/Change instead of just manually editing text?

_____

_____

4. What are the two filters available in Find/Change?

_____

_____

5. Name the two ways of getting to the top of a search process so you won't miss any instances of the target.

_____

_____

6. Name the keyboard shortcut for Find/Change.

_____

_____

7. Name the signal QuarkXPress gives you when all the finds have been made during a search operation

_____

_____

8. What's the advantage of the Find/Change dialog box being non-modal?

_____

_____

9. What condition must be true before you can use Change?

_____

_____

10. What is the drawback of the Skip and Replace commands?

_____

_____

Check It

Multiple Choice

Please circle the correct answer for each of the following questions.

1. To define the spell search area, you can press what keys in combination with Ⓛ (Mac) or Ⓦ (Win95)?

    a. ⌘ (Mac) or Ctrl (Win95)

    b. ⌘+Option (Mac) or Ctrl+Alt (Win95)

    c. ⌘+Option+⬆Shift (Mac) or Ctrl+Alt+⬆Shift (Win95)

    d. All of the above

2. During a QuarkXPress session, the Find/Change command is _____.

    a. Sticky

    b. Always open once opened

    c. Running in the background

    d. All of the above

3. You can really speed up spell checking by _____.

 a. Leaving it open all the time

 b. Holding down Option (Mac) or Alt (Win95) when checking

 c. Using keyboard shortcuts

 d. All of the above

4. To first establish an auxiliary dictionary, you must _____.

 a. Create a new one and then open it

 b. Associate it with your publication

 c. Save it from Edit Dictionary

 d. All of the above

5. Once you have found some text, you can change it by clicking _____.

 a. Change button

 b. Change Then Find button

 c. Change All button

 d. All of the above

6. Almost all of the search codes for invisible characters are preceded by _____.

 a. ⃞ /

 b. ⃞ \

 c. ⌘ (Mac) or Ctrl (Win95) key

 d. ⃞ ∧

7. A gray type style button means _____.

 a. Find this style

 b. Change this style

 c. Ignore this style

 d. Alert to any instances of this style

8. If you only need to do a Find operation, not a Change operation _____.

 a. Hold down Option (Mac) or Alt (Win95) while opening

 b. Hold down ⌘ (Mac) or Ctrl (Win95) while opening

 c. Don't turn on any of the Change options

 d. All of the above

9. To activate Find First, with Find/Change open you hold down _____.

 a. ⇧Shift

 b. Option (Mac) or Alt (Win95)

 c. ⇧Shift+Option (Mac) or ⇧Shift+Alt (Win95)

 d. Return (Mac) or ⏎Enter (Win95)

10. When trying to find or change specific text styles, you must make sure the buttons are _____.

 a. Black (Mac) or pushed in (Win95)

 b. Gray

 c. White (Mac) or Black (Win95)

 d. Same on both sides of dialog box

True or False

Please circle *T* or *F* to indicate whether the statement is true or false.

T　F　**1.** You can find or change virtually any text character or paragraph formatting.

T　F　**2.** QuarkXPress automatically shifts the view so you can see the results of your search or spell check.

T　F　**3.** You must hold down Option (Mac) or Alt (Win95) to get the Change dialog box.

T   F   **4.** Whole word and ignore case don't have any effect when you are searching for a symbol or punctuation.

T   F   **5.** It's always handy to change a suspect spelling and try Lookup again to see if you can get the spelling correct.

T   F   **6.** You must always make invisibles visible before you can Find/Change them.

T   F   **7.** In Edit Auxiliary, you have buttons to Add, Delete, or Change a word.

T   F   **8.** You might sometimes have to drag a Find/Change or spelling checker dialog out of the way to see found text.

T   F   **9.** The Find Case filter will help you find capitalized words.

T   F   **10.** Once you establish an auxiliary dictionary for a document, the document will always try to open the dictionary for you.

Design It

The copy editing tools in this chapter may not have much to do with how you design pages, but they have a lot to do with how fast you can bend a project to your will. Spend some time practicing with these tools now, before moving on to the next chapter.

■ Conduct a search and replace that will convert the italic text to plain text, reduced to 10 points.

■ Figure out a way to convert all the menu item headlines such as "Hamburgers," "Chicken," and "Drinks" to bold type.

■ Make up some new menu items with unusual names, unlikely to be in the spell check dictionary. Then run a spell check, and add the new words to your auxiliary dictionary.

Real World Work

Advice—Avoid Student Portfolios

One of the main pieces of advice we gathered from our group of design professionals was this: "Do whatever you can to keep your portfolio from looking like a collection of student work." They told us one of the biggest problems with student portfolios is the fact that they look like what they are—student portfolios.

Werner Berghofer: Most of the portfolios I saw pretty much looked like "study objects" which had little or no connection to something which actually gets printed and published. They looked like examples showing how to use certain techniques or styles, but just for the sake of demonstration, and not for some "real world" use.

Ann Clarkson: I don't know what the tip off is about student exercises, unless it is the fact that when you are doing a real job, there are always some constraining factors—the budget, the deadline, the content, or the client's taste. But the difference is usually obvious.

With real live jobs, there are usually several of these constraining factors, and working within them involves some real sweat on the part of the designer. There is usually more than one round of sessions with the client, so the project has several stages. In each stage, the focus shifts slightly to reflect the interaction between the client and the designer. And since the client is paying the designer to produce something that will sell a product, he/she has a vital interest in the outcome.

Exercises, on the other hand, while they may have a constraining factor, tend to be done as a result of instructions from a teacher, who may or may not have used a real live project as a model. But the end product lacks the interaction and dependence on an outcome which give a real live project its character.

Patricia Olson: I think that's a big part of it. A project done for a client very often reflects the personality, likes, and dislikes of both the client and the designer, along with budget and time constraints. By the time any project is finished, it's truly a composite of what the designer thinks and knows will work, and what the client thinks and knows will work. Then there are the constraints of the particular industry that the piece is produced for. I don't have as much freedom designing a piece for the medical/disability industry as I do designing a restaurant menu.

We'd all love to show pieces which could be printed in process color, with a PMS color accent, with varnish and die cutting, etc. I'd love to have a few show-stopping pieces in my portfolio that the client could actually afford to print. But that is almost never the case.

For instance, if I design a piece that uses a distinctive die-cut, then I usually have to forgo additional colors, varnish, etc., because I can rarely convince a client to pay for all of those effects. So portfolio pieces designed for paying clients are usually a study in playing up the one or two embellishments we can afford to make. Often, if I have a little budget to play with, the first thing I recommend is higher quality paper.

If I were creating pieces to simply show off what I could do, I am certain all these constraints would be out the window.

David Rozansky: I suspect student portfolios suffer because they contain too many amateur class projects. There is not much cure for this other than to go out and get as many real professional projects under your belt as possible. I guess what gives a student portfolio away the fastest is that it is a hodgepodge of projects that show no development of career or no unique ability.

Exercise—Produce for a "Client"

In the absence of a portfolio full of completed professional work, maybe the best thing for you to do is provide one concrete example of how you can think in terms of communications goals, then execute those goals in a graphic design within time and budget limits. The work might still be a student project, but at least it will have some connection with the way a real graphic arts assignment works, rather than being a technique learning exercise.

Simply put, this exercise consists of finding a client and producing some actual work. At the end of this Portfolio Builder exercise, you want to be able to speak in a very specific way about how you met the challenges of a real project, and back up the story you have to tell by showing a finished portfolio piece. Here are some ideas for you to try.

- See if a department at your school needs some design and layout done—a graduate student's play needs a program, the student union coffee shop needs a menu, the school newspaper needs some ad designs.

- Better yet, go off campus looking for your client. Talk to some local businesses and ask if they need some design work. Perhaps a local bank or real estate office would like to start a newsletter. A new cafe might need some table topper signs to advertise specials.

- Study Appendix D from the CD-ROM, the Master Checklist for Desktop Publishing Projects. In it you will find a comprehensive list of issues that you will want to consider as you collaborate with your client. Especially, focus on the items at the front of the master checklist that help you define a communications goal for a project—analyzing the potential audience, defining the messages, and determining the constraints such as budget and deadline.

- As you go through the client interaction process, notice how the professionals were correct. There are constraining factors, as well as a back and forth interaction with the client, that give your project a real-world feel.

- Document the process of developing the design. Identify the constraints that made this particular job a challenge. No money for color? A 12-hour deadline? Personal taste of the client? Making sure the design fit in with the existing graphic identity of the business?

7

Automatic Formatting Using Style Sheets

Part III

Working Systematically

What You Will Learn

Paragraph and character styles are pre-defined collections of text formatting information. You "tag" text with these styles to apply the formatting. You can then edit a definition at any time and—as if by magic, even over hundreds of pages—change the formatting of all of the text that has been tagged with that style.

We should mention here that QuarkXPress refers to styles as style sheets. That's twisted from the rest of the publishing world, so in this chapter we'll use the industry standard terminology. You'll get some more details about this QuarkXPress idiosyncrasy in an upcoming section.

In this chapter, you will learn how to make new styles and edit existing ones. More importantly, you will learn how to use styles as extremely powerful—yet easy to use—production tools. They will save you tons of time in formatting text. They will help you easily achieve a consistent look in your publications. And, because you save so much time and they are so easy to use, styles will set you free as a designer so you can feel relaxed about experimenting with the look of your publication, even in the face of a crushing deadline.

This chapter's exercises will help you learn how to:

➤ Apply styles to text

➤ Decide when to use character styles versus paragraph styles

➤ Define new styles

➤ Edit styles to reformat text

➤ Nest styles so one definition can be multiplied into many

➤ Import styles

Hamburgers
Classic – tomato, sweet onion 4.00
Deluxe – bacon, cheddar 4.00
Mexican – napoles, jalapeno 4.00
Salmon – mayonnaise, capers 4.00
Soy – roasted eggplant, scallions 3.00

Chicken
Southern – dipped and fried 4.50
Barbecue – howlin' hot sauce 4.50
Date Night – roasted with garlic 4.50
Caesar – chopped, tossed, romaine 4.50
Mediterranean – tomatoes, basil 4.50

Drinks
Cuppa Coffee .75
Grande Latte 2.50
Cappuccino 1.50
Shot of Syrup – 15 flavors .20
Domestic Beer 1.50
Imported Beer 2.00
Wine – red, white, blush 2.00

Desserts
Pie – fresh three times a day 2.50
Ice Cream – new flavors daily 2.25
Croissant, Sweet Rolls, Brioche 2.00
Chocolate Sin 3.00

111 Timberline Road, Wenatchee, (514) 876-3001

Harvest Moon Bistro

Hamburgers
Classic – tomato, sweet onion 4.00
Deluxe – bacon, cheddar 4.00
Mexican – napoles, jalapeno 4.00
Salmon – mayonnaise, capers 4.00
Soy – roasted eggplant, scallions 3.00

Chicken
Southern – dipped and fried 4.50
Barbecue – howlin' hot sauce 4.50
Date Night – roasted with garlic 4.50
Caesar – chopped, tossed, romaine 4.50
Mediterranean – tomatoes, basil 4.50

Drinks
Cuppa Coffee .75
Grande Latte 2.50
Cappuccino 1.50
Shot of Syrup – 15 flavors .20
Domestic Beer 1.50
Imported Beer 2.00
Wine – red, white, blush 2.00

Desserts
Pie – fresh three times a day 2.50
Ice Cream – new flavors daily 2.25
Croissant, Sweet Rolls, Brioche 2.00
Chocolate Sin 3.00

111 Timberline Road, Wenatchee, (514) 876-3001

Harvest Moon Bistro

Hamburgers
Classic – tomato, sweet onion 4.00
Deluxe – bacon, cheddar 4.00
Mexican – napoles, jalapeno 4.00
Salmon – mayonnaise, capers 4.00
Soy – roasted eggplant, scallions 3.00

Chicken
Southern – dipped and fried 4.50
Barbecue – howlin' hot sauce 4.50
Date Night – roasted with garlic 4.50
Caesar – chopped, tossed, romaine 4.50
Mediterranean – tomatoes, basil 4.50

Drinks
Cuppa Coffee .75
Grande Latte 2.50
Cappuccino 1.50
Shot of Syrup – 15 flavors .20
Domestic Beer 1.50
Imported Beer 2.00
Wine – red, white, blush 2.00

Desserts
Pie – fresh three times a day 2.50
Ice Cream – new flavors daily 2.25
Croissant, Sweet Rolls, Brioche 2.00
Chocolate Sin 3.00

111 Timberline Road, Wenatchee, (514) 876-3001

Figure 7.1

You will use styles to make quick work of transforming the menu on the top left to look like the menu on the top right, and then into the one on the bottom.

Design Notes

This version of the menu, for the Harvest Moon Bistro, has a lot more flair than the one in the last chapter. As you can see in Figure 7.1, there are two main reasons for that. First, the artwork has been jazzed up with the moon motif. Second, for the first time, we have incorporated a much more decorative font into the design.

In fact, even though we have retained the body copy font used in the last chapter, Caslon, these changes in its graphic environment give it a new kick. As you work on building this new design, notice how its attitude shifts when it is combined with another typeface.

That other typeface is Mistral. It has an informal snap to it that just seems to fit in with the idea of a bistro, especially one with a down home harvest moon-type name.

Mistral is a script style font. In the Digital Type Design Guide, Sean Cavanaugh has some good advice about using script typefaces...

Script fonts are some of the most beautiful typefaces available, but they are also some of the easiest to misuse. Part of the reason for this is emotional: A person might become enamored with a certain script face and attempt to use it for everything—memos, letters, brochures, newsletters, etc. Don't let this happen to you. Script faces work very well in formal documents like invitations, and as decorative fonts for use in packaging, signs, titles, menus and logos, and as initial drop caps. They do not work well as text fonts, or for long lines of text. Script faces look best with tight letter spacing. Avoid setting them in all caps.

As a matter of fact, we'd like to rephrase Sean's last sentence to make it even stronger. Never, ever, set a script face in all caps. It's one of the worst typographic sins you can commit, for the very simple reason that script faces are virtually unreadable in all caps.

Getting Set Up

Copy all the files for this chapter from the CD-ROM to a work area on your hard drive. They are all in the **Steps** folder in the folder labeled **07**.

You will need to have the Caslon and Mistral fonts installed on your computer for this chapter's menu redesign. For an exercise near the end of the chapter, you will also need two fonts you used in previous chapters, Goudy Sans and Opus.

You can see the beginning and end point of the makeover you will perform in Figure 7.1. The menu that we are going to redesign has been stored in its beginning form as file **07BASE01.QXT** on the CD-ROM. The starting point file has all the graphics and text you will need but the text has not been formatted. It also contains some pre-defined styles you will use in this chapter.

Introducing...Styles

Think of a style as a group of text formatting commands gathered into a single definition. This definition might include dozens of text format attributes—any text attribute whatsoever—from alignment to H&J settings, and from paragraph rules to typeface and type size.

If you tried to assign all those text attributes manually one at a time, you would need to work your way through half a dozen dialog boxes and perform many intricate entries in each one. And then, for the next text that called for that collection of formatting, you would need to do that same tedious, repetitive work again.

However, styles enable you to automate the process. You can collect all those attributes into a single style definition, and apply all the collected formatting commands with a single click of the mouse or with an assigned keyboard shortcut.

Furthermore, once you have tagged all your many text passages with a particular style, you can automatically and globally change the formatting of all those text passages by simply editing the style definition in one central location.

Styles Save Time and Prevent Tedium

Exactly why are we emphasizing styles? Why should you use styles instead of just formatting text with multiple menu commands?

■ **Save time by automating production.**

The power of styles goes way beyond the ability to apply a collection of formatting attributes in one mouse click or keyboard shortcut.

You can assign styles in advance to text in your word processor. Then, when you import the text, it comes into QuarkXPress with most of the formatting already in place. People have automated the production of entire books using this pre-assigned styles technique.

In fact, that's one way styles helped the layout team that produced this book. As I wrote, I assigned styles to the paragraphs. When the text was brought into the page layout program, 90% of it was already formatted.

- **You can design once and consistently apply that design work many times.**

  Creating a style to format your text allows you to multiply your complex formatting work over dozens or hundreds of locations. Do the formatting once in the style definition, and from then on you can apply your collection of formatting commands with one click of the mouse on the Styles palette. (In this chapter, you are working on a short publication, a menu. However, you will often work on much longer documents, and that's when you will really appreciate this benefit of using styles.)

- **You can easily experiment with your designs.**

  With styles, you can experiment to your heart's content, knowing that changes require only a quick, easy, and simple style edit. This is a great aid to creativity. After all, how creative can you be if you know that any experimentation with a hard-formatted publication (not using the power of styles) would require you to tediously reformat every paragraph in your publication?

Styles Are Style Sheets

QuarkXPress has a little idiosyncrasy when it comes to styles. Everyone else in the desktop publishing software world uses the simple term "style" for this kind of collection of formatting parameters. But in QuarkXPress, it's called a style sheet.

So, when you leave this classroom and go out into the job market, you need to be aware that the words style and style sheet are pretty much synonymous. Most everyone who uses them refers to them as styles, even most designers who work primarily in QuarkXPress. In this book, we will generally refer to them as styles.

Styles Are for Paragraphs...and Characters, Too

For a long time, QuarkXPress styles only worked at the paragraph level. A style was a paragraph attribute just like alignment or H&J settings. You could click in a paragraph and, without selecting any text, format the whole thing. You could not apply a style to just a few of the words in a paragraph.

That has now changed. QuarkXPress 4.0 has added character styles to your production repertoire. You can apply a paragraph style, then select some text inside that paragraph and specially format it with a character style.

Character styles in QuarkXPress act just like local formatting, not unlike bolding or italicizing text. Of course, a character style definition can apply many character attributes including both bolding and italicizing.

Apply with the Style Sheets Palette

It couldn't be much easier to apply paragraph styles. You click your insertion point or select some text to identify the text to receive the formatting. Then you click the style in the Style Sheets palette you see in Figure 7.2.

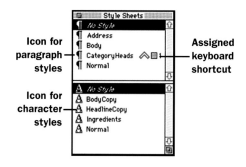

Figure 7.2

Apply styles using this palette.

There are commands for applying character and paragraph styles in the Style menu, but it's hard to see why you would use them when the palette is so much easier and faster to use.

Notice that the same palette displays both paragraph and character styles.

You can get to the Style Sheets palette through the View>Show Style Sheets command, F11.

Manage Styles with the Style Sheets Dialog Box

You use the command **Edit>Style Sheets**, (⬆Shift)+(F11), to get to the dialog box in Figure 7.3. You can use this dialog box to do pretty much everything else there is to do with styles.

Details of selected style definition   **Select which styles will display in dialog**

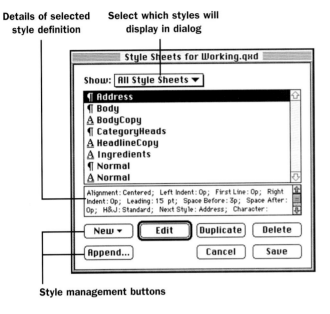

Style management buttons

Figure 7.3

Manage your fonts here in this central dialog box.

As you can see, there are style management buttons to allow you to define new styles, edit existing ones, duplicate existing styles (so you can create variations), delete styles, and append (import) existing styles from another QuarkXPress document.

Again, notice the symbols next to each style, indicating whether each one is a paragraph or a character level style.

Applying Styles

Actually putting styles to work may seem a bit anticlimactic. In this exercise, you will easily format most of the text on this page in less than two minutes of work—probably less.

1. To get started, open **07BASE01.QXT** in QuarkXPress and save the new document under a new name in your work directory.

Opening the Style Sheets Palette

2. Open the Style Sheets Palette, (F11).

3. With the Content tool, click an insertion point in the first headline, "Hamburgers."

   As you know, since paragraph styles are paragraph attributes, you don't need to select the entire paragraph. You only need to select a tiny portion of the text in the paragraph—even an insertion point will do.

Applying Styles with Palette

4. In the Style Sheets Palette, click the CategoryHeads style.

   The entire paragraph takes on the definition described in that style. In this single step, you just applied many formatting attributes—tabs, alignment, typeface, type size, and more.

Applying Styles from Menu

5. You do have the option of applying a style using a menu command.

   Click an insertion point in the next headline, "Chicken."

6. Use Style>Paragraph Style Sheet, as in Figure 7.4, to choose the CategoryHeads style.

   If you look in the Style Sheets palette, you will notice that two styles are highlighted. That's because the HeadlineCopy character level style is part of the CategoryHeads paragraph level style definition.

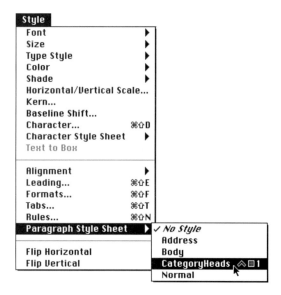

Figure 7.4

Using the menu to apply a style.

Applying Styles with Keyboard Shortcuts

7. When we built the CategoryHeads style we included a keyboard shortcut.

    Click an insertion point in the next headline, "Drinks."

    Press `Ctrl`+`F1` (Mac) or `Ctrl`+1 (Win95).

    (Win95) Make sure `Num Lock` is on, if you are using Windows, so you can type the numbers on the numeric keypad. Otherwise this keyboard shortcut won't work for you.

    You will have a chance to assign a shortcut to a style later on in this chapter. As we will discuss then, only certain keys can be used for style shortcuts. The Macintosh has more options available than on the Win95 platforms. The numeric keypad is available for style shortcuts on both platforms.

8. Use the same keyboard shortcut to finish up formatting the category headlines.

    Click an insertion point in the "Desserts" headline and press `⌘`+`F1` (Mac) or `Ctrl`+ Keypad 1 (Win95) to apply the CategoryHeads style.

Styling Many Paragraphs at Once

9. You can apply styles to multiple paragraphs.

    Go to the "Hamburgers" section of the menu. With the Content tool active, click "Classic" and drag down through the other items in this category, selecting at least a little part of the "Soy" paragraph.

    You don't need to select the entire group of paragraphs, but you should have touched somewhere in all five paragraphs under the "Hamburgers" category.

10. Use the Style Sheets palette to apply the style "Body" to the selected paragraphs.

11. Use this same technique to apply the style "Body" to all the rest of the menu items under each of the category headlines.

Applying Character Styles

12. Unlike paragraph styles, character styles apply only to text that has actually been selected.

    Select the ingredients text in the "Classic" item under "Hamburgers."

    You can click and drag over the words, but the best way to do this is probably to navigate to the line and then select the words you want with `Shift`+`⌘`+`→` or `Shift`+`⌘`+`←` (Mac) or `Shift`+`Ctrl`+`→` or `Shift`+`Ctrl`+`←` (Win95).

13. When you have the text selected, apply the Ingredients character style from the Style Sheets palette.

    Applying the character style over the top of a paragraph style is an example of local formatting, which is sometimes called hard formatting. Local formatting is any character-level formatting that you apply to text that has a style assigned to it.

    It is sometimes called hard formatting because it overrides the paragraph style formatting instructions. We'll talk more about how local formatting interacts with paragraph styling in the next few steps.

    As you see in Figure 7.5, even though the paragraph style is still applied to the menu item paragraph, the character style has overridden its formatting in the selected text. There's a plus sign next to the paragraph style name to indicate that there's some local formatting in place, in this case the character styling.

14. Go ahead and apply the Ingredients character style to the rest of the locations. Apply it to any text that follows an en dash in the items under each of the menu categories. (This will be the same text that was formatted with italics in the last chapter.)

Removing Local Formatting

15. As an experiment, go back to the "Classic" item in the Hamburgers section and click an insertion point in the paragraph.

Try to reapply the Body paragraph style by clicking it in the Style Sheets palette. You will find that nothing changes. The local (hard) formatting doesn't budge.

Here's the trick. Hold down the Option (Mac) or Alt (Win95) keys as you click in the Style Sheets palette on the Body paragraph style. That will allow the paragraph style sheet to wipe out the local formatting. That's all local formatting, including character-based styles and any other manually applied text formatting.

Don't forget to reapply the Ingredients style to the text that you de-formatted during this experiment.

16. Apply the Address style to the last line of the menu, the one that shows the bistro's location.

The menu, now in Caslon and Mistral, has been almost completely formatted in just a couple of minutes with roughly a dozen mouse clicks.

The progress so far on the redesign menu has been saved on the CD-ROM in a file named **07BASE02.QXT**. Your menu should look like the one in Figure 7.6.

Plus sign indicates local formatting

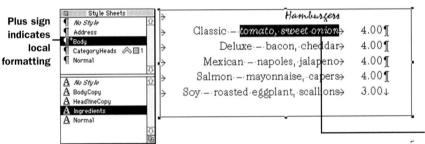

Figure 7.5
Character styles behave just like local formatting.

Character style overrides paragraph style

Figure 7.6
Progress so far with style assignments indicated.

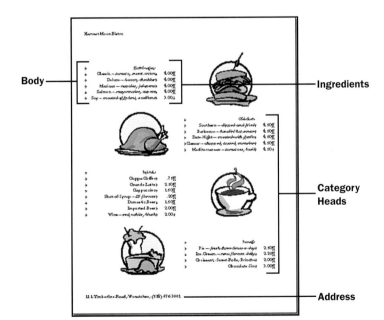

Body — **Ingredients**

Category Heads

Address

Editing Styles

You are about to get your first real taste of the power of styles. It's good to be able to quickly and consistently format text. But to really enjoy your new knowledge about styles—to use them as a supercharged technique for revising or experimenting with the design of a publication—you need to be able to modify existing styles.

You have two basic ways to edit styles. You can:

■ Edit Multiple Styles in the Main Dialog

Use the Edit>Style Sheets menu command or its keyboard shortcut, (◆Shift)+(F11). You can also get the same result by (⌘)+ Click (Mac) or (Ctrl)+ Click (Win95) on any item in the Style Sheets palette. (However, the Style Sheets palette will be grayed out and unavailable unless you have a text box selected with the Content tool.)

■ Go Directly To Editing a Single Style

(Ctrl)+ Click (Mac) or right-click (Win95) on the style you want to edit in the Style Sheets palette.

You'll use both methods in this exercise.

Shortcut to Edit Single Style

1. The italicized ingredients items need to be brought down in size a bit. At their present size, they are fighting visually with the menu items.

There are more than a dozen of these locations and it would be tedious to reformat every single one of them by manual methods. Fortunately, we can simply edit their style definition.

Magnify your view, maybe to actual size, so you can see the type well enough to evaluate your formatting changes.

2. Click an insertion point anywhere in some text so the Style Sheets palette will become active. Otherwise, it will be grayed out and you won't be able to use it.

3. (Ctrl)+ Click (Mac) or right-click (Win95) on the Ingredients style and choose the pop-up menu to edit the style as in Figure 7.7.

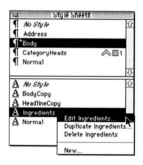

Figure 7.7

Use this shortcut to directly edit a single style.

Editing a Character Style

4. You will be taken directly to a familiar dialog box where you could make modifications to the style you chose, as shown in Figure 7.8.

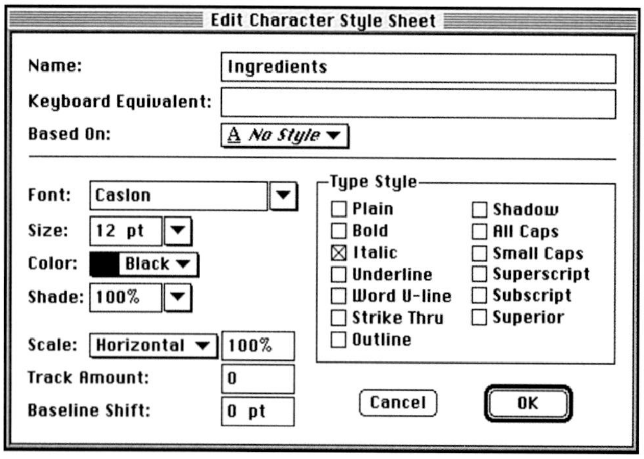

Figure 7.8

Edit character style definitions here.

Edit Character Style Sheet

Name: Ingredients

Keyboard Equivalent:

Based On: A No Style ▼

Font: Caslon ▼

Size: 12 pt ▼

Color: Black ▼

Shade: 100% ▼

Scale: Horizontal ▼ 100%

Track Amount: 0

Baseline Shift: 0 pt

Type Style
☐ Plain   ☐ Shadow
☐ Bold   ☐ All Caps
☒ Italic   ☐ Small Caps
☐ Underline ☐ Superscript
☐ Word U-line ☐ Subscript
☐ Strike Thru ☐ Superior
☐ Outline

Cancel   OK

The reason this dialog box looks familiar is because you used it repeatedly in earlier chapters to format text. It has a few items added at the top so you can manage your character level style, but otherwise it is a nearly exact copy of the Character Attributes dialog box.

Throughout the style editing process, you will discover that you already know how to use the style editing dialog boxes because they mimic the familiar formatting dialog boxes for character and paragraph attributes. That goes for character attributes as well as paragraph attributes, such as alignment and tabs.

Change the font size from 12 to 11.5 points and click OK. The chage will ripple through your document.

5. Pan your view, Option | Click and Drag (Mac) or Alt + Click and Drag (Win95) so you can see the address at the bottom of the menu. That's what you will work on next.

Accessing the Main Style Edit Dialog

6. One drawback of the single style shortcut you just used is that you now can't work on other styles.

Open up the main style editing dialog box. You can either use the menu, Edit>Style Sheets, or you can use the keyboard shortcut ⬆Shift + F11.

Editing a Paragraph Style

7. Select the Address style (it's probably already selected since it should be at the top of the list) and click the Edit button, or just press Return (Mac) or ⏎Enter (Win95).

8. This text should be centered.

⌘ + Tab↹ (Mac) or Ctrl + Tab↹ (Win95) to get to the familiar paragraph formats dialog box.

Change left Alignment to centered.

9. The text should also be bold, to visually anchor the page.

⬆Shift + ⌘ + Tab↹ (Mac) or ⬆Shift + Ctrl + Tab↹ (Win95) to get back to the General style editing tab of this dialog box.

In the Character Attributes section, notice the word "Default." That means this paragraph style has a built-in default character style definition. (An alternative that you will learn about in the next section would be to base the paragraph style on a character style.)

10. Click Edit to access the Character Attributes dialog box, again a familiar face from several earlier chapters.

Turn on the checkbox for Bold.

11. Click OK twice to get back to the main style sheet editing dialog.

Click Save.

When you are back to the menu, you will see that the address has been centered and boldened.

The progress so far on the menu has been saved on the CD-ROM in a file named **07BASE03.QXT**. Your menu redesign should look like the one in Figure 7.9.

Points for Ingredients style   Centered and bold for Address style

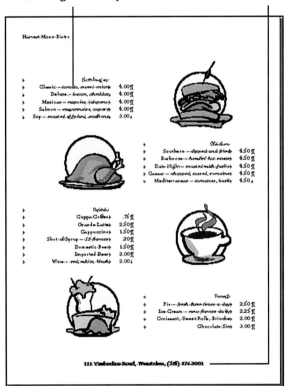

Figure 7.9

The menu redesign so far.

Working with Based On Styles

One very powerful, yet potentially dangerous, style editing and construction technique is the "Based On" style. That means you can base a style on another style.

So here's a very, very important concept. If you edit the format of an underlying based on style, you will cause that exact same formatting change to cascade through every other style that has been based on the style you have edited.

In the exercises you are about to do, that's exactly what you want. But you must use caution when editing styles that have been used to create other styles—based on styles. If you aren't aware of all the ways a based on style has been used, you could unwittingly trigger formatting changes that could wreak havoc on your publication.

1. Shortcut your way to edit the CategoryHeads style.

    Click an insertion point in some text to activate the Style Sheets palette.

Ctrl + Click (Mac) or Right Click (Win95) on the CategoryHeads style in the palette and choose to edit it.

Two Kinds of Based On Styles

2. Take note in the Edit Paragraph Style Sheet dialog box that the Category Heads style has been based on a character style named HeadlineCopy, as you see in Figure 7.10.

This is a common technique when working with styles, to set up underlying basic character formatting styles for headlines and body copy. These underlying character formatting styles make it easy to make major revisions in a piece's design by editing one or two underlying styles instead of dozens of them.

There are actually two kinds of based on styles in QuarkXPress. There's the kind you are working with here, where a paragraph style has been based on a character style. In addition, there's the QuarkXPress official type of based on style where you base a paragraph style on another paragraph style, using the Based On box you see in the upper portion of the dialog box in Figure 7.10.

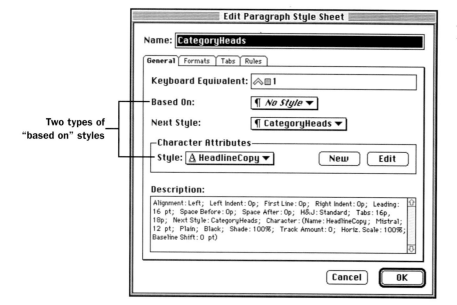

Two types of "based on" styles

Figure 7.10

Beginning to edit a based on style.

Editing a Based On Style

3. Edit the HeadlineCopy style.

Bump the type size up to 14 points and click OK twice and finally click Save, until you have cleared the dialog boxes from the screen.

Have a look at the change in the headlines.

Stylistic Experimentation

4. There's still not enough emphasis for these heads. However, as you now know, it is easy to experiment.

Use the same technique you used in the last couple of steps to again adjust the type size of the CategoryHeads style.

However, this time there's no need to go to CategoryHeads. You know that you can make the change you want by directly editing the underlying based on style, HeadlineCopy.

Use the Ctrl+ click (Mac) or right-click (Win95) shortcut to open up the HeadlineCopy style for editing.

5. Bump the type size up to 15 points, from 14 points.

Take a moment while you are here to notice all the power you have to make a style do text formatting work for you. You could assign a keyboard shortcut, or even color the type or set its tracking (actually, range kerning).

6. Click OK and then Save to get back to your layout and evaluate the new headline look based on your editing of this underlying style.

● The progress so far on the redesigned menu has been saved on the CD-ROM in a file named **07BASE04.QXT**.

Creating a New Style

The easiest way to create a new style is to model the style on some existing text formatting. You could, of course, create your new style from scratch in the dialog boxes that you have been using in this chapter. However, creating your new style by basing it on some existing formatted text recycles existing formatting work and can save you many steps.

1. Begin by formatting the title of the menu.

Click an insertion point with the Content tool in the topmost text box on the page and select all the text, ⌘+Ⓐ (Mac) or Ctrl+Ⓐ (Win95). (We can use Select All in this case because this text box isn't threaded to the rest of the text on the page, otherwise we'd be selecting too much text.)

Use the Measurements palette or keyboard shortcuts to format the title text in Mistral, to center it, and to increase it to 60 points in size.

You may need to adjust the size of the text box to hold the increased text size.

Shortcut to New Style

2. With the title text still selected, Ctrl+ click (Mac) or right-click (Win95) on the No Style paragraph style.

Choose New.

Naming the New Style

3. Type in a new name for your style. Make it **Title**.

Notice in the Description section of the dialog box that all your formatting attributes have automatically been adopted into this new style definition, including the centering of the text and the large type size as in Figure 7.11.

Assigning a Keyboard Shortcut

4. Also, notice that you can assign a keyboard shortcut to this style, just like the one you used earlier in this chapter when formatting text with the CategoryHeads style.

Click in the Keyboard Equivalent box and press, being careful to use the numeric keypad for the number 2.

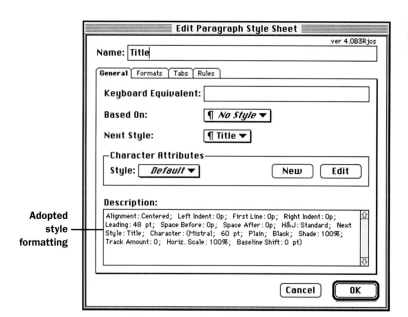

Figure 7.11

Creating a new style from pre-formatted text.

The Macintosh and Windows versions of QuarkXPress behave a bit differently when it comes to keyboard shortcuts for styles.

Macintosh/Windows Keyboard Shortcut Differences

(Win95) For Windows machines, you must have the Num Lock *on or the keypad shortcuts won't work. Your only two available modifier key choices are* Ctrl *or* Ctrl+Alt. *Unlike the Macintosh, you can use these modifier keys only with the numeric keypad, not with the function keys. In the windows Style Sheets palette, the keyboard shortcuts are spelled out with a "KP" to indicate keypad, where Macintosh users get keycaps-style icons to indicate the shortcut keys.*

(Mac) It doesn't matter on the Mac whether the Num Lock *is on or off; you can still use the numeric keypad keys for style shortcuts. On the Mac, you also have a much wider range of keys at your disposal than you do in Windows. You can use any*

combination of the Ctrl, ⬆Shift, Option, *or* ⌘ *modifier keys. And you have a choice of the numeric keypad keys or any of the function keys. In the Macintosh Style Sheets palette, the keyboard shortcuts are indicated with keycaps style icons. When using function keys, be extremely careful not to duplicate one of the QuarkXPress built-in keyboard shortcuts.*

Applying the New Style

5. Click OK to return to layout view and see your brand-new style in place on the Style Sheets palette.

   There's one last step. Even though you defined the style based on the formatting of the selected text, it still has not been tagged with the style.

   Use your Ctrl+ Keypad 2 (Mac) or Ctrl+ Keypad 2 (Win95) and assign the Title style to the title text.

The redesigned menu should now look like the one in Figure 7.12 and it has been saved on the CD-ROM in a file named **07BASE05.QXT**.

New Title style

Figure 7.12

Redesign progress so far, with the menu almost completely formatted.

Tip

Save Often So You Can Undo by Reverting

By now you may have come to rely on QuarkXPress's Edit>Undo command, ⌘+Z (Mac) or Ctrl+Z to get you out of mistakes you make during the layout process. But there are a number of situations where the Undo command just won't work, edits to paragraph styles being one important example. That's why many designers have had to learn the hard way to save their work before making any major changes in their publication. If you save frequently, you will always be able to use the File>Revert To Saved command to get back to your last saved version.

Importing Styles

There are two basic ways you can bring styles into QuarkXPress, aside from creating new ones from scratch.

■ You may very well, intentionally or not, import styles when you Get Text, copy/paste, or drag/drop text into your publication.

During any of these operations, QuarkXPress tries to keep as much formatting information as posible, including style definitions, and if there are any styles in the inbound text, they will be imported and loaded into the Style Sheets palette.

This is a very powerful and important tool for automating production. If the person writing the text uses styles in their word processor, particularly if it is Microsoft Word, the imported text can easily be formatted using that style system.

■ You can use the QuarkXPress style management system. In the dialog box where you have been editing styles, there's an Append button that will help you import just the styles from other QuarkXPress documents—no text import needed.

That last option, involving the Append button, is the technique you'll try in the following steps. In a very few steps, you will completely transform your menu text from Mistral and Caslon to an entirely different typeface design using Goudy Sans and Opus.

1. With the current version of the menu open, the version you had produced as of the end of the last exercise, open the Edit>Style Sheets command, ◆Shift+F11.

Appending Styles

2. Click the Append button to open the Append Style Sheets dialog you see in Figure 7.13.

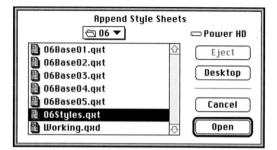

Figure 7.13

Selecting the file containing the inbound styles.

Choosing a Style Source File

3. Double-click the file **07STYLES.QXT**. This is a file you should have copied to your working folder on your hard drive at the beginning of the chapter.

The result will be the dialog box in Figure 7.14.

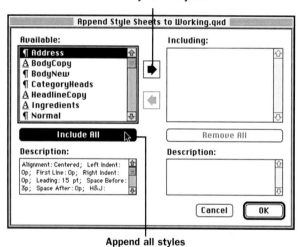

Figure 7.14

Selecting the individual styles to be appended (imported).

Embedded Import and Conflict Warnings

4. Click on the Include All button and click OK.

You will then need to click OK in the warning dialog shown in Figure 7.15.

You get this warning for all QuarkXPress append operations, not just for styles. In this case, it's warning you that importing styles that have been based on other styles will also import the underlying styles.

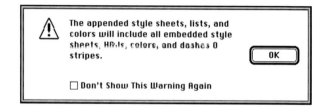

Figure 7.15

Warning, you may import more than you expected.

5. You will then get another warning, that you are importing new styles that have the same name as the existing styles but with different definitions, as you see in Figure 7.16.

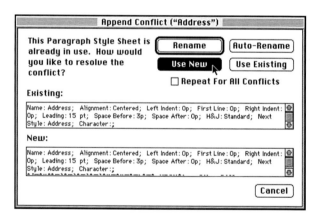

Figure 7.16

Dealing with style name conflicts.

You can choose to give the new, inbound style a new name, or have QuarkXPress think up a new name for it. You can also decide to use the new style's definition and override the existing style, or vice versa.

Turn on the Repeat For All Conflicts checkbox so you won't get this dialog box for each conflict.

Click the Use New button to allow the inbound new styles to override the existing ones.

Adopting the Appended Styles

6. Get ready for magic.

Click the Save button in the style editing dialog box and your menu will be transformed from Mistral and Caslon to Goudy Sans and Opus, as in Figure 7.17.

From Mistral to Goudy Sans

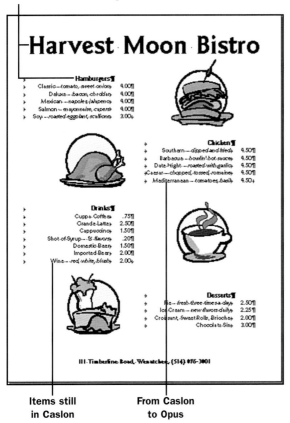

Items still in Caslon   **From Caslon to Opus**

Figure 7.17

The magic transformation, thanks to appended styles.

Find/Change Style Formatting

7. You have probably noticed, however, that the menu's food items are still in Caslon. And you now have two similar styles, the old Body style plus the new imported style named BodyNew.

Use a Find/Change operation to search out all the text formatted with the Body style and change it to the BodyNew style.

If you need to review the Find/Change process, go back to the Chapter 5 section called "Formatting Text With Find/Change."

Don't forget to turn off Ignore Attributes to expand the Find/Change dialog box. Then use the Style Sheet boxes to find the Body style and change to BodyNew. Once you find the first instance, use Change All.

Deleting a Style

8. You no longer need the Body style, so you can delete it. Use the shortcut technique you've already used several times in this chapter.

Ctrl + Click (Mac) or Right Click (Win95) on the Body style and select the delete option from the pop-up menu.

Click OK when you get an alert dialog box asking if you really want to delete this style.

The final version, actually a second redesign of the menu using the Goudy Sans and Opus typefaces, has been saved on the CD-ROM in a file named **07BASE06.QXT**. You can see what it should look like in Figure 7.18.

Figure 7.18

The new look of the menu, the final redesign, after appending the new style definitions.

Summary

In this chapter, you learned more than the nuts and bolts of using QuarkXPress styles. You also learned—by actually experiencing it—that styles can save you time when building and revising a project, help you achieve design consistency, and give you the freedom to experiment with the design of a piece.

Bottom line advice: Never design any QuarkXPress project, one page or hundreds, without using styles. It's the professional way to manage the formatting of a publication.

Review It

As a review of what you have learned in this chapter, please answer the following questions.

1. What is the difference between a style and a style sheet?

2. Name at least two advantages of styles that improve production efficiency or aid creativity.

3. What is the keyboard shortcut to open the Style Sheets palette? To the Edit Style Sheets dialog box?

4. Name some examples of local or hard formatting. How can you apply a style and remove local formatting.

5. What does a plus sign mean next to a style name in the Style Sheets palette?

6. How should you decide between the Edit Style Sheets dialog and the click on the palette methods of editing and defining styles?

_____

_____

7. What is the effect if you edit a style that has been used as a based on style?

_____

_____

8. What are the two ways you can import styles into PageMaker?

_____

_____

9. After you create a new style by creating some sample text, what's the next step?

_____

_____

10. There are two answers to this question. How much text must be selected before you can apply a style to it?

_____

_____

Check It

Multiple Choice

Please circle the correct answer for each of the following questions.

1. You can use a style to wipe out local formatting if you hold down _____ keys while clicking in the Style Sheets palette.

   a. Option (Mac) or Alt (Win95)

   b. ⬆Shift

   c. Ctrl (Mac) or Ctrl (Win95)

   d. ⌘ (Mac) or Ctrl (Win95)

2. Use a character style when you _____.

   a. Need to format only part of a paragraph

   b. Might change a project's type design

   c. Have many styles that share similar typeface formats

   d. All of the above

3. To apply a style to some text, you have a choice of _____.

   a. Importing or appending the style

   b. Palette or menu

   c. Keyboard shortcut, menus, palette

   d. None of the above

4. Editing a style definition will _____.

   a. Retroactively change all text tagged with the style

   b. Affect all publications using that style

   c. Affects only based on styles

   d. All of the above

5. You can find out all the details of a style definition by _____.

   a. Printing out a style sheet report

   b. Looking at the description in the Edit Style Sheets dialog box.

c. Appending a new style to see if there's a conflict

d. All of the above

6. You can always tell which are paragraph and which are character styles by _____.

a. Checking their icons in the Style Sheets palette

b. Noting where they are listed in the palette

c. Using the Show list in the Edit Style Sheets dialog box

d. All of the above

7. Macintosh users, when it comes to keyboard shortcuts, can _____.

a. Use both the function keys and numeric keypad keys

b. Choose among four modifier keys

c. Create shortcut conflicts by using function keys

d. All of the above

8. To go directly to editing a single style, you can _____ on the Style Sheets palette?

a. Double-click

b. ⌘+click (Mac) or Ctrl+click (Win95)

c. Ctrl+click (Mac) or right-click (Win95)

d. All of the above

9. To create a new style you can _____.

a. Click on New button in the Edit Style Sheets dialog box

b. Use the Duplicate button in the Edit Style Sheets dialog box

c. Format text and use it as model

d. All of the above

10. To get back from a mistaken style edit, you can _____.

a. Use **Edit**>**Undo**

b. Press ⌘+Z (Mac) or Ctrl+Z (Win95)

c. Use **File**>**Revert To Saved**

d. All of the above

True or False

Please circle *T* or *F* to indicate whether the statement is true or false.

T F **1.** When appending styles from another document you can choose to rename conflicting styles

T F **2.** Appending styles means you must accept all the new styles at once.

T F **3.** Fortunately, editing a based on style has no retroactive effect on text.

T F **4.** To apply a character style you only need to click an insertion point at the beginning and end of the text.

T F **5.** Fortunately, you can select many paragraphs at a time and apply styles to them all.

T F **6.** The Find/Change method of applying a different style has no effect on local formatting.

T F **7.** Unfortunately, there's only one way to apply styles, using the Style Sheets palette.

T F **8.** There's just no way to rescue yourself if you make a mistake editing a style.

T F **9.** If you create a new style you still have one step left, applying it to the text.

T F **10.** There are only a few, but it's impossible to do certain text formatting tasks with styles.

Design It

Using paragraph and character styles, develop several alternate designs for this menu. As you develop your designs, make absolutely sure the text—the main point of a menu—is readable and holds center stage.

- In one of your designs, use the same basic layout but develop a new theme and title for a restaurant. Incorporate different clip art from sources at your school.

- Try at least one design approach that breaks away from the squared-away, checkerboard format of the menu you've been working with the last two chapters. Search out a way to blend text and graphics in an unusual way, perhaps by using one large graphic as a thematic focus, instead of suggesting menu categories.

As you work, do your best to use styles and the Find/Change command to quickly manipulate your text. The point is to take advantage of styles to support your creativity with experimentation and exploration.

8
Organizing Many Pages

Setting Up a Book Project

What You Will Learn

Most of the time, people think of design as the process of making a page look attractive and pleasing to read. However, design is also very much about organizing information, not only on a single page but across many pages. When constructing a long form document—a book, an annual report, a catalog, a software manual—organization becomes a crucial element of publication design.

In this chapter, you will learn about:

➤ Adding many pages automatically when importing large quantities of text

➤ Using master pages to add repeating information to pages

➤ Adding page numbers on master pages

➤ Sectioning off parts of your document for special page number formats

➤ Building a table of contents using your paragraph styles system

➤ Indexing your text

➤ Assembling "chapter" files into a book using a QuarkXPress book file

MANAGING LITIGATION
The Insider's Guide

A Cavalcade Deskbook

Produced By
Martin L. Dean, Esq.
Editor of the Deskbook Series

Special Subject Matter Author and Editor
Anne Kemp

Associate Editor
Lauren Kerr

Written By
Rick Wallace

401 Francisco Street, San Francisco, CA 94133
(415) 986-3700 ¥ Fax: (415) 986-2110

LITIGATION SUPPORT

Fundamentals Of Litigation Support

Litigation support and information retrieval are mutually dependent functions. Litigation support is the management of information — screening, analyzing, indexing, and summarizing. Those functions enable you to retrieve specific factual and legal information easily and quickly during discovery, other pre-trial preparation and during the trial itself.

For example, using basic litigation support techniques, you will be able to quickly locate all correspondence between plaintiff and defendant regarding a key issue during a particular time period. And you will be able to retrieve specific passages in depositions for the purpose of impeaching a witness or precisely framing a probing question.

You will first learn about litigation support methods which apply whether you are using manual methods or are implementing a computerized litigation support system. These fundamentals include screening and indexing documents, summarizing depositions, and managing files of documents. Then, in building-block style as the chapter progresses, you will acquire the knowledge needed to computerize these litigation support functions — automated litigation support.

We'll end this chapter with a section on demonstrative evidence, a specialized form of summarizing information and presenting it at trial using visual demonstration techniques.

Litigation Support Management Functions

The process of litigation support includes these major functions, covered in the corresponding sections of this chapter.

▸ **Document Screening And Indexing**

In screening your own client's documents as well as discovered documents, you will be performing multi-faceted tasks such as reviewing for privilege, "hot" documents, key case parties, document types, new discovery leads, and even faulty photocopying and otherwise illegible documents. By numbering documents and abstracting information regarding their content, you will be indexing them so they can be retrieved as needed.

▸ **Deposition Summaries**

You will prepare indexed summaries of depositions, making it possible to find critical passages during the preparation of trial questions and attempts to impeach a witness.

1

Figure 8.1

In this chapter, you will be working with the files for a real published book (actually, just the first few pages of each chapter for convenience sake and to keep file sizes down). You see here the title page (left) and a chapter body page (right) from Managing Litigation, *published by attorney Martin Dean of San Francisco (copyright 1994–1996). It's a handbook for attorneys in small law offices.*

Design Notes

In addition to design elements such as page numbers, tables of contents, and an index, there are other important organization elements to this design.

If you flip through the pages of the working file you use for this chapter, for example, you will see a set of icons down the left side of the main text (the body copy). These icons are symbols taken from a special typeface called Sean's Symbols that we'll discuss in a moment.

Each of these symbols has been set up in a headline constructed with what's called a hanging indent which, in effect, creates a companion column.

For the hanging indent, the whole paragraph—except for the first line—is indented on the left. The first line would hang out to the left of the rest of the paragraph except for some tabs. It is those tabs that align the icon in the space to the left of the main body of the paragraph.

This formatting causes the icons to ride in a companion column. Even though there is actually no column, in the sense of a dual column text box, the hanging indent creates the visual effect of a column. The companion column is simply a narrow strip of space that rides along one edge of the main body copy column, a space where information (such as the icons) can be positioned to visually emphasize the structure of a page.

About the typeface Sean's Symbols—it is on the CD-ROM and is another one of the fonts from Sean Cavanaugh's *Digital Type Design Guide*. It's called a dingbat font. If you look this word up in a dictionary you will find it defined typographically as "an ornamental piece of type for borders, separators, decorations, etc." But we liked the other, non-typographical, definition listed in our Random House Unabridged Dictionary: "An object of unknown or unspecified description; thingumbob; dingus."

Sean's Symbols closely resembles the ubiquitous Zapf Dingbats, a font built into almost every laser printer ever made, or the Wingdings font that comes with Windows 95. But Sean says he constructed this version because of the numbers-in-circles characters it contains. They are also found in Zapf Dingbats and Wingdings but not with their proper keys for some strange reason. In Sean's Symbols, when you press the number 1, you actually get a dingbat of a circle with a 1 in it.

The other two fonts used for this book design are Opus and URW Palladio, a font combination that you used in earlier chapters.

Getting Set Up

Copy all the files for this chapter from the CD-ROM to a work area on your hard drive. They are all in the **Steps** folder in the folder labeled **08**.

You will need to have the Sean's Symbols, Opus, and URW Palladio fonts installed on your computer for the exercises in this chapter.

Introducing...Master Pages

To understand why you will love master pages, imagine a couple of scenarios for me.

First, imagine you carefully positioned numbers for every page of a 1,000-page book. And after you had tediously gone through and manually numbered each and every page, the client decided to remove pages 19 and 20, making all the numbering on 980 pages useless. Imagine blowing a deadline and repeatedly banging your head against the computer screen in frustration.

Now, instead, imagine a QuarkXPress master page. On it is an automatic page number character. Imagine the client deciding to remove pages 19 and 20 and imagine that page marker updating all the page numbering automatically without you even thinking about it. Imagine feeling relaxed and making your deadline with no problem at all.

That's what master pages will do for you. Anything that repeats on many pages can be put on a master page—automatic page numbers, chapter headings, ruler guides, and so on. And you can create many different master pages to adjust a page layout for certain situations. For example, you might want to use different margins or different text box and column layouts on a title page, compared to body copy.

In this chapter, you will get a quick introduction to using master pages by applying and adding elements to them. You will create your own master pages in Chapter 9.

Before going ahead to the next section, it will be very helpful for you to review the information on inserting, deleting, and navigating between pages in Chapter 1, especially the part about the Document Layout palette.

Automatic Page Insertion

When you are laying out a book with dozens or even hundreds of pages, it would take far too long to manually insert each page. QuarkXPress saves you from that with a special kind of text box kept on a master page. It's called an automatic text box.

The easiest way to set up an automatic text box is in the New Document dialog box when you are first creating a new publication file, as in Figure 8.2.

Check here for automatic text boxes

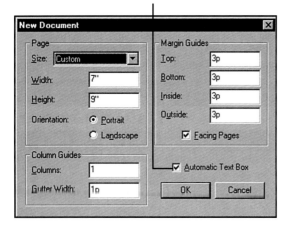

Figure 8.2

Automatic page insertion requires automatic text boxes.

For the following exercise, we've set up a template for you to use. We have already set up the automatic text box on a master page using this technique.

1. Notice that you have two files in your work folder that have very similar names but different ending extension letters. They both begin with **02INITIATE.**

    You have a QuarkXPress template, **02INTIATE. QXT**. And you have a special text file named **02INITIATE.XTG**. The XTG extension indicates that the file is a QuarkXPress tag language file. This is a bit like a word processor file, except it is specially designed for exporting/ importing with QuarkXPress.

    Open up **02INITIATE.QXT** and save the resulting new file as **02INITIATE.QXD**. (The file name will become important later on when you assemble multiple chapter files using a book file.)

Using the Document Layout Palette

2. Open up the Document Layout palette, F10 (Mac) or F4 (Win95). You should be familiar with this palette from your work in Chapter 1. Figure 8.3 gives you some basics for review.

    Remember, the Macintosh and Windows versions of the Document Layout palette are cosmetically a bit different. For example, the deletion icon is a trash can on the Macintosh platform instead of a slash "X" in Windows 95. Also, for the Macintosh, the current page number is indicated in outlined type instead of bold as it is in Windows 95.

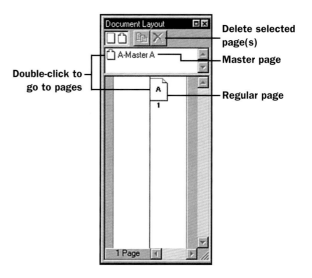

Figure 8.3

The Document Layout palette.

Navigating to a Master Page

3. Double-click the A-Master A icon in the master page section at the top of the Document Layout palette.

Understanding Automatic
Text Links

4. Notice in Figure 8.4 that this template already has text boxes on the left and right master pages.

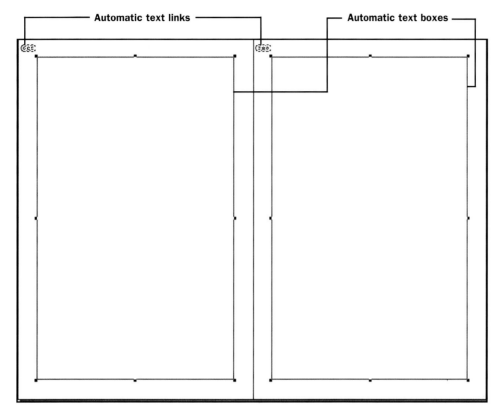

Automatic text links ——————— Automatic text boxes ———————

Figure 8.4

Master page with automatic page insertion elements in place.

Notice also that there are some chain links in the upper-left corner of each page. That means these text boxes are able to act as text placeholders.

When you insert text on a regular page that has been assigned this master page, the text will flow right into it. More importantly, if there's too much text for a single page, the text will just keep on flowing onto the next page with a linked automatic text box, and the next one after that, and so on until all the text is on pages. And if QuarkXPress runs out of pages, it will create enough new ones to hold all the text.

If the chain in the upper corner of the master page is broken, there is no automatic text box link in place. If it is intact, then an automatic text box has been established. In that case, you will be able to activate the Linking tool and see a linking arrow from the chain to any selected text box.

Tip

Customize Your Automatic Text Boxes

Automatic text boxes can be sized, just like regular ones. You can also have more than one on a page and link them with the Link tool. In fact, the automatic links in the corners of your master page in Figure 8.4 are quite similar to the text box links you have already been using in your previous work in this class. You can break them, if you must. Just click the chains with the unlink tool. You can also manually create automatic text boxes if you need to, without using the checkbox in the New Document dialog box.

Page Navigation Pop-Up

5. Use the page navigator pop-up menu at the bottom of the QuarkXPress window to return to the first page of your document, as you see in Figure 8.5.

Page navigation pop-up

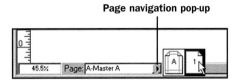

Figure 8.5

An alternative to the Document Layout palette for page navigation.

Automatically Inserting Pages

6. Click the Content tool inside the margins of this page.

 You will see that the automatic text box from the master page shows up here as well. For every page you add using this master, there will be one of these text boxes. That's the point of a master page, to replicate items onto many pages.

7. Use the Get Text command, ⌘+E (Mac) or Ctrl+E (Win95).

 Select the text file **02INITIATE.XTG** and make sure the Convert Quotes and Include Style Sheets checkboxes are turned on. That will cause QuarkXPress to import the styles from the text file. In addition, any quotes in the file will be converted to professional-looking curly typographer quotes instead of amateurish straight typewriter-style quotes.

8. Double-click the text file, **02INITIATE.XTG** and watch what happens as the text is imported and pages are added to your document.

 Now have a look at the Document Layout palette. It should look like Figure 8.6, with lots more pages automatically added to this file, which will be the second chapter of the practice book we are assembling.

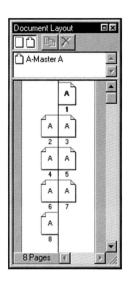

Figure 8.6

Pages automatically added by importing text.

A copy of the second chapter file has been saved on your CD-ROM, just in case you have trouble with this exercise and need to have a look at what it should look like. The name of the file is **02DONE.QXT**.

Setting Page Numbers

For any long form publication, page numbers will be the fundamental, essential, universally understood way of organizing a publication.

You've probably done page numbering in a word processor before. That means you are used to just turning page numbering on or off, and allowing the word processing software to automatically position the numbers on the pages without any intervention from you. But QuarkXPress is a sophisticated page layout program. In this kind of a professional typesetting situation, you take control of the numbering process.

In the following steps, you will create a text box on a master page and include within the box the special code that tells QuarkXPress to display the page number. (You can put this page number code on regular pages, but it is almost always used on master pages to automate the page numbering process.)

1. Open the template file **00FRONT.QXT** and save the resulting new file as **00FRONT.QXD**, a document file.

2. Notice that there are two master pages in this file. You can see why if you look at the first page of this document. The title page of the book, obviously, needs a different layout than the text pages.

Navigate to Master A by double-clicking its icon in the Document Layout palette.

Constructing a Master Page Footer

3. Footers are text information that repeats along the lower edge—the foot—of the pages of a long form document like a book. Headers are at the top—the head—of the pages.

Draw out a text box in the lower-left corner of the left-hand page using the Rectangle Text Box tool. Use the Modify command to make it 4 picas wide and 1p3 tall and nestle it right below the intersection of the left and bottom margin guides.

4. Type the page number marker in this text box, ⌘+3 (Mac) or Ctrl+3 (Win95).

These page number markers, even though they look a bit odd, are just text and you can format them just as you would any other text.

The page number should be left-aligned in the text box. Format it as 10-point Opus.

When you get to this point, the lower-left corner of your Master A page should look like Figure

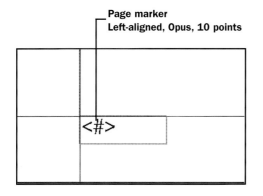

Page marker
Left-aligned, Opus, 10 points

<#>

8.7.

Figure 8.7

Setting a page number, the Master page view.

Numbering Opposing (Facing) Pages

5. Use the Item tool to select the page number text box.

Copy it and Paste it. Then drag this duplicate page number text box to the lower-right corner of the right-hand page and position it just as you did the first one, beneath the intersection of the bottom and right-hand margin guides.

6. Set this new page number to be right-aligned instead of left-aligned, so it will force itself against the outer margin of the right-hand page.

Understanding Multiple Master Pages

7. Use the Document Layout palette or the page navigation pop-up to get to the first page of the document, the title page that is formatted using the Master B master page.

Notice that there is nothing along the lower edge of the page, no page number.

8. Now go to page two, which is formatted with Master A, the master that you just equipped with a page number marker.

Observe that the page number marker is no longer a funny-looking symbol. It's an automatically updating page number. It appears on every page assigned to the Master A master page.

The title and regular text pages differ from one another because their underlying master pages are different.

Creating Footer/Header Styles

9. The page numbering has already been done on most of the files assembled into this book, but you need to apply page numbers to two more files.

Return to the Master A master page where you will begin by creating styles for your two kinds of footer text. You should always use styles wherever you can. It makes it much easier to keep the formatting of book elements consistent, and it makes it easier to change the formatting if you need to do so at some future date.

You probably remember the procedure for creating a new style from the last chapter, but we'll give you the basics here to refresh your memory.

Click the Content tool in the right footer text box. Ctrl + click (Mac) or right-click (Win95) on the No Style selection in the Style Sheets palette. Name it **FOOTERLEFT**.

Do the same for the right-hand page number footer except you should name it **FOOTERRIGHT**.

Don't forget to apply the new styles to the text.

Copying Footers to Additional Publications

10. Use the Item tool to select one of the footer text blocks and then ⬆Shift+click the other one so you have them both selected. Copy them to the Clipboard.

11. Open the file **01STRATEGY.QXT**, a template file, and save it as **01STRATEGY.QXD**, a document file.

12. With the Item tool still selected, navigate to Master A in **01STRATEGY.QXD** and Paste the footers onto the master.

With both text boxes still selected, use the Item tool to move them into position at the lower edge of the page.

Navigate back to page 1 of the document and note that you have page 1 numbered automatically.

13. Perform the same operation for **02INITIATE.QXD**, the file you were working with in your previous exercise.

Open up the file and navigate to Master A.

With the Item tool still selected, paste the footer text boxes (which are still on the Clipboard) onto the master page.

Position the text boxes at the lower edge of the page.

Navigate back to page 1 of the document and note that you have page 1 numbered automatically.

14. After saving all your open files, close down QuarkXPress. (It can get pretty confusing with a book's worth of files open and this will get us back to scratch for the next exercise.)

You should now have page numbers in all six book files, the ones you did that begin with 00, 01, 02, and the ones we have already set up with page numbers, up through 05.

Special Page Numbering Using Sections

It's common to number the front matter of a book, the copyright, preface, and acknowledgements, with small roman numerals. In order to accomplish this specialized page numbering, you mark QuarkXPress files into sections. In fact, that's pretty much the only reason you would ever want to use sections, to set up some specialized page numbering as you will in this next exercise.

1. Open the file **00FRONT.QXD**. It's the file with two master pages in it, the one you saved as a document in the last exercise after adding page numbers. (Don't get the template file that ends in .QXT by mistake.)

2. Navigate to the third page of this file.

As you'd expect, it's numbered page 3. But in this case it shouldn't be. Practices vary, but editors often decide against starting page numbering with the title page or even the copyright page. They sometimes begin numbering with the acknowledgments page and that's what we'll do here. (Besides, this is a good way to show you how to work this command.)

Also, you'll notice that page 2 is numbered in Arabic instead of with a small roman numeral.

3. We'll fix that by setting a section.

Make sure page 3 is the one that is indicated as your position in the Document Layout palette. On the Mac, the page number will be in outline type. In Windows 95, the page number will be bolded.

Activating a Section

4. Use the **P**age>Section command to open the Section dialog box.

5. Click the **S**ection Start checkbox and, as you see in Figure 8.8, the Page Numbering part of the dialog box will become active. (It was grayed out when you first opened the dialog box.)

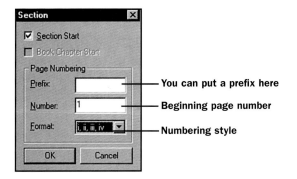

You can put a prefix here

Beginning page number

Numbering style

Figure 8.8

Setting a section for special page numbering.

Setting Page Number and Format

6. The starting page number should be 1, which is the default choice for this command.

   Choose from the list the small Roman numeral format you see in Figure 8.8.

7. Click OK and have a look at the page number in the lower-right corner of the page. Also notice the numbering change in the Document Layout palette. All the numbers from actual page number three on are numbered with small Roman numerals beginning with "i."

   You will also notice that the page number at the beginning of the section is marked with an asterisk wherever it appears, including in the lower-left corner of the QuarkXPress window and the Document Layout palette.

Editing Master Page Items on Text Pages

8. Now what do you do about page 2? It's still numbered, and worse yet it has an out-of-order number.

   The solution is easy. Just select the Item tool and delete the page 2 footer text block.

   In QuarkXPress, you can edit any master page item from the text pages without affecting the underlying master page. (You'll notice, if you happen to be familiar with it, that this works entirely differently from the PageMaker approach to master pages.)

9. As usual, save your work before shutting down QuarkXPress to be ready for the next exercise.

A copy of **00FRONT.QXD** as it should look after this exercise has been saved on the CD-ROM in a file named **00DONE.QXT**.

Combining "Chapters" into a Book

Almost any long form publication ought to be broken up into smaller pieces. You might call them chapters, just for convenience sake, but they could be book sections, preface, introduction, appendixes, tables of contents, indexes, or any of the other many parts of a long document.

When you use a QuarkXPress Book file to combine a series of files into one publication, you reduce the overall size of any one piece of the publication as you work on it, thus reducing the demand on system resources—always a safer way to run. By breaking the job into pieces, you also limit the extent of potential disaster if a file goes bad.

In this exercise, you will assemble the book chapter files you have been working on by building a list of them in a special kind of QuarkXPress file called a book file.

1. Open QuarkXPress. Don't double-click a file, just launch the program.

Making a Book File

2. Choose File>New>Book to get the dialog box you see in Figure 8.9.

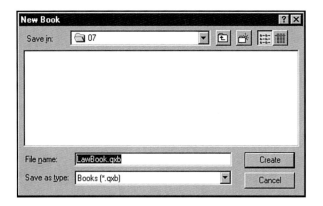

Figure 8.9

Creating your book file.

Navigate to your work folder and type in a name for your new book file, **LAWBOOK.QXB**.

Press ⌈Return⌉ (Mac) or ⌈⏎Enter⌉ (Win95) to create your book file.

Building a Book List

3. You will next see a dialog box where you will actually put together a list of the files you are assembling into a book. Notice that the name of the book file is at the top of the dialog box.

Figure 8.10 maps out the functions of all the icons. It also lists for you the order of the chapter files you will be selecting for your book list.

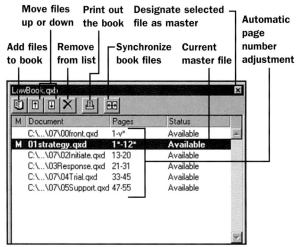

Figure 8.10

The book list in the order you should assemble it.

Adding to the List and Sorting It

4. Build your book list by clicking the Add Files icon in the upper-left corner of this palette, matching the list in Figure 8.10. The palette provides you with a standard file selection dialog box where you can pick out the files you need. Click the Add button to put selected files on your book list.

   The first file you select will be designated the Master file. That means you should select **01STRATEGY.QXD** first. (Alternatively, you can select the files in any order and change the master file designation later.)

   You designate a master by selecting it and clicking the "M" just to the left of the word "Document," as in Figure 8.10.

   Adjust the order of the files as needed by using the up or down buttons.

Tip

Develop a Standard File Naming System

Notice that we have named the files for the book list with leading numbers so that they naturally sort themselves into order. That makes it very easy to compile the book list in the proper order.

Automatic Page Numbering

Take a good look at the list of page numbers. It automatically takes care of consecutive page numbering across files, depending on how you set up your sections.

Notice that the numbering for **01STRATEGY. QXD** restarts page numbers at number 1 after the small Roman numeral section is finished in file **00FRONT.QXD**. That's because there's a section setting at the beginning of that file.

Synchronizing Styles (and More)

5. Synchronizing means every file in the book will be modified to match the designated master file. The styles, H&Js, colors, and so on will be copied from the master file to all the others on the list. That means, if a style with the same name already exists but has a different definition, its definition will be changed to match the master style.

   The file **01STRATEGY.QXD** should already have been designated as the master. The designated master will be the file name with the "M" next to it, listed in bold in the list.

   The synchronizing icon is the one at the right end of the row of icons across the top of the book list palette. Click it now.

   Watch the status column of the palette as QuarkXPress goes through the files, briefly opening each one in turn to do its work. (You won't see that happen except for the indication in the palette).

6. You may have noticed earlier that **02INITIATE.QXD** had quite a different look from **01STRATEGY.QXD**. The strategy chapter had reversed out, white on black, headlines. Open it now to see how its styles have been updated.

Tip

Print Books from Book File

To print a book, you work from the book file. To print the entire book, make sure you don't have any individual chapters selected and click on the Print icon. To print one or more individual chapters, select them and click on the Print icon.

7. Close QuarkXPress to get out of the book and close out all the book files, in preparation for a fresh start in the next exercise.

Introducing...Tables of Contents and Other Lists

You could build a table of contents the old-fashioned way, by going through the publication and making a list of all the items to be included in the table along with their page numbers. Then you would type the table of contents item by item. You would also be dreading any editing changes that caused the page numbering to shift.

But there's no need for dread. QuarkXPress can automatically compile your table of contents for you if you set things up properly. In fact, QuarkXPress refers to this compilation as a list, and that's good. It means you are not limited to tables of contents and you can create many differing kinds of lists for your publications: illustration lists, lists of tables, and so on.

QuarkXPress lists are built around paragraph styles. The list feature compiles all the paragraphs that have a designated style from a file (or a book) into a list. In the course of compiling these paragraphs, usually headlines or captions, it also formats the entries so they look good in list form. You have a great deal of flexibility—lots of power—in commanding QuarkXPress to perform this compilation and formatting.

This process of creating a list in QuarkXPress has some basic steps to it that work the same regardless of the kind of list you are creating. First you define the list in a list dialog box. Then you build the list from a list palette.

Here's an overview of how it works:

- Given that you can have more than one list, your central command center for list definition and editing is reached through the Edit>Lists command, which gives you a dialog box like the one in Figure 8.11.

- When you click the New button, you get the powerful dialog box in Figure 8.12 where you can specify the parameters of your list.

- After your new list has been defined, build the list by using the Lists palette in Figure 8.13.

  Select the list you want to compile in the palette, use the Contents tool to select a text box where QuarkXPress can dump the compiled list text, and click the Build button.

Your list of defined lists

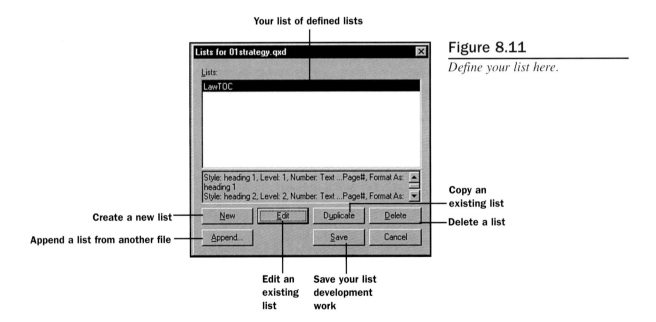

Figure 8.11

Define your list here.

Create a new list

Append a list from another file

Copy an existing list

Delete a list

Edit an existing list

Save your list development work

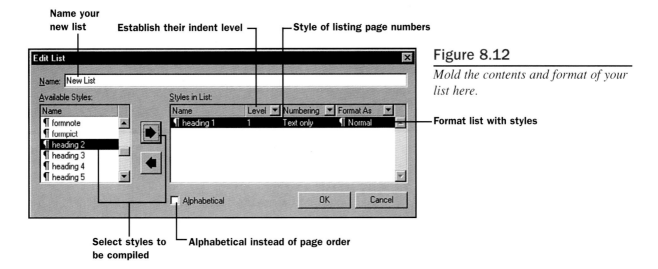

Name your new list

Establish their indent level

Style of listing page numbers

Figure 8.12

Mold the contents and format of your list here.

Format list with styles

Select styles to be compiled

Alphabetical instead of page order

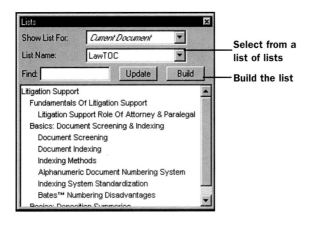

Select from a list of lists

Build the list

Figure 8.13

Build the list with the Lists palette.

Generating Tables of Contents

Now that you have the basic idea of how to build a list, you can get practice by building the most common list of all—a table of contents.

1. For convenience sake, we will build a table of contents for just one chapter rather than for an entire book.

You should have shut down QuarkXPress at the end of the last exercise. Open it again and open up **01STRATEGY.QXD**.

Inserting Pages

2. In order to put a table of contents list at the head of this chapter, we will need to add some pages.

Navigate to the first page of the document.

Use the Page>Insert command you learned to use in Chapter 1 to add two pages before the first page of the document, as in Figure 8.14.

Two pages

Before first page

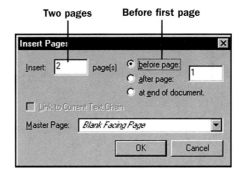

Figure 8.14

Inserting pages.

3. Navigate back to the first document page, the beginning of the chapter's body copy.

Appending List Styles

4. You will want some special paragraph styles to format your table of contents. We have already constructed them for you.

You learned how to use the **File>Append** command to import styles in Chapter 7. Use that command now to import the TOC styles from the file **TOCSTYLES.QXT** from the CD-ROM.

As with all the other working files from this chapter, you should have copied it into your work folder at the beginning of the chapter.

Defining a New List

5. Use **Edit>List** to reach the Lists dialog box to define your list as you see it in Figure 8.15.

Name the new list **LawTOC**.

Select the top three headline styles and use the right facing arrow button to move them onto the right side of the dialog box for inclusion in the list.

Set up the hierarchy of your list by assigning level 1 to Heading 1, level 2 to Heading 2, and level 3 to Heading 3.

You want the list page numbering style that puts the page number after the item.

Format the list entries with your special appended TOC styles as in Figure 8.15.

6. Click OK to close the Edit List dialog box.

Notice that you use basically the same dialog box for both making a new list and editing an existing one. The operations are very similar.

7. Click Save to keep the list development work you have just completed.

Building a List

8. If you aren't already there, navigate to the first page in the document so you can build your list.

9. Draw out a text box on this page. Make it the size of the margin guides.

10. Click the Content tool in the text box.

11. In the Lists palette, notice that the Build button became active when you clicked the text box.

Also, notice that you have a preview window in the palette that you can renew by using the Update button.

You can also find text within the preview by using the Find box.

12. Click the Build button and your table of contents list—already neatly formatted—will pour into the new text box. It should look like Figure 8.16.

Tip

You Can Compile Lists from an Entire Book

You've been compiling a table of contents for a single chapter file. Of course, in the real world, you would be compiling a table of contents for many files assembled into a book. The trick for building a book-level list is to create the list in the designated master chapter. Then, in the list palette, select the book file in the Show List For pop-up menu.

A copy of the strategy chapter with the completed table of contents inserted has been saved on the CD-ROM in a file named **01TOCDONE.QXT**.

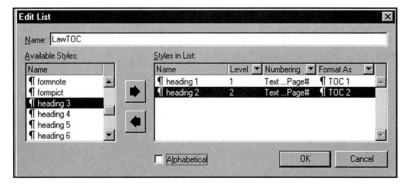

Figure 8.15

Use this as a model for defining your list.

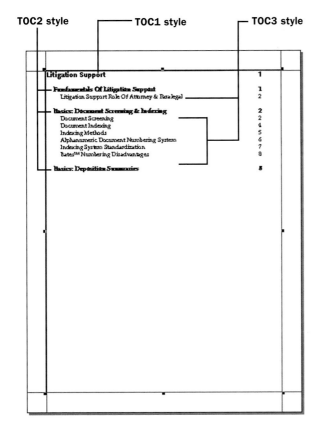

TOC2 style ── **TOC1 style** ── **TOC3 style**

Figure 8.16

The finished, compiled table of contents list.

Introducing...Indexing

Use of the QuarkXPress indexing feature will have a lot to do with the type of index you want to create. Much depends on what level of quality is desired.

Concordance or True Index?

Often, when somebody talks about an index in the computer world, they are thinking of a simple word list. There are some add-on utilities (Xtensions in QuarkXPress jargon) that will help you with this job of compiling a word list. Sonar Bookends is one of them. Such word lists are called *concordances*, an alphabetical list of the principal words of a book.

You can make a much better index than that, if you want to, in QuarkXPress. It has been designed for craftsmen who construct truly useful indexes that go beyond simple word lists. You can use the QuarkXPress indexing feature to delve into the fundamental nature of a book—its concepts, broad topics, and multiple references to a single topic.

Such an index requires more work and more thought, even using an automatic index compilation tool like the one in QuarkXPress. Clearly, however, this is the best quality approach. One dictionary calls an index "Something serving to point out; a sign, token, or indication."

The rigorous indexer attempts to think the way the reader will be thinking when attempting to find some bit of information. A complete index includes cross references and cites important themes of discussion whether or not they actually appear as words in the text.

A book on mammals that offers only a concordance might include references in its index for every species named in the text. But a mere concordance might omit useful references to endangered species or habitats or even quotes from poems that mention the animals. Also, an index has cross references so that someone finding whale in the index would also be referred to endangered species issues.

So, while a concordance can be automated, a true index requires human attention, using a tool like the indexing facility in QuarkXPress.

Importance of Master Topic List

One rule of thumb for index creation is consistency. All the entries for a certain topic should appear in one location in the index. You shouldn't, for example, have a listing for "whale" as well as an entry for "whales." Also, it is good to have a standardized structure for thinking about entries so that you use the same cross references throughout the indexing process. Consistency makes finding a specific index entry much easier for the reader.

This standardization can be achieved by creating a master topic list. In fact, a concordance list of all the unique words in a publication can be a useful starting point for creating such a master list. If you know all the unique word items in a book, you have an idea of the topics that need to be indexed.

Also, once you have a master topic list, you can type it up in QuarkXPress and select items from the list as you tag index locations, another aid to standardization. Using such a standard topic list prevents strange index entries, such as three different spellings of a person's name. When you make an entry, you instead choose from the standard list, which is a boon to consistency.

Introducing the QuarkXPress Index Palette

Most of your indexing work revolves around the palette in Figure 8.17.

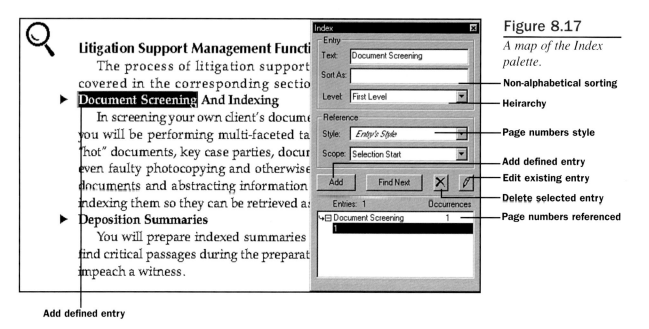

Figure 8.17

A map of the Index palette.

Non-alphabetical sorting

Heirarchy

Page numbers style

Add defined entry

Edit existing entry

Delete selected entry

Page numbers referenced

Add defined entry

This Index palette is rich with power and that means it is fairly complex. Follow along, using the illustration as a "map," as we talk our way from top to bottom of this sample entry.

The figure illustrates the creation of the simplest possible type of index entry. Some text has been highlighted, so that it automatically appears as a possible entry.

You have the option, not taken here, to force the entry to adopt some non-standard (non-alphabetical) sorting. For example, you could put a letter "s" here if you wanted "Document screening" to be sorted by its second word (which begins with an "s").

This entry is a first-level entry but you can establish entries as one of four levels, for a hierarchical listing of items. Bolognese, for example, might be a second-level entry under the first-level entry of pasta sauce.

For this simple entry, the choice has been made to use the same style sheet for the page number as the style already being used for the index entry. You could also select a special style for the page number, perhaps using italic for all references where there's an illustration.

The scope determines how many pages, and which pages, will be listed after the entry. Here, only one page will be listed. But you could choose from a variety of options, including all pages covered by the selected text; all pages until the next occurrence of a particular style; or all pages from the entry to the end of the current story. There are lots more scope options.

From left to right, the buttons along the middle of the palette allow you to: add your entry to the index when you've got it defined; search for the next occurrence of the entry text in the document; delete an existing index entry; and edit an existing entry.

Last, but hardly least, all your index entries are automatically updated as you create them—in real time, which is a big deal. Other indexing systems in page layout programs and word processors usually require a two-step process where you mark your entry locations and then generate the index.

Exploring the Build Index Dialog Box

Instead of the build button you have when compiling a list, the indexing facility has an entire build dialog box, shown in Figure 8.18.

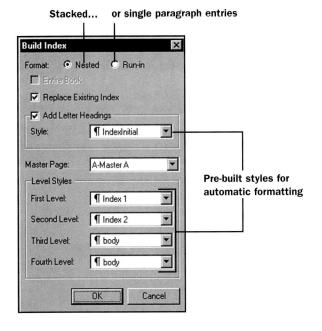

Stacked... **or single paragraph entries**

Pre-built styles for automatic formatting

Figure 8.18

After marking entries with the Index palette, you switch to this dialog box to actually build the index.

Again, as with the Index palette, follow along top to bottom of the Build Index dialog box while we take a quick tour.

You will almost always use a nested index where various index levels are stacked and indented. The run-in format puts a list of the entries under each topic in a single paragraph.

When you build the index, you can save yourself a lot of time by automatically overwriting the old index text.

Letter headings are the letters of the alphabet, inserted between the various sections of the index. You can format them with a paragraph style.

You can also set predefined styles for each level of index entry so that your automatically compiled index entries will be put down on the page virtually entirely formatted—automatically.

Coding and Compiling an Index

This exercise will get you familiar with the basic QuarkXPress indexing procedure, now that you understand some of the basic concepts. With this powerful tool in hand, the thought that goes into making a high-quality index will be up to you from here.

1. Keep working in the **01STRATEGY.QXD** document for this indexing process. If you closed it after compiling your table of contents in the last exercise, open it now.

Making a Quick Index Entry

2. For your first entry, perform the same indexing operation as illustrated in Figure 8.17.

    Begin by opening the Index palette.

    There's no keyboard shortcut for it, unlike most of the other QuarkXPress palettes. Use the View>Show Index command.

3. Highlight the words Document Screening on the first regular text page of the document, about ¾ of the way down the page.

    Notice that the text appears automatically in the Index palette, ready to be added as an entry.

4. Click the Add button and the entry will appear in the palette list.

    Thin red brackets will appear, indicating that the bracketed text has been placed in the index.

Editing an Index Entry

5. However, there's something wrong with this entry. Both words have been capitalized because it was drawn from a headline.

    Select the entry in the list and click the pencil icon.

6. Edit the S on-screen to be lowercase and click the edit icon again to accept the edited version.

Scoping an Entry

7. Scoping means creating an entry that refers to a group of pages where the topic is covered.

Highlight the words Support Management Functions from the headline on the first page right above the last entry you created.

If you have the Styles palette open, you will notice that this paragraph is tagged with the Heading 4 paragraph style.

8. Don't click the Add button yet.

Before moving ahead, correct the capitalization so that the second and third words are all lowercase.

9. Use the pop-up menu for Scope to select the To Style option.

A second pop-up appears with the word Next in it. That means this index entry will include all the page numbers from this location to the next instance of the current paragraph style.

You could also select some other style from this pop-up list.

10. When you click the Add button, your new entry should look like the one in Figure 8.19.

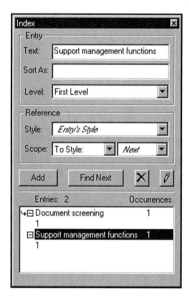

Figure 8.19

An index entry with scope.

Composing a Custom Entry

11. You don't always want to make an entry from some specific wording in text. In fact, if you are really compiling a conceptual index, a true index, you will have many entries that don't even appear verbatim in your book.

Click a text insertion point in the second bullet point on this first page of the document, after the words Deposition Summaries.

12. With no entry selected in the list, type the words **Deposition summary** into the Index palette text box. (Notice that it is not plural.)

Click the Add button to make your custom entry official.

The red index marker in the text this time isn't bracketing a section of indexed text. Instead, it is a tiny red mark in the text.

> **Tip**
>
> **Customize Your Index Feature**
>
> You can customize the text index marker color. Go to Edit>Preferences>Index. Click the color square in that dialog box to reach a custom color picker. Also, note that you can customize the punctuation that appears between multiple index entries.

Setting an Entry's Hierarchy

13. Notice the tiny curved arrow out to the left of one of the entries in the palette. That's the pointer that tells QuarkXPress where you want a lower hierarchy entry to go.

Double-click just to the left of the entry for Support management functions and the hierarchy arrow will move there.

14. Click in the body text again in the same spot as the last step, after the words Deposition Summaries. (If you don't click a second time, you will get an error message saying there's already an entry there.)

15. Again, with no entry selected, type in another custom entry, the same words as the last one, Deposition summary.

16. Set the hierarchy at Second Level.

Make sure you change the scope back to Selection Start. QuarkXPress tries to help by repeating the last entry. That can be very convenient, but watch for this trait because you could easily forget to change your entry setting and make an entry with the wrong scope setting.

17. Click the Add button and notice, as you see in Figure 8.20, that the new entry is indented slightly underneath the top level entry.

Making a Cross Reference

18. You often need to refer the reader to somewhere else within the index itself, as opposed to a page number within the text. That's a cross reference entry.

Click a new index insertion point in your body text.

With the hierarchy pointer still set next to the entry for Support management functions, keep the hierarchy level for this cross reference entry at Second Level.

19. Type in a custom entry for Screening.

20. Select a scope of X-Ref and choose See Also from the adjacent pop-up menu that appears just to the right of X-Ref.

21. You now need a specific cross reference, which should be an existing index entry.

Click in the blank provided, just to the right of the scope choice for See also.

Click the index entry for Document screening and that will be entered into this blank box—no typing required and you are sure of an exact spelling.

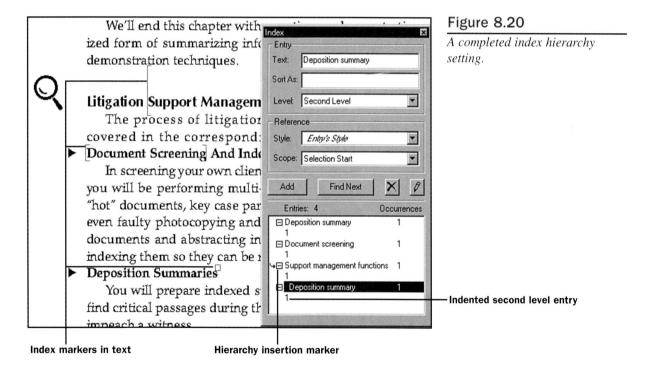

Index markers in text   **Hierarchy insertion marker**

Figure 8.20

A completed index hierarchy setting.

Indented second level entry

22. Click the Add button to complete the cross reference and your Index palette should look like the one in Figure 8.21.

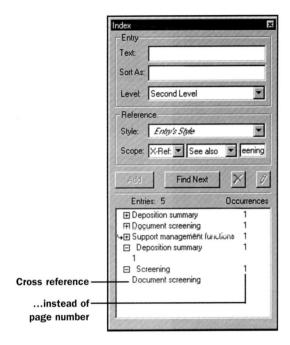

Cross reference ——
...instead of ——
page number

Figure 8.21

Cross reference index entry.

Notice that you have been building a list of page numbers for each entry or topic. (All the page numbers are 1 because we've been working exclusively on page one.)

You can also delete individual entries underneath each topic, including the one for your new cross reference.

Building the Index

23. Once you have all your entries in place, you must actually build the index. This process is quite similar to the process for building a list.

You might want to review the instructions at the end of the table of contents exercise to help you through the next couple of steps.

Now that you have achieved an important level of knowledge about QuarkXPress, we'll be asking you to go on your own a bit more, without

detailed step-by-step instructions. The point is to help you learn how to apply concepts you've learned in previous lessons to specific tasks. That's an important skill in the job world! No one will be providing you with step-by-step guided exercises when you have a design challenge and a deadline ahead of you.

24. Append the index styles you will use in the index from the file **INDEXSTYLE.QXT**.

25. Add a page at the end of your document. You will need to draw a text box on this page to hold the index text.

Now you are all set to build your index onto this page.

26. Click the Contents tool in a text box to get started with the build index operation. As with lists, you must be in an active text box before the whole thing will work.

Use Utilities>Build Index to reach the dialog box in Figure 8.22. It's the same one you saw in the tour of the Build Index dialog box earlier in this chapter.

Figure 8.22

Creating the format for an index.

27. Duplicate the settings in this dialog box before you actually build your index.

Choose Nested entries for your format.

You don't have a book open at the moment, but if you did, the check box for Entire Book would be active.

Likewise, there's no index in place so you don't have the option of replacing it.

From there to the bottom of the dialog box, everything is about choosing styles and page designs that will automatically format your index entries.

28. Click OK to go ahead and compile your index. It will be popped into place in the index text box where you directed it.

Your finished index should look like the one in Figure 8.23.

The file with the finished index work in it has been saved on the CD-ROM as **01INDEXDONE.QXT**.

Summary

It takes a lot of skill and effort to accurately manage all the elements of a long form document—a book, annual report, recipe collection, school yearbook, sales brochure. With QuarkXPress, you have powerful tools to help you perform these tasks, to make sure that page numbers don't get out of order, that styles are consistent between documents, and that indexes and tables of contents have accurate page references. And with master pages and auto page insert, you can quickly and efficiently whip a long document together and accurately and consistently shape it to convey information to the reader.

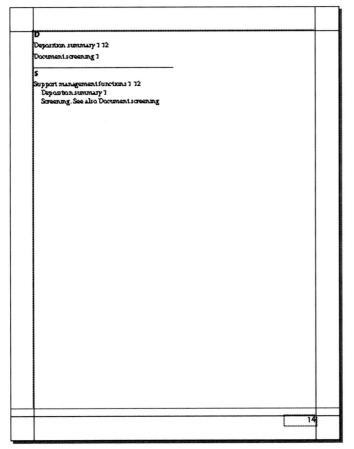

Figure 8.23

A completed index job.

Review It

As a review of what you have learned in this chapter, please answer the following questions..

1. Where would you usually place the page number code in a QuarkXPress document? And what is the code for the page number character?

_____

_____

2. What is the absolutely essential formatting ingredient in order to compile a table of contents or list?

_____

_____

3. How do you designate what items will be compiled into a list?

_____

_____

4. Name two ways you can mark an index entry location.

_____

_____

5. If you've already got an index in place, what's the quickest way to update it?

_____

_____

6. What are the two essential ingredients for auto-pagination?

_____

_____

7. How can you make sure all the styles in the files of a book list match up?

_____

_____

8. Why would you section a document?

_____

_____

9. If you are building a true index, a good first step would be…?

_____

_____

10. To make page numbers from a master page show up on body pages, you need two things. And they are…?

_____

_____

Check It

Multiple Choice

Please circle the correct answer for each of the following questions.

1. You use master pages to achieve _____.

   a. repeating body text page elements

   b. consistent margins on many body text pages

   c. body text page numbering

   d. all of the above

2. Before building an index or a list, you should always _____.

   a. define index entry paragraph styles

   b. set your index marker color

   c. create a concordance list

   d. all of the above

3. The scope setting determines an index entry's _____.

   a. depth of hierarchy

   b. style in Build Index

   c. page number reference range

   d. all of the above

4. How many styles should you have to compile a well-formatted list?

   a. One, to pick up the list text

   b. Two, to gather source entries and format the target

   c. Unknown, depending on number of entry types

   d. Double the number of entry types, for source and target

5. To go to a page in a document, you _____.

   a. double-click on page in Document Layout palette

   b. select in page navigation pop-up

   c. use Page>Go To

   d. all of the above

6. If you want prefix numbering for your pages, the solution is to use _____.

   a. manual edits of master page numbers

   b. section dialog box

   c. master page prefix command

   d. all of the above

7. You break big projects into chapters because it _____.

   a. reduces risk of loss if there's a crash

   b. lowers system load for faster operation

   c. helps organize material

   d. all of the above

8. When defining a list, the first file you select will _____.

   a. be designated master file

   b. be listed in bold

   c. have an "M" next to it

   d. all of the above

9. You set the hierarchy of index items by _____.

   a. choosing top item first

   b. selecting them in book list

   c. double-clicking to set hierarchy marker

   d. all of the above

10. A high-quality index helps the reader find _____.

    a. specific words in the text

    b. concepts and cross references

    c. concordance items

    d. all of the above

True or False

Please circle *T* or *F* to indicate whether the statement is true or false.

T   F   **1.** Master page items are locked and uneditable on body copy pages.

T   F   **2.** Automatic text links can be broken.

T   F   **3.** Automatic text boxes can be resized.

T   F   **4.** The key command for an automatic page number is ⌘+③ (Mac) or Ctrl+③ (Win95).

T   F   **5.** Paragraph styles are optional but desired for defining a list.

T   F   **6.** Sectioning a document reduces its size and thus helps compile a book more efficiently.

T   F   **7.** Synchronizing a book shares index entries between the files.

T   F   **8.** To compile a book list, you must select the book file in the List palette.

T   F   **9.** You must have a scope for every index entry, including a cross reference.

T   F   **10.** You must select book files in the correct order when adding them to a list definition.

Design It

For this chapter's independent work project, focus on information design as opposed to "just looking good" design.

Set up some practice chapter files of your own, similar to the ones you used for exercises in this book. The point is that you should focus on material you can visually organize. Use your design skills to make the information presentation as clear as possible.

- Design a strongly formatted table of contents or table of illustrations list, creating paragraph styles so that the entries have a very clear hierarchy.

- For your list, utilize some organizational styling such as reversed out text or borders. (Be careful not to overdo this since a little bit of this kind of formatting goes a long way.)

- Create left and right facing master pages for the body copy. Explore ways that footers and headers can be used to help visually organize the information.

- For your footers/header design, don't forget that you can use reversed-out type, special typefaces, or even some graphics icons from Sean's Symbols to give the reader visual cues about the organization of information.

Using a Design Grid

What You Will Learn

In the last chapter, we talked about creating a structure for a book or other long form documents. In this chapter, we talk about the structure of a page—and how QuarkXPress can help you create that structure.

In this chapter, you will learn about:

➤ Setting up a design grid to structure your pages with column and margin master guides

➤ Augmenting that page structure by locking your type to a baseline grid and setting a customized zero point for your rulers

➤ Building the grid into a new master page definition and applying it to your body copy pages

➤ Creating a fancy newsletter nameplate with a typeface choice plus some kerning and baseline adjustments

➤ Four advanced techniques for constructing columns, even ones with uneven widths and headlines hanging outside their perimeters

➤ Using the QuarkXPress anchoring feature to lock a headline or graphic to text

➤ Raising and lowering type on a line using baseline adjustment

➤ Setting good-looking numerals in body copy using a special old style figure font

➤ Putting a frame around a text box

Figure 9.1

In this chapter, you will use a design grid and other techniques to create this newsletter design.

Design Notes

Although the main point of this chapter is using a design grid to structure a page, you will be exploring another area as well—the use of special purpose type.

Have a look at Figure 9.1 and notice that, even though there are no imported graphics in this newsletter design, the page has a real graphic flair. That's due to a few characters from a special decorative dingbat font called Deanna Flowers. (We will be adding imported graphics to the newsletter in the next chapter, which is why the second page looks empty.)

In the nameplate at the top of the newsletter's first page, the area that many people mistakenly call the masthead, we used a leafy character from Deanna Flowers to make a flowing ersatz capital letter T. It works well here because there's no doubt about the name of the newsletter. The rest of the letters in the title have been set in an extra bold weight of a popular typeface called Futura. We use a variant of Futura here, which is named Function on your CD-ROM.

You will set the body copy of the newsletter in a variant of the Sabon typeface. It's called Savoy on your CD-ROM. Sean Cavanaugh calls Sabon "lively and interesting…a romantic design married to Teutonic sensibility."

Another new typographical nicety that you will learn in this chapter is the use of old style figures. Old style figures don't sit on the baseline like the numbers you are used to seeing. They fit in with body copy much better than the usual numbers because they act more like lowercase alphabetical characters. A portion of some of the letters hangs down below the baseline of a line of text. These professional typesetter's numeral characters come in special augmented versions of regular typefaces and you will make use of one in this chapter. It's called Savoy SC+OsF. The initials SC+OsF tell you that this augmentation to the regular Savoy font contains the old-style figures we have just discussed as well as an alphabet of specially-designed small caps (lowercase capital letters). In fact, another name for old-style figures is lowercase figures.

Getting Set Up

Copy all the files for this chapter from the CD-ROM to a work area on your hard drive. They are labeled **09** in the **Steps**.

You will need to have the Deanna Flowers, Function, Function Heavy, Savoy, and Savoy SC+OsF fonts installed on your computer for the exercises in this chapter.

Each exercise in this chapter builds on the previous one. Except where we've indicated otherwise, you should save your work at the end of each exercise so you can pick up where you left off at the beginning of the next exercise.

Before you open QuarkXPress, it is very important that you go through the following steps to set up some standard defaults and preferences. You will get unexpected results if your preferences don't match up with the ones we had when initially building the newsletter design.

1. Delete or rename your preferences file, XPRESS PREFERENCES, in your main QuarkXPress program folder.

2. Start up QuarkXPress but do not open a new document. You want to set your preferences so they will apply to any new document you set up, as you learned in Chapter 1 in the section called "Understanding QuarkXPress Defaults."

3. Use ⌘+Y (Mac) or Ctrl+Y (Win95) to open up Default Document Preferences.

   In the General tab, set the horizontal and vertical measuring systems to Picas.

   Set Master Page Items to Delete Changes. This means a new master page will wipe out any existing master page items on a body copy page (unless you have edited them at some point). You will make use of this setting in an upcoming exercise.

   Check that Points/Inch has been set at 72.

   Change the greeked type setting to below 4 points.

4. Switch to the Paragraph tab, ⌘+Tab↹ (Mac) or Ctrl+Tab↹ (Win95).

   Make sure leading is in Typesetting mode.

   Set hyphenation to Expanded.

   Take note of the Baseline Grid setting in this dialog box. We'll be coming back to set that one in an upcoming exercise.

5. Switch to the Character tab.

   Check that Auto Kern Above is set to 4 points.

   Standard Em Space should be turned on so you won't be using QuarkXPress' odd double-zero basis for calculating the width of an em.

6. Move to the Tool tab.

   Select the Rectangular Text Box tool and click Modify.

   In the Box tab, set the Box Color to None.

7. Still in the Modify dialog box for the Rectangular Text Box tool, select the Text tab.

   Set Text Inset to 0 points. That means text will snug directly up against the edges of a text box, not inset.

8. Move to the Runaround tab. Any object with a runaround setting will push type away from its perimeter. It is often used on graphics so they won't be obscured by surrounding type. You will make extensive use of it and learn a lot more about it in the next chapter when you add graphics to the newsletter design you create.

Turn off runaround by selecting a Type setting of None.

The no runaround setting, along with a color of none in your text boxes, will make it easier to overlap text boxes in this chapter's exercises.

9. Click OK twice to close out of document preferences.

10. Open Application Preferences, ⬆Shift+⌘+ Option+Y (Mac) or ⬆Shift+Ctrl+Alt+Y (Win95).

    Go to the Save tab and set Auto Save to every 15 minutes. Set Auto Backup to keep two revisions.

    Click on OK to get out of the Preferences dialog box.

11. Quit QuarkXPress, so these new default settings will be safely stored away in the program's preferences file.

Now that you have set up QuarkXPress for the upcoming exercises, it's time to learn about constructing a design grid.

Introducing...QuarkXPress' Built-In Grid System

In many desktop publishing situations—some would insist that this should apply to all DTP projects—you will create an underlying structure of various kinds of guides to help you consistently position objects on the page.

You create this structure by setting up a grid of column guides, ruler guides, and standard increments for line spacing (leading).

Setting up a design grid means thinking ahead about the form your pages will take. What will be the maximum number of columns on a page and how wide should they be? How far apart should your lines of type be? How much white space should you allow around the edges (margins) of your pages, and how open will you want the live area of your pages to be?

It will be tempting to not bother with this design grid. Maybe you will think that your design sense will come through and you can just free-form the placement of columns of type and pictures together on a page. You may well be right. But you will get to an attractive and logical page layout much faster if you first set a design grid in place and use it as a starting point.

This isn't a new concept of the computer age, by the way. The kind of electronic paste-up design grid tools we have in QuarkXPress simply mimic old-fashioned paste up sheets. Years ago, art supply stores did a big business in these sheets, printed up with various kinds of grids of light blue lines on them. Layout artists would use these non-reproducing blue lines as guides to paste up columns of type and art. You can still buy them, in fact.

So how does it work, this construction of a design grid? You build up a design grid in steps.

Master Guides: Columns and Margins

Begin with column and margin guides, master guides, as you see in Figure 9.2.

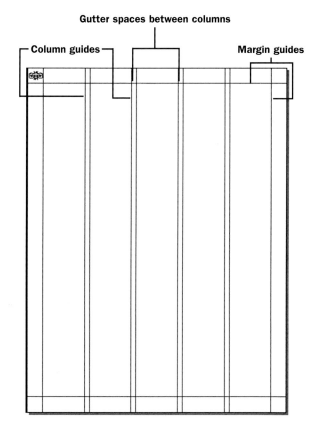

Gutter spaces between columns

Column guides

Margin guides

Figure 9.2

Master guides form the basis of a QuarkXPress design grid.

These margin and column guides are called master guides because they can only be set on master pages. That's only right, too, since the whole point of them is to act as a template or guide for use throughout a document.

You can set margin and column guides for the default master page of your document in the New Document dialog box, **File>New>Document**, in Figure 9.3.

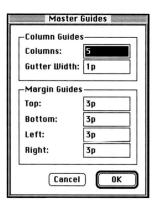

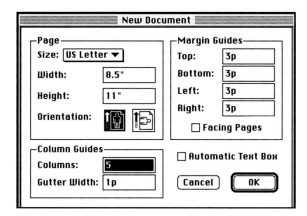

Figure 9.3

Set margins and columns when first creating a document.

After a document has been created, you can change existing guides, or add guides to brand new master pages, by navigating to the master page where you want the guides. You then use the **Page>Master Guides** command to reach the Master Guides dialog in Figure 9.4.

Figure 9.4

After a document has been created, come to this dialog box to set or change margin or column guides on each master page.

Ruler Guides

You already know about ruler guides, having already set a few in previous chapters. However, you may not have realized that you can set ruler guides on master pages. They can thus become an important part of setting up your design grid.

Standard Leading and a Baseline Grid

Another important way to give structural integrity to your pages is to settle on a standard amount of leading for body copy lines. That will make it easy, for example, to align the baselines of type in adjacent columns.

It helps to make a baseline grid part of your design grid, like the one you see in Figure 9.5.

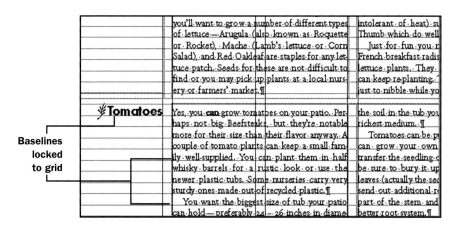

Baselines locked to grid

Figure 9.5

Align lines of type using a baseline grid.

Once you decide, for example, to make your body copy leading 13 points, you control the baseline grid feature of QuarkXPress in three locations.

The grid is always there, but you can turn its display on and off with the View>Show/Hide Baseline Grid command, Option+F7 (Mac) or Ctrl+F7 (Win95). (This works just like the command for turning guides on and off, except you use just plain F7 for that.)

You set the location of the first gridline (usually equal to your top margin) and the spacing of the grid (usually equal to your body copy leading amount) in Document Preferences, as in Figure 9.6.

Once the baseline grid has been established, put it in effect on the individual paragraph level. As in Figure 9.7, you set paragraphs (or paragraph styles) to lock to the grid or not in the Paragraph Attributes dialog, ◆Shift+⌘+F (Mac) or ◆Shift+Ctrl+F (Win95).

Zero Point

Once you have the design grid set up, it's easier to use if you customize the QuarkXPress zero point. The zero point is also called the ruler origin, and it's the point where the zero marks on the vertical and horizontal rulers intersect.

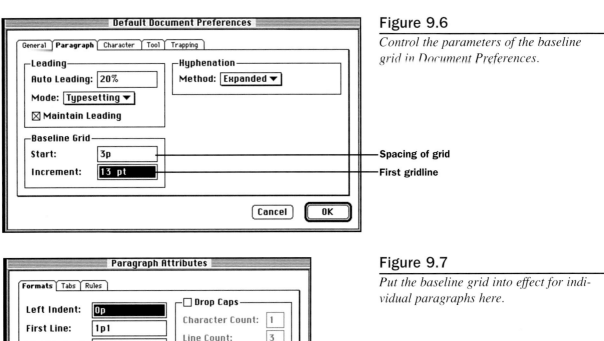

Figure 9.6

Control the parameters of the baseline grid in Document Preferences.

Spacing of grid
First gridline

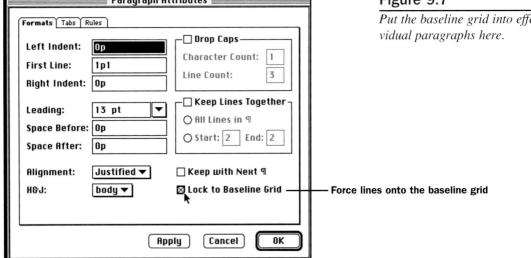

Figure 9.7

Put the baseline grid into effect for individual paragraphs here.

Force lines onto the baseline grid

Normally, when you start a new document in QuarkXPress, the zero point is set for the upper-left corner of your page. However, it is often very helpful to move it to the intersection of your top and left margin. That way, your left and top margins start from zero and make it easier to figure out spatial relationships. You can then set objects into place in relation to the columns of your design grid rather than the edge of the page.

To change the zero point, click and drag from the box in the upper-left corner of the QuarkXPress window, where the rulers intersect, as in Figure 9.8.

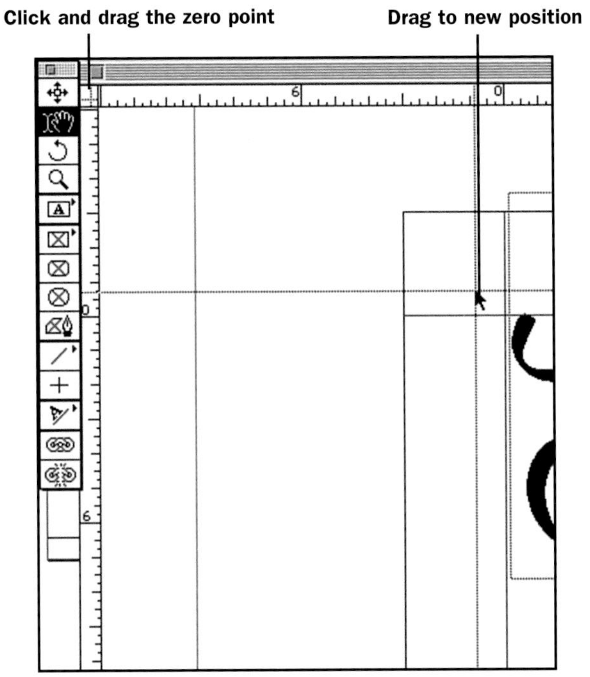

Click and drag the zero point   **Drag to new position**

Figure 9.8

Setting the zero point to match your master guide margins.

Together—the master guides, master page ruler guides, the baseline grid, and the customized zero point—make up your design grid system. In this next exercise, you will actually create one yourself.

Setting Up a Design Grid

Design grids belong on master pages where you can apply them to many pages at once, thus giving your design work consistency throughout a publication. So, in this exercise, you will first create a master page, where you will set up a design grid, and then apply the grid to the body copy pages of the newsletter.

1. Start a brand new QuarkXPress publication. It will, as you know, adopt all the defaults you set in this chapter's setting up section.

   After you open QuarkXPress, press ⌘+Ⓝ (Mac) or Ctrl+Ⓝ (Win95).

2. Leave all the master margin and column guide settings as they are (because you will be creating a new master page with your own settings in a minute).

   Turn off the Automatic Text Box option.

   Press Ⓡeturn (Mac) or ↵Enter (Win95) to OK the dialog box.

   Set Snap To Guides to on, ⬆Shift+Ⓕ7. This is a very important step for later exercises.

3. Save this new document in your working folder, giving it a name of your choice.

Creating a Master Page

4. Open the Document Layout palette, Ⓕ10 (Mac) or Ⓕ4 (Win95).

5. Click and drag the blank single-page icon down into the master page area of the palette, as shown in Figure 9.9.

   Drag it down past the existing master page and notice that the pointer changes to a horizontal line with a downward-pointing arrow. Release the mouse button when the pointer makes that shift.

   If you had chosen the other new page icon, you would have created a new facing page master for situations like a magazine spread or the facing pages of a book.

Figure 9.9

Clicking and dragging down a new master page.

Adding a Body Copy Page

6. Adding a new page in the Document Layout palette works just like creating a new master page.

Click and drag the new single page icon again.

This time, don't stop in the master page section of the palette. Drag the icon all the way down below the existing page one.

Naming a Master Page

7. You may have noticed that the new master page you created was automatically named B-Master B.

The prefix, the part of the name before the hyphen, is the identification that QuarkXPress brands onto body copy pages in the Document Layout palette. It can be up to three letters long.

8. Double-click the B-Master B name, the text and not its icon. The name will be highlighted and you can type in a new name.

Type the new name **Bod-Body** and press (Return) (Mac) or (⏎Enter) (Win95) to apply the new name.

Applying a Master Page

9. You can apply your new page to both pages of the newsletter at the same time.

Click page one, then (⇧Shift)+ click on page two so they are both selected.

10. With both pages selected, apply the master page using (Option)+ Click (Mac) or (Alt)+ click (Win95) on the master page Bod-Body.

If you are applying a master page to a single page, not multiple pages, you can also click and drag the master page down over the body copy page.

Master Margin Guides

11. Now you are ready to create your design grid on your new master page.

Navigate to your new Bod-Body master page by double-clicking its icon—not its name—in the master page section of the Document Layout palette.

12. Open up **P**age>Master Guides and notice that the master margin guides have all been correctly set, 3 picas around the edges of the page.

Master Column Guides

13. To set up column guides, work in the same dialog box.

At the top of the dialog box, tell QuarkXPress you want five columns. The gutter width is fine at 1 pica.

14. Click OK and have a look at the beginning of your design grid, as you see it in Figure 9.10.

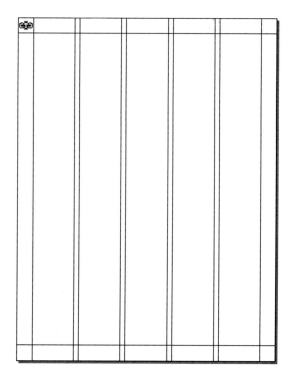

Figure 9.10

The basic design grid in place, with margin and column master guides.

Ruler Guides

15. You can also have ruler guides on your master pages.

Turn on the Measurements palette, if it isn't already active.

Pull down a ruler guide from the top ruler and set it at 11p6. This will be the mark where you will first put copy on the page, just below the newsletter nameplate.

> **Tip**
>
> **Drop Point Controls Ruler Guide Visibility**
>
> **If you release the ruler guide while the pointer is over a page, the ruler guide will only be visible on that page. If you make the release over the Pasteboard, the ruler guide will extend over the entire Pasteboard and on all the pages in a spread.**

Zero Point

16. Click and drag the zero point to the intersection of the top and left margin guide.

> **Tip**
>
> **Double-Click to Reset Zero Point**
>
> **To set the zero point back to its default location, double click the zero point box in the upper left hand corner of the QuarkXPress window. For non-facing pages, the default location is the upper-left corner of the page. For facing pages, the default is along the top edge of the pages where the two facing pages meet. You choose between these two defaults in Document Preferences.**

17. Now have a look at your body copy pages by double-clicking them in the Document Layout palette. You should see that they both have been outfitted with the design grid you set up on the Bod-Body master page.

The progress so far in setting up a design grid for the newsletter has been saved on the CD-ROM in a file named **09BASE01.QXT**.

Setting a Baseline Grid

There's one last element to be set in the design grid—your baseline leading grid.

Setting Baseline Grid Spacing

1. The standard leading for body copy text in the newsletter will be 13 points. That will be the spacing interval you use for the grid so the text can be locked to those gridlines.

To set the grid spacing, go to Document Preferences, ⌘+Y (Mac) or Ctrl+Y (Win95).

Select the Paragraph tab.

2. In the Baseline Grid section of the dialog box, Figure 9.11, type in a new **I**ncrement setting of `13 pt`. Again, the spacing of the baseline grid should match the leading of your body copy.

Notice that we are keeping the default setting for the **S**tart of the baseline grid. This setting should nearly always match the top master column guide. If you set it to a different location, the baseline gridlines will be out of sync with the other guides in your design grid.

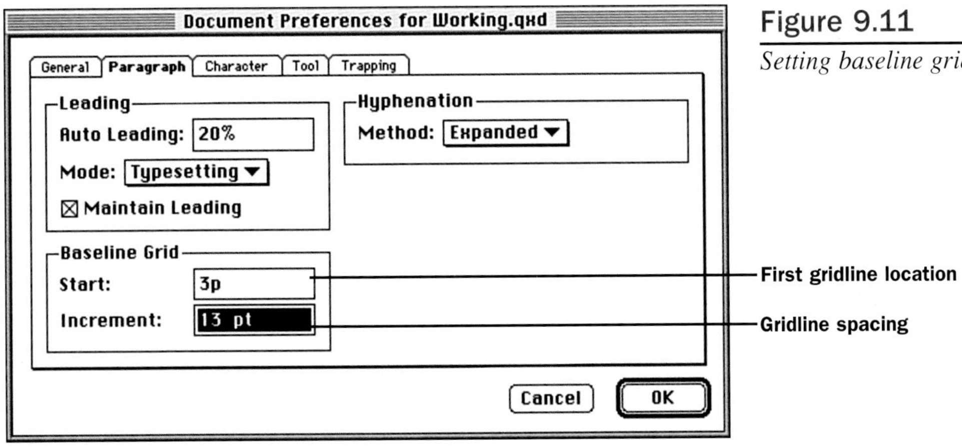

Figure 9.11
Setting baseline grid locations.

Displaying the Baseline Grid

3. As you know, you can turn the display of guides on and off by using the keyboard shortcut F7.

The baseline grid display command is similar, Option+F7 (Mac) or Ctrl+F7 (Win95).

Turn on the display now, just to see what your grid looks like. It should look like Figure 9.12.

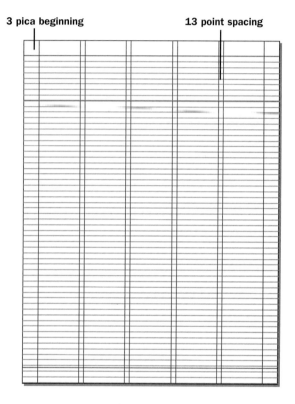

3 pica beginning   13 point spacing

Figure 9.12

Completed baseline grid.

Keep in mind that the baseline grid now being displayed on your screen has no effect on any of your text unless you take one additional step. You must turn on the Lock To Baseline Grid setting in the Paragraph Attributes dialog box for each paragraph you want to conform to the grid. (You can turn the setting on manually or you can include it in a style definition.)

In the next several steps of this exercise, you will experiment with the effect of the Lock To Baseline Grid setting and how it relates to the amount of leading you set in a paragraph.

Precise Positioning with the Design Grid

4. Draw out a rectangular text box across the second through fifth columns, snapping the top of the text box to the ruler guide (the one you drew on the Bod-Body master page). Make it about 7 or 8 picas tall.

Right away, you can see one of the benefits of a design grid. You can precisely draw out a page element, and it can be positioned exactly where you want it on the page without any additional steps with the Modify command or the Measurement palette.

Mismatched Leading and Grid Interval

5. The text box tool should have automatically reverted to the Content tool after you drew the text box and there should now be an insertion point blinking in it.

Get Text, ⌘+E (Mac) or Ctrl+E (Win95) and import the file **INTRO.TXT**. Make sure the checkbox to Include Style Sheets is checked on.

Notice that the lines of type are not on the grid. One or two might accidentally be sitting on their gridlines, but most are not.

Turning on Baseline Grid Locking

6. With the insertion point still blinking in the intro paragraph, go to Paragraph Attributes, ⌘+Shift+ F (Mac) or Ctrl+Shift+F (Win95).

In the Formats tab, turn on Lock to Baseline Grid. Click the Apply button.

Your text will probably spring into much wider spacing. It will look like Figure 9.13, with the lines shoved apart as they try to seek out and lock onto the gridlines. That's because the text is set at autoleading and that has forced the leading to be too big for the grid. The factory default for auto-leading is 120% and your type is at 12 points. Therefore, the leading is 14.4 points and that is too wide to fit on the baseline grid.

So, here's a key concept about how a baseline grid works. When a line of type doesn't naturally fall on the leading grid, QuarkXPress forces it down to the next available baseline.

Line pushed down to next gridline ⌐

This Month...Vegetables! In previous editions of the newsletter we've dealt			
with structural shrubbery and floral accents. Now, for those of you who crave ⌐			
just a bit more — here's your chance to grow fresh vegetables just outside your			
door. This month we'll plant the basics, best suited to this time of year. Next			
month we'll tackle more esoteric varieties.			

Figure 9.13

Extra leading forces baselines off the grid.

Matching Leading and Grid Interval

7. The Paragraph Attributes dialog box should still be open from the last step since you used the Apply button instead of OK.

Set the leading of this paragraph to 13 points and click **A**pply again.

The baselines of the lines of type all snap to the grid because the leading now matches their spacing.

Close this dialog box once you have the leading set correctly.

8. Finish formatting this paragraph before moving on to the columns of text below it.

Use the **F**ile>**A**ppend command and import the styles from the file we included in this chapter's work files, **NEWSLETTERSTYLES.QXT.**

If you need to brush up on the steps for importing styles with the Append command, you can review them in Chapter 7 in the section called "Importing Styles."

Deliberately Departing from the Grid

9. Apply the paragraph style called intro to this paragraph of text but use a slightly different technique than usual. Hold down the [Option] (Mac) or [Alt] (Win95) key while applying the style. That will force the style to take force completely, even if there is some local formatting in place.

The text will fall back off the grid again but will have normal spacing. That's because this style application technique allowed the style to turn off the Lock To Baseline Grid setting. The new style also set the leading to 14 points, which is just a bit off the baseline grid spacing.

As we build the rest of this page in the other exercises in this chapter, you will see that this slight leading adjustment makes a big difference in the look of the page.

All the other body copy on the page will be set at 13 point leading. By slightly opening up the leading on this introductory paragraph, you really call it to the reader's attention. It will contrast to the rest of the text, since it will be slightly off the leading grid.

That's an important concept about working with a design grid. If you generally adhere to the grid, you can use subtle departures from it to accomplish special design goals.

10. To complete the formatting of this paragraph, highlight the text "This Month...Vegetables!"

Format the text with the character style called head cutin.

11. Resize the intro text box by sliding its bottom edge up to the baseline gridline, just below the main part of the text.

As always, save your work in readiness for the next exercise.

Your formatted text should look like Figure 9.14. The newsletter, including all the steps so far in this chapter, has been saved on the CD-ROM in a file named **09BASE02.QXT.**

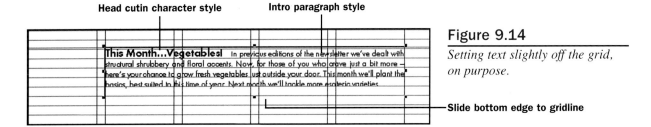

Head cutin character style

Intro paragraph style

This Month...Vegetables! In previous editions of the newsletter we've dealt with structural shrubbery and floral accents. Now, for those of you who crave just a bit more – here's your chance to grow fresh vegetables just outside your door. This month we'll plant the basics, best suited to this time of year. Next month we'll tackle more esoteric varieties.

Figure 9.14

Setting text slightly off the grid, on purpose.

Slide bottom edge to gridline

Setting Uneven Columns...Stretch Technique

One of the design features of this newsletter is the companion column, the narrow column down the left-hand side of the pages that holds the headlines for the stories.

The question is, how do you set uneven columns in QuarkXPress? As you know, it's easy to set columns in QuarkXPress by using the Modify command on a text box. (You used the technique in Chapter 5, in the section called "Setting Columns, Advanced Tabs, and Indents.") However, there's no way in QuarkXPress to set uneven columns within a text box. They all must be the same width.

The answer to the question is to use your design grid. In this exercise, and several other that follow, you will explore all the ways you can set uneven columns in QuarkXpress. In the process, you will learn a lot more about how to use your design grid to maintain consistency in a layout.

1. Draw out a rectangular text box just below the intro paragraph.

   Since Snap To Guides is still turned on from previous exercises, it should be no trouble to get the Rectangular Text Box tool crosshair to snap to the left column guide at 0 picas. Draw the box all the way from the left margin guide to the right margin guide at 45 picas.

   Make the box around 32 picas deep. We will make a final adjustment later in this exercise.

2. Use File>Get Text to import the next portion of text into this text box. You want the file called **BODY.TXT** and don't bother to turn on the Include Style Sheets checkbox.

3. Select all the text in the text box, ⌘+Ⓐ (Mac) or Ⓒⓣⓡⓛ+Ⓐ (Win95), and apply the paragraph style named body.

   You may need to Ⓞⓟⓣⓘⓞⓝ+click (Mac) or Ⓐⓛⓣ+ Click on the style name to remove local formatting applied automatically as you imported this plain text. The text should be formatted as Savoy, 11 points on 13 points leading.

   Notice, by the way, that the baselines of this text, since it is set at 13 points leading, have all snapped perfectly to the baseline gridlines.

Setting Equal "Unequal" Columns

4. Set this text box to 3 equal columns (that's right, equal columns, but we'll make them "unequal" in a few steps). To set the columns, as you will recall, you use the Text tab of the Modify command, ⌘+Ⓜ (Mac) or Ⓒⓣⓡⓛ+Ⓜ (Win95).

   Leave the standard 1 pica gutter between the columns. Your text box should also have 0 inset and should have a color of None, and runaround should be turned off, since you set those as defaults in the beginning steps of this chapter.

5. Turn on Show Invisibles, ⌘+Ⓘ (Mac) or Ⓒⓣⓡⓛ+Ⓘ (Win95) and navigate your text insertion point to just in front of the paragraph marker following the first word in the text, the word "lettuce."

   As always, adjust your view magnification so you can properly see what you are doing.

Inserting a Column Break

6. Force the text following the word lettuce into the adjacent columns by inserting a column break, Ⓡⓔⓣⓤⓡⓝ (Mac) or ⏎Enter (Keypad) (Win95).

Press the ⌦ (Mac) or ⌦ (Win95) key to remove any extra paragraph endings which now sit at the top of the second column.

7. Finish applying styles to this text.

   Apply the body first graph style to the current paragraph, the one that now sits at the top of the second column.

   Navigate back to the word lettuce and apply the paragraph style called head column.

   This word isn't misspelled, even though it might appear so. Highlight the letter b at the beginning of the word and apply the character style named leaf. This applies the Deanna Flowers font and turns that b into a pretty floral figure to decorate this headline.

Stretching Out "Unequal" Columns

8. Back out to a wide enough magnification to be able to see the entire top of the text block and a good bit of the pasteboard to the left of the page.

Turn off all baseline gridlines so you can get a better view of the page without clutter, Option+F7 (Mac) or Ctrl+F7 (Win95).

9. Click and hold for a beat the sizing handle on the left edge of the text box. Wait for a dark line to appear beneath the hand pointer (Mac) or a rectangle to appear around the hand pointer (Win95).

Tip

Customize Your Live Refresh Settings

This click and hold technique relates to a QuarkXPress feature called live refresh. You can customize the delay period for this feature, the amount of time you must hold your click before it kicks in, in the Interactive tab of the Application Preferences dialog box.

The following instructions will be easier to follow if you glance at Figure 9.15.

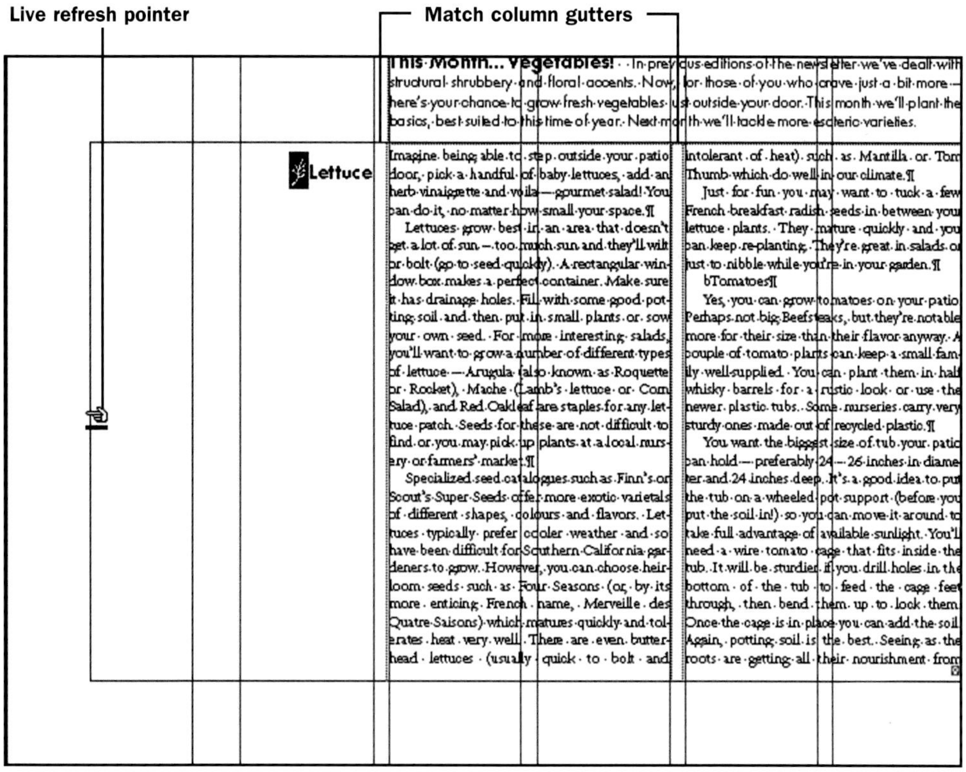

Live refresh pointer   Match column gutters

Figure 9.15
Stretching the text box into "unequal" columns.

When you are in this live refresh display mode, drag to the left on the sizing handle and match up the second and third columns of the text box with the design grid. By stretching the left side of the text box off the page and onto the pasteboard, you will, in effect, set this text box in unequal columns.

The right edge of the first column should line up on the right edge of the design grid's first column, putting the headline where it belongs in the narrow companion column.

The second column of the text box will then match the narrower second and third columns of the design grid. And the third text box column will line up on the fourth and fifth columns of the design grid.

It's almost impossible to get the columns to fit absolutely perfectly on the grid. The geometry of three columns into five columns just won't work out. However, it will be very close indeed, good enough for most design situations.

10. Again in live refresh display mode, click and drag up on the bottom of the lettuce text box until you have just the lettuce text showing.

As you raise the lower edge of the text box, you will find a point where the tomato headline disappears that goes with the next text block. The final words in the text box will be "while you're in your garden." You will also have a red overset text marker at the end of the text box, which should look like Figure 9.16 when you are done.

The point is, you want to keep the tomato headline out of this text box. You may need to insert a column break to make sure this happens.

● The progress so far on the newsletter layout in this chapter has been saved on the CD-ROM in a file named **09BASE03.QXT**.

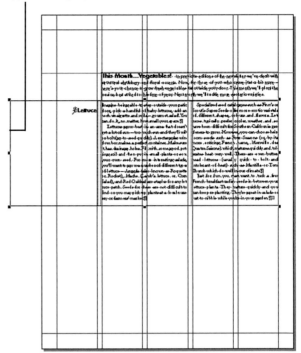

Approximately -9p2.7

Figure 9.16
The finished stretched "unequal" triple column approach.

Setting Uneven Columns...Linked Boxes

One way to build uneven columns is to simply split one of the columns off into its own text box. In this exercise, you build a text box to hold the companion column information, and another one to hold the other two columns of body copy. You control what appears in the first column text box by using a new box character.

Creating "Column" Text Boxes

1. You will need two text boxes to hold the first portion of the tomatoes article.

   Draw out a narrow box in the first column of the design grid. It should extend from the bottom of the box for the lettuce article down to the bottom margin guide.

   Draw a second box of the same height, covering the second through fifth columns of the design grid.

   The two boxes should look like Figure 9.17.

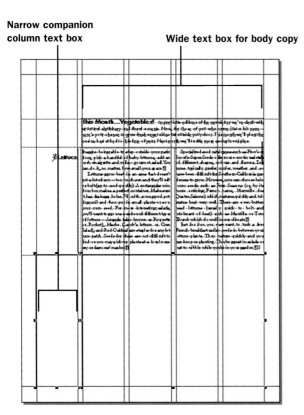

Narrow companion column text box

Wide text box for body copy

Figure 9.17

Two different width text boxes will be used to create unequal columns.

2. Use the Modify command to set two columns in the wide text box.

Linking Text Box "Columns"

3. As you know, to make text flow between your text box "columns," you must create a link between the text boxes.

   Select the Linking tool, holding down the (Option) (Mac) or (Alt) (Win95) key in order to keep the tool selected between uses. By doing so, it won't revert to the Content tool.

4. Click with the Linking tool on the lettuce article text box and it will become active, indicated by the animated dotted line around it.

   Click the narrow text box to indicate where the link should go.

   Notice that the overset text flows down into the narrow text box.

5. The Linking tool should still be selected, so click the wide text box one more time to flow the text there.

   Your Linked text boxes should look like Figure 9.18.

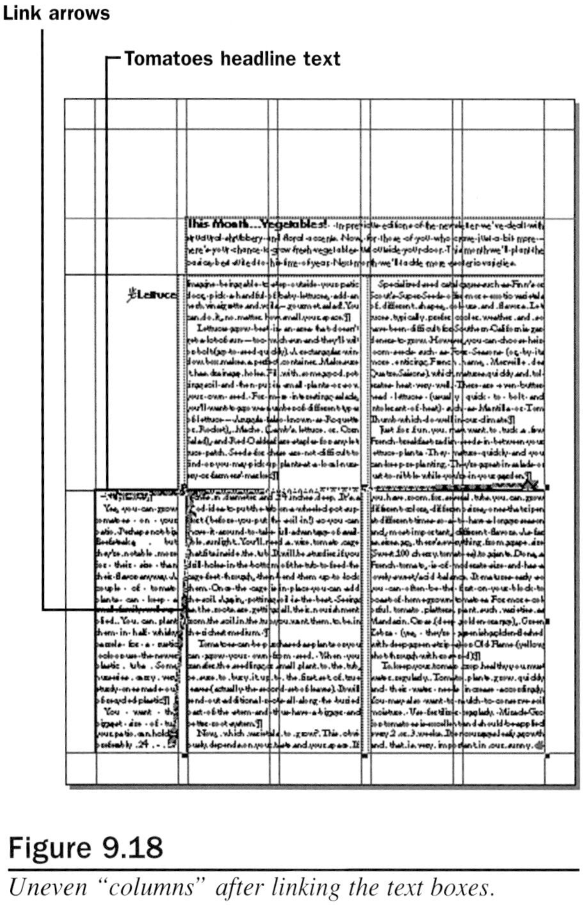

Link arrows

Tomatoes headline text

Figure 9.18

Uneven "columns" after linking the text boxes.

Breaking Text into Columns

6. The technique for forcing the text into proper positions in your text box columns is similar to the one you used in the last exercise.

Click the Contents tool to deactivate the Linking tool.

7. Navigate to a point just before the paragraph ending on the headline for the tomato article.

Insert a next box character (as opposed to the next column character you used for this purpose in the last exercise), ⏏Shift+Return (Mac) or ⏏Shift+↵Enter (Keypad) (Win95).

Remove the excess carriage return at the top of the wide text box.

Formatting Column Text

8. The formatting for the headline and body copy for the tomato article is identical to the formatting in the lettuce article.

Apply the paragraph style called body first graph to the first paragraph in the body copy, beginning with the words "Yes, you can."

Also, highlight the word "can" in the first line of the body copy and bold it.

Apply the paragraph style head column to the tomatoes headline.

Highlight the letter b at the beginning of the headline and format it with the character style named leaf.

Adjusting Text to Baseline Grid (Sizing Text Box)

9. It can sometimes be a bit touchy getting text to align to the baseline grid. Notice that the headlines on both articles so far have quite a bit of space above them.

Activate the display of the baseline grid, Option+F7 (Mac) or Ctrl+F7 (Win95).

You can see that the leaf character set in Deanna Flower on both the lettuce and tomato headlines is so big that it is forcing the headline down onto a lower baseline grid.

This is a characteristic of the way QuarkXPress deals with the first lines in text boxes. In fact, it's a law of the universe: Nothing can go outside the perimeter of a box—nothing at all, period. In this case, in order to keep everything inside the text box, the program forces the first line down to make the fit.

10. Work on the tomatoes article first.

Click and hold the top edge sizing handle for the narrow companion column text box until you are in live refresh mode.

Drag up, not too far, until the box is tall enough that the headline pops up to the next baseline above, as in Figure 9.19.

Adjusting Text to Baseline Grid (Adjacent Runaround)

11. The tomato headline was easy to adjust because there are two separate text boxes used to make the uneven columns and they could be aligned by resizing. The lettuce headline is a different story because all the text is contained in a single text box.

You can use the QuarkXPress runaround feature to push text around on a page. When runaround is set for an item—including a text box—that item will fend off any other text it overlaps.

Select the intro text box and go to the Runaround tab of the Modify command, ⌘+M (Mac) or Ctrl+M (Win95).

12. Change the runaround setting from None to Item and click OK.

13. Click and hold (to get live refresh mode) on the sizing handle for the upper edge of the lettuce story text box (not the intro story).

Drag the top edge of the lettuce story up and the intro text (which now has runaround set) will force the lettuce body copy down while the headline follows your upward text box stretching move.

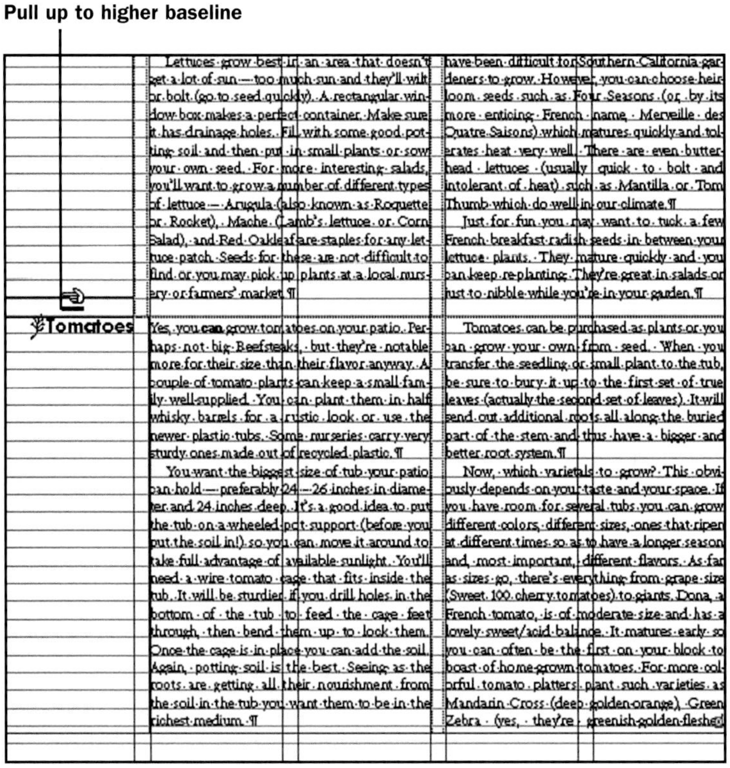

Figure 9.19

Pulling a headline text box up to fit the baseline grid.

A very small movement should force the body copy text down onto the correct baseline and allow the headline to rise up, as in Figure 9.20.

Tip

Runaround Facts—Standoff and Stacking Order

When you set a runaround, you also must take into account two important factors. There's a standoff for the distance text is kept from the runaround item and that standoff is adjustable, although here you are relying on the default of 1 pica. Also, runaround only works on text boxes that are in front of the item with the runaround.

You will work more with the runaround feature when you position graphics within some of your newsletter columns in Chapter 10.

Linking Text Between Pages

14. Draw out a text box at the top of the second page, one that duplicates your wide column text box for the tomatoes story. It should cover the design grid's second through fifth column, and the new text box should be set for two columns.

Try hard to simply remember how you did it last time, but if you need to do so, go ahead and review the steps earlier in this exercise.

15. Again following the same steps you used earlier in this exercise, select the Linking tool and forge a link between the tomatoes story and your new text box. The text flows onto the second page, like Figure 9.21.

16. Size the bottom edge of the text box so it doesn't contain any of the herb story. The last words in the text box should be "to prevent sunscald."

Adjust upward to force text down

Figure 9.20

Using runaround to force text onto the baseline grid.

Text block set to runaround

Text link onto second page

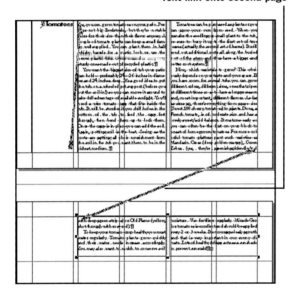

Figure 9.21

Taking the text onto the second page of the newsletter.

The newsletter, as it should look after all the exercises so far, has been saved on the CD-ROM in a file named **09BASE04.QXT**.

Setting Uneven Columns...Hanging Indent

If you only need two columns, not three, you can use an old trick for setting up companion columns. It's the same sort of formatting used to set bullet points, called a hanging indent.

It's called a hanging indent because the first line, the one that is often indented for the beginning of a paragraph, is given a negative indent so that it hangs out to the left of the main body of the paragraph. You use hanging indents for numbered steps like the ones for the exercises in this book, or for bulleted lists. You will build a hanging indent format for the first paragraph of the next article, and the hanging indent will hold a one word headline, positioning it in the companion column.

1. Draw out a new text box just below the existing one on the second page. It should be the width of all five columns on the design grid. It will have an X/Y position of 0p/7p7 and be 45 picas wide.

   Don't set any columns in this text box. You will be using the hanging indent and tabs to make text columns.

2. Use the Linking tool to make a path for the text to flow from the end of the tomatoes story into the new text box.

Hanging Indent Requires Two Tabs

3. If Show Invisibles isn't on, turn it on by using ⌘+I (Mac) or Ctrl+I (Win95).

   Notice that there are tabs before and after the "Herbs" headline.

4. Format the headline.

   Highlight the word "Herbs" and format it with the character style named head cutin.

Highlight the letter "b" just before "Herbs" and format it with the character style called leaf.

5. Open up the Tabs dialog box, ⌘+Shift+T (Mac) or Ctrl+Shift+T (Win95).

6. For the following steps, you will want to get to a high enough view magnification level to see the effects of your commands.

   You will be setting up your tabs and indents as you see them in Figure 9.22.

Setting Hanging Indents

7. Set the indents first.

   Click and drag the bottom margin icon, the one that controls the overall left indent for the paragraph. Position it on the right edge of the gutter—where you want the body copy of this paragraph.

   Position the first line indent icon all the way out on the left margin. Hold down the Shift key and click and drag the upper margin icon to the left, all the way out to the left margin.

   Click Apply to put your hanging indent margin into effect.

Setting Hanging Indent Tabs

8. Set a right tab on the left edge of the gutter. Click the Set button and then click Apply, which will bring the headline into position.

   Complete the hanging indent by following the same process, this time setting a left tab on the right edge of the gutter, shoving the first line of body copy into position.

   Click OK and have a look at your hanging indent headline.

   If you have trouble getting this hanging indent arrangement set correctly, a paragraph style has been included that will do an instant formatting job for you. It's called hanging first.

9. Format the two remaining body copy paragraphs in the story on herbs with the paragraph style called hanging body.

   Get back to a normal magnification so you can see the overall look of the hanging indent story, and so it will be easier to position the story on the baseline grid. Turn on the grid if it isn't already active.

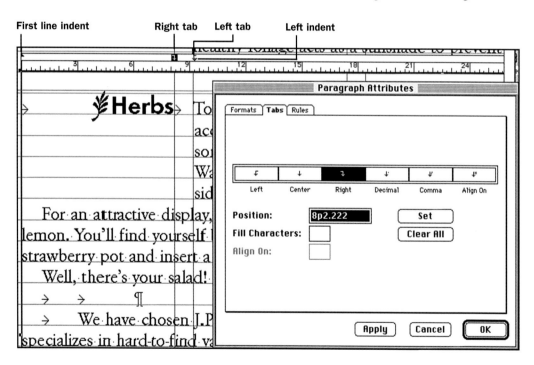

Figure 9.22

Setting up a hanging indent headline.

10. Using the live refresh mode, click and hold for a moment on the sizing handle on the top edge of the herbs story text box. Then drag it up until the first line of the story sits one baseline interval below the previous story.

11. When you turn off the baseline grid display, the whole page should now look like Figure 9.23.

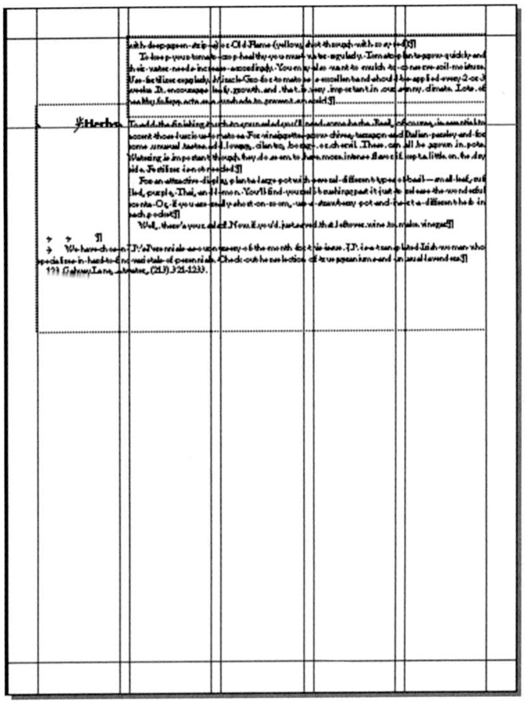

Figure 9.23

The second page of the newsletter, so far.

● The newsletter in its present form has been saved on the CD-ROM in a file named **09BASE05.QXT**.

Setting Uneven Columns...Anchored Headline Box

One of the great QuarkXpress tricks is to anchor an item to some text. It allows you to edit the text above that point without worrying about the position of a graphic or, in the case of this exercise, a headline. If you shorten or lengthen the text above the anchored item, it just slides up or down with the text as it changes position.

Creating the Headline Box

1. Begin by building a headline in its own text box.

   Draw out a small text box on the pasteboard just to the left of the nursery of the month story.

   It should be 8p6 wide and 4p8 high. You can set those dimensions in the Measurements palette or with the Modify command.

2. Type out the headline text, including a small letter n at the beginning, **nNursery of the Month**.

   Insert a carriage return after the "y" in "Nursery" so the headline is in two paragraphs.

3. Format both paragraphs of the headline with the paragraph style called head column.

   Select the small letter "n" at the beginning of the headline text and format it with the character style named leaf.

   Your headline text box should look like Figure 9.24.

Anchoring the Headline

4. Select the headline text box with the Item tool and Copy it to the Clipboard.

5. Switch to the Content tool and click an insertion point between the two tabs, in the empty paragraph between the herbs story and the nursery of the month story.

6. Paste the headline text box.

Tip

Anchor Ritual: First Item and Then Content

Just remember, anchoring always works exactly the same way. First you use the Item tool, then you use the Content tool. You first select the item with the Item tool and copy it to the Clipboard. Then you move to the Content tool and make a text insertion point before you Paste the item into place.

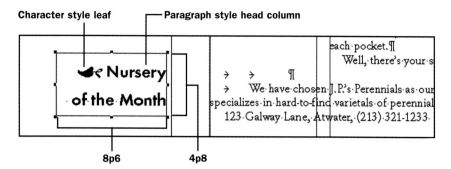

Character style leaf   Paragraph style head column

8p6   4p8

Figure 9.24

The headline text box before being anchored to the body copy text.

Setting an Anchored Item Hanging Indent

7. You need the same kind of hanging indent you used in the last exercise, except this time you are "hanging" an anchored text box.

 We saved the hanging indent setup you used in the last exercise in a paragraph style.

 Format the first two paragraphs of this nursery of the month story with the paragraph style called hanging first.

 Format the last paragraph with the paragraph style called body.

8. Use the Modify command to set the headline text box to Ascent rather than Baseline alignment with the text in which it is anchored.

 You may also need to slightly resize the width of the headline text box so its right edge sits squarely on the left side of the gutter.

 Your completed anchored text box headline should look like Figure 9.25.

If you have had any trouble following all the steps, you can open the version of the newsletter that has been saved for you on the CD-ROM in a file named **09BASE06.QXT**.

Setting a Framed Box onto the Grid

Many people call the title of a newsletter the masthead even though its proper name is the nameplate. However, many newsletters do include a masthead, which is actually the publishing information. It's common to include this information in a box on an inside page of the newsletter. In fact, that's one of many, many situations where you will want to put a box around some text. It's a very easy thing to do in QuarkXPress, as you'll learn in this exercise.

See how much you remember from the first several text importing and formatting steps in this exercise. You have done each of these steps many times by now and we're not even going to prompt you with keyboard shortcuts or menu commands.

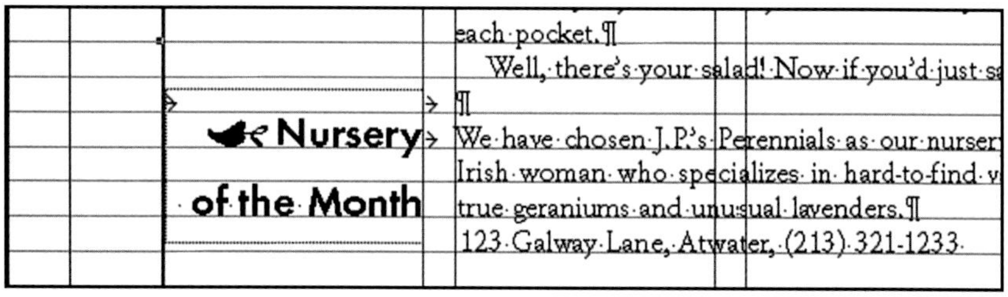

Figure 9.25

Completed anchored text box headline.

Text Handling Review

1. On page 2, draw out a text box across the second through fifth columns, extending approximately 16 picas high above the bottom margin guide.

2. Set the text box for two columns.

3. Get the text for this box by importing the file **MASTHEAD.TXT**.

4. Select all of the text in the box and format it with the paragraph style named info body.

5. Format the headlines with the paragraph style called info head. The headlines are the lines "The Patio Gardener is published monthly," and "The Patio Gardener."

6. Insert a column break so the headlines are each at the top of their own column.

   When you are done with these first several steps, your masthead text should look like Figure 9.26.

Setting the Text Box Frame

7. With the masthead text box still selected, open up the Modify command, ⌘+Ⓜ (Mac) or Ⓒtrl+Ⓜ (Win95).

8. In the Text tab, set the inset to 4 points.

   The inset is the distance QuarkXPress will force between the inside edge of the box frame and the contents of the box, in this case the text although it could also be a graphic.

Setting the Text Box Frame Width

9. In the Frame tab, set the width of the frame to 1.5 points.

   Click OK to finish the frame.

10. Use live refresh to size the text box so it is just high enough to hold its first column of text, which is the tallest of the two.

    When you are finished, the masthead should look like Figure 9.27. We've turned off Show Invisibles.

The progress so far on the newsletter has been saved on the CD-ROM in a file named **09BASE07.QXT**.

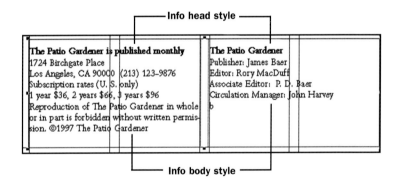

Info head style

Info body style

Figure 9.26
Masthead text box, ready to be framed.

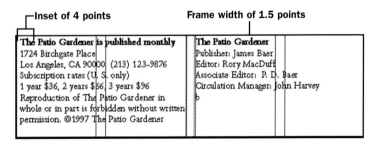

Inset of 4 points

Frame width of 1.5 points

Figure 9.27
Finished text box frame.

Baseline Adjust

You probably noticed the letter "b" on the last line of the second column of the text box. That's going to be a floral decoration for the newsletter masthead. You already know how to format the character in the decorative dingbat font, but in this exercise, you will learn more about how to position the character on its line. The process you will use to do that is called baseline adjustment.

1. Magnify the view of the text box so you'll be able to work accurately.

2. Select the character "b" in the masthead text box and format it with the character style named leaf.

3. Size this character to a very large 110 points.

4. To solve the resulting colliding text problem, right align this paragraph, ⌘+⬆Shift+R (Mac) or Ctrl+⬆Shift+R (Win95).

   You now need to adjust this big floral character down in the text box. It should flow around a portion of the masthead text, but also run down into the empty space in the second column.

   You do that with Baseline adjustment.

Dialog Box Baseline Adjustment

5. You can make very precise baseline adjustments using a dialog box, where you can type in exact locations down to fractions of points.

With the floral character selected, open the Character Attributes dialog box, ⌘+⬆Shift+D (Mac) or Ctrl+⬆Shift+D (Win95).

6. Set the baseline adjustment of the floral character at -15.5. As you might expect, a negative number adjusts the character down in relation to the baseline.

   At this point, you could click the Apply button and experiment with various baseline adjustments. However, there's a better way to do this kind of experimentation.

   Click OK.

Keyboard Baseline Adjustment

7. With the floral character still selected, continue adjusting the baseline down. Press ⌘+⬆Shift+Option+- (Mac) or Ctrl+⬆Shift+Alt+((Win95).

   Each key press of this command moves the selected text down one point in relation to the baseline. To move up one point at a time, use the same key combination except with + (Mac) or) (Win95).

8. Adjust the character down until it seems right to you. We ended up at -20.5 baseline adjustment and it looked like Figure 9.28. (We've turned off Show Invisibles and Show Guides.)

The Patio Gardener is published monthly
1724 Birchgate Place
Los Angeles, CA 90000 (213) 123-9876
Subscription rates (U. S. only)
1 year $36, 2 years $66, 3 years $96
Reproduction of The Patio Gardener in whole or in part is forbidden without written permission. ©1997 The Patio Gardener

The Patio Gardener
Publisher: James Baer
Editor: Rory MacDuff
Associate Editor: P. D. Baer
Circulation Manager: John Harvey

Right aligned
110 points
-20.5 baseline adjustment

Figure 9.28
The baseline adjusted floral figure.

> **Tip**
>
> **Set Baseline Adjustments in Styles**
>
> **As with any character attribute, you can include baseline adjustments in character or paragraph styles. In fact, every time you have applied the style named leaf in this chapter, you have been applying a baseline adjustment.**

So far, your newsletter design should look like the one we've saved on the CD-ROM in a file named **09BASE08.QXT**.

Old Style Figures

As we indicated in the Design Notes section of this chapter, professional typesetters often replace the regular numeral characters with special old style numbers. There are several sets of numbers in the body copy of the newsletter that would benefit from using these "lowercase" numbers and, in this exercise, you will see how they improve the look of the newsletter.

1. Navigate to the nursery of the month story and select the numbers in the Galway Lane address.
2. Format the numbers with the font Savoy Small Caps.

   Often, the old style figures in a font family are contained in the version of the font that also has specially-built lowercase all caps characters.
3. Select the phone number in that same line.
4. Format the phone number with the font Savoy Small Caps.

   Have a look at Figure 9.29 to see the difference between regular numerals on the top and old style figures on the bottom. There's a pretty big difference, isn't there?

   The reason there's such a difference between the regular and old style figure forms of the number characters is shown in Figure 9.30. The regular numbers (top) stick up on the line because they sit completely above the baseline. The old style figures (bottom) look more like their neighboring characters because they act like lowercase letters, some of them even having descenders. Descenders are the "tails" of letters such as "p" or "g."
5. Go through the remainder of the copy now and format the rest of the numbers as old style figures.

   That would include the numbers in the phrase "2 or 3 weeks" in the tomatoes story.

   Don't miss the numbers in the name of the tomatoes, "Sweet 100."

   Also in the tomatoes story is the measurement information for the tubs, in the second paragraph.

   And, finally, format all the numbers in the framed masthead text box as old style figures. Notice, in the phone number, the old-style numbers "6" and "8" have ascenders, meaning they are as tall as capital letters, similar to a lowercase letter "h" or "d."

The progress so far on the redesigned menu has been saved on the CD-ROM in a file named **09BASE09.QXT**.

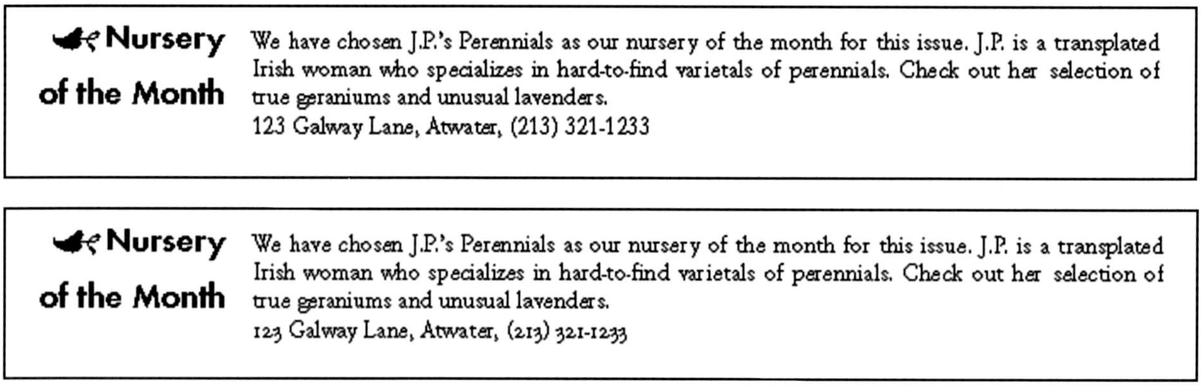

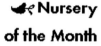

Nursery of the Month
We have chosen J.P.'s Perennials as our nursery of the month for this issue. J.P. is a transplated Irish woman who specializes in hard-to-find varietals of perennials. Check out her selection of true geraniums and unusual lavenders.
123 Galway Lane, Atwater, (213) 321-1233
Nursery of the Month
We have chosen J.P.'s Perennials as our nursery of the month for this issue. J.P. is a transplated Irish woman who specializes in hard-to-find varietals of perennials. Check out her selection of true geraniums and unusual lavenders.
123 Galway Lane, Atwater, (213) 321-1233

Figure 9.29

Before (top) and after (bottom) using old style figures.

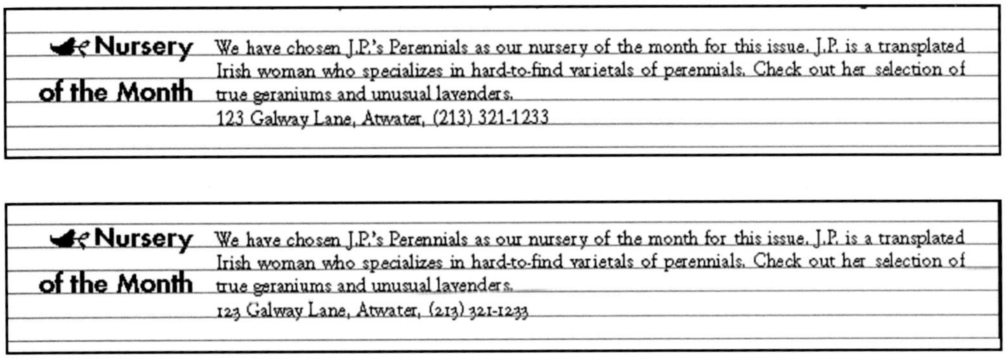

Nursery

of the Month

We have chosen J.P.'s Perennials as our nursery of the month for this issue. J.P. is a transplanted Irish woman who specializes in hard-to-find varietals of perennials. Check out her selection of true geraniums and unusual lavenders.

123 Galway Lane, Atwater, (213) 321-1233

Nursery

of the Month

We have chosen J.P.'s Perennials as our nursery of the month for this issue. J.P. is a transplanted Irish woman who specializes in hard-to-find varietals of perennials. Check out her selection of true geraniums and unusual lavenders.

123 Galway Lane, Atwater, (213) 321-1233

Figure 9.30

A baseline view of regular (top) numerals versus old style figures (bottom).

Building a Fancy Nameplate out of Type...Typesetting Review

In this exercise, you will use baseline adjustment, paragraph rules, indents, and kerning to create a graphically ornate nameplate for the newsletter strictly out of type.

The point of this exercise is to demonstrate how you can combine a variety of very different effects to create an overall graphic look. As a guide, you are aiming to create a nameplate that looks like Figure 9.31, which is located at the end of this exercise. You can see it in wide view in Figure 9.1 at the beginning of the chapter.

None of the text formatting features in this exercise are new to you. This exercise is a review of basic QuarkXPress keyboard shortcuts and menu commands you'll need to know in your daily work as a designer. We'll be giving you tasks, but not providing super-precise step-by-step instructions.

1. Draw out a text box at the top of the first page.

   It should extend from the left to the right margin guides (45 picas wide).

   The text box should be completely above and not touching the intro text (which has a runaround set on it). Also, it should be around 12 picas tall and extend up above the top margin guide (although we'll adjust the size and exact position later).

2. Import the text from the file **NAMEPLATE.TXT** into this text box.

3. Working at a high enough magnification that you can get a good view of your text, format the first of these two paragraphs of text.

   Set the name "Patio Gardener" and its preceding space in Function Heavy at 63/72, 63 points high on 72 points of leading.

   (Win95) Fonts work a bit differently in Windows 95 compared to the Macintosh. On the PC, in order to get Function Heavy, you select FunctionLH and style it as bold.

   Set the letters "he" in Function Heavy, 36/72.

   The letter "a" should be set in Deanna Flowers, 128/72.

4. You will need some tracking and kerning in this title paragraph in order to make it look right, and to close it up enough to fit on a single line.

   If you need to temporarily widen the text block in order to access all the text in this paragraph, go ahead. You can resize when the formatting has been completed.

   We applied -6 units of tracking to the words "Patio Gardener." Heavy display text at a large size like this often requires tracking.

5. Tighten the kerning between the letter "h" and the floral character we are using as a stylized "T." They should snug in tight together.

We ended up with kerning of -22 units for this pair of characters.

Also, other character pairs need tightening, notably the space between the "t" and the "i" in "Patio."

Take care to kern the capital "P" to the left so that its stem lines up with the edge of the second column master guide.

6. Format the second paragraph of the nameplate in Function Heavy as well, 16.5 points on 26 points leading.

7. Indent the second paragraph by at least 3 picas (we used 3p3) so it is lined up on the right with the outside edge of the stem on the letter "r" above it.

8. Adjust the baseline of the floral figure down so it really looks like it is replacing a letter "T" and the most bulbous part of its lower portion is mimicking the arch of the letter "h."

9. Adjust the baseline of the second paragraph so it centers vertically on and nestles into the sweeping curve of the floral figures lower portion. We settled on a +2 baseline adjustment.

You would usually use reduced leading to accomplish this same task but for this exercise we are using baseline leading to give you experience with that typographical tool.

10. Add a rule above the second paragraph.

It should be a 1-point wide rule set to indents mode.

You may need to experiment with the offset and indents. We ended up with a 1p6 offset with a 1 pica left indent and a 1p3 right indent.

Tip

Use Fixed Offset for Paragraph Rules

QuarkXPress, by default, offers to let you set the offset of a paragraph rule by percentage. However, it is almost always better to use a specific amount of offset. It's the same concept as using fixed leading instead of autoleading—both can work, but with a fixed amount of offset (or leading) you can be much more precise. Also, if a rule above has been set with a percentage of offset, the rule disappears when the paragraph sits at the top of a text box (or at the bottom of a text box for a rule below).

11. Select the nameplate text block with the Item tool and use the arrow keys to nudge it into final position.

You may also need to adjust the text block vertical height in order to work out this positioning move.

The upper left point of the floral character should be set right into the inside corner of the left and top margin guides.

The final newsletter, without the graphics you will be adding in the next chapter, has been saved on the CD-ROM in a file named **09BASE10.QXT**.

Figure 9.31

A close-up of the completed nameplate.

Summary

The tools of which you learned in this chapter—master page guides, snap to guides, lock to baseline grid—will help you structure your pages. Page-level structural integrity improves the communication power of your designs. They provide visual cues to the reader where to focus attention and as well as the logical reading order of the information on a page. In addition, page structure gives you a visual consistency that permits you to create contrast through subtle rule breaking, a way to attract attention to especially important content.

Review It

As a review of what you have learned in this chapter, please answer the following questions.

1. Thinking about structuring pages in QuarkXPress, name at least three of the half-dozen visual organization tools you learned about in this chapter.

2. What are the three essential elements you need to make a baseline grid work for you?

3. Name three special-purpose types of typefaces you used in this chapter.

4. Name the main ways you can adjust the horizontal and vertical position of a character in relation to its neighbor.

5. What is the purpose of the pre-hyphen letters in the name of a master page?

6. What are the four techniques for setting uneven width columns?

7. What power does an item have if it has a runaround set?

8. How long must you wait before Live Refresh kicks in?

9. What does the inset setting do when setting content in a box?

10. What is the "law of the universe" for QuarkXPress boxes?

Check It

Multiple Choice

Please circle the correct answer for each of the following questions.

1. A hanging indent always has _____.

    a. one tab

    b. offset first line indent

    c. a dingbat or number

    d. all of the above

2. To anchor a text or picture box in a text box, what tools do you need, and in what order?

    a. Text box, then Content

    b. Content, then Text box

    c. Item, then Content

    d. Content, then Item

3. When you turn on Show Baseline Grid _____.

    a. it is in effect

    b. you can click and drag the interval

    c. it is on display

    d. all of the above

4. The main difference between regular and old style figures is _____.

    a. baseline position

    b. weight

    c. serifs

    d. all of the above

5. You generally set the same amount in _____.

    a. box inset and rule offset

    b. kerning and baseline adjustment

    c. body copy leading and baseline grid interval

    d. all of the above

6. You generally match up _____.

    a. first gridline and top margin

    b. fixed leading and autoleading

    c. baseline grid interval and autoleading percentage

    d. runaround amount and baseline grid interval

7. In order to set text box "columns," you must use what tools?

    a. Linking tool, one of text box tools

    b. New column tool, Zoom tools

    c. Item tool, Content tool

    d. All of the above

8. In order to apply a master page to a body page, you _____.

    a. ⬆Shift + click

    b. Ctrl + click (Mac) or Ctrl + click (Win95)

    c. Option + click (Mac) or Alt + click (Win95)

    d. all of the above

9. The default percentage for autoleading is _____.

    a. 120% of font size

    b. 125% of font size

    c. 120% of baseline grid interval

    d. 125% of baseline grid interval

10. If you need three or more "columns," you can use _____.

    a. modify dialog on text box

    b. linked text boxes

    c. stretch columned text box

    d. all of the above

True or False

Please circle *T* or *F* to indicate whether the statement is true or false.

T   F   **1.** The title of a newsletter is called the masthead.

T   F   **2.** You normally set the baseline grid interval to equal the distance of the top margin.

T   F   **3.** If you set preferences to Delete Changes, applying a new master page will wipe out any old master page items.

T   F   **4.** You can set baseline adjustments in character and paragraph styles.

T   F   **5.** To get the most use out of master guides and ruler guides you should always turn on Snap To Guides.

T   F   **6.** You set guides on a default master page when you start a new Document.

T   F   **7.** Setting a baseline grid interval will cause lines to snap to the grid intervals.

T   F   **8.** You can set master guides from a body copy page.

T   F   **9.** The contents of an anchored text box can be formatted and edited.

T   F   **10.** The first line of a hanging indent paragraph is set with a negative indent.

Design It

Many people, when they first hear about the concept of a design grid, see the grid as a constraint. However, instead of limiting your design, it helps you experiment with your design. You can now find the best way to lay out your elements for most effective communication. Try some experiments yourself right now.

■ Select three magazine advertisements—each very different from the other in terms of style. Photocopy them. Use a ruler to try to understand what underlying design grid was used in producing the ads.

■ Cut apart the graphic elements of each ad and try to reassemble them in a different way. Experiment with positioning of elements based on your view of the original designer's design grid.

■ Open up QuarkXPress and create three new master pages, each one set up with master guides and ruler guides that duplicate the design grids from the ads.

■ Building on those three new master page design grids, construct a new design for the newsletter (or any one of the projects from previous chapters).

Idea Generator

Advice—Portfolio as Starting Point

Mike Cotterell: My experience is that prospective customers are more interested in talking about their job than looking at a portfolio. I do, however, find a portfolio of projects that contain interesting ideas is useful both for discussion with customers and for ideas when I'm stuck in a pit. I actively scavenge for junk mail and ask colleagues to give it to me when they get more interesting items than I do.

Elyse Chapman: The last time my portfolio was requested and I brought it to a face-to-face meeting, before I could offer to show my work, we began discussing the project at hand. I started tossing out ideas and thumbnail sketches, and they never got around to asking to see the portfolio. As the meeting was ending I finally saw a chance to offer it to them and they replied, "No, thanks, that's fine. We can see you know what you're doing."

I should add, however, that during the course of the meeting I sensed I might not get a chance to do a formal portfolio presentation. With that in mind, I looked for opportunities to pull out a few samples and use them as visual aids, to help me make some point. When discussing, for example, a particular color, I'd pull out one piece or another asking, "Is that the red you're after or something more like I used here?" I wasn't formally showing the pieces, but I ensured they saw at least some of my best stuff.

David Rozansky: The best use of a portfolio is to spur clients with new ideas. It is more a catalog of possibilities than a proof of ability. For non-publishing-industry work, such as a newsletter design for a corporation, I find the client has no idea what they really want, and so my portfolio also acts as an idea generator. It also shows the client that they have no one on staff who can handle the project, although they may have thought so before seeing me.

Exercise—Build an Ideas Portfolio

As these professionals have indicated, there are actually two purposes for a portfolio—particularly if you are working freelance. One purpose is to show off your skills. In addition, your portfolio can be a source for ideas and discussion when you are working with a client.

So, for this Portfolio Builder exercise build a collection of samples.

- Collect commercial graphics pieces that you think are effective or contain striking or creative graphic approaches—menus, handbills, newsletters, business forms, play programs, sporting event programs, annual stockholder reports, calendars, price sheets.

- Go through all the direct mail you receive looking for effective design elements. Is there something interesting there in the way of a headline, a type treatment, die cut paper, central graphic image, a melding of type and graphics that might help you explain a particular concept to a client?

- As you collect, focus particularly on type treatments—use of color, pleasing typeface combinations, unusual or striking typefaces that help communicate an idea or a business identity.

- Search out paper samples, often available at no charge or nominal expense from paper manufacturers. In addition, collect interesting treatments of paper from finished pieces—deckled edges, die cuts, paper textures of all sorts.

Let's be clear about one thing. We aren't suggesting that you pass someone else's work off as your own. That's not the point. The point is, by having a portfolio of samples to show a client or prospective employer during an interview, you can demonstrate how you can think through their challenges. You can use the samples as a communications tool, examples of the kinds of approaches that the client might like or dislike. Even though you don't have a bulging portfolio of professional work, you can use a portfolio of samples to illustrate how you might approach a job in a professional manner. You are illustrating yourself by showing how you think through a communications challenge.

Mike Cotterell: I still remember interviewing a candidate years ago who arrived with a superb portfolio of work. We didn't question him much about it but just took it at face value. We were on the point of selecting him for the job when his references arrived. He had given his boss as a reference.

The boss said "I have seen the work that he is presenting to you. None of it is, in fact, his own. It is all mine." Unfortunately, the boss wasn't looking for a job.

Working With Graphics Files

What You Will Learn

You have already imported graphics files into QuarkXPress—for the stationery file, for the price list, and the menus. In this chapter, you will be getting more practice with that important skill and gaining new insight into how QuarkXPress helps you manage graphics files during layout. In the next few pages, you will learn about:

➤ The two main graphic file types used in desktop publishing: EPS and TIFF

➤ Keeping graphics and other items handy in a library for quick access during production

➤ Sizing pictures and picture boxes

➤ Cropping pictures

➤ Framing pictures

➤ Forcing text to run around the edges of a graphic box

➤ Creating fancy runarounds so the text follows the edge of a complicated object in a graphic

➤ Rotating pictures

➤ Controlling the display of graphics as you work

Adding Pictures to the Newsletter

Part IV

Adding Graphics

Figure 10.1

The front (left) and back (right) of the two-page newsletter, as it will look when you are finished with the exercises in this chapter.

Design Notes

Check out Figure 10.1 and you'll see that adding a couple of graphics to your pages makes a big difference in the look of a piece.

Part of the reason the added graphics make such a big difference, in this case, is their interaction with the text. After all, that's what QuarkXPress is for—electronic pasteup, combining text and graphics together into great looking pages.

The geranium on the second page has been set into place with a runaround, a concept that you were exposed to in the last chapter. The runaround, set to the box containing the picture, has pushed the text away so that the picture sits on the design grid and maintains the columns of text.

On the front page, you might at first think that we've fractured the design grid you worked so hard to create in the last chapter. In fact, however, the front page still adheres closely to your system of master page guides. The bottom of the tomato graphic has been cropped to the bottom margin, for example. More importantly, the text that follows the outline of the tomatoes stays strictly within the column guides.

This tomato runaround is a good example of one thing we discussed in the last chapter—a design grid can provide a source of attention-getting contrast in a design. The vertical stripes of text interact with the jagged outline of the tomatoes, and both elements are the stronger for it. That effect wouldn't be possible without the underlying structural foundation of the design grid—much more powerful than a scattered hodge podge of elements tossed haphazardly onto the page.

Getting Set Up

Copy all the files for this chapter from the CD-ROM to a work area on your hard drive. They are all in the **Steps** folder in the folder labeled **10**.

You will need to have installed on your computer the same fonts we used in the last chapter. They are Deanna Flowers, Function, Function Heavy, Savoy, and Savoy SC+OsF.

Each exercise in this chapter builds on the previous one. Except where we've indicated otherwise, you should save your work at the end of each exercise so you can pick up where you left off at the beginning of the next exercise.

You should have the same defaults in place as the last chapter. If there's some question in your mind, you might want to go back and review the setting up section in Chapter 9.

Introducing...Two Types of Graphics

One of QuarkXPress's great strengths is its ability to help you combine type with imported graphics—a piece of clip art, a stock photograph, your own scan of a photograph, a drawing from Illustrator or FreeHand, or a digital painting from Photoshop, just to name a few possibilities.

That means you must deal with a variety of graphic files, potentially with dozens of different file formats. It can, at times, feel like a cocktail party at the United Nations—with no interpreters.

However, all the various graphic file formats you ordinarily come across can be boiled down to two basic kinds—resolution-dependent and resolution-independent. I've chosen these terms because they suggest the practical results you achieve with each sort of graphics image. You will also hear resolution-dependent graphics referred to as *bit-mapped*, *paint*, or *raster* images. Resolution-independent graphics are often called *object-oriented*, *draw*, or *vector* images.

Preventing Jaggies with Resolution Independence

If you run a resolution-independent graphic through a laser printer or the high resolution imagesetter at your service bureau, you get a smooth reproduction with no jaggies, no matter how much you magnify the graphic. As you can see in Figure 10.2, object-oriented images yield resolution-independent results.

Figure 10.2

A resolution-independent eye at two magnifications.

You produce resolution-independent files when you work with drawing programs such as Illustrator and FreeHand. (The boxes, lines, circles, and polygons you create in QuarkXPress are also resolution-independent.)

Resolution-independent images are not stored as a bunch of dots; they are stored on disk as a set of equations, sometimes called vectors because the equations describe vectors—lines that add up to arcs, circles, and boxes. The equations for each intricate line, curve, and angle in the image can be sent right to the printing device to appear on paper or film at the device's full resolution. So, when you enlarge a resolution-independent graphic and then send the result to the imagesetter or laser printer, the output device uses these resolution-independent vectors or equations to draw a crisp new version of the graphic at whatever size might be needed. It is resolution-independent because the resolution of the final output is independent of the size of the graphic. You can pretty much adjust the size of a resolution-independent graphic within QuarkXPress in any way you like with no harm done. The same is not true of a bitmapped, resolution-dependent graphic.

The main resolution-independent format in desktop publishing is *EPS*, which stands for *Encapsulated PostScript file*. EPS files contain PostScript code. A company named Adobe invented PostScript, the same company that makes the main competitor to QuarkXPress, PageMaker, as well as Illustrator and Photoshop. The PostScript page-description language virtually dominates the desktop publishing market and provides the central technology for the laser printers and imagesetters in most DTP applications.

Please take note that you *can* bundle up a resolution-dependent image inside an EPS file. The part of the EPS file that is resolution-dependent stays that way. It's just that the EPS format was designed primarily for the purpose of containing resolution-independent PostScript descriptions of graphic information.

Your computer can't use the PostScript graphic itself to create an image on the screen. So, when you see an EPS file positioned on a QuarkXPress page, the image you see on-screen isn't the same as the vectors transmitted to the laser printer or imagesetter. The EPS actually contains, encapsulated within the file, a representation of what's in the file. It's a screen preview, there so you can see what you are doing when you position the graphic on a page.

The Windows and Macintosh forms of EPS graphics use slightly different file formats to accomplish this screen preview business. The underlying PostScript is the same for both platforms but not the previews. This difference in screen previews is why EPS graphics exchanged between Mac and Windows platforms often look like a plain gray box on-screen, but print just fine to a PostScript printer. The Mac EPS preview (PICT file format) is usable only on a Mac, and the Windows EPS preview (TIFF or WMF file format) works only in Windows. Many graphics programs give you the option to save an EPS with a variety of preview formats to help you transport EPS images between different types of computers.

If you are printing an EPS graphic to a non-PostScript printer, QuarkXPress tries to print your page using the screen preview—a poorer quality, resolution-dependent file format. If you are printing an EPS PostScript image to a PostScript printer, the preview image is purely for on-screen display and isn't used for printing.

Working with Resolution-Dependent Images

Scanners create resolution-dependent graphics, as do paint programs such as Photoshop and Fractal Painter. These programs produce files made up of dots rather than vectors. The total number of dots that make up any particular resolution-dependent image is fixed and constant. Therefore, when you magnify the image, the dots get bigger and farther apart. In other words, the quality of the image depends on its resolution.

For this reason, resolution-dependent images produce quite different results from EPS graphics. If you blow up resolution-dependent graphics into larger sizes, their fixed-resolution dots can look lumpy and ugly, like a badly damaged tile mosaic. Take a look at the eye in Figure 10.3, and then at the accompanying close-up. Both images have the same number of dots devoted to the eyeball, but as you might expect, the magnified image reveals those dots to the…well, to the naked eye.

The main resolution-dependent file format in desktop publishing is TIFF. TIFF stands for Tag Image File Format. Most scans are saved in TIFF file format, for example. High-end painting and photo-retouching programs such as Photoshop commonly use TIFF for graphics. TIFF files are capable of conveying simple black-and-white picture information, more complex shades of gray, and colors. Gray-scale files have up to 256 levels of gray. Color TIFF files are…in color.

TIFF files, although resolution-dependent, are capable of extremely fine resolution—if you are willing to pay the price in hard disk space. Highly detailed TIFF images create huge files. The more visual information in a graphic file (resolution, grayscales, and colors), the bigger it will be.

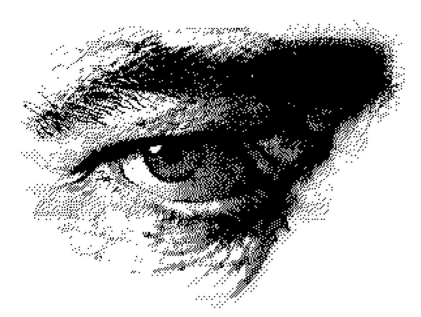

Figure 10.3

A resolution-dependent eye, from a paint program graphic.

Often, resolution is expressed in dots per inch. This business of dots per inch can be confusing. Keep in mind that, in this section, we are discussing the resolution of a file when it arrives in QuarkXPress. That's not the same as the dots you get when you take the pages containing these graphics to a commercial printer for final production on a printing press.

Those dots in a magazine picture or illustration are called *halftones*. That topic is another discussion, involving the concepts of line screens, dots, pixels, cells, and dot gain. All these topics are covered in Chapters 14 and 15.

Tip

Use EPS or TIFF Files for Professional Results

No matter the source for the images in your publication or how they are originally created, you should use EPS and TIFF graphics files wherever possible. These two formats have become solidly entrenched as the standards for professional desktop publishing. You may encounter a virtual alphabet soup of other file formats (PNT, PCX, WMF, CGM, BMP, to name a few). The main thing to remember is that QuarkXPress works best when outputting PostScript language to a printer or imagesetter. QuarkXPress has been optimized to do that job.

Tip

EPS/TIFF Except...With A Non-PostScript Printer

On the other hand, there's one time you would consider ignoring this advice. That's if you are producing a job you know will be output on a non-PostScript printer—something like an office newsletter, where your artwork will be produced on a Hewlett Packard PCL type printer or most Apple inkjet printers. In that situation, an EPS may not give you the best results because you will simply get the screen preview instead of a full resolution file at output time. If your job will never need to be run on a PostScript device, you may be better off with other graphic file formats such as PCT (Mac) or PCX and WMF (Win95).

Working with a Library

You are going to love libraries because they make your production work go much more quickly.

■ Keep items you will use over and over again in a library. For example, when you produce a newsletter on a monthly basis, you regularly use and re-use certain elements such as the newsletter nameplate. Keep the nameplate in a library.

■ Use libraries to organize and keep track of large quantities of page elements. For example, if you were working on a book, you may have dozens or hundreds of illustrations such as the screenshot illustrations you see on these pages. Keep the illustrations in a library, labeled so you can find them quickly and easily.

Putting a library to work couldn't be simpler. You can click and drag items (actually copies of items) in and out of a library. Or, you can use the regular Copy, Cut, and Paste commands instead of drag and drop.

In the following exercise, you will try it for yourself by storing the newsletter nameplate, two illustrations, and a caption in a library…ready for re-use as you add elements to the newsletter you constructed in the last chapter.

1. Open the file **GRAPHICSONLY.QXT**, one of the files you copied from the CD-ROM to your working folder in the Getting Set Up section at the beginning of this chapter.

   As you can see in Figure 10.4, this page contains the familiar newsletter nameplate, as well as some graphics and some caption text. You are going to store these things in a library so you can use them during the remainder of this chapter.

   You don't need to bother saving this file, by the way. You will only have it open temporarily. It's not going to be your main working file for this chapter.

Creating a Library

2. Creating a new library isn't very different from creating a new QuarkXPress document.

   Use File>New>Library, ⌘+Option+N (Mac) or Ctrl+Alt+N (Win95) to get to a New Library dialog.

   Give your new library file a name and click the Create button, or press Return (Mac) or Enter (Win95). We used the name NEWSLETTER (Mac) and NEWSLETTER.QXL (Win95).

Figure 10.4

The "books" you will be shelving in your library.

Tip

Libraries Don't Cross Platforms

It's a bit unfortunate, but Macintosh QuarkXPress libraries can't be opened by the Windows version of QuarkXPress, and vice versa. (That means, technically, the QXL file name extension is only needed on the Windows side.)

Drag and Drop a Library Addition

3. With the Item tool selected, click and drag the tomato so that it is over the new library palette you just created.

   As in Figure 10.5, some black arrowheads appear in the palette to show you where the item will be listed in the library. Since this is the first item, it's located at the top. When you start adding more items, these arrow indicators will tell you where items will be in the palette.

Notice, by the way, that after you release the mouse button, you now have two tomato images. The original one in your source document is unchanged and there's a new copy of the original stored in the palette.

Here's an important concept about the nature of this new copy. You haven't really stored a complete copy in the library. It's a low resolution placeholder. The significance of this point will become more clear later on in this chapter when we discuss picture links. For now, you should understand that giving a QuarkXPress library file to someone who will be doing production on a job isn't nearly the same as actually giving that person a copy of the graphics files.

Copy/Paste a Library Addition

4. Still with the Item tool selected—the Content tool can't do this job—click the purple geranium once

and Copy it to the Clipboard, ⌘+C (Mac) or Ctrl+C (Win95).

5. Click in the Library palette and the position indicator arrowheads will display, showing where your library addition will go in the palette.

Paste the item into the library palette, ⌘+V (Mac) or click the palette's special Edit menu and choose Paste (Win95).

(Win95) When it comes to a library palette, the usual Cut, Copy, and Paste keyboard commands (as well as the Del key) don't work for the Windows version of QuarkXPress. You must use the palette's Edit menu for those functions.

(Mac) On the Macintosh side, you don't have an Edit menu for a library palette. Use the normal keyboard commands for Cut, Copy, and Paste. Use the Del key to erase an item from a library without putting it on the Clipboard.

6. Use drag and drop (or Copy/Paste if you prefer) to add the rest of the items, the nameplate and the caption text, into the library.

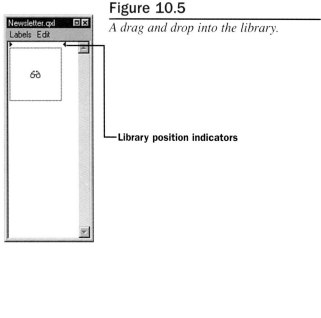

Figure 10.5
A drag and drop into the library.

Library position indicators

Autosave Your Library

7. There's no save command for the library. So, in the normal course of things, the only way your library will get saved is if you shut down the palette (by clicking the palette's close box) or when you shut down QuarkXPress.

    However, you can set a preference to save your library work as you go along. Always set this preference to on. Otherwise, a crash could wipe out an hour's (or a day's) worth of library entry work, including all the labels you created.

    Get to Application Preferences, ⌘+Shift+ Option+Y (Mac) or Ctrl+Shift+Alt+Y (Win95).

    In the Save tab, turn on the checkbox for Auto Library Save.

Resizing Library Palettes

8. With those items added to the library palette, you may need to resize the palette to see them all. Just click and drag the lower-right hand corner of the palette. It works just like the Styles palette and several other palettes of a similar nature.

Labeling Library Items

9. To label an item in the library, double-click it.

    Double-click the tomato illustration and you will get a Library Entry dialog box like the one in Figure 10.6.

Label this illustration by typing in **Vegetable** and press [Return] (Mac) or [↵Enter] (Win95).

Figure 10.6

Labeling a library palette item.

Narrowing the Palette Choices

10. Click the pull-down menu for labels in the library palette and you can choose between seeing all of your library items, selecting only the items that have no labels, or just the ones with certain labels.

    Choose Vegetable, as in Figure 10.7, and you will see that the only item showing will be the tomato picture.

Figure 10.7

Selecting palette items by label.

11. Return the labels pull-down menu to All.

12. Now you are ready to put your new palette to work.

Close the graphics only document.

Shut down the Library palette by clicking its close box in the upper left corner (Mac) or upper right corner (Win95).

This palette closing will automatically save the palette. As we've explained, other than autosave, there's no other way for you to proactively save your palette work.

13. Open the file named **NOGRAPHICS.QXT**. Save it under a name of your choice in your working folder. We just called ours WORKING.QXD.

Opening a Library Palette

14. Open the library palette you created, in our case we named it NEWSLETTER.QXL.

You simply use **File>Open** to get to a normal file selection dialog box where you can double-click the file name of your library.

Copying From a Library Palette

15. With either the Item or Content tool selected (either one works for getting stuff out of the palette), click and drag the newsletter nameplate in the library palette and drop it onto the newsletter page.

Maneuver the nameplate right to the top of the first page, as in Figure 10.8.

Snap the text box to the left master margin guide you built into the master page of the newsletter in the last chapter. Position the decorative dingbat "T" so that it snugs into the intersection of the top and left margins.

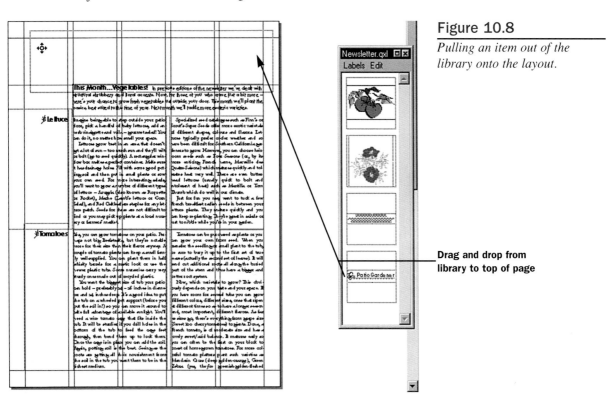

Figure 10.8

Pulling an item out of the library onto the layout.

Drag and drop from library to top of page

16. Save your work and exit QuarkXPress. (Don't close the library first.)

We want you to specifically leave the program before the next exercise so that you can see one of the great features of the library palette in action. The next time you open this document, you won't need to take explicit action to open the library. It will open automatically because it was open the last time QuarkXPress was closed.

The progress so far on the newsletter project has been saved on the CD-ROM in a file named **10BASE01.QXT**.

Making a Simple Text Runaround

The simplest kind of text runaround is a box shape. You insert a rectangular item into one or more columns of text, set a runaround, and watch the item push away the text so the text runs (or wraps) around the sides of the item.

In this exercise, you will drag a graphic out of the library you just created and insert it into a column of text. You will then set a runaround on the graphic.

1. Open the working file of the newsletter design, the one you closed at the end of the last exercise.

As we promised, notice that the library re-opens automatically with the document.

2. Navigate to the second page of the newsletter so you can work on the section called "Nursery of the Month."

Importing an Item from the Library

3. Click and drag the purple geranium out of the library and drop it near the bottom of page two, on the right side, just above the masthead (the text containing the publisher's name).

Snug it into the fourth and fifth columns, as you see in Figure 10.9, and notice that it collides with the text, letting the text show through.

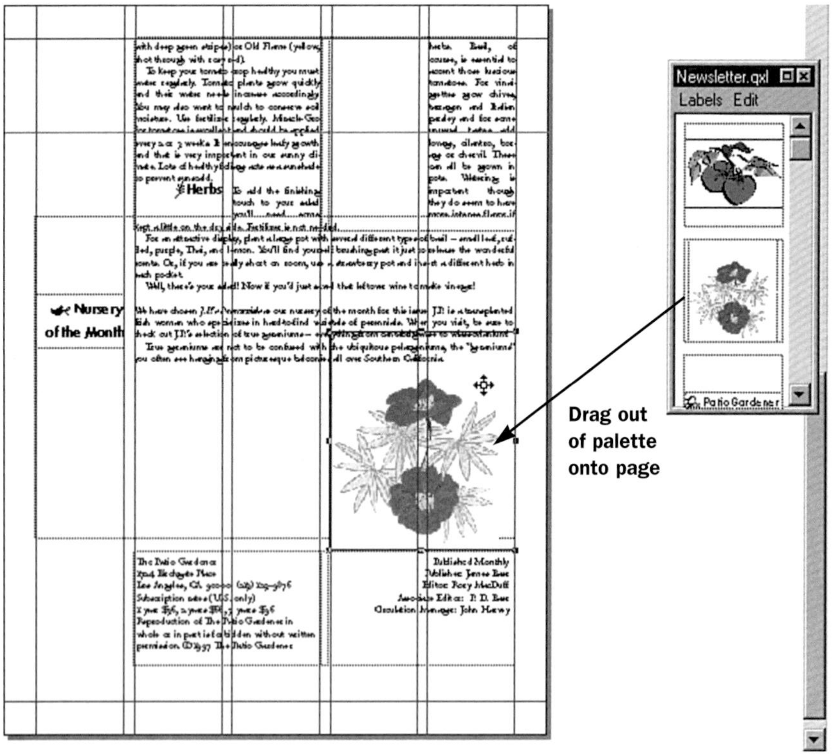

Figure 10.9

Dragging a graphic out of the library.

Drag out of palette onto page

Setting a Runaround

4. With the geranium still selected, open the Modify command and go to the Runaround tab.

Use the **Type** pull-down menu and choose Item for the type of runaround.

5. Set the amount of the runaround for 1 pica (12 points) on the left and right (equal to the column gutters), with zero runaround distance on the top. On the bottom, make the runaround amount 13 points.

Your dialog box should look like the one in Figure 10.10.

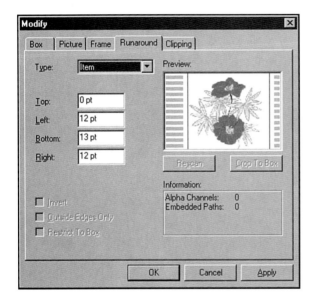

Figure 10.10

Setting a runaround on a picture.

6. Click OK and watch the text push away.

Notice that since you set the left side runaround amount at the gutter distance, the text is pushed precisely into the third column.

Live Refresh Positioning of Runaround Item

7. With the Item tool still selected, click and hold the geranium graphic until live refresh is activated.

Remember, you will get a bar under the pointer on the Mac or a square around it in Windows 95.

8. Position the graphic so that it pushes down the masthead text. The bottom line of the line of text about the circulation manager should be even with the copyright line in the left hand columns at the bottom of the page.

Having live refresh activated is really helpful when you have a runaround situation, so you can evaluate the effects on the text as you slide the graphic into position.

The other thing that helps here is the fact that you set the masthead paragraphs for Lock To Baseline Grid in the last chapter.

You have probably noticed that the text in the columns above the nursery of the month story is badly out of kilter and not in its proper columns. That's because you still have another graphic to position on the front page. We have pre-positioned the newsletter text elements, at least approximately. So, when you add the graphic to the first page, the text should be pushed into roughly the correct locations.

Setting a Frame on a Picture

9. With the geranium graphic still selected, open the modify command again and go to the Frame tab.

10. Setting a frame on a picture box works exactly like setting a frame around a text box. You'll recall that you set a frame on the masthead text in the last chapter (although we removed it for this chapter's variation on the design).

Set a 1.5-point width frame, solid pattern, 100% black. Your dialog box should look like the one in Figure 10.11.

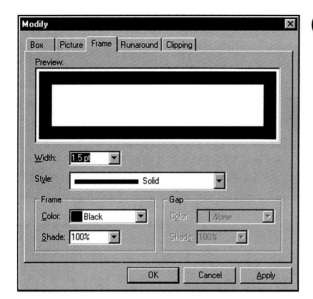

Figure 10.11

Setting a frame on a picture box.

Adding Caption Text to a Graphic

11. Click and drag the caption text box out of the library onto the geranium, positioning it at the bottom of the picture box.

The caption text has been centered and the text box is the exact width of the picture box. Line up the left and right edges of the caption text box with the left and right edges of the graphic.

12. With the Content tool selected, position the geranium picture toward the top of the picture box, so the graphic and the caption text aren't colliding with one another. Your geranium and its caption should look like Figure 10.12.

Figure 10.12

Final arrangement of graphic with caption.

QuarkXPress gives you a number of tricks so you can center, size, and otherwise position graphics within their text boxes, as in Table 10.1.

● The newsletter design so far, with the geranium and its caption in place, has been saved on the CD-ROM in a file named **10BASE02.QXT**.

Making a Fancy Text Runaround

Sometimes, a square-edged runaround just isn't enough. You may want to create a runaround where the text fits to the outline of the item in the picture, oozing around its edges.

In this exercise, you will use some of QuarkXPress' powerful automatic runaround capabilities. These features will make it easy to form the front page text around the complex outline of the tomato plant.

1. Navigate to the first page of the newsletter.

2. Click and drag the tomato graphic out of the library and onto the first page.

   Just so we have a common point of reference, align the lower left corner of the picture box precisely with the lower left corner of the page. (You may want to go to a high magnification view for this alignment operation.)

Rotating a Graphic

3. We need to rotate the tomato graphic a little bit so that the leaves form more of an arch. That's what we'll be using for the runaround shape.

   You have several options for rotating items or their contents but, for this exercise, let's use the Measurements palette. Open the Measurements palette now, F9.

4. With the Contents tool chosen, click the tomato graphic to select it.

Table 10.1   Keyboard shortcuts and mouse moves for sizing and positioning graphics

With Content Tool Selected You Can...	Mac	Win95
Center picture in box	⌘+Shift+M	Ctrl+Shift+M
Fit to box	⌘+Shift+F	Ctrl+Shift+F
Fit to box, maintain proportions	⌘+Option+Shift+F	Ctrl+Alt+Shift+F
Nudge 1 point	Any Arrowkey	Any Arrowkey
Nudge 1/10 point	Option+ Any Arrowkey	Alt+ Any Arrowkey
Scale picture up 5%	⌘+Option+Shift+>	⌘+Alt+Shift+>
Scale picture down 5%	⌘+Shift+Option+<	⌘+Alt+Shift+<
Resize box, constrain box shape	Shift+ Click/Drag	Shift+ Click/Drag
Resize box, maintain aspect ratio	Option+Shift+ Click/Drag	Alt+Shift+Click/Drag
Resize box, scale picture	⌘+ Click/Drag	Ctrl+ Click/Drag
Resize box, scale picture, constrain box shape	⌘+Shift+ Click/Drag	Ctrl+Shift+ Click/Drag
Resize box, size picture, maintain proportions	⌘+Option+Shift+ Click/Drag	Ctrl+Alt+Shift+ Click/Drag

Click the far right hand end of the Measurements palette, next to the angle symbol, which is the symbol for the field where you can enter an angle of rotation. Minus numbers are for clockwise rotation, positive for counter-clockwise.

Type **-10** and press Return (Mac) or ⏎Enter (Win95) to spin the tomato.

5. Adjust the position of the tomato picture as it relates to the picture box. The Content tool should still be selected.

Again, work with the right hand end of the palette (the end with the scaling percentages) and adjust the X+/Y+ coordinates. They should be 3p3/1p9.

You may make some more manual adjustments later, but this initial positioning information will help us synchronize the following steps.

The bottom edge of the tomato should be off the bottom of the page, and the leaves on the left side of the graphic should be draped out to the left edge of the page into the companion column. Your tomato and Measurements palette setting should match up with Figure 10.13.

Cropping a Graphic

6. Trimming an edge off a graphic—cropping it— couldn't be simpler.

Simply click and drag one of the picture box sizing handles until you have sliced off the part of the graphic that you don't want showing.

Do that now, but if you don't have Show Guides turned on you better turn them on first. Click and drag up the bottom edge sizing handle of the tomato graphic picture box. Cut the picture off at the bottom margin guide. (You should automatically snap to the guide as you drag the sizing handle up.)

Save for Possible Revert

7. The following process of setting a complex path runaround can be a bit ticklish. It might be important to be able to get back to the state your publication is in right now, before you attempt this operation.

Do a Save. That way, if you need to return to this point, you can use **File>Revert To Saved** to get back to the last saved version of your work.

Tip

Incremental Backups Can Save You

During a project, it's a good idea to give yourself an extra level of protection beyond Revert To Saved. Periodically, use File>Save As to preserve interim versions of your document. We often save successive versions of a document by adding the time into the file name at each save, "Working0613AM" for example. After a project is completed, you can delete the extra files.

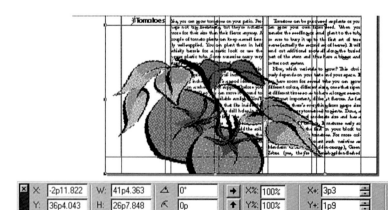

Figure 10.13

Initial positioning of the graphic.

| X: -2p11.822 | W: 41p4.363 | △ 0° | → | X%: 100% | X+: 3p3 | △ -10° | — Minus rotation is clockwise |
| Y: 36p4.043 | H: 26p7.848 | ⦧ 0p | ↑ | Y%: 100% | Y+: 1p9 | ⬛ 0° | — Contents settings at this end |

Setting a Complex Runaround

8. Make sure you've selected the tomato graphic (either the Content or Item tools will do) and open the Runaround dialog box.

You could get to it through the Modify command, but an even better method is to open it directly, ⌘+T (Mac) or Ctrl+T (Win95).

Exploring Runaround Types

9. Follow along as we now try each type of runaround offered in this dialog box.

Move the Modify dialog box aside so you can see all of it but also see the tomato graphic in the background. That way, you can select each runaround alternative and click the Apply button to see the effect without closing the dialog box.

10. First, select Item from the runaround type pull-down menu and click the Apply button.

Observe what happens in the Preview box. It creates a square-edged text runaround based on a picture box or a text box—as opposed to its contents.

You have already used Item runaround on the geranium graphic as well as on a text box in the last chapter.

11. Try Auto Image. Select it, observe the Preview box, and click Apply.

QuarkXPress 4.0 (this is brand new) has a sort of automatic tracing engine built into it. It can go into a picture and try to draw an outline around the main subject in a picture. It works best on a picture like this one, where the object in the picture stands alone against a white background.

It may take a bit as QuarkXPress tries to find the edges of the tomato graphic and calculates a path around them. But the Auto Image will chug along and do its best to draw a runaround that follows the outline of the object in the picture.

The next two runaround items, Embedded Path and Alpha Channel, will be grayed out and unavailable. They are quite similar in concept to Auto Image. Instead of QuarkXPress drawing the outline, the outline is built into the graphic file—created in a paint or drawing program and before you import it into your document. This picture doesn't have either an embedded path or alpha channel.

12. Try Non-White Areas. Select it, check the Preview, and Apply it.

The result of this type of runaround looks a lot like Auto Image. That's because this graphic happens to have a white background. Non-White Area runarounds purely look at white to decide where to trace their outline, whereas Auto Image will try to work on even the non-white portions of a graphic to find an edge.

The next runaround item, Same As Clipping, has to do with the fact that there's no such thing as a picture with jaggedy edges. Basically, all digital graphics files are rectangular. If you want to clip around the edges of an object in such a file—to cut out the object in the picture—you need a clipping path. Until now, you had to build an embedded path into your graphics file before you imported it, as we discussed a few steps ago. But now QuarkXPress gives you the power to build a clipping path right inside the program.

13. Have a look at Picture Bounds (select, check the Preview, Apply) and you will see that this is a rectangular runaround, very similar to Item. However, it works on the contents of the picture box, not the picture box itself.

Building an Automatic Runaround

14. Select Non-White Areas as your runaround type.

15. Outset is the amount of distance QuarkXPress will try to maintain between text and the runaround line.

Set the Outset at 3 points.

16. In the tolerance section, the noise setting determines how big an object QuarkXPress will try to outline. If you had a tomato worm crawling loose in this picture and it was only 6 points across in size, you might want to set the noise tolerance at 7 points to make sure the worm didn't get outlined.

Set the Noise tolerance at 5 points.

17. Smoothness tolerance determines how many points there will be on your runaround outline. QuarkXPress draws a kind of connect-the-dots outline. The more dots on the outline, the more complex the outline. If you get the outline too complex, it gets very difficult to edit during the fine tuning of your runaround. Also, an outline with a large number of points can create such a complex outline that it will cause trouble when you try to print the file.

Set Smoothness to 25 points.

18. The threshold won't have any effect on this graphic. It defines what would be considered white in a graphic for the purposes of drawing the outline.

Leave Threshold set to 20%.

The Outside Edges Only checkbox tells QuarkXpress not to go looking for any outline opportunities in the light area inside the main part of the graphic.

Restrict To Box keeps all the runaround effects inside the picture box.

Your runaround settings should look like the ones in Figure 10.14.

19. When all the settings are in place, click OK to set your runaround path in place.

Editing the Runaround

20. It stands to reason that a machine would have a bit of trouble doing a perfect job of cutting an outline around a complex picture, such as a tomato vine. You've got to fine tune the outline by editing it.

Check to see that runaround editing is turned on and if it isn't turn it on through **Item>Edit> Runaround** or Option+F4 (Mac) or Ctrl+F10 (Win95).

Tip

Experiment with Tolerance Settings to Fine Tune Runaround

It usually pays off to spend some time experimenting with the tolerance settings on a complex runaround, to try to get the text to break as well as possible. This experimentation, which can be done very quickly if you use the Apply button to check your results, may save you a lot of time by reducing the number of nodes that must be manually adjusted to get a good runaround path.

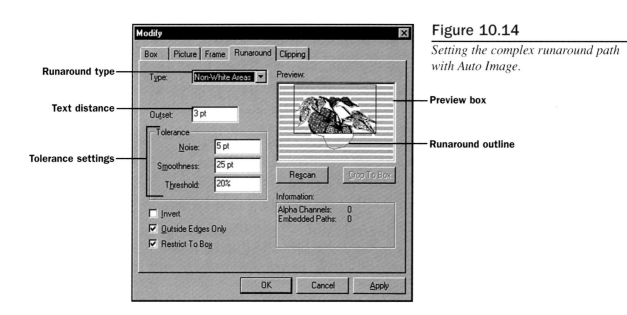

Figure 10.14

Setting the complex runaround path with Auto Image.

21. You can see on this pink outline all the node points QuarkXPress used to draw this line. You need to adjust these points so that scraps of text aren't scattered all over the place.

With the Content tool selected, spend a moment experimenting with your pointer. Drag it over a line. Drag it over a node point. Hold down the Option (Mac) or Alt (Win95) keys as you maneuver the pointer over a line and a point.

You will see how the pointer changes in these different situations in Figure 10.15.

22. As you can see in Figure 10.16, you can adjust node points and lines by clicking and dragging them.

Try moving one point now, holding down the mouse button a beat before moving to activate live refresh. Notice how moving the runaround path affects the text, shoving it aside or guiding it in towards the graphic, depending on which way you maneuver.

You can also add points to line segments, or delete points, by holding down Option (Mac) or Alt key (Win95) as you click them.

Learning about line segments and nodes takes you halfway towards drawing lines in QuarkXPress, special lines called Bezier curves. We will be doing more work with Bezier points and curves in Chapters 11 and 12. Consider this as a brief introduction to the concept.

23. Go to work now, adjusting the runaround outline. You should be looking to create an even text spacing while still getting the text to roughly follow the outline of the tomato foliage.

This will probably feel a little like shoveling Jello, since pinching in the runaround path in one spot will force the text into another area where you need to make another adjustment. The best tactic is to start making adjustments at the top of the graphic and work your way down.

Don't hesitate to nudge the entire graphic to the right or left a bit to reach the best compromise. You can even change the rotation adjustment to see if that helps.

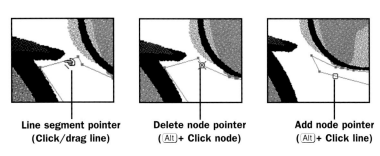

Line segment pointer
(Click/drag line)

Delete node pointer
(Alt + Click node)

Add node pointer
(Alt + Click line)

Figure 10.15

Editing pointers for runaround outline nodes and lines

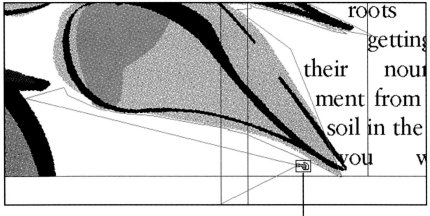

Live refresh in effect while moving a node

Figure 10.16

Click and dragging a node point to adjust runaround path

When you are done making adjustments, your runaround path should resemble the one in Figure 10.17. There are too many variables here for you to match ours exactly, but the basic idea is to avoid creating major gaps in text spacing while still following the outline of the graphic.

If you have trouble adjusting the runaround path, you can have a look at ours. The progress so far on the newsletter has been saved on the CD-ROM in a file named **10BASE03.QXT**. The layout in the version on the CD-ROM also has been adjusted to take into account the text that was shoved around by adding the tomato graphic on the first page.

Summary

Looking ahead, the path and node editing you did towards the end of this chapter will be very important for you during Chapters 11 and 12, as an introduction and some hands on experience with the very basic aspects of working with Bezier curves. In addition, you will want to get a firm hold on the quality consequences of re-sizing resolution-dependent graphics. The library palette capabilities in QuarkXPress will save you lots of time during production.

Figure 10.17

A finished, edited, text runaround.

Review It

As a review of what you have learned in this chapter, please answer the following questions.

1. What are the two main categories of computer graphics?

   _____

   _____

2. In terms of quality, what is the practical difference between the two versions?

   _____

   _____

3. For professional situations, what are the two preferred, specific file format types?

_____

_____

4. You create and open a library just like…?

_____

_____

5. How many node points does QuarkXPress use when building a runaround?

_____

_____

6. An item's runaround path affects all objects…?

_____

_____

7. Labels for items in the library can be filtered or selected by…?

_____

_____

8. The two simplest text runarounds are…?

_____

_____

9. To add a caption to a graphic you…?

_____

_____

10. To rotate an item you use which palette?

_____

_____

Check It

Multiple Choice

Please circle the correct answer for each of the following questions.

1. The Measurements palette settings for contents of an item are always _____.

    a. centered in the palette

    b. at the right side of the line in the middle of the palette

    c. in picas

    d. none of the above

2. You can turn off the display during runaround adjustment by _____.

    a. setting picture greeking in preferences

    b. holding down ⌘ (Mac) or Ctrl (Win95)

    c. holding down Spacebar

    d. all of the above

3. Before undertaking an intricate operation you should always consider _____.

    a. taking notes on current settings

    b. doing a Save for **File>Revert**

c. clearing the Undo command

d. all of the above

4. Control the number of points in a runaround by setting _____.

    a. noise

    b. smoothness

    c. threshold

    d. all of the above

5. When you want to add or delete a point you hold down _____.

    a. Option or Alt

    b. ⌘ (Mac) or Ctrl (Win95)

    c. ⬆Shift

    d. none of the above

6. While selecting a type of runaround path you can look at what dialog box feature to evaluate effects?

    a. Apply button

    b. Preview box

    c. Pull-down menu

    d. None of the above

7. What's the best way to quickly fine tune a complex runaround outline?

    a. Experiment with tolerance settings

    b. Increase number of points in outline

    c. Reduce noise setting

    d. Reduce threshold setting

8. To import an item from a library, you _____.

    a. drop and drag from library to page

    b. copy and paste

    c. cut and paste

    d. all of the above

9. To crop a graphic you _____.

    a. resize the picture box

    b. activate cropping tool

c. hold down ⌘ (Mac) or Ctrl (Win95) while resizing picture box

d. none of the above

10. A resolution-dependent graphic has how many pixels?

    a. Determined by vectors

    b. 1,024

    c. Fixed number

    d. None of the above

True or False

Please circle *T* or *F* to indicate whether the statement is true or false.

T F **1.** A plus rotation setting will rotate an item counter-clockwise.

T F **2.** Another name for resolution-dependent graphics is bitmapped graphics.

T F **3.** One time you might not want to use EPS would be if you have a non-PostScript printer.

T F **4.** Every item in a library must have a unique name.

T F **5.** You can swap QuarkXPress library files at will, even between Macintosh and Windows machines.

T F **6.** If you copy a selection of multiple items into a library they come in as a single item.

T F **7.** Only pictures can have text runarounds.

T F **8.** Unlike a mouse resize operation, if you use the Modify command to resize a resolution-dependent graphic, there will be no degradation of image quality.

T F **9.** The Non-White Areas runaround type builds an outline by tracing the main object in a picture.

T F **10.** The Auto Image runaround type builds an outline by tracing the main object in a picture.

Design It

Wrapping text around an object can be a powerful visual tool, but not if it's poorly done—causing type to look ugly due to unsightly gaps or line crowding. To learn more about runarounds...

■ Pick up at least three magazines and examine the type around runarounds they have built.

Were the runarounds executed well? What type of runaround approach did they take, rectangular or complex path? Does the text around the runaround look normal or has the spacing been distorted?

■ Working on a copy of the newsletter file, remove the frame from the geranium graphic and set a complex runaround on it.

How could you improve on it by manipulating the tolerance settings? How much difference is there in the text wrap if you change the number of nodes?

Try deleting a great many nodes to see what the minimum number might be.

11 Drawing in QuarkXPress

What You Will Learn

QuarkXPress, in this latest version, now gives you drawing tools—the ability to craft freeform lines, curves, and combinations of objects. That's what this chapter is all about.

However, you should keep in mind that it would not be a good idea to make a general practice of creating complex drawings in QuarkXPress. It's likely to take longer to do a complex drawing in QuarkXPress, and you probably won't be able to achieve the same high quality in QuarkXPress, because it doesn't have near the capabilities of a real drawing program like Illustrator, FreeHand or CorelDRAW. That being said, there's real power in the new drawing tools and, used wisely and sparingly, they can really add a lot to a page layout.

In this chapter, you will learn about:

➤ Drawing complex lines (and boxes) with Bézier curves

➤ Carving out a piece of a picture with a clipping path

➤ Curving type by building it on a text path line

➤ Gluing items together with the Group command

➤ Creating custom dashes and stripes (lines)

➤ Setting a drop or initial capital letter

➤ Rotating text

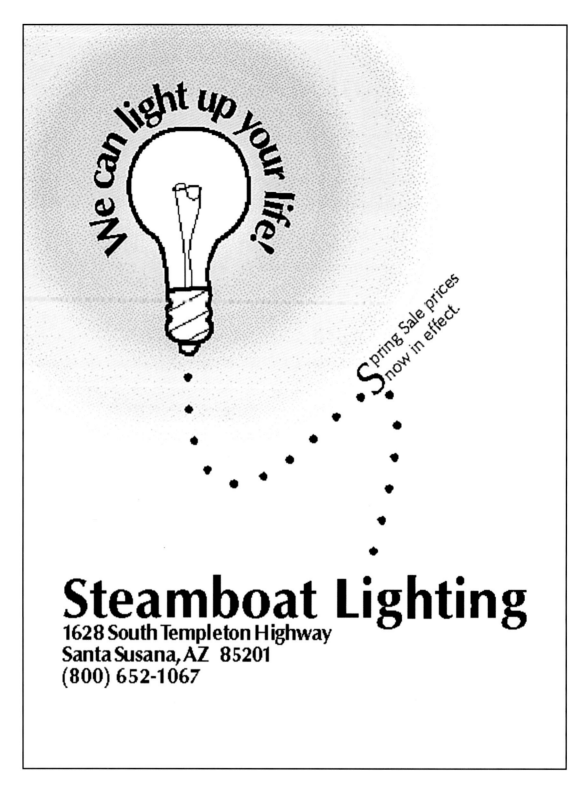

Figure 11.1

In this chapter, you will create this magazine advertisement, relying heavily on Bézier curves, a technique for drawing complex curved lines.

Getting Set Up

Copy all the files for this chapter from the CD-ROM to a work area on your hard drive. They are all in the **Steps** folder in the subfolder labeled **11**.

You will need to have the Opus font installed on your computer for the exercises in this chapter. It's one you've used in several other chapters.

After you finish the first exercise in this chapter, each following exercise builds on the previous one. Except where we've indicated otherwise, you should save your advertisement design project at the end of each exercise so you can pick up where you left off at the beginning of the next exercise.

For the exercises in this chapter to work best, you should have certain QuarkXPress defaults set. They are the same ones you have set in previous chapters, so the process should be familiar. In fact, all these preferences should already be set, assuming nobody has changed them on your copy of QuarkXPress since you last used it. Here's a checklist of defaults that you can set in the Document Preferences and Application Preferences:

■ Set the horizontal and vertical measuring systems to Picas.

■ Check that Points/Inch has been set at 72.

■ Change the greeked type setting to below 4 points.

■ Make sure leading is in Typesetting mode.

■ Set hyphenation to Expanded.

■ Check that Auto Kern Above is set to 4 points.

■ Standard Em Space should be turned on.

■ Set the text box default color to None.

■ Set Text Inset to 0 points. That means text will snug directly up against the edges of a text box, not inset.

■ Turn off runaround by selecting a runaround Type setting of None.

■ Set Auto Save to every 15 minutes. Set Auto Backup to keep 2 revisions.

Now it's time to learn about QuarkXPress's fancy Bézier curve drawing feature, a new addition with version 4 of the program.

Introducing...Bézier Curves

If you think you couldn't draw a smooth curve in a million years, you are going to love Bézier curves. By click and dragging levers attached to points in Bézier items—lines, polygons, clipping paths, runaround outlines—you can easily create graceful arcs and swirls.

The simple truth is, there's no better way to learn about Béziers than sitting down and trying them out. Fortunately, you've already begun that process. The runaround you shaped when you were working on the tomato graphic in the last chapter was a Bézier item, although you didn't get a full experience of how Béziers work. However, you already have worked on points and have deleted and added them to lines. (It's not an official QuarkXPress term, but sometimes we like to think of these Bézier points as node points. It seems descriptive of the way they behave, as focal points for changing the shape of a line.)

In this exercise, you will get some more hands-on experience with Bézier lines before you put them to work in this chapter.

1. Open up the file **11BASE01.QXT**. You should have already copied it to a working directory on your computer from the CD-ROM, along with the other elements you'll need for constructing the advertisement.

If guides are not showing, turn them on by pressing (F7), and turn on Snap To Guides, (⬆Shift)+(F7).

You will notice that there's not much in this file except for some text. You will soon be adding other elements.

Another thing you might note is the size of this document. It isn't a regular paper size. It has been set up to the specifications of the magazine that will run this full page ad—8 1/2 inches wide by 10 inches tall. This is a common situation you will face as a designer, having to think about the different shapes your work may need to fit, depending on publication specifications, special brochure sizes, or other special sizing needs.

Bézier Tools

2. Have a look at Figure 11.2 and you will see that there are three tools you use for creating Bézier items. We've set it up so they all show in the illustration but, of course, they don't all show in the default Tool palette.

    You want the Bézier Line tool, so select it now, using the popup menu behind the regular Line tool, fifth one up from the bottom in the palette.

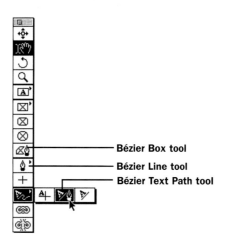

Figure 11.2

Create Bézier items with these three tools.

Drawing a Bézier Line

3. We need a Bézier line with which to work, so draw one now.

Click with the tool someplace on the document page and you will get a point on the screen.

Click a second time and you will have a line segment with a hollow square point at the new end of it. That's to indicate that you are drawing a multi-segment line and your next click will add a segment from the hollow point.

Double click to end the line while adding a second segment.

Just like when you draw a box, you will be switched to the Item or Content tool, whichever one was most recently active. You should have a line that looks something like Figure 11.3.

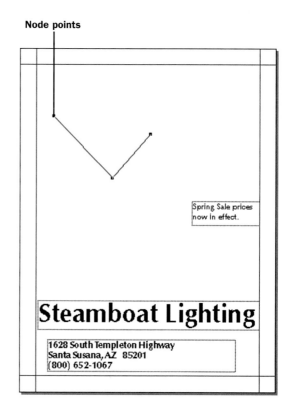

Figure 11.3

Clicking a multi-segment Bézier line into place.

Line Pointer

4. With the line still selected, move your pointer over your new line and observe how it changes. You have seen these pointers before, the ones shown in Figure 11.4, when you adjusted the runaround in the last chapter.

Figure 11.4

Line pointer (left) and Point pointer (right).

The Line pointer, which looks like a hand with a slanted line below it, can be used to move or change the shape of line segments.

Hold down Option (Mac) or Alt (Win95) while you have the Line pointer active. It will change to a round cornered square.

With the round cornered square pointer active, click at some point in the line. You will create a new node point on the line with a couple of levers poking out of it, breaking a single line segment into two.

Point Pointer

5. Maneuver the pointer over your new point. You will see that it changes to the Point pointer.

Hold down Option (Mac) or Alt (Win95) and the pointer will change to a round cornered square with an "X" through it. That's the point deletion pointer.

Click the new point with this pointer to remove the point from the line, joining the two segments back into one.

Tip

Use Del or +Backspace To Delete Points

If you have the Item tool active and points selected, you can delete them using Del (Mac) or +Backspace (Win95). This is also the way to delete a Bézier line segment.

Selecting a Point

6. Hold the pointer over the middle point in your line so that you have the Point pointer.

Click once and the point will turn into a blue triangle, indicating that it has been selected.

Selecting All Points

7. Double click one of the points in the line to select all of them. (Actually, it takes a triple click to do

this for most multi-segment lines, but a double click works here because you only have two segments.)

Corner and Curve Points

8. Pull down the Item>Point/Segment Type menu command, as in Figure 11.5.

Item	
Modify...	⌘M
Frame...	⌘B
Runaround...	⌘T
Clipping...	⌘⌥T
Duplicate	⌘D
Step and Repeat...	⌘⌥D
Delete	⌘K
Group	⌘G
Ungroup	⌘U
Constrain	
Lock	F6
Merge	▶
Split	▶
Send to Back	⇧F5
Bring to Front	F5
Space/Align...	⌘,
Shape	▶
Content	▶
Edit	▶
Point/Segment Type	▶

✓Corner Point	⌥F1
Smooth Point	⌥F2
Symmetrical Point	⌥F3
✓Straight Segment	⌥⇧F1
Curved Segment	⌥⇧F2

Figure 11.5

Use this menu (or the keyboard shortcuts) to change points and lines from one type to another.

Notice that all the points in this line are corner points and the line is made up of straight segments.

Corner points generally make sharp, angular turns. They can be associated with straight or curved lines, but they certainly don't make smooth or symmetrical curves, which are the other two kinds of points you can have.

In the next few steps, we'll be changing these corners and straight lines to curvy ones, so take note of the keyboard shortcuts indicated here and repeated in Table 11.1.

Table 11.1   To convert a Mac Win95 point or line to...

	Mac	Win 95
Corner point	Option+F1	Ctrl+F1
Corner from smooth	Ctrl+ Click point	Ctrl I Shift+ Click point
Smooth point	Option+F2	Ctrl+F2
Smooth from corner	Ctrl+ Click/drag handle	Ctrl+Shift+ Click/drag handle
Symmetrical point	Option+F3	Ctrl+F3
Straight segment	Option+Shift+F1	Ctrl+Shift+F1
Curved segment	Option+Shift+F2	Ctrl+Shift+F2

Making a Smooth Curve

9. Here's where you make a beautiful smooth curve, even if you can't draw and your fist shakes every time you hold a pencil.

    Ctrl+ Click/drag (Mac) or Ctrl+Shift+ Click/drag (Win95) the point at the right end of your line, as you see in Figure 11.6.

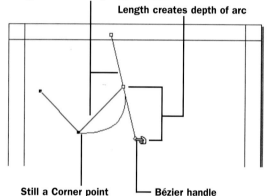

Angle creates sharpness of curve

Length creates depth of arc

Still a Corner point   **Bézier handle**

Figure 11.6

Drawing out a Bézier curve.

The triangle shaped point will turn to a square, indicating it has changed from a corner point to a smooth or symmetrical point.

And you will have dragged out some Bézier curve handles that you can use to "draw" a curved line. Pull the handle out away from the line and swing it around a bit and you will discover how easy it is to make a curved line using Bézier points. You will also see that when you move one curve handle, the other one moves with it.

(You could have converted the point from a Corner point to a Smooth point first using a keyboard shortcut, and then done a Click/drag one of the handles, but this is quicker.)

If you draw the handle out a long way from the point, you get a very deep arc in the line segment.

If you drag the handle to the side quite a ways, you will create a sharp curve, and you can even make it loop back onto itself.

When you are done experimenting, release the mouse button.

Measurements Palette and Bézier Items

10. Turn on the Measurements palette, if it isn't on already, F9.

    Since you still have a Bézier point selected, notice that you could completely control it from the Measurements palette, as you see in Figure 11.7.

Corner Points

11. Click and drag the middle point to pull out some Bézier handles and convert the point from a Corner point to a Smooth point.

    Press Option+F1 (Mac) or Ctrl+F1 (Win95) to convert it back to a Corner point.

    (You can see the button change from Smooth to Corner point in the Measurements palette. You could have, of course, clicked that button to accomplish the same thing.)

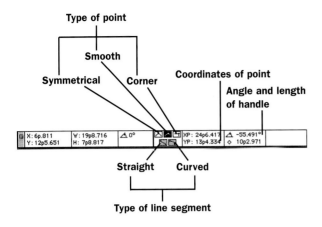

Figure 11.7

Measurements palette controls over Bézier curves.

12. Click/drag one of the handles of the point.

Notice that you can move one handle independently of another. That's what makes it a corner point. While one line segment is being manipulated in a curve, the other one is staying the same, as in Figure 11.8.

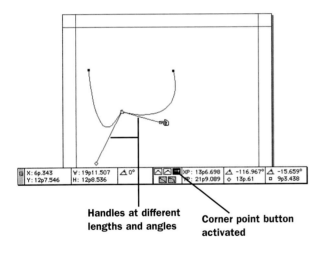

Figure 11.8

Corner point handles are not symmetrical or smooth.

Smooth Points

13. Convert the Corner point back to a Smooth point by clicking the middle point control button in the Measurements palette.

Notice that the curves snap into a smooth line instead of making a corner, although the handles are still not the same length.

If you swing one or the other handles, you can see that you are able to make a very unsymmetrical set of curves, as in Figure 11.9.

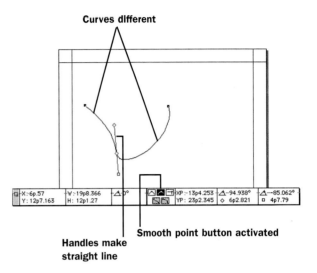

Figure 11.9

Smooth points make lines with no corners.

Symmetrical Points

14. A Symmetrical point makes the most even and graceful curves of all the points.

Press Option+F3 (Mac) or Ctrl+F3 (Win95) to convert the Smooth point into a Symmetrical point.

As in Figure 11.10, you can see that the curve is quite symmetrical and stays that way as you swing the handles. The handles will always be an equal distance from the point when you are working with a Symmetrical point.

As you can see, the handles may be symmetrical but Symmetrical points do not necessarily make symmetrical curves. The points on either side of the Symmetrical point have an influence on the shape of the line segments.

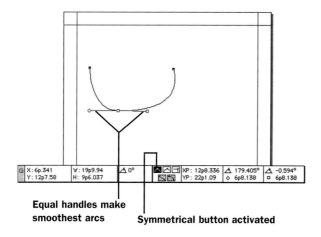

Equal handles make smoothest arcs

Symmetrical button activated

Figure 11.10

Symmetrical handles extended from a Symmetrical point.

Directly Shaping a Line Segment

15. One of the beauties of the QuarkXPress Bézier curve system is that you can shape a line segment directly, without using handles.

Maneuver your pointer to one of the line segments until it turns into a Line pointer. Then just click and drag the line to change the depth and sharpness of its arc.

Since you were only using it for experimentation, don't bother saving this document. You will start fresh in the next exercise, using the same template file you used to start the exercise you just completed. So, close this exercise without saving it.

Cutting a Clipping Path Silhouette

A clipping path works like a text runaround. You create an outline around the item and you can shape the outline by working with its points. In fact, you can tell QuarkXPress to use a clipping path as a runaround outline.

A clipping path, like a runaround, also helps you position an item in front of another item. In building a runaround, you wrap text around the item. For a clip-

ping path, you "clip" away extraneous material from a graphic so you can see what's in the background.

Both clipping paths and runaround outlines can be rectangular around a box or around the contents of a box, but they can also be constructed out of and shaped with Bézier points.

In this exercise, you will have QuarkXPress automatically construct a clipping path around the light bulb you see in Figure 11.1 so it will be silhouetted against the glow graphic in back of it. You will manually tweak the outline of the clipping path using Bézier points.

1. Open up the file **11BASE01.QXT**. It should already have been copied to a working directory on your computer from the CD-ROM.

Make sure your guides are showing and that Snap To Guides is activated.

2. Draw a rectangular picture box down from the upper left corner of the page to cover about two-thirds of the page. Take some care to get the box snugged into the upper left corner (use the Measurements palette to set the X/Y coordinates to 0). The size isn't that critical but you should draw out the box to be roughly as wide as the page. You will be making further adjustments to the size and shape of the box in a few steps.

> **Tip**
>
> **Sometimes JPG Files Work Just as Well as TIFs**
>
> You may notice that you have two glow image files on your CD-ROM. They are both bitmapped, resolution-dependent files, which tend to be quite large compared to vector, resolution-independent files. However, GLOW.JPG is less than 300 kilobytes, whereas GLOW.TIF is huge—over 8.5 megabytes. That's more than 25 times as big! The JPG file format (pronounced jay-peg) is a "lossy" compression scheme. That means it compresses a file by eliminating "unnecessary" information. For that reason, you can get some terrible looking graphics results by overdoing a JPG compression. On the other hand, for a single color image like this yellow glow, JPG file format can be a great, disk space saving, alternative to TIF format.

3. Import the file **GLOW.JPG** into this new box using the Get Picture command, ⌘+E (Mac) or Ctrl+E (Win95).

4. Draw a second rectangular picture box on top of the glow image. It should be around 13 picas wide by 23 picas tall. Roughly center it on the glow box.

5. Use the Item>Modify command, Box tab, to give this box a color of none instead of white, so the yellow glow graphic will show through the box.

Graphics Obscure Background

6. Import the file **BULB.EPS** into this box.

Notice, as in Figure 11.11, that the light bulb graphic is shaped like a rectangle. All graphics are shaped like rectangles and, unless you set a clipping path, will obscure whatever is behind them.

Setting a Clipping Path

7. Go to the Modify command again and click the Path tab. Look at Figure 11.12 and you will see just how much the clipping path and runaround functions resemble each other. This tab has many of the same types of settings as the Runaround tab.

8. Set the path type to Non-White Areas and click OK. The result should look like Figure 11.13.

9. The bulb needs to be bigger in order to make a statement inside this design.

Re-open the Modify command and select the Picture tab. Set Scale Across and Scale Down at 140%, then click the Apply button to put the setting in effect.

Exploring Clipping Path Options

10. Move back to the Clipping tab so you can get an idea of the degree of automatic control this feature gives you over clipping paths. Follow along with Figure 11.14.

Outset will let you trace an edge around the graphic. In this case, it would allow you to leave some of the white background as a visible outline around the light bulb.

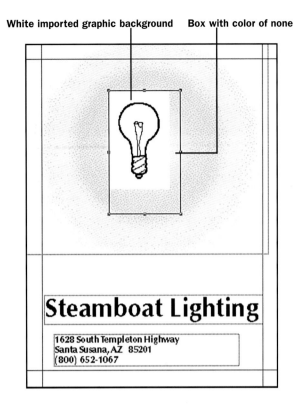

Figure 11.11

Imported graphic obscures item behind it.

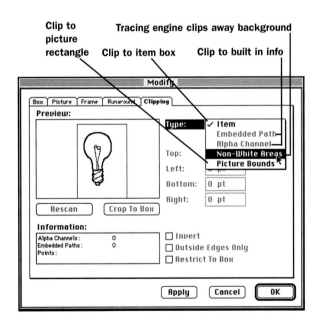

Figure 11.12

Clipping path options resemble runaround options.

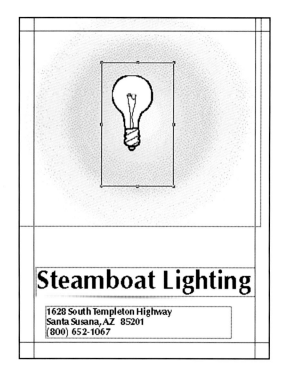

Figure 11.13

Clipping path in place, allows background item to show through.

The Tolerance settings work like they do in Runaround. It's particularly important to keep an eye on the number of points you generate in Non-White Areas mode. Creating an ultra-complex path can create a virtually unprintable file, choking the memory of the printer or the high resolution imagesetter at your service bureau.

You can check the number of points (try to keep it in double digits, if you can) in the Information box. That's also where you can get information on any clipping information built into the imported graphic file.

It's a bit hard to see at this point but there's a green line that shows the clipping path. (The runaround path was pink or magenta.)

11. Click Invert. In this mode you can see that you can create a light bulb shaped hole. Instead of clipping away the background in the light bulb graphic, you can eliminate the picture, leaving the graphic's rectangular background material visible.

Click Invert off before moving on.

The Outside Edges Only setting tells the tracing engine to stick to the outside edges of a complex object area (such as the tomato vine in the last chapter). In this mode you won't get any little holes carved out inside the basic outline perimeter of a graphic.

Restrict To Box violates the law of the universe that we described in the last chapter. If you have set a clipping path on a picture, you can have that picture show outside the edges of its item box. (You might use this if you wanted a graphic to overlap the edges of a frame, yet still be silhouetted against a background.)

Crop to box will cut off any part of the clipping path that falls outside the item box perimeter.

When you are done checking out these clipping path options, click OK.

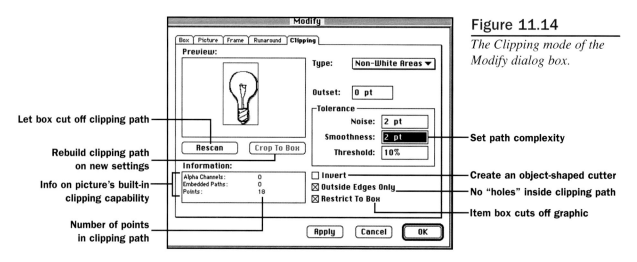

Figure 11.14

The Clipping mode of the Modify dialog box.

Adjusting Clipping Path with Béziers

12. With the bulb graphic selected, magnify your view so the graphic fills your screen.

Notice that there are tiny white edges around the bulb where the clipping path didn't snug as tightly as it might have against the outline of the bulb.

13. Open this clipping path for Bézier curve editing with the Item>Edit>Clipping Path command, ⬆Shift+Option+F4 (Mac) or Ctrl+⬆Shift+F10 (Win95).

You can see that the clipping path is a green line with lots of points in it. Those points are all Bézier items.

14. Use these Bézier points to adjust the shape of the clipping path, trying to fit the clipping path better to the outline of the bulb. Don't forget all the keyboard commands in Table 11.1 and the different kinds of pointers you learned in the previous exercise.

You will probably find that you can improve the outline somewhat, although the QuarkXPress tracing engine does a pretty good job on a simple graphic like this one.

A key part of success is deciding which kind of point to use among the three different kinds you explored during your Bézier point experimentation in the last exercise. For the smooth arc of the bulb itself, Symmetrical points will probably be helpful, as in Figure 11.15.

When you are done experimenting, move on to the next exercise.

> ### Tip
>
> **Path Adjustments Only as Accurate as EPS Preview**
>
> When adjusting a clipping path on an EPS graphic, as the light bulb is, you need to keep in mind that you are working with a low resolution preview of the actual PostScript vector graphic. That's why the on-screen image has the jaggies in Figure 11.15. These screen previews are generally pretty accurate, but on really critical work you will need to print a copy of your work on a PostScript printer to be certain that you have cut the path in the right spot.

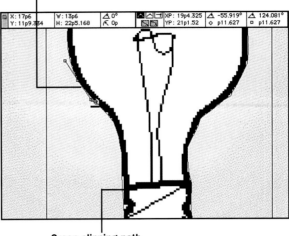

Symmetrical Bézier handles

Green clipping path

Figure 11.15

Adjusting a Bézier point on the clipping path.

The progress so far on the advertisement has been saved on the CD-ROM in a file named **11BASE02.QXT**.

Converting Item Types

As you can see from Figure 11.1, you will need to curve the headline slogan of this advertisement around the light bulb. You accomplish this by putting the text on a special kind of QuarkXPress line called a text path. You can then shape the line any way you like, often by using Bézier points, so that the text follows the desired path. That would be a straightforward way to accomplish this effect, but it would not be the easiest way. QuarkXPress has the ability to change item types. You can make a line into a text path, for example, or convert a box or a circle into a Bézier curve.

For this exercise, you will draw a perfect circle. Then you will convert that to a Bézier item. You will then convert the Bézier item to a perfect curved text path. (You'll add and format the text in the next exercise.)

Centering a Picture in a Box

1. Select the light bulb picture box with either the Item or Content tool and center the graphic in it, ⌘+M (Mac) or Ctrl+M (Win95). (If your bulb is bigger than the box, adjust the box so the bulb is completely showing first.)

2. Before you draw your perfect circle, you need to set your tool so it will draw a see-through box.

Double click the Oval Picture Box tool. That will take you to the familiar Tool tab for Document Preferences.

Click the Modify button and, as you have done before for other picture box tools, change the color of the box from white to none.

Click OK.

Drawing a Perfect Circle

3. With the Oval Picture Box tool selected, hold down ◆Shift and draw a circle around the bulb part of the light bulb.

Start drawing from the upper left corner of the picture box and pulling down and to the right until you have a circle like the one in Figure 11.16.

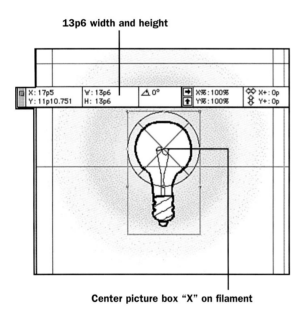

13p6 width and height

X: 17p5　W: 13p6　△ 0°　X%: 100%　X+: 0p
Y: 11p10.751　H: 13p6　　　Y%: 100%　Y+: 0p

Center picture box "X" on filament

Figure 11.16

Shift plus Oval Picture Box tool yields perfect circle.

4. Use the Measurements palette to set the circle to 13p6 width and height. (You must get the size just right before converting it to Bézier curves because the conversion breaks the circle into line segments that can't be adjusted as a symmetrical "perfect circle.")

Arrow Key Nudging for Position

5. With the Item tool selected, use the arrow keys to nudge the circle into precise position over the bulb, centering the "X" of the picture box on the filament.

Converting Box to Bézier Item

6. Any box can be converted to a Bézier item.

Use the **Item>Shape** menu, as in Figure 11.17, and notice the checkbox next to the circle symbol. Choose the Bézier symbol instead.

This will convert the circle into eight perfectly equal and perfectly symmetrical Bézier line segments. You could, we suppose, call it a Bézier circle.

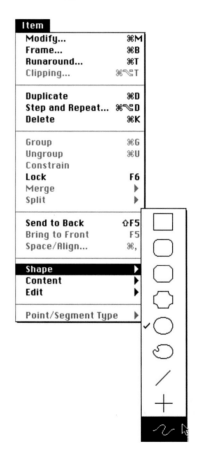

Item	
Modify...	⌘M
Frame...	⌘B
Runaround...	⌘T
Clipping...	⌘⌥T
Duplicate	⌘D
Step and Repeat...	⌘⌥D
Delete	⌘K
Group	⌘G
Ungroup	⌘U
Constrain	
Lock	F6
Merge	▶
Split	▶
Send to Back	⇧F5
Bring to Front	F5
Space/Align...	⌘,
Shape	▶
Content	▶
Edit	▶
Point/Segment Type	▶

Figure 11.17

Converting a box into a Bézier item.

Deleting Bézier Line Segments

7. Save your work before doing the next few steps so you can use **File>Revert To Saved** if you accidentally delete the wrong thing.

8. Maneuver the pointer over the Bézier point at the bottom of the circle until you get a Point pointer.

    Click to select the bottom most point in the circle. The Bézier handles should extend if you did select the point.

    If you accidentally select the bulb instead, click off to the side to deselect the bulb and try again, making sure you have the Point pointer before clicking. (If you have the Item tool active, you can also press Tab⇆ to deselect everything.)

9. Press Del (Mac) or ⌫Backspace (Win95) to delete the line segment to the left of the selected point.

10. Select the same point again and delete it, which will delete the line segment to the right of the selected point.

    You now have a three-quarter circle, ready to hold your text except for one last detail.

Converting a Bézier Line to a Bézier Text Path

11. Any line, including a Bézier line, can be converted to a text path.

    Use **Item>Content>Text** to change this line's content from none to text, which will make it a text path. As you see in Figure 11.18, it's all ready for you to add text, which you will do in the next exercise.

⬤ The current status of the advertisement has been saved on the CD-ROM in a file named **11BASE03.QXT**.

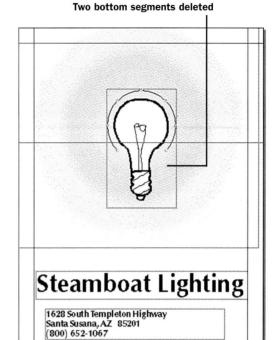

Two bottom segments deleted

Steamboat Lighting

1628 South Templeton Highway
Santa Susana, AZ 85201
(800) 652-1067

Figure 11.18

Three-quarter circle text path.

Curving Type on a Path

Adding text to the curve you created over the light bulb in the last exercise couldn't be simpler.

Adding Text to Text Path

1. Select the Content tool and click the curve.

    It might be a little hard to see against the yellow glow graphic in the background, but you will get a blinking text insertion point just like you would if this was a text box.

2. You can even import text, just like a text box.

    With the insertion point blinking use the Get Text command, ⌘+E (Mac) or Ctrl+E (Win95) and import the file **SLOGAN.TXT**.

Formatting Text on a Path

3. Formatting text works normally, as well.

   Select All, ⌘+Ⓐ (Mac) or Ctrl+Ⓐ (Win95).

4. Go to Character Attributes, ⌘+Ⓓ (Mac) or Ctrl+Ⓓ (Win95), and format the text as Opus, 50 points, Bold.

5. The text will be a bit too big, and will show a red overset symbol. Again, a text path behaves just like a text box in nearly every way.

6. Adjust the point size of the text down until it is all showing.

   You can do that using the keyboard shortcut, ⌘+⬆Shift+Option+< (Mac) or Ctrl+⬆Shift+Alt+< (Win95). A size of 42 points worked for us.

Exploring Text Path Effects

7. You don't want the line showing under the text, so open up the Modify command.

   Set the color of the line to none, instead of black.

8. Go to the Text Path tab as shown in Figure 11.19.

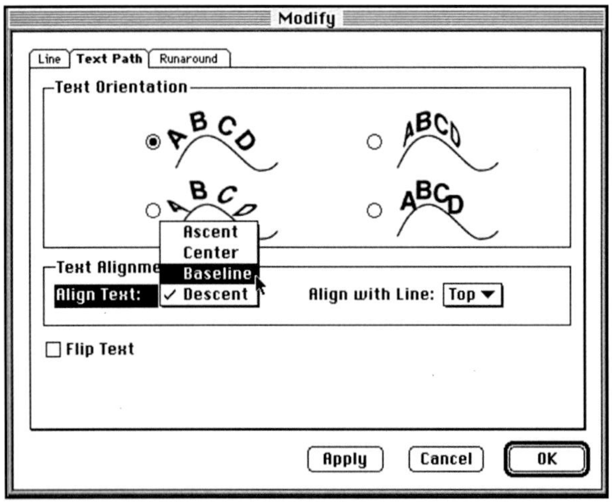

![Modify dialog box showing the Text Path tab with Text Orientation options, Text Alignment with Align Text dropdown showing Ascent, Center, Baseline, Descent options, Align with Line set to Top, and a Flip Text checkbox. Apply, Cancel, and OK buttons at bottom.]

Figure 11.19

Setting text path options using the Modify command.

You now have a number of possibilities for shaping text on a path. We'll just use the baseline option.

Set Align Text to Baseline, so the base of the letters will rest on the text path. You would probably use the Descent option instead if you had a visible line so the descenders of the letters (the tail of the "y" or "g") would rest above the line and not collide with it.

You can combine some of these options to make some striking effects. Text orientation can be used, for example, to make text look as if it has been printed on a ribbon. If you set a wide line for your text path and reversed out the type, it really would look like a ribbon, especially if you set the Align With Line option to Bottom so the text was resting on the bottom edge of the thick line.

When you are done with the Modify command text options, click OK.

Centering Text on a Path

9. You still need to center the text so it arcs over the top of the light bulb.

   You center text on a path in the same way you would center any other text. Press ⌘+⬆Shift+Ⓒ (Mac) or Ctrl+⬆Shift+Ⓒ (Win95).

   When you are done, your advertisement design should be taking shape like the one in Figure 11.20.

Figure 11.20

Centered text on a perfect semi-circle path.

• The advertisement, as it should appear with all the steps so far, has been saved on the CD-ROM in a file named **11BASE04.QXT**.

Grouping Items

The positioning of the bulb and the text are crucial and it would be very easy to knock them out of position. That's why this is one of those cases where we can be really glad that QuarkXPress gives us a way to lock them together. It's called grouping and this exercise will show you how to use it.

1. With the Item tool active and guides showing, select the text path. It may take you a couple of clicks to select the path, but try clicking several times on the base of the letters until you get it.

2. Hold down ⬆Shift and click the light bulb picture box (not the yellow glow picture box).

3. Group them using **Item>Group**, ⌘+G (Mac) or Ctrl+G (Win95). It's that simple.

   You can tell grouped items because they have a dotted line around them, as in Figure 11.21.

Dotted lines indicate group

Steamboat Lighting

1628 South Templeton Highway
Santa Susana, AZ 85201
(800) 652-1067

Figure 11.21

Grouping items.

Tip

You Can Edit Contents of Grouped Items

Even though items have been grouped together as if they were a single item, the fact is they aren't totally locked. You can use the Content tool on individually grouped items to edit text or shift the position of a picture inside a box. That's probably why QuarkXPress is set up so that you can only use the Item tool when moving a group—to make sure you don't accidentally shift the position of contents in one of the items.

Tip

Select Hidden Items "Through" Stacked Items

When you have a bunch of items stacked up, it can be very difficult to select an item that is towards the bottom of the stack. In situations like that, use ⌘+Option+⬆Shift+ Click (Mac) or Ctrl+Alt+⬆Shift+ Click (Win95). Each time you click with this key combination, you will select items in the order they are stacked, from front to back.

4. With the Content tool selected, move the yellow glow graphic towards the upper left corner of the advertisement.

   Position it as you see in Figure 11.22, with the lighter colored edge of the rim off the upper left corner of the page. In our Measurements palette, the picture was at X/Y coordinates of -8p/-8p inside the glow picture box.

5. Now you can see the power of grouping items.

   With the Item tool selected, click and drag the bulb and text group. With the two items grouped, it's easy to move them as a unit.

   Slide the group so that the bulb is centered on the light colored center of the glow, as if the light bulb was generating the glow. In our Measurements palette, the group was at X/Y coordinates of 8p/7p.

6. Click/drag the lower right corner of the glow picture box so it is as small as possible but still shows all of the glow along the right and bottom sides.

   Slide the spring sale text out of the way if it is colliding with the glow picture box.

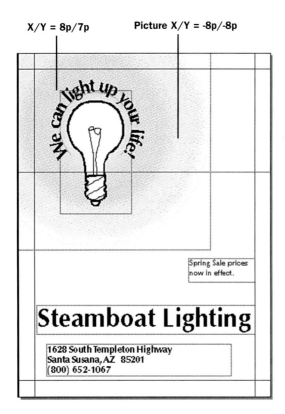

X/Y = 8p/7p

Picture X/Y = -8p/-8p

Steamboat Lighting

1628 South Templeton Highway
Santa Susana, AZ 85201
(800) 652-1067

Spring Sale prices
now in effect.

Figure 11.22

Grouped items moved as a unit, centered on the glow.

● The progress so far on the redesigned menu has been saved on the CD-ROM in a file named **11BASE05.QXT**.

Creating Custom Dashes and Stripes (Lines)

The old-fashioned pull chain that's part of the Steamboat Lighting brand identity is a series of widely spaced dots. A regular dotted line won't do, so in the past the line would have been composed out of many small black circles grouped together. In QuarkXPress version 4, you can create custom dashes and stripes. In this exercise, you will create a widely spaced dotted line just for use on this client's projects.

Editing Dashes and Stripes

1. Use the **E**dit>Dashes & Stripes command to reach the dialog box you see in Figure 11.23. In many ways, it resembles the Style or List dialog boxes with its append, duplicate, new, save, and delete functions.

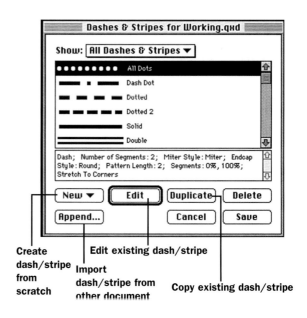

Create dash/stripe from scratch

Import dash/stripe from other document

Edit existing dash/stripe

Copy existing dash/stripe

Figure 11.23

Setting Dashes & Stripes definitions for current document.

Basing New Dash Definition on Existing One

2. With the All Dots dashes definition selected, click **D**uplicate and you will be able to assign a new name to your custom dots, **Steamboat Dots**.

Spacing Dashes

3. To space these dots wider, change the **R**epeats Every setting in Dash Attributes from 2 times width to 3.75 times width and you will see the dots in the Preview section space themselves wider, as in Figure 11.24.

If you wanted to add dots or change their length, you would set new arrow positions (or move existing ones) on the repeating pattern "ruler." This works a little bit like setting tab stops in the tab ruler, except instead of tabs you are setting the number and length of dots (or the stripe pattern if you are editing a stripe).

Click arrows to set length or number
of dots in repeating pattern

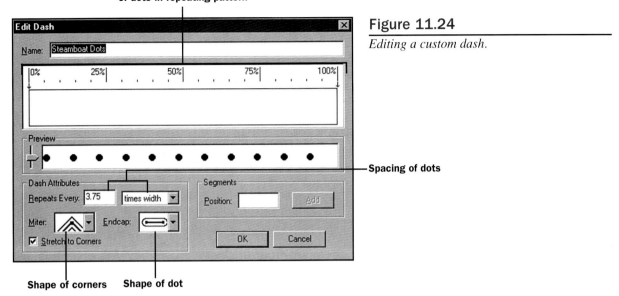

Figure 11.24

Editing a custom dash.

Spacing of dots

Shape of corners   Shape of dot

Saving Dash Definition

4. Click OK when you have your dash edited, then click **S**ave to add the new dash definition to your list of dash and stripe options.

Setting Bézier Line Defaults

5. Select the Bézier Line tool and then double click on it so you can set a default for drawing the pull chain line for this advertisement.

    In the dialog box, choose Modify. Then, in the Line tab of the Modify dialog box, select the Steamboat Dots dash you just created from the pop-ups in Figure 11.25, and set it for a width of 9 points.

    (You could also, of course, draw the line first and then format it with your new custom dash definition.)

    These dash and stripe definitions work a great deal like paragraph and character styles. You can edit a custom dash definition and all the lines styled with that definition will change appearance to match the new definition.

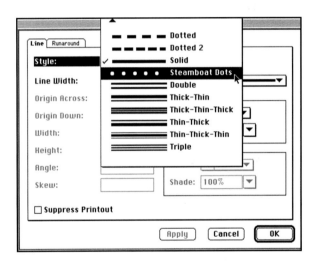

Figure 11.25

Selecting the new custom dash definition.

Drawing a Bézier Dashed Line

6. With the Bézier Line tool selected, click a point just below the light bulb, another one below it and to the right, and a finishing point just above the dot in the letter "i" in "Lighting." Your line should look something like Figure 11.26.

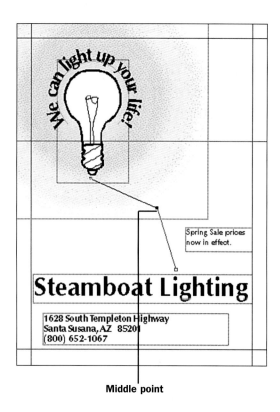

Middle point

Figure 11.26

Drawing the initial line.

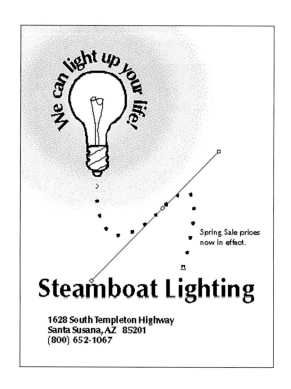

Figure 11.27

Making the middle loop in the "chain pull" dotted line.

7. Click the Item tool to end the line (or you could double click as you set the last point).

   The line-in-progress in Figure 11.26 will become a line composed of your custom Steamboat Dots pattern.

8. Adjust the ending point of the line so it is spaced away from the dot in the "i" about the same distance as the space between dots, as if one of the dots in the line was actually forming the dot of the "i."

   Likewise, adjust the spacing of the first dot from the base of the bulb so it is the distance of the dot on the "i" at the other end of the line.

9. Drag out some Bézier handles from the middle point on the line by Ctrl+ Click/dragging (Mac) or Ctrl+◆Shift+ Click/dragging the middle point in the new line.

   Create a loopy curve that looks something like the one in Figure 11.27. Ours looked best when the angle of the handles was about 45 degrees.

> **Tip**
>
> **Automatic 45 Degree Angles with ◆Shift Key**
>
> If you hold down ◆Shift while click/dragging Bézier handles, you will constrain their angles to increments of 45 degrees. Note that, as a general rule of thumb, the ◆Shift key works to constrain drawing tools in some way. For example, you have already used ◆Shift to constrain the Oval Picture Box tool to a perfect circle.

> **Tip**
>
> **Move Bézier Item in Bounding Box**
>
> You may be wondering how in the world you could click/drag a Bézier item to move it. Every kind of click/drag move you make seems to shift the shape of the line. The answer is to put the Bézier to bounding box mode and click/drag with the Item tool. You do that with the Item>Edit>Shape command, ◆Shift+F4 (Mac) or F10 (Win95).

The advertisement as it looks so far, in Figure 11.27, has been saved on the CD-ROM in a file named **11BASE06.QXT**.

Setting Initial or Drop Caps

You set initial caps by formatting the first initial letter of the first word of a paragraph larger than the rest of the text, or with some different looking type.

The typographical roots of this practice probably stem from the medieval practice of "illuminating" capitals as fancy miniature pictures when books were copied out by hand on parchment in European monasteries.

It's not as pretty as illuminated capitals, but QuarkXPress has a paragraph attribute that can automatically create drop caps for you, a particular style of initial caps where the capital letter is set (dropped) down into the body text. In this exercise, you will use this drop cap paragraph attribute on the advertisement's spring sale blurb.

1. With the Content tool selected, click in the paragraph where you want the initial cap. Actually, you can click anywhere in the spring sale text box in this case because there's only one paragraph in this text box.

2. Open up the Paragraph Attributes dialog box, ⌘+⬆Shift+F (Mac) or Ctrl+⬆Shift+F (Win95).

3. As in Figure 11.28, set the **D**rop Cap attribute.

   You could drop cap many characters, by many lines, but in this case set the drop cap for a Character Count of 1, and a Line Count of 2 lines deep (which is the number of lines in this text box).

4. Click OK to finish setting the drop cap. It's that quick and simple.

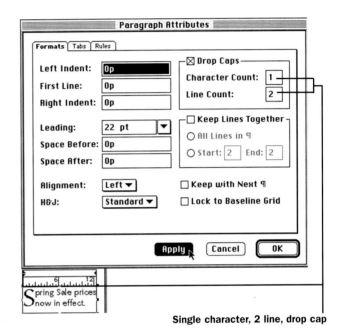

Single character, 2 line, drop cap

Figure 11.28

Setting and applying the drop cap.

The advertisement with the drop cap set has been saved on the CD-ROM in a file named **11BASE07.QXT**.

Rotating Text

Rotating text can be done with the Rotation tool, or in the Measurements palette, or in the Modify dialog box—all the places you would normally go to modify the look of a QuarkXPress item. In this exercise, you will use the Rotation tool.

1. Using the Item tool, click/drag the spring sale text box up so that its lower left corner is near the peak of the loop in the dotted line.

   Notice that some (or maybe even all) of the text is obscured by the yellow glow image.

2. You could try to cut a clipping path around the glow image but it has fuzzy, gradated edges and it would probably spoil the effect.

Instead, bring the text box forward all the way in the stacking order using the **I**tem>**B**ring To Front command, (F5).

It will now be completely showing in front of the glow image.

3. Select the Rotation tool, the third one down from the top, located below the Contents tool.

4. The secret of using the Rotation tool is to think about the "axle" around which you'd like to rotate your object. The first point you click during a rotation move will be the point around which the selected object will rotate.

Click the lower loop of the drop cap "S" in "Spring" and drag to the right and up, as in Figure 11.29.

Hold down (◆Shift) while you drag, to constrain the rotation angle to 45 degrees. That will help you match the angle of the text to the angle of the dotted line coming into the loop, making it look like the spring sale blurb has been tossed off the light bulb "pull chain" at the peak of the loop.

Click rotation point

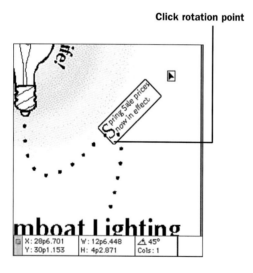

Figure 11.29

Rotation tool in action.

5. Make final adjustments of the position of the spring sale blurb on the chain, again trying for the effect of the text being tossed off the dotted line as if someone had given it a big yank and let go.

You can make fine adjustments by selecting the text box with the Item tool and then using the arrow keys to nudge it into place.

You can also get a temporary Item tool for click/drag purposes by holding down (⌘) (Mac) or (Ctrl) (Win95) while any tool is selected.

6. Finally, position the address text under the name of the business in a manner that pleases you.

In our finished version, the address information snugs fairly tightly under the word "Steamboat" and the two text blocks are lined up on the left. In our version, we left a fair amount of white space at the bottom of the ad so it would look like the company was flying loose, hanging at the end of the light bulb's pull chain.

Your finished advertisement should look like the one in Figure 11.1.

The finished advertisement has been saved on the CD-ROM in a file named **11BASE08.QXT**.

Summary

QuarkXPress doesn't have full power drawing tools, but the ability to manipulate Bézier items makes it possible to really spark up a simple design—even one with just a few elements like the advertisement in this chapter.

When you combine Bézier power with other QuarkXPress capabilities such as clipping paths and text paths, you have major power to manipulate images and text. And during production, you can use grouping, rotation, custom dashes and lines, and drop caps to quickly and automatically accomplish tasks that would otherwise require tedious and time consuming hand work.

Review It

As a review of what you have learned in this chapter, please answer the following questions.

1. What are the three Bézier tools?

   _____

   _____

2. What are the two main kinds of pointers for Bézier objects?

   _____

   _____

3. What are the different pointers for dealing with Bézier points?

   _____

   _____

4. How do you convert an item from one type to another?

   _____

   _____

5. What three main keys are used, along with modifier keys, to convert points or line segments from one type to another?

   _____

   _____

6. Aside from manual adjustment, what is the main way you can tune a Non-White Area clipping path or runaround outline?

   _____

   _____

7. What three techniques can you use to rotate an item?

   _____

   _____

8. For what kind of situation would you use the Group command?

   _____

   _____

9. What are the three kinds of Bézier points?

   _____

   _____

Check It

Multiple Choice

Please circle the correct answer for each of the following questions.

1. If you had unsymmetrical curves to build, with a sharp turn at the point, what kind of Bézier point would you use?

   a. Curved

   b. Angled

   c. Corner

   d. None of the above

2. For a curve with no sharp turns, which two kinds of points would you choose from?

   a. Smooth or Symmetrical

   b. Curve or Smooth

   c. Symmetrical or Even

   d. None of the above

3. To hold a Bézier handle or rotation angle at 45 degree increments you would hold down _____.

   a. ⌘ (Mac) or Ctrl (Win95)

   b. Option (Mac) or Alt (Win95)

   c. ⬆Shift

   d. all of the above

4. You can stop drawing a line by _____.

   a. lifting mouse

   b. double clicking or clicking on a tool

   c. ⬆Shift + Clicking

   d. all of the above

5. To convert a point from one type to the other, which modifier key do you use along with a function key?

   a. Option (Mac) or Ctrl (Win95)

   b. Option (Mac) or Alt (Win95)

   c. ⬆Shift

   d. none of the above

6. To delete a Bézier point, you use Del (Mac) or ⬆Backspace, or you can _____.

   a. ⌘ + Click (Mac) or Ctrl + Click

   b. double click

   c. Option + Click (Mac) or Alt + Click

   d. none of the above

7. You can have a graphic extend outside a picture box by _____.

   a. impossible

   b. setting clipping path, turn off Restrict To Box

   c. ⬆Shift + Contents tool click/drag

   d. none of the above

8. To change a Bézier line to a text path, you use _____ command.

   a. Item>Shape

   b. Item>Contents

   c. Item>Edit

   d. none of the above

9. For dashes, the "ruler" in Edit>Dashes & Stripes determines _____.

   a. width of dash

   b. length and spacing of dash

   c. shape of dash

   d. none of the above

10. The colors of clipping paths and runaround outlines are _____.

   a. pink and green

   b. blue

   c. black and green

   d. none of the above

True or False

Please circle *T* or *F* to indicate whether the statement is true or false.

T F **1.** You can adjust the style of an existing dotted line by editing it in Dashes & Stripes.

T F **2.** In order to format text on a path you must take a special extra step first.

T F **3.** To temporarily get an Item tool, when any other tool is selected, you hold down ⌘ (Mac) or Ctrl (Win95).

T F **4.** You can manipulate Bézier items from the Measurements palette.

T F **5.** Once you group some items, you can still edit their contents.

T F **6.** To center text on a path you use the text alignment command.

T F **7.** You can select an item hidden behind another by using a special keystroke combination while clicking.

T F **8.** Simple graphics files (like a light bulb) take on the shape of their contents so you can see through their backgrounds.

T F **9.** The first step in using the Rotation tool is to click a rotation point.

T F **10.** You can bring an item all the way to the front in the stacking order by pressing ⬆Shift+F5.

Design It

After all our work in the previous chapters with design grids, you may feel like a bit of a traitor having worked on such a free form advertisement. The fact is, however, there is still a grid of sorts in effect. The space was used as an artificial window, with the glow graphic cropped in the upper left corner and the other items positioned in relation to that window. Not much of a design grid, we'll admit, but still a structure nonetheless.

Experiment with this layout and see how many different ways you can put the elements together, even though there are basically only seven items.

■ Try centering the graphic on the page. Why does this not work as well as off to the side and cropped?

■ What happens if you rotate the grouped text and bulb, but also maintain the pull chain motif? How much of a problem is it that the curved text becomes less readable that way?

■ Develop some longer sales copy in place of the short blurb about the spring sale. Where could you put it on the page? Is it too "heavy" to be launched by the pull chain? How can you get the longer text on the page and still maintain all the elements of the brand identity?

Combining and Manipulating Graphics

Revising the Advertisement

What You Will Learn

In addition to the drawing capabilities you explored in the last chapter, QuarkXPress provides you with some powerful tools for assembling graphics and text on pages. Some of these—especially alignment and step/repeat—allow you to accomplish in just a few seconds some complex layout tasks that might otherwise take hours to complete.

In this chapter, you will learn:

➤ Aligning and spacing graphic and text items

➤ Making multiple copies of an item with the Step and Repeat command

➤ Locking items to the page once they are in position so you can't accidentally bump them out of position

➤ Turning text characters into boxes that can be colored or hold graphics

➤ Combining simple QuarkXPress boxes and lines together with the Merge command to compose complex shapes

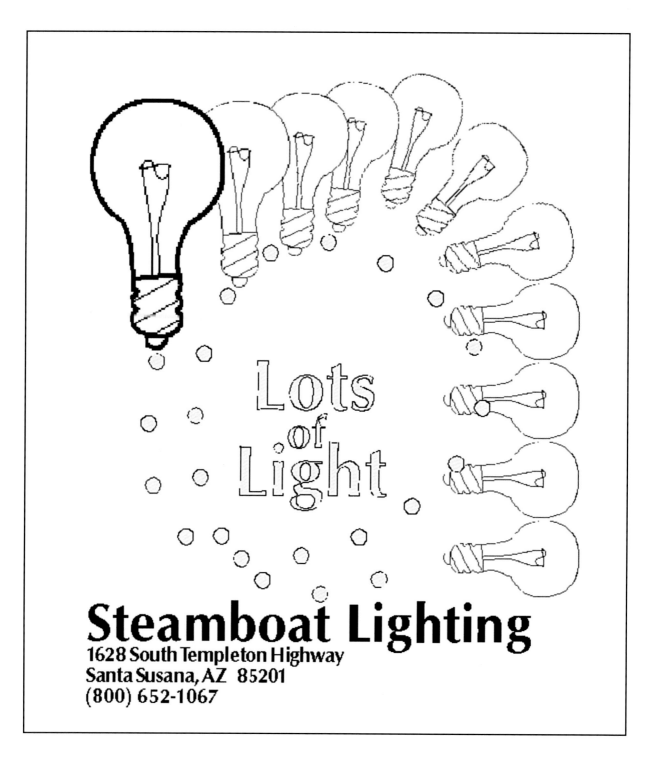

Figure 12.1

You create a new advertisement in this chapter, building on many of the elements you used in the last one.

Getting Set Up

Copy all the files for this chapter from the CD-ROM to a work area on your hard drive. They are all in the **Steps** folder in the subfolder labeled **12**.

You will need to have the Opus font installed on your computer for the exercises in this chapter. It's the one you've used in several other chapters, including the advertisement you created in Chapter 11.

Following each exercise, save your project to a work area on your hard drive. Each succeeding exercise builds on the previous one, so saving at the end of each exercise will enable you to pick up where you left off if you aren't able to complete the chapter exercises in one sitting. Also, on the CD-ROM, we have provided saved versions of the project as it should exist at the end of each exercise. You can fall back on those interim versions of the advertisement as reference points if you are having trouble with one of the exercises.

Aligning and Spacing Items

You might want to think of the QuarkXPress Space/Align command as a remote control box for automatically maneuvering items on a page. You could, if you wanted to take the time, manually align items by clicking and dragging them with your mouse and using ruler guides to get them lined up or by matching up item coordinates using the Measurements palette. But it's a great deal faster if you use your remote control. With the Space/Align command, you can establish a few settings and click a button.

By the way, the space part of the Space/Align command refers to its ability to precisely set the distance—the space—between selected items. It works almost exactly the same way as alignment, so the two functions have been combined in one dialog box.

In this exercise, you will adjust the positions of the small, gray light bulb and the name of the shop so they line up exactly on the page. In the process, you will learn how you can take control of the Space/Align command remote control panel.

1. Open the file **12BASE01.QXT** and save the new document in your work folder under the name of your choice.

Choosing Items for Alignment

2. Select the text box containing the shop's name and address, and ⬥Shift + click the small light bulb to add it to the selection. You can use either the Content or Item tools for this.

    You can select any number of items for alignment—except one. The Space/Align command will not be available if you only select one item.

Space/Align Command

3. Open Item>Space/Align, ⌘+⟨,⟩ (Mac) or Ctrl+⟨,⟩ (Win95).

4. Slide the dialog box up or to the side so you will be able to see the two selected items. You want to be able to see the effects of your moves as you use the Apply button.

In the next several steps, where we call for using the **Apply** button, try to be careful not to use OK by mistake.

Setting Horizontal and Vertical

5. Most of the Space/Align Items dialog box will be a dim gray when you first open it.

   You can choose to align or space items either in the horizontal or vertical, or both.

   Click the **H**orizontal checkbox and the left half of the dialog box will come to life.

   Figure 12.2 will help to give you an overview as we run through a little experimentation to show you the concepts behind the Space/Align command.

Setting Relationship Points

6. In addition to telling QuarkXPress whether you want to set horizontal or vertical spacing (or both), you must also give the Space/Align command a relationship point. In other words, how can the program set space between objects unless you tell it what to use for measurements?

   In QuarkXPress, you select this reference point in the **B**etween pull-down menu. Click it now to see what options you have. Should the spacing be based on one of the edges, or the center? (On the vertical side of the dialog box you have a choice of top or bottom edges. For horizontal, it's left or right edges.)

Aligning Edge Reference Points

7. Select Right Edges from the **B**etween menu. You should still have **S**pace set at zero and only the **H**orizontal side of the Space/Align Items dialog box should be active.

   Click Apply and see how the light bulb snaps its right edge into alignment with the right edge of the text box. You have aligned these items (set zero space) on their right edges.

   In Figure 12.3, notice that the light bulb moved into place while the text stayed put. When you are setting horizontal spacing, the leftmost item controls the move. It becomes the guidepost for measuring horizontal spacing (and alignment).

Aligning Centers

8. Select a Centers relationship in the **B**etween menu of Centers and click **A**pply.

   Again the light bulb moved, centering itself on the leftmost item, the text, as in Figure 12.4.

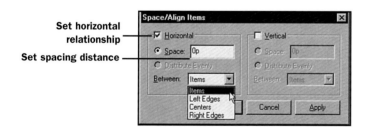
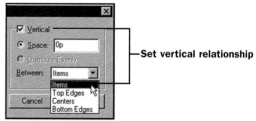

Set horizontal relationship
Set spacing distance

Set vertical relationship

Figure 12.2

Horizontal (left) and Vertical (right) setting possibilities for Space/Align.

Zero space alignment on right edges

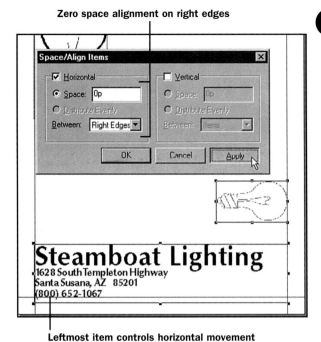

Leftmost item controls horizontal movement

Figure 12.3

Aligning on an edge.

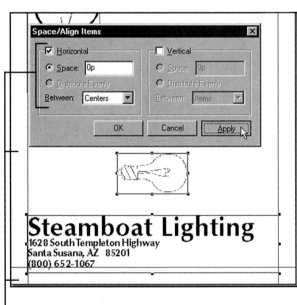

Zero space alignment on centers

Figure 12.4

Aligning horizontal centers.

Tip

Generally...Zero Space Equals Alignment

Here's a key concept about the Space/Align command. When you align items in QuarkXPress you are simply setting zero space between them.

In fact, they could just as well have named it the "Space" command because that's all it really does—set space. And by default, you will always find a zero in the Space box when you first open Space/Align Items dialog box. That's because its most common use is for alignment.

The only time this doesn't apply is when you set a relationship of Item. In that case, the items will be butted together, rather than aligned in the way most of us usually think of the term.

Spacing Items

9. You can also use the Space/Align command to set specific amounts of space between items.

Set the relationship **B**etween on Left Edges and **S**pace at 3 picas and click **A**pply. You should get the same effect as you see in Figure 12.5, the objects spaced 3 picas apart based on their left edges.

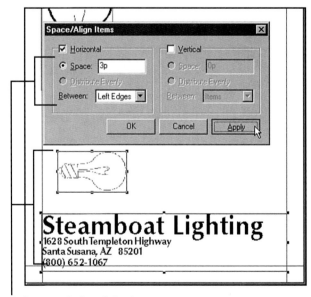

3 picas apart along left edges

Figure 12.5

Left edge alignment with a space setting.

Setting Both Vertical and Horizontal Spacing

10. It's easy to combine two moves in one.

As you see in Figure 12.6, you can simultaneously make horizontal and vertical moves.

Set **H**orizontal at zero **S**pace and a relationship **B**etween of Right Edges.

Set **V**ertical at zero **S**pace and a relationship **B**etween of Items.

Click OK this time instead of **A**pply.

Notice that the light bulb, as before, moved in the horizontal axis because it must line up with the text, which is the leftmost item.

This time, the text also moved. In the vertical axis of the Space/Align command, the topmost item controls the alignment and spacing process.

When you move both at once, the topmost and leftmost items control their respective directions. The topmost item dictates vertical movement and stays in its vertical axis. The leftmost item dictates horizontal movement and stay in its horizontal axis.

11. Both of the items should still be selected as you come out of the Space/Align Items dialog box.

With either the Item or Content tool, click/drag the two items down so that the baseline of the telephone number text rests on the bottom margin.

You may need to temporarily switch off **S**nap To Guides so QuarkXPress won't try to force the bottom edge of the text box to the guide instead of the baseline of the text. You can do that with ⬆Shift)+(F7).

At this stage, the new advertisement project should look like the one saved on the CD-ROM in a file named **12BASE02.QXT**.

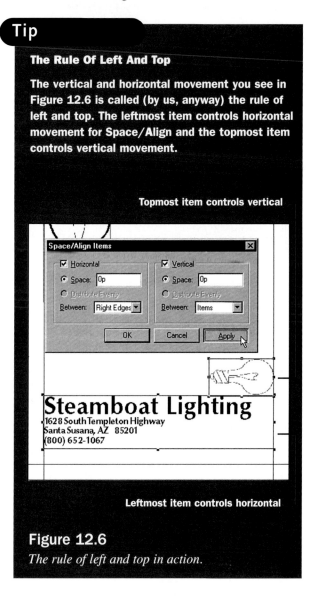

Figure 12.6

The rule of left and top in action.

Duplicating Items with Step and Repeat

By now you know how to Copy and Paste. It's a fundamental part of the operating system for both Macintosh and Windows 95 and you use it in word processors, spreadsheets, drawing programs, and so on. QuarkXPress has two very powerful commands that will save time when you need to perform copy and paste operations.

Item>Duplicate, ⌘+D (Mac) or Ctrl+D (Win95) will instantly, in a single step, copy and paste an item.

Item>Step and Repeat, ⌘+Option+D (Mac) or Ctrl+Alt+D (Win95) will, in a single step, perform as many as you tell it. At the same time it allows you to set the horizontal and vertical distance for positioning the copies from each other (almost like it had a built in Space/Align command).

In this exercise, you will use both commands to multiply the single small light bulb in the lower right quadrant of the page into many light bulbs.

1. Select the small light bulb, using either the Item or Content tool.

Setting Step and Repeat Offsets

2. Call up the Item>Step and Repeat command and tell it to make four copies.

3. Set the horizontal offset at zero so they all line up in the same horizontal axis (just like aligning with the Space/Align command).

4. The vertical offset should be set to minus 7 picas. (That's the width of the rotated light bulb picture box. If you wanted to overlap the bulbs, you would set the distance at less than the width of the box.)

   You may be asking yourself why this measurement has a minus in front of it. It's because we are step and repeating in an upward direction, from the bottom of the page. If we were duplicating down from the top we would be using a positive number.

   The offset is measured from the origin point of the item that you are duplicating. If you added space, you would be adding 7 picas to the Y coordinate of the existing item. That would position the new duplicate bulbs down below the existing one instead of above. (It would also, by the way, try to position the item off the available pasteboard and QuarkXPress would give you an error message.)

   Your Step and Repeat dialog box should look like the one in Figure 12.7.

Figure 12.7

Stepping and repeating with horizontal and vertical spacing offsets.

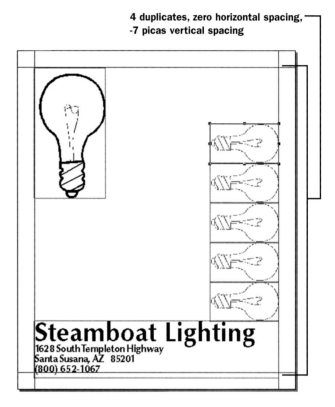

Figure 12.8

A completed Step and Repeat operation.

Performing Step and Repeat

5. Click OK and you will instantly have a vertical row of light bulbs along the right hand side of your advertisement. It's that fast and easy and it should look like Figure 12.8.

Setting Duplicate Offset Spacing

Don't do it, but if you pressed ⌘+D (Mac) or Ctrl+D (Win95) right now, you would create a fifth duplicate with exactly the same offsets. You would get these offsets on your duplicate because the Duplicate command's offsets are always the last ones used in the Step and Repeat dialog box. (If you haven't used the command in the current work session, the defaults are .25 inch horizontal and .25 inch vertical.)

6. We are going to use a combination of the Duplicate command and Step and Repeat several times to create the row of rotated bulbs across the top of the advertisement.

   So let's use Step and Repeat now to set new default offsets for the Duplicate command. You should still have the topmost light bulb in the vertical row selected.

   Call up Step and Repeat, ⌘+Option+D (Mac) or Ctrl+Alt+D (Win95).

7. Set the Repeat count to just one.

   Horizontal offset should be -5 picas.

   Vertical offset should be -4p6.

   Click OK.

Duplicating an Item

8. Press ⌘+D (Mac) or Ctrl+D (Win95) and you will get a duplicate copy with exactly the same offsets.

Resetting Duplicate Offsets

9. To adjust the offsets for the Duplicate command, go back to Step and Repeat.

   Leave the count at one and the Horizontal offset at -5p.

   Change the Vertical offset to 1 pica.

   Click OK.

10. Use the Duplicate command two more times using this new offset, ⌘+D (Mac) or Ctrl+D (Win95).

When you are finished, your roughed-in row of light bulbs should look like Figure 12.9. (They still need to be rotated and then manually tweaked for effect).

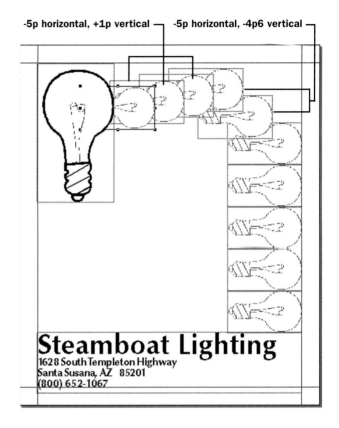

-5p horizontal, +1p vertical — -5p horizontal, -4p6 vertical —

Steamboat Lighting
1628 South Templeton Highway
Santa Susana, AZ 85201
(800) 652-1067

Figure 12.9
Duplicating, using Step and Repeat offsets.

11. The rest of this exercise involves finishing this multiple light bulb effect.

    Use the Measurements palette to set rotations on each of the picture boxes containing the top row of light bulbs as indicated in Figure 12.10. (Rotate the picture boxes, not the contents.)

    Don't forget that you can either explicitly set the rotation, or you can get QuarkXPress to calculate the finished rotation by literally adding or subtracting a given number of degrees from the set rotation.

    The point is, there's a progression of the "speed" of rotation of these light bulbs that makes it seem as if they are accelerating and then slowing down as they seem to "morph" into the big light bulb in the foreground.

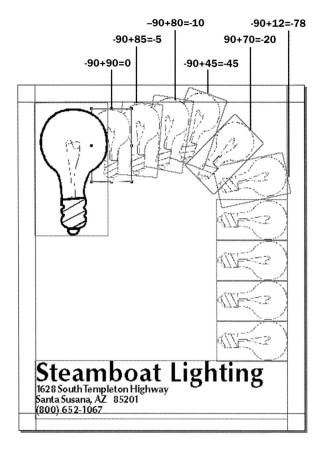

Figure 12.10

Progressive rotation to give the sensation of moving to foreground.

Scaling Pictures to Boxes

12. Another aspect to this effect of the light bulbs morphing into a foreground bulb is to increase their size as they "come toward" the reader.

Select the third gray bulb box from the left (the fourth one counting the big bulb). It's the one that you rotated to -10 degrees.

In the Measurements palette, add 1 pica to the W/H measurements for this box.

13. Select the next one over to the left and add 2p6 to its W/H measurements.

14. Select the final gray box, the one just to the right of the big bulb, and add 4 picas to its W/H measurements.

15. When you have resized all the text boxes, you can apply a special keyboard command to resize the pictures inside them to fit.

Select each of the resized boxes and press this keyboard command, (⌘)+(Option)+(⬆Shift)+(F) (Mac) or (Ctrl)+(Alt)+(⬆Shift)+(F) (Win95). This command resizes a picture to fit its box, maintaining the picture's normal proportions.

If you leave off (Option) (Mac) or (Alt) (Win95) the picture will be resized to fit the box without regard to proportions.

When you are done, the result should look something like Figure 12.11.

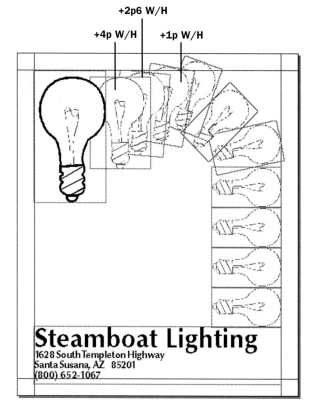

Figure 12.11

Resizing pictures to fit boxes.

It's okay to resize these images because they are vector-based, resolution-independent EPS graphics. We would not be using this technique if they were bitmapped, resolution-dependent TIFF graphics.

16. Finish by tweaking the position of the light bulbs so they achieve the morphing effect to your satisfaction. Feel free to experiment with degree of rotation or size in order to maximize the effect.

The progress so far on the redesigned advertisement has been saved on the CD-ROM in a file named **12BASE03.QXT**.

Locking Items to the Page

When you have spent as much time tweaking the position of something as this light bulb morphing effect, you want to try to make sure you don't lose the work.

QuarkXPress can help you with this by allowing you to lock the position of an item on the page, which is what you will learn about in this next brief exercise.

1. With the Item tool activated, select all the items on the page, ⌘+Ⓐ (Mac) or Ctrl+Ⓐ (Win95).

2. Lock them using the **Item>Lock** command, F6.

3. Maneuver your pointer over any selected item on the page and you will get a pointer shaped like a padlock, indicating that it has been locked into place.

Tip

Sometimes Locked Isn't Locked Tight

Actually, you can move locked items in two ways. You can select them and then use the Space/Align command to move locked items. Or, you can move them using the Measurements palette. You can also move the contents of locked boxes and edit text inside locked text boxes. The point is, QuarkXPress does not make it impossible to move a locked item on purpose but does make it very difficult to move a locked item accidentally.

The advertisement as it should look at this stage has been saved on the CD-ROM in a file named **12BASE04.QXT**.

Converting Letters to Boxes

There are times when you would just like to treat text as if it was a graphic item. You might like to fill some letters of type with color, or outline them with a line (called stroking), or even fill the letters with a picture.

In this exercise, you will learn how to use QuarkXPress' new feature for converting text to boxes.

1. Draw a rectangular text box roughly in the center of the advertisement. We made ours about 40 picas wide and 8 picas high.

2. Type the text **Lots of Light** into the new text box.

3. Select all the type and format it as Opus, Bold, 78 points.

   You can only convert one line of text at a time so the text should all fit on one line. If it doesn't, adjust the text box width.

Converting Text to Box

4. With all the text still selected, use the **Style>Text To Box** command.

   The result will be as you see in Figure 12.12, a duplicate of the text except it will be in the form of a very complicated QuarkXPress box. (All those points are Bézier points so you could, if you wanted, work on the shapes of these letters.)

Stroking and Filling Letters

5. One nice thing you can do with text once it's converted to a box is outline it with one color (stroke it) and color it with another (fill it).

   (We are going to spend a lot more time on color, starting in the next chapter.)

   Use the Modify command, Box tab and where the box is colored white, use the pull down menu to select yellow instead.

   Navigate to the Frame tab, still with the Modify dialog box, and put a 1-point line around this box so you'll be able to see it better on the page while you are working.

   Click OK and you will have letters stroked in black and filled with yellow.

6. With the Item tool, select the original text box and delete it.

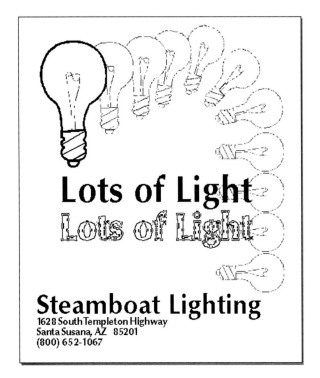

Figure 12.12

Text converted to a box.

At this stage of redesigning, the advertisement your project should look like the one saved on the CD-ROM in a file named **12BASE05.QXT**.

Introducing...Merge

In QuarkXPress, merging means combining boxes and lines into new forms. You could, for example, combine two overlapping circles into a figure-eight shape. It gives you the power to make complex shapes out of simple ones—complex shapes that you would otherwise be forced to try to draw freehand.

For this exercise, you will diverge from the advertisement redesign and do some experimentation on a file we've built specially for this purpose. In the next several steps, you will learn about all the different variations of merging and actually experience each one of them for yourself.

1. Open the file **MERGE.QXT**.

2. With the Item or Content tool active, drag a marquee around the three colored items. They are red, green, and blue.

Notice that the green polygon is behind the other two items. That's important because it is the rearmost item that determines what happens when you merge.

3. With all three of these items selected, go to Item>Merge, as you see in Figure 12.13.

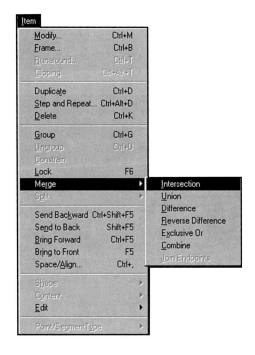

Figure 12.13

The Merge command options.

Intersection

4. Select the Intersection merge option.

We have gathered all the various merge options together into one illustration so you can easily compare their effects, as in Figure 12.14.

As you can see, the Intersection option removes any areas of the back item that are not "selected" by the forward items. It is as if the forward items were cookie cutters and punched out material from the back item.

You will also notice as we go along that the final product of every one of these merge commands is a green box. That's because the back item controls the result so the new merged box item takes on the attributes of the back item, in this case a fill color of green.

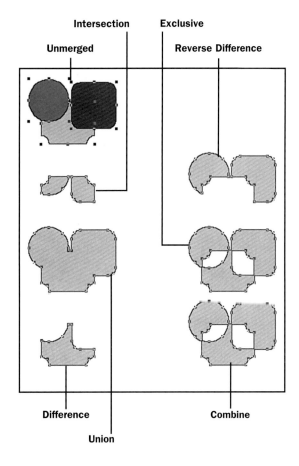

Figure 12.14

A sampler of all the QuarkXPress Merge command options.

Press ⌘+Z (Mac) or Ctrl+Z (Win95) to undo this merge move so you can start again.

Union

5. Select **I**tem>**M**erge>**U**nion.

With this merge you get a big box that follows the outside perimeter of the all the selected items. Again, it's a green box because the back item is colored green.

Press ⌘+Z (Mac) or Ctrl+Z (Win95) to undo this merge move so you will be ready for the next step.

Difference

6. Choose **I**tem>**M**erge>**D**ifference.

This merge is basically the reverse of **I**ntersection. The only areas of the back item that remain are the ones that were not covered by the front items.

Press ⌘+Z (Mac) or Ctrl+Z (Win95) to undo this merge move so you can try the next merge option.

Reverse Difference

7. Try **I**tem>**M**erge>**R**everse Difference.

As you might expect, this one is the reverse of **D**ifference. The back item has been deleted and the remaining area follows the shape of the front selected items, although they are still green.

Press ⌘+Z (Mac) or Ctrl+Z (Win95) to undo this merge move so you can start fresh.

Exclusive Or

8. Next choose **I**tem>**M**erge>**E**xclusive Or.

This one removes any areas where the front items and the back item overlap one another.

Press ⌘+Z (Mac) or Ctrl+Z (Win95) to undo this merge move so you can begin with a new merge option.

Combine

9. With **I**tem>**M**erge>**C**ombine, you get a result that looks exactly like **E**xclusive Or.

The difference between the two is the number of Bézier points available to you if you wanted to further shape this merged box. Combine gives you only one point per intersection. Exclusive Or provides two points.

Press ⌘+Z (Mac) or Ctrl+Z (Win95) to undo this merge move so you can try the splitting command.

Join Endpoints

10. Select the two lines that are located right below the boxes with which you have been experimenting.

    Try the Item>Merge>Join Endpoints merge option.

    You will get an error message saying the endpoints aren't close enough.

11. Maneuver one end of each line over the other so that they have two overlapping endpoints.

    Now try the Item>Merge>Join Endpoints command again and it should work this time.

    As you can see, this is how you join two lines into a single line. The joined point is a Corner point, which you could now convert to a Smooth point or a Symmetrical point just as with any other Bézier point.

    Feel free to simply close this experimental document without saving it and move on to the next exercise where you will be back working on the revised advertisement.

Merging and Splitting Items

It would be hard to imagine a real world graphics project that would use more than one or two of the various merge options you just experienced. But in this exercise, you will put merging and splitting to work, and will make some interesting use of merging in connection with the custom dotted line you built for our hypothetical lighting company in the last chapter.

1. If you closed it while we were doing our merge experiments, reopen your working file of the revised advertisement. You could also work from **12BASE05.QXT** from the CD-ROM, which should be one of the files you copied to your working folder at the beginning of this chapter.

Text Converted to Box Is One Item

2. Right now, the text you converted to a box is just that, a single box, even though the letters don't touch. In fact, it is just like a merged item.

   Click on one of the letters with the Item tool and you'll see that the entire group of letters is selected.

Splitting Box Into Discrete Parts

3. Go to Item>Split and notice that you have two options.

   All Paths will break a merged box down into every possible component. In this case, it would break the letters "o" into several parts, making an item out of the outer circle and another item out of the center "donut hole."

   Outside Paths will split a merged box into its separate components based on the outermost edge of each item that was merged. In this case, the text will be split into discrete letters, each one having been converted into a QuarkXPress box.

   Choose Outside Paths.

Rejoining Split Boxes

4. Again, each letter is now a separate box and only the first one is selected after the Split operation.

   Drag a marquee around the boxes that spell out "Lots" and select Item>Merge>Combine. This will have the effect of putting these pieces back together into a single box.

5. Combine the boxes that spell out "of," just as you did in the last step.

6. Combine the boxes that spell "Light" in the same way. Use ⬆Shift + Click to select them, rather than a marquee, so you won't also be selecting the light bulbs in the background.

You now have three word-sized boxes.

7. With the Item tool, select the word "of."

    Reduce its size to 65%. You can do that by typing ***.65** after the W/H coordinates in the Measurements palette and pressing ⌐Return⌐ (Mac) or ⌐Enter⌐ (Win95).

8. Using the Item tool—and being careful not to accidentally grab a Bézier point and stretch a box out of shape—stack up the boxes as in Figure 12.15. You should try to nestle the word "of" down between the ascenders of the letters in "Light."

9. Select all three "word" boxes and again use Item>Merge>Combine on them, merging them back into a new and restructured single box.

Merging Lines

10. In addition to the Join Endpoints option, you can also merge lines and boxes for some useful effects.

    Using the Bézier Line tool, draw out a line similar to the one in Figure 12.16. With some special treatment, this will become the pull chain dotted line.

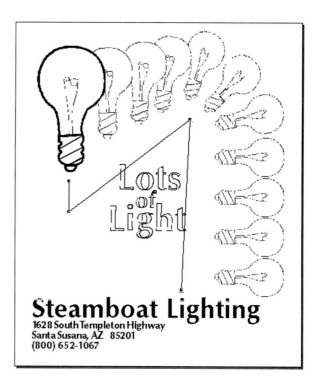

Figure 12.16

The initial Bézier line, before converting to curves.

11. Triple-click the line to select all its points and use Item>Point/Segment Type to convert the points to Smooth points. Our line flipped into the curves you see in Figure 12.17. (Yours may vary since it's hard to duplicate a Bézier exactly.)

Appending Dash and Stripe Definitions

12. Use the familiar File>Append command to import into your working file the Steamboat Dots dash definition, as in Figure 12.18.

    You can append from the final file from Chapter 11, **11BASE08.QXT**. It contains the definition and it should already be in your working folder from when you copied the Chapter 12 files from your CD-ROM.

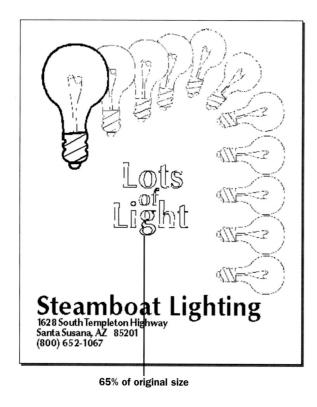

65% of original size

Figure 12.15

Stacking "word" boxes.

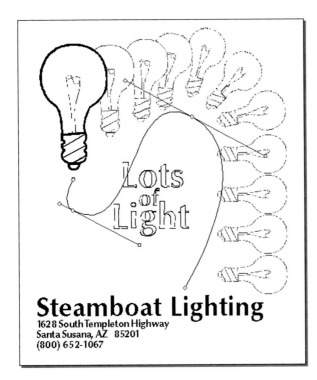

Figure 12.17

The line after converting to curves by changing Corner points to Smooth points.

13. Format the Bézier line with the Steamboat Dots definition.

14. Set the line at 18 points width.

15. As always, before beginning a tricky move, save your file so you can **File>Revert** To Saved. If your Bézier curve adjustments in the next few steps don't go quite right you'll be able to easily return to this point.

16. Use the Bézier points to form the pull chain dotted line into a loop as in Figure 12.19.

    You will need to use the Bézier handles on the topmost point of the line to do this. Simply grab one of the handles (we used the one to the right) and rotate it completely around.

17. As in Figure 12.20, draw out a rectangle picture box, big enough to cover all the dotted line.

    Send it all the way to the back of the stacking order with ⬧Shift+F5 and use the Modify command to color it yellow.

    Any kind of merge requires two objects and you will recall that the back one controls the outcome of the procedure. This yellow box will be the back object when we merge it with the dotted line.

Figure 12.18

Appending a custom dash definition from an old working file.

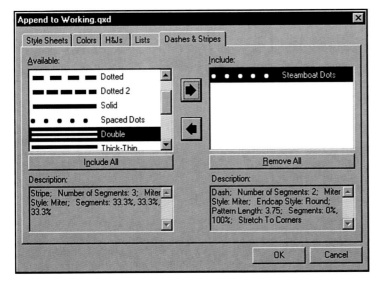

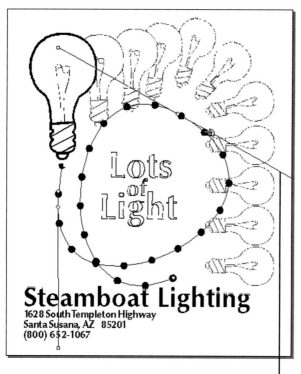

Rotate Bézier handle to form loop ⏤

Figure 12.19

Looped dotted line.

Merging a Box and a Line

18. Save your file again once you have the line adjusted and the yellow box in place, just in case you need to Revert To Saved.

19. Select both the yellow box and the dotted line.

20. Apply **I**tem>**M**erge>**I**ntersection. You've got yellow dots as in Figure 12.21.

Just as with the Type To Box command, the elements of the item—in this case the dots—are turned into a single box. (If you split this box now, just like when you broke up the converted type into individual letter boxes, the dots would be broken down into individual items.)

21. You may have figured out by now that you could simply have colored the dotted line yellow to achieve this effect much more simply. However, you would not have been able to put a stroke on these dots, something you need to do to help the yellow dots stand out. Yellow, being a light color, needs this kind of help when used alone or it tends to just disappear on the page.

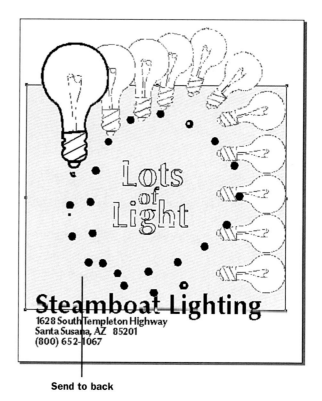

Send to back

Figure 12.20

Creating a back item before merging the dotted line.

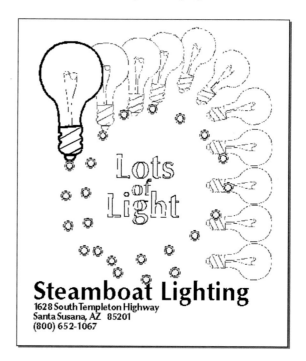

Figure 12.21

Dots merged into box yield a box made up of dots.

With the dotted box selected, use Modify to put a 1-point "frame" around the box, outlining each dot in black.

22. Where the light bulbs cover dots, send the bulbs to the back using ⬆Shift+F5.

● The final revised advertisement has been saved on the CD-ROM in a file named **12BASE06.QXT**.

Tip

Be Cautious About Complex Boxes And Bézier Items

Fundamentally, these, like Clipping Path and Runaround, generate Bézier points—potentially a lot of them. We will talk more about preparing files for output in Chapter 15, but for now it is important that you understand that the Type To Box and Merge commands are capable of creating items that are so complex that they simply can't be printed, even on the most sophisticated of equipment. The situation can get even worse

if you put a picture or some other graphic item inside one of these complex boxes. That isn't to say you should never do it, but you should exercise caution and follow proofing precautions you learn about in Chapter 15 when building pages with these complex items.

Summary

This chapter has been about saving time. Aligning, spacing, merging, splitting, locking, duplicating, stepping, and repeating—these are all production tools designed to automatically perform jobs that would take you a very long time indeed if you had to do them by hand. Instead of lining items up by hand or maybe with ruler guides you can align or space them automatically using Space/Align. Instead of a two step Copy/Paste operation you can just Duplicate an item. And the Step And Repeat command will allow you to duplicate an item many times at once.

Review It

As a review of what you have learned in this chapter, please answer the following questions.

1. Name the three parameters you need to set in the Space/Align Items dialog box.

2. How do you give QuarkXPress a measurement reference point for Space/Align Items?

3. QuarkXPress bases its Space/Align move on what in the horizontal direction? And for vertical Space/Align moves?

4. The Duplicate command and the Step and Repeat command are one-step versions of what standard operations?

5. What can you do if you want to move or modify locked items (and leave them locked)?

6. Text To Box and Merge both generate a general category of item, which is…?

7. What are the three parameters you set for Step and Repeat?

_____

_____

8. When merging items, what determines the attributes of the resulting box?

_____

_____

9. If you want to break a merged item down into individual components you use which command?

_____

_____

10. As a general rule, you should do what before beginning a tricky operation?

_____

_____

Check It

Multiple Choice

Please circle the correct answer for each of the following questions.

1. In order to create a Bézier line loop you _____.

   a.   select all points, convert to Symmetrical

   b.   rotate point handle

   c.   convert to curved segments

   d.   all of the above

2. The offset for the Step and Repeat and the Duplicate commands is measured from _____.

   a.   origin point

   b.   chosen edge

   c.   topmost edge

   d.   none of the above

3. If you select a single item and set the Step and Repeat count at seven you will end up with _____ items.

   a.   seven

   b.   eight

   c.   depends on offset amount

   d.   minus one

4. When you first use it, the offset for the Duplicate command will be _____.

   a.   based on current Step and Repeat setting

   b.   last session's offset in Step and Repeat

   c.   .25 inch

   d.   none of the above

5. Converting text to a box will let you _____.

   a.   fill the box with color

   b.   stroke the box with a frame

   c.   get a picture

   d.   all of the above

6. Which of the Merge command options can be used on a line?

   a.   All of them

   b.   Join Endpoint

   c.   Line Intersection

   d.   all of the above

7. The keyboard shortcuts for the Duplicate and the Step and Repeat commands are _____.

   a.   ⌘+D, Ctrl+D for Duplicate and ⌘+Option+D, Ctrl+Alt+D for Step and Repeat

b. ⌘+U, Ctrl+U for Duplicate and ⌘+Option +R, Ctrl+Alt+R for Step and Repeat

c. ⌘+D, Ctrl+D for Duplicate and ⌘+Option +S, Ctrl+Alt+S for Step and Repeat

d. none of the above

8. If you wanted to double the size of an item, you could _____.

a. type *2 after the W/H parameters in Modify

b. type *2 after the W/H parameters in Measurements palette

c. ⬆Shift+Click/drag on size handle until twice the size

d. all of the above

9. The various merge options differ by _____.

a. amount of area cut out of back item

b. amount of area delete from front items

c. treatment of overlap with back item

d. all of the above

10. The controlling factor in a vertical Space/Align move is _____.

a. leftmost item

b. topmost item

c. center item

d. none of the above

True or False

Please circle *T* or *F* to indicate whether the statement is true or false.

T   F   **1.** When stepping and repeating in an upward direction on the page use a negative offset value.

T   F   **2.** To open the Align/Space command, the keyboard shortcut is ⌘+, (Mac) or Ctrl+, (Win95).

T   F   **3.** If the back box in a selection is filled with red and stroked with a frame, the merged box will be framed but not read.

T   F   **4.** There's no way to set the offset for the Duplicate command.

T   F   **5.** The leftmost item will control the vertical positioning of selected items in a Space/Align move.

T   F   **6.** Once you split a merged item you can't merge it again.

T   F   **7.** You use the upper left corner of an item as the measuring point for a step and repeat move.

T   F   **8.** If you do a save first, you can undo any QuarkXPress move with Revert To Saved.

T   F   **9.** Once you lock an item you can't change it in any way.

T   F   **10.** There's no way to use the Text To Box command on more than one line of text.

Design It

Using some of the bag of tricks you learned in this chapter could get to be an exercise in excess. You can compose some horribly complicated files using such commands as Step And Repeat on a large graphics image, or converting a lot of text to boxes. Try to avoid making those mistakes in this independent work exercise.

■   Search out a number of different kinds of light bulb images and change the message in this ad to one of variety instead of quantity. Try a search of your school computer lab's clip art library or scan some images from a catalog. Try to compose a layout that morphs one type of bulb to another and then to another.

■   Is there another way you could use the pull chain motif for this ad? What about a necklace of lights? Or perhaps a string of light bulbs linked by the pull chain dotted line?

Case Studies

Advice—Show Your Range

Ann Clarkson: One technique that has helped me in the past is a "before & after" section, where I've been able to take on a bad or mediocre product and improve it.

Patricia Olson: I did do a few newsletter makeovers and brought them to those who produced them. They became clients.

David Rozansky: Another suggestion is to go for a personal portfolio that has no reason other than for art's sake. Pretend to be Ansel Adams and create an art portfolio using the techniques learned from school. In other words, show me insight into how you think and what is important to you.

Exercise—Create Case Studies

In the previous Portfolio Builders, we have spoken a good deal about telling your story, of how you think, of your creative aesthetic, of how you can solve communications challenges.

One portfolio technique you could try is to create a series of case studies. These case studies are designed to openly acknowledge that you are a student with limited professional experience, but that you have potential for thinking creatively.

- Identify two to four (any more would probably be more than you could talk about in a portfolio interview) examples of graphics work that you would like to explore.

- For each project, identify the communications goal—trying to sell something to a particular audience, trying to persuade a group of people of the rightness of a political position, informing a reader about important information. Each of your chosen projects should have a different communications goal.

- Don't just change for change sake. Try to explore new ways to use the visual elements—or to slightly modify the same elements—in order to meet the communications goal.

- Consider picking some graphic element out of each case study project to retain through each of the designs. That will illustrate your ability to tackle a project from a number of different perspectives while sticking to the communications goal.

These case studies will clearly be student exercises, not real work for hire. However, instead of being a hodgepodge of technique exercises, like many student portfolios, they will have a focus and will illustrate that you can not only work in QuarkXPress, but also that you can think creatively.

Understanding and Defining Color

What You Will Learn

There may be no bigger thrill in desktop publishing than creating color right on your computer—especially for those who started out in the business using only pre-computer traditional color techniques. Using those old ways, it often took hours to create what you can now do on your computer in a few minutes. That same new computer power has its dark side, though. Working faster doesn't necessarily mean working better, and the new ways make it easy to create an unprintable mess in just a few minutes—also much faster than the traditional methods.

So, it's crucial that you spend some time in the next three chapters learning the fundamental technology of getting colored ink onto paper.

In Chapter 14, you put all this color theory to work, creating several versions of an annual report cover using three different techniques for producing color.

In Chapter 15, you learn how to proof your job and bundle it up to take it to a commercial printer for final production.

In this chapter, you will learn:

➤ Why your computer screen will only rarely—if ever— match the results you actually get from the printing press

➤ The difference between spot color and the four-color process

➤ How your printer and service bureau get the printing press to achieve halftones—shades of gray and color intensities that allow you to reproduce highlights and shadows

➤ How to define a color in QuarkXPress

➤ The importance of using standard color libraries to try to maximize color accuracy

Creating an Annual Report Cover

Part V

Getting Colorful

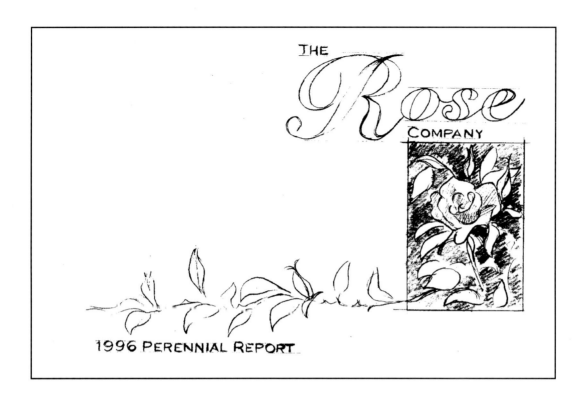

Figure 13.1

You will, by the end of this chapter and the next one, turn the pencil sketch at top into the full-color layout you see below it.

Getting Set Up

Copy all the files for this chapter from the CD-ROM to a work area on your hard drive. They are all in the **Steps** folder in the subfolder labeled **13**.

You will need to have the Vivaldi and Function Small Caps fonts installed on your computer for the exercises in this chapter.

Vivaldi is a new font and the final one to be introduced in the book. (You used the Function Small Caps font when you set old style figures in the newsletter in Chapters 9 and 10.) You might like to review the information on script fonts in the Design Notes section of Chapter 6 where we introduced another—very different—script font called Mistral.

Following each exercise in this chapter, save your project to a work area on your hard drive. Each succeeding exercise builds on the previous one, so saving at the end of each exercise will enable you to pick up where you left off if you aren't able to complete all the chapter exercises in one sitting. Also, on the CD-ROM you will find saved versions of the project as it should exist at the end of each exercise. You can fall back on those interim versions of the advertisement as reference points if you are having trouble with one of the exercises.

Your Screen Doesn't Match the Printing Press

In the world of digital color—in the world of any kind of color—there's no such thing as perfect accuracy. Certainly, there's no such thing as a perfect match between your computer screen and the results you achieve when you hire a printer to put ink to paper on a printing press. Call up a picture of a dewy pink rose on any dozen computers and you are apt to get a dozen subtly different shades of pink. And the color you get on paper from a printing press probably won't perfectly match any of them.

There are some standard color-matching systems, such as the Pantone systems that we will discuss shortly, and those colors can be depended upon to be close to one another, even if they are run on two different printing presses (unless someone screws up when mixing the ink, or does a bad job of cleaning the press between jobs). But even though you get consistent colors on the printing press with these standard color systems, your computer screen still won't match your printed color.

In the last few years, there have been significant improvements in the ability to calibrate and synchronize the color reproduction from your computer screen, your color printer or proofing system, and the printing press. These new color management systems are helping a great deal in the search for color accuracy.

However, no matter how much color management systems improve, it will take a lot of innovation for a calibration system to ever conquer one central difficulty: The way your computer produces color on the video screen and the way a printing press produces color on a page simply do not compare.

As illustrated in Figure 13.2, the computer screen shoots light at you by making phosphor glow inside a glass picture tube—projected light. A printing press puts ink on paper so you only see it from light that bounces off the paper—reflected light.

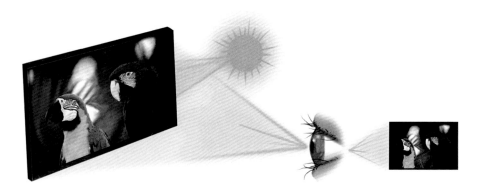

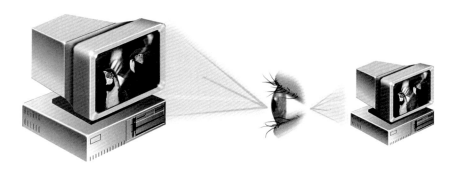

Figure 13.2

Reflected light (top) and projected light (bottom) reach the eye in completely different ways, resulting in major differences in how you see the "same" color. (Also reproduced in the color section.)

Here's a list of the variables that hinder your computer screen from displaying the same color you will get off the printing press:

- Computer monitors build up colors from red, green, and blue (RGB) light, whereas printing presses build colors out of inks.

- Instead of RGB, printing presses use either pre-mixed ink colors (as if you had bought a can of a particular color of paint) or they compose colors from a mixture of four colors—cyan, magenta, yellow, and black. (There are a few other printing press color systems, but those are the two main ones.)

- The computer can use any one of a dozen or so methods of describing colors—called color spaces. When scanning color images or creating custom colors, it is possible to mix these color spaces. However, the translations between different color spaces can create major inaccuracies.

- Printing press results will be inconsistent due to batch variations in the "same" ink colors and variations in the way different press operators produce the printing press plates.

- Phosphor varies from one computer screen to the other, resulting in inconsistent display of colors.

- As it ages, a computer monitor screen sprays a varying number of electrons at the phosphor, resulting in brightness and contrast inconsistencies from monitor to monitor, even if they are plugged into the same computer and even if they are made at the same factory, using the same batch of phosphor.

- Paper makes a major difference in the color of your final printed product, absorbing more or less ink (depending on the weather and storage conditions) and adding its own underlying tint to the color mix.

- The systems that provide color proofs—as good as they are—aren't perfect. So when the service bureau pulls a proof, you can't rely on a perfect match with the final printed page.

- You may not be publishing on paper. If you are using QuarkXPress to create a slide or overhead presentation, other factors can create variations in color. Fundamental differences occur when you shine light through transparent material. For slides, many other variables are introduced by the operator of the film recorder and the slide developing process. And for overheads, the range of color printer options—from an inexpensive inkjet to an ultra-expensive dye sublimation printer—introduces yet more variables.

- And finally, your brain constantly makes judgments, so you see colors differently. What you see may depend on all sorts of environmental factors, such as the amount and type of overhead lights and the color of the walls in your design studio. Neutral colors are best.

The point is: Don't trust the color you see on your monitor. So, how do you deal with this color accuracy problem?

- Keep in mind that you can't choose or edit colors based purely on what you see on the computer screen. Be constantly aware of the challenge you face in translating color from the computer screen to some other medium.

- Learn about all the technology—the old-fashioned printing press technology as well as the new color management systems. Use the new technology to the limit in order to achieve results, but remain cautious about relying on color management.

- Rely on experience—the experience of your service bureau and print shop managers. Nothing will take the place of collaboration with the experts on your color production team. These people have been trained by years of expensive mistakes and they see more jobs in a week than most graphic designers see in six months.

Understanding Spot Color

When you use a rubber stamp or pick up a brush to paint the trim of your house, you are using spot color. In printing, *spot color* means you are smearing a solid swatch of ink onto the printed page. In a sense you are printing with spot color, even when you print an all black-ink publication—in that case, the spot color being the color of black ink.

Usually, though, when someone says, "I just did a spot color job," they mean they have run a job on a printing press using black ink plus one or more additional spot colors. The spot colors are premixed ink, concocted by the printer or by the print shop's supplier, almost always using one of the standardized color-matching systems. That's how you choose your color and achieve color accuracy—by selecting from standard color swatches.

Spot Color Means Accurate Color

Spot color is accurate because you are actually selecting the ink that will be used by the printer, in much the same way you would select a particular color when painting a room. So, because you are working with premixed ink colors, spot color pretty much solves the challenge of achieving accurate color on the press.

You still can't see the color accurately on your computer, but you can see what you will get. You buy a book of color swatches similar to the paint chips you get at the paint store. For a PMS (Pantone Matching System) swatch book for example, the Pantone company mixes its standard colors of ink under scientifically controlled circumstances and puts them down on paper so you can select a color and specify its use by the commercial printer.

Of course, there are still some variables. Your paper choice will influence the results from the press, and your perception of the colors varies because of the ambient light as you examine the color swatch (fluorescent, sunshine, incandescent, and so forth). However, by and large, spot color means accurate color.

You *could* create a spot color in QuarkXPress without using one of the standard color matching systems. You *could* "mix" a color on your computer screen and designate it as a spot color. But don't do it with any expectation that you will get that color on paper from a printing press. You could have puce on screen and specify that the printer use chartreuse ink. The result won't be puce. It will be chartreuse. In spot color work, everything depends on the ink used by the print shop, no matter what color you use on your computer screen.

Spot Color Overlays and Press Plates

When you work with spot color you generally use two or three inks, although you could have many more. The printer makes up a plate for black ink, a plate for your second color, and another for your third, then prints your pages by running the paper over all those plates. You can have as many inks as your printer can handle on the press during a single run. The print shop can even run the paper through more than once to add still more colors (at some point, however, it makes more sense to use process color, a discussion coming up in the next section).

In order to create these plates—one for each color you are specifying for the job (including black)—you need to make up paper or film *overlays*. Each overlay mimics the printing press plate by isolating every little bit

of its particular assigned color onto a single sheet of paper or film that the printer can use to photographically expose a plate (Figure 13.3).

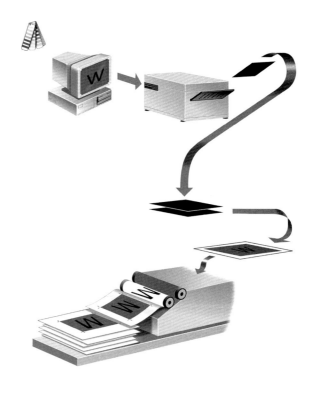

Figure 13.3

The work flow for creating spot color, from color-matching system swatches, to computer layout, to imagesetter output, and then finally on the press. (Also reproduced in the color section.)

Why are these spot color mechanicals called overlays? Because that was the term traditionally used when a graphic artist pasted up a project for the printer. The type was mechanically (instead of electronically) pasted down on a stiff board and each spot color was represented by acetate overlays mounted in layers.

We now paste up our pages electronically, in the computer, instead of using an Xacto knife, T-square, Rubylith, acetate, and poster board or foam-core.

QuarkXPress will then automatically produce your spot color overlay mechanicals. In Chapter 14, you will print some overlays on a desktop printer just to see the effect of splitting a publication into these layers of color. (You will use the Output tab in QuarkXPress's Print dialog box to produce these overlays.)

Understanding Process Color

Think of process color printing as playing a major hoax on your eyes and brain. Process color uses the four CMYK colors—cyan, magenta, yellow, and black—to create the effect of thousands of colors.

Some people think of four-color process printing as mixing these four ink colors to create the new colors, but that's not quite so. In actuality, each of the four-color plates prints nearly microscopic separate dots of ink onto the paper. Speaking in general terms, these dots of ink don't physically mix together on the paper (other than the inevitable situation where some dots land on top of each other). Instead, your eye sees all these dots and they are actually mixed by your brain to create the effect of a rainbow of color. In short, process color printing is an optical illusion.

Another reason the illusion works, in addition to breaking the images up into dots, is the fact that process color inks are transparent. That helps the eye to mix colors when dots inevitably overlap. Spot color inks, by comparison, are dense and opaque.

Images get converted into these dots by turning your publication into four-layered *halftones*, one for each color. You'll need to understand more about halftones, a discussion that's coming up in the section titled "Understanding Halftones and Screens."

Separating the Four Process Colors

At some point, if your full-color (as opposed to spot color) publication is heading for a printing press, you must get it into CMYK four-color process color.

Instead of one or two or three spot color overlays, you must separate the publication into four overlays, one for each of the standard process colors.

In desktop publishing, you separate your color work electronically by using a software program that breaks an image down into four separations—four layers of color that together compose a full-color image. QuarkXPress does this for you, or it may be done by special software at your service bureau or print shop. Sometimes the scanned photographs you import into QuarkXPress have been pre-separated into CMYK color. (Most scanners operate in the same kind of color you see on your computer screen, RGB for Red, Green, and Blue.)

Before computers, this separation of color into four component parts was done photographically in a print shop darkroom. The process is called *separating* and the resulting screens are called *separations*. (See Figure 13.4)

Separating the image into the four CMYK colors of cyan, magenta, yellow, and black is just one part of the job. Those layers of color must be turned into halftones called *screens*. Again, we'll talk some more about halftones in an upcoming section. For now, it is important to understand that halftone screens create the dots that are essential to the process color optical illusion. Your brain conveniently ignores the fact that the color image is just a bunch of individual colored dots, and it blends adjacent dots into a perceived color. (See Figure 13.5)

It's important that you understand this point: Dots of cyan, magenta, yellow, and black can be mixed together to create almost any color you like, but they aren't actually mixed together except in your brain. They create these colors through optical illusion.

Here's another important point: The apparent color and the intensity of that color on your printed page is determined by the relative percentages (size and number of dots) of each of the four colors on a scale of zero to 100 percent.

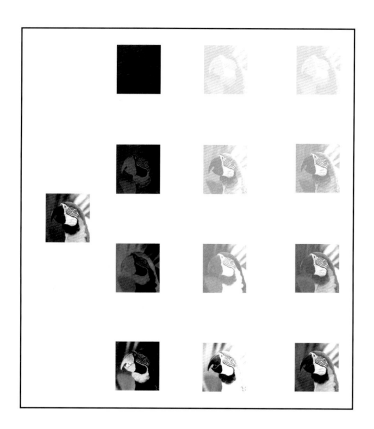

Figure 13.4

From left to right, the original picture, the four CMYK negative films (the separations), the printing press impressions from each separation in the proper CMYK colors, and finally the way the four colors combine to produce a final full-color image. (Also reproduced in the color section.)

Figure 13.5

The eye perceives the dots of different colors all together, not as individual dots, and "mixes" the color. (Also reproduced in the color section.)

Deciding between Spot and Process Color

So now you know that there are two basic methods for creating color on a printing press—spot color and process color. How do you choose between them?

To some extent, you choose between spot color and process color because of money. Basically, you want to use the minimum possible number of color plates on the press because the price goes up with every additional ink color (additional printing press plate). That means that if you have any more than three colors, then you probably want to use process color techniques. As long as you have that many press plates in play, you might as well go to process colors, which only require four plates. When you are paying for four colors, you might as well use process color instead of spot color and have the freedom to design with as many colors as you like.

That's over-simplified, of course, because in some circumstances you need the accuracy of the pre-mixed inks used in the spot color method. However, the basic idea holds true—the more inks you use, the more complicated the job on the press and the more money you spend.

Sometimes, despite expense issues, you have no choice in methods. You have to use process color to reproduce a color photograph, for example, because spot color simply can't do it. Conversely, for some jobs you absolutely must use spot colors. For those jobs, you use standard inks from one of the color-matching systems. The Pantone Matching System (PMS) has become ubiquitous since its invention back in the early 1960s, but other systems for achieving standard color do exist. Some other spot color-matching systems are Dainippon (or DIC) and Toyo. Also, some color-matching systems bridge the gap between premixed inks and process color printing, since these process color matching systems give you swatches printed with particular percentages of the four process colors.

When might a spot color-matching system be essential? Well, you need inks from one of the color matching systems to create certain unusual ink effects, such as fluorescent yellow, pearlescent blue, or metal-flake tangerine. There are also some colors that simply can't be reproduced through the process color technique and you would need to use spot colors to get those colors.

Also, companies or brands sometimes are very picky about their signature colors, and you must have a spot color plate to get that color exactly right—the color for a consumer packaged goods brand like soap or cough medicine is a good example. This sometimes results in jobs with five plates, four CMYK plates plus a spot color specified with a PMS number. It's also common to print high quality maps with six or eight spot colors rather than process colors.

Understanding Halftones and Screens

It's crucial that you understand halftones and screens. Otherwise you won't be able to clearly understand how you go about creating process color. And you need to know how that process works—and make some decisions about how you will implement it—right from the beginning of building a color publication. Ignorance could cause you to build fundamental mistakes into your project, mistakes that could require expensive make goods and require you to redo your work. So, let's cover some theory and then we'll get to some bottom line advice about halftones and screening.

There's No Gray on the Printing Press

To understand halftones, screens, and dots, you need to start with the fact that the whole point of these three things is to make it possible for a printing press to print shades of gray (or shades of yellow, or blue, or any other color).

Let's hit that point again: Without halftones, screens, and dots, a printing press can't actually print shades of gray.

You might not think being able to print gray or shades of colors would be a big deal. But, in fact, it is an absolutely huge big deal.

Here's why. You can't reproduce a photograph without being able to print gray. One name for bitmapped images, in fact, is grayscale image. And you could pour all the gray ink you want onto the printing press plates and you still wouldn't be able to print that photograph. You need the illusion of gray, and that means you need halftones, screens, and dots.

When someone says a photograph has 256 shades of gray—a grayscale image—there's no gray ink in that image at all. By screening inks—by making halftones—you can achieve the optical illusion of gray. Figure 13.6 shows two ways of creating gray with dots of ink.

To drive this point home, have a look at Figure 13.7 where you can see two versions of the same picture, one with solid ink and the other broken up into halftone dots by screening. Of course, we've kept this simple by using just a single ink. If it was a color photo, we would be screening the separated overlays of the four CMYK process colors.

Figure 13.6

These two squares of gray have been created with two different processes. The one on the top is a halftone gray, a "tint" of black made up of dots created through screening. The one on the bottom is actually a gray made up of the CMYK process colors, also by creating halftones of cyan, magenta, yellow, and black. (Also reproduced in the color section.)

Figure 13.7

Solid ink can't be used to reproduce a photograph because it can't give you a range of gray values—a grayscale. The top photo was scanned as line art, without halftoning so all the areas that would normally be printed in gradations of tone have been inked in solid. The same photo was scanned in the bottom version, but the bottom scan has been broken up into dots—a halftone. (Also reproduced in the color section.)

Before Digital Halftones, There Were Process Cameras

To understand what happens in the digital halftone world, it helps to understand the old way of producing halftones. Traditionally, before we had computers doing this work, halftone spots were all literally created by a screen. A screen would be shoved between the original photograph and the film or paper used to photographically create the plate for the printing press. That screen would break up the original image into halftone spots (Figure 13.8).

The screen in this depiction of the traditional process is a piece of glass etched with crisscrossing lines. More commonly today—in those infrequent cases where the procedure is still used—the screening is accomplished by making a sandwich of the original photo negative, the screen, and the film for making the plate. In that case, the screen is made up of dots instead of crisscrossing lines, but the end result is the same.

You can still have a photograph traditionally screened, by the way. The world hasn't gone entirely digital yet. Like the debates between those who still love vinyl records and CD aficionados, some designers still prefer the look of the rounder and softer dots created for a traditionally halftoned photograph. It just means doing mechanical pasteup or stripping instead of using desktop publishing to its fullest extent.

Why do they call them *halftones*? The idea comes from the concept of removing "half" the information from the original image—a halftone. It doesn't literally work this way, but that's the idea behind the term. The original photograph is called a *contone*, or continuous tone image.

Image **Lens** **Halftone screen** **Film to make printing press plate**

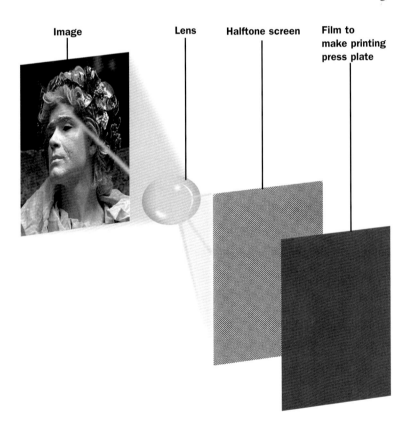

Figure 13.8

This conceptual diagram shows how a printer's process camera works. The camera is set up to make halftones by putting a screen between the lens and the film. (Also reproduced in the color section.)

Now It's PostScript Digital Screening

How does a laser printer or an imagesetter make a halftone? These machines don't have a glass screen hidden inside them, but they produce halftones all the same. They produce halftones with cells, dots, and spots.

Each of the dots in a digital halftone is made up of a bunch of imagesetter or laser spots. Each dot is contained within a halftone cell, which is the square area bounded by the vertical and horizontal lines of the digital "screen," as shown in Figure 13.9.

All this dot and spot business gets confusing because in discussions, people tend to blur the meaning between laser spot and halftone dot. It helps to think of this in terms of a hierarchy:

- The screen divides the image—the halftone—into *cells* which are the equivalent of the traditional screen's grid.

- These cells contain *halftone dots*, the equivalent of the dots created by a traditional photo-optical, mechanical screening process.

- For digital screening we go one level of detail deeper. The digital dots are made up of *spots*.

In a laser printer, the spots are microscopic bits of plastic toner that are fused under heat to the paper, usually 300 or 600 dots per inch (dpi) in resolution.

Instead of a laser printer, your service bureau or commercial printer will use a high resolution photographic imagesetter to create films to be used in "burning" printing press plates. An imagesetter can achieve much higher resolution, 2450 dpi or better.

This dpi business is unfortunately a bit confusing because the resolution of printers and imagesetters is traditionally expressed in dpi, or dots per inch. But those dots per inch are—in our halftone hierarchy—actually spots per inch.

Remember those terms, from largest to smallest: Cells contain halftone dots, which are in turn made up of microscopic spots.

But how does the imagesetter or laser printer make the screen that breaks the image up into cells and dots in the first place? The screening capability is built into PostScript, a special programming language that lives inside laser printers and imagesetters. Digital halftone dots are done mathematically instead of photographically.

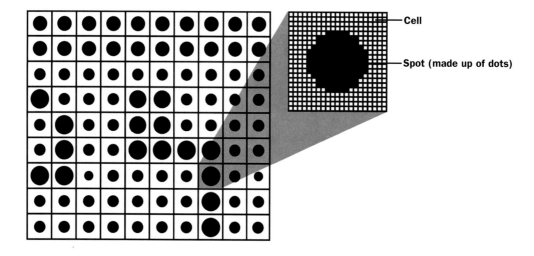

Figure 13.9

Dots, spots, and cells, and how they all relate to one another. (Also reproduced in the color section.)

You Get Gray from the Size of the Halftone Spot

Most people intuitively think that gradations of gray or color intensity are achieved by the total number of dots in a halftone. They think more dots would make a darker gray. But that's not the way it works.

For a given screen, there are always exactly the same number of cells, and hence the same number of potential dots. You can understand this by looking at a close-up of a cell. The cell in a 30 percent gray area of an image is the same size and has the same number of dots (one) as the cell from a 70 percent gray area of the same image. But, as you see in Figure 13.10, the dot inside the cells varies to produce a lighter or darker point on the scale of gray.

More Grays from Larger Cells

This may be the most confusing part of the halftone concept. For any given imagesetter resolution, a coarser screen will give you more gradations of gray (gray levels). You would usually think that a finer screen would somehow give you finer results, so this is a bit counter-intuitive. But it's true, the larger the cells, the more gray levels.

It's true because, in order to achieve more levels of gray, you need to be able to put inside a cell a wider range of dot sizes. In order to vary the size of the dot, you need to be able to vary the number of spots in a dot. However, the spots created in a laser printer or an imagesetter are always the same size.

That means you can get more levels of gray by increasing the size of the cell so it can hold a wider range of total dots. The coarser the screen—the larger the cells—the more levels of gray you can portray. (Or, you could go to a higher resolution laser printer or imagesetter that can print smaller spots and therefore be able to print a wider range of dots sizes for a given cell size (or line screen).)

Screening (Tinting) Color

Halftoning is the process of screening an image in order to reproduce it with ink and paper. Screening also refers to producing tints of a color. You could, for example, specify that you wanted type in 100% black against a 20% screen of pink. Screening or doing percentage tints of solid colors helps you make many colors out of a single one when you do spot color. As with halftones, you break the color into dots, and the size of the dots equates to the percentage of the screen, as shown in Figure 13.11.

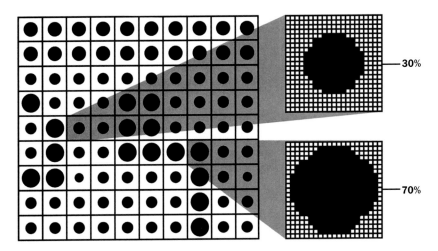

Figure 13.10

What makes these halftone cells 30 and 70 percent? The percentage of gray equals the percentage of the cell area that has been covered by the dot, which is made up of laser spots. It's the relative size of the dots that determines the level of gray (or of color intensity). (Also reproduced in the color section.)

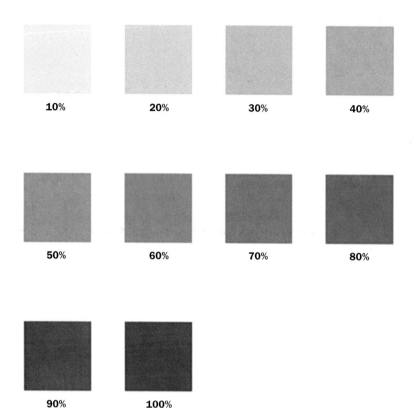

Figure 13.11

A range of percentage tints of the same color. (Also reproduced in the color section.)

10% 20% 30% 40%

50% 60% 70% 80%

90% 100%

Screen Angles and Process Color

The screens in all these illustrations have been at 45 degree angles. That's because making the dots run horizontally or vertically emphasizes their linearity and makes the lines stand out to the eye. The traditional angle for any black or spot color ink screen is 45 degrees, chosen years ago as the best angle for the halftone effect.

Why do you care about the angle of the screens? Well, you will almost never need to care about it. But the question comes up a lot because most desktop publishing and graphics programs allow you to set the angle of the screen for each color. It almost *invites* you to change screen angles. So, naturally, people say, "What screen angle am I supposed to use?" They say, "It's there as if I'm supposed to use it. Why else would they put it there, if I'm not supposed to tweak it?"

Resist that impulse and don't change screen angles. The angles you see there have been standardized over decades of printing halftones and color images with the printing press. Unless there's some really special reason for changing screen angles, and you are doing it in consultation with your print shop, don't mess with the screen angle setting. If you are running color, chances are good that you are going through a service bureau that will do the output anyway. You'll just be setting a booby trap for them. And even if you think there's a better angle for a certain color, it would almost certainly throw off the printing press crew. The project would be booby-trapped; both the printing crew and the service bureau would expect to see the standard angles rolling off the press.

Screen angles become an even more important issue when you do process color work. There are two reasons why and you can see them in Figure 13.12.

Understanding Color, Trapping, and Halftones

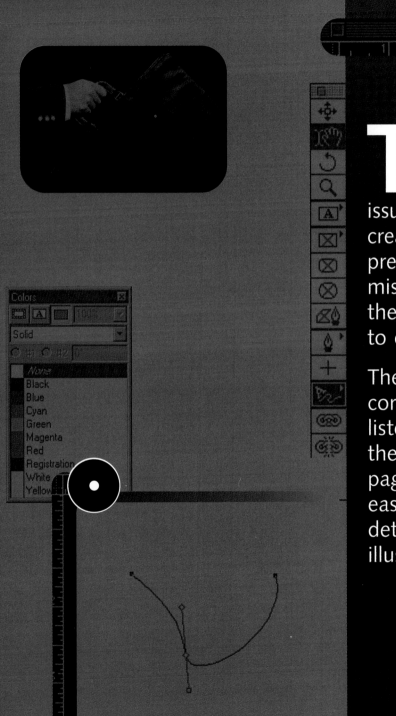

This special section gathers all the illustrations that have to do with color issues into one central location—creating color on the printing press, trapping the color to mask misregistration problems, and the theory behind screening halftones to create grayscale images.

The figure captions listed here correspond to the figure captions listed in the actual chapters of the book. You are also given page numbers so that you can easily refer to the text for a more detailed discussion about these illustrations.

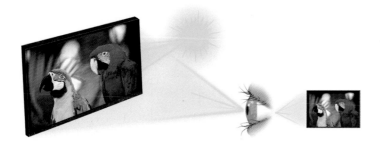

◀ **Figure 13.2** **(Page 302)**

Reflected light (top) and projected light (bottom) reach the eye in completely different ways, resulting in major differences in how you see the "same" color.

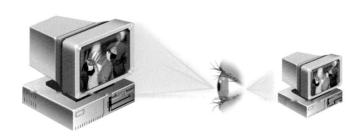

◀ **Figure 13.3** **(Page 304)**

The work flow for creating spot color, from color-matching system swatches, to computer layout, to imagesetter output, and then finally on the press.

Figure 13.4 ▲ (Page 306)

From left to right, the original picture, the four CMYK negative films (the separations), the printing press impressions from each separation in the proper CMYK colors, and finally the way the four colors combine to produce a final full-color image.

(Page 306)   Figure 13.5   ▶

The eye perceives the dots of different colors all together, not as individual dots, and "mixes" the color.

◀   Figure 13.6   (Page 308)

These two squares of gray have been created with two different processes. The one on the left is a halftone gray, a "tint" of black made up of dots created through screening. The one on the right is actually a gray made up of the CMYK process colors, also by creating halftones of cyan, magenta, yellow, and black.

(Page 308)   Figure 13.7   ▼   ▶

Solid ink can't be used to reproduce a photograph because it can't give you a range of gray values—a grayscale. The top photo was scanned as line art, without halftoning so all the areas that would normally be printed in gradations of tone have been inked in solid. The same photo was scanned in the bottom version, but the bottom scan has been broken up into dots, that is, screened into a halftone.

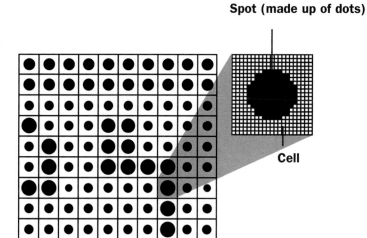

Figure 13.9 ▲ (Page 310)

Dots, spots, and cells, and how they all relate to one another.

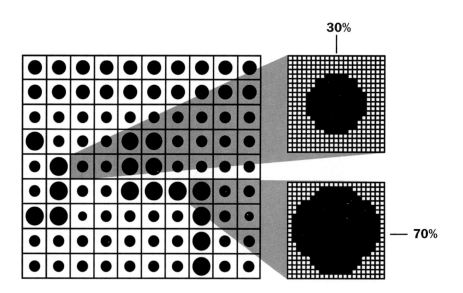

Figure 13.10 ▲ (Page 311)

What makes these halftone cells 30 and 70 percent? The percentage of gray equals the percentage of the cell area that has been covered by the dot, which is made up of laser spots. It's the relative size of the dots that determines the level of gray (or of color intensity).

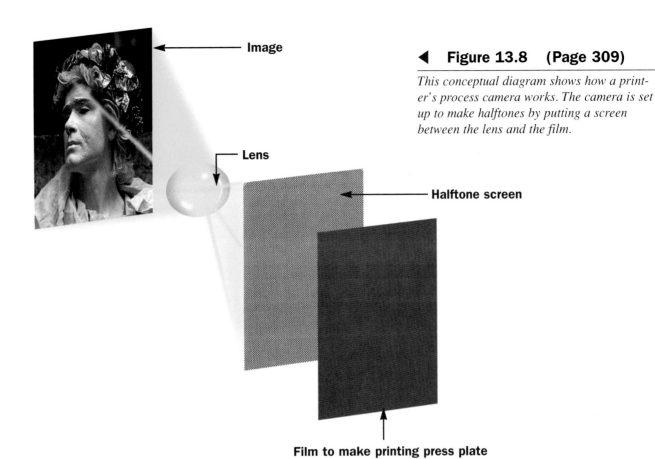

Image

Lens

Halftone screen

Film to make printing press plate

◄ **Figure 13.8** (Page 309)

This conceptual diagram shows how a printer's process camera works. The camera is set up to make halftones by putting a screen between the lens and the film.

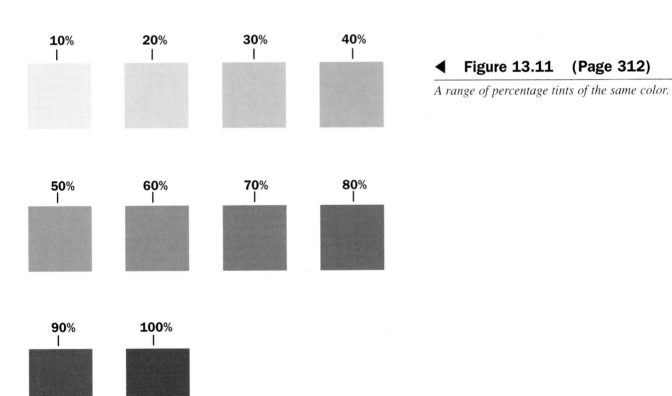

10%   20%   30%   40%

50%   60%   70%   80%

90%   100%

◄ **Figure 13.11** (Page 312)

A range of percentage tints of the same color.

Color Section

Figure 13.12 ▲ ▼ (Page 313)

Process color screen angles keep dots from piling up on one another as in the top illustration of a dot pattern. However, as you can see in the bottom illustration, if you don't use the correct angles you can get a bad moiré pattern.

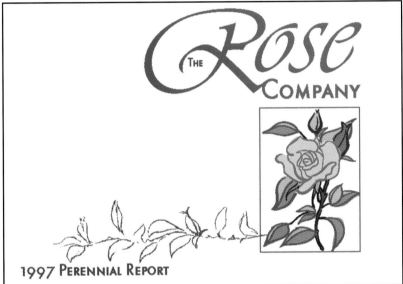

◀ Figure 14.1   (Page 322)

The annual report cover for The Rose Company will go through a design evolution in this chapter. The top cover, with the hand-sketched rose drawing, has been colored using spot colors you defined in the last chapter. The center version of the cover contains an EPS graphic drawing of the rose, with colors adopted from that computer-drawn sketch. The bottom version contains a scanned photo of the rose.

The two "black" overlays (top and center), when burned onto printing press plates and coated with spot color inks, will come together into the color composite final publication (bottom).

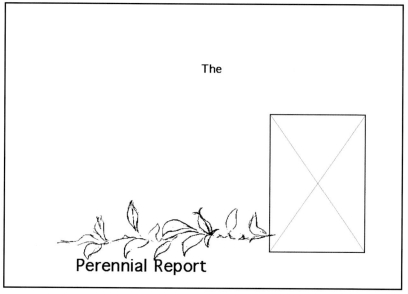

COMPANY

1997

The three spot color plates for the pink rose (top), green leaf (middle), and brown stem (bottom), along with the color composite of the page with the rose drawing (next page).

THE

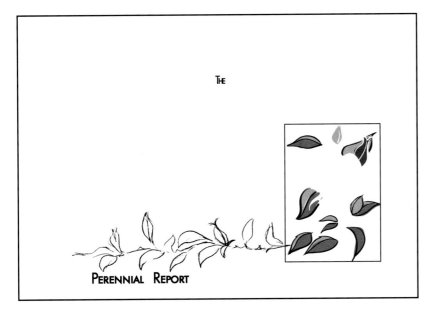

PERENNIAL REPORT

(Page 333)   Figure 14.13 ▶

The four process colors will be used to make the printing press plates. Together, they combine to make up a full-color photograph and the former spot colors.

THE

PERENNIAL REPORT

THE CROSE COMPANY

1997 PERENNIAL REPORT

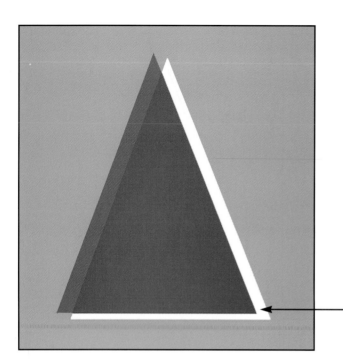

White paper shows through

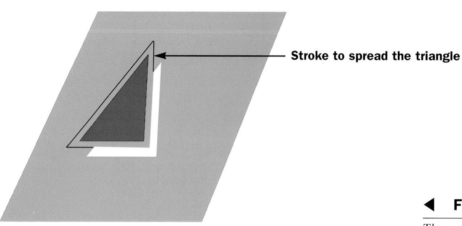

Stroke to spread the triangle

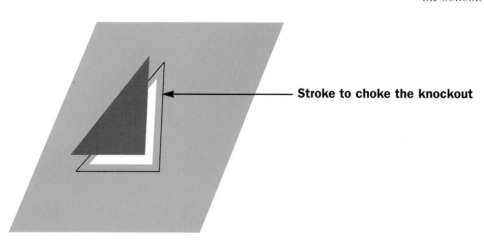

Stroke to choke the knockout

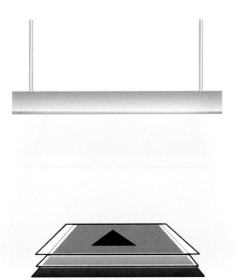

◄ **Figure 15.8** (Page 364)

The light sandwich method used by strippers to create a trap.

◄ **Figure 15.9** (Page 365)

An object stroked with a trapping line, a spread, drawn around the object being trapped.

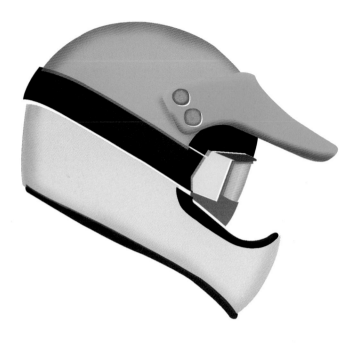

◄ **Figure 15.10** (Page 366)

You must trap imported graphic objects in the programs that created them.

◄ **Figure 15.11** (Page 367)

Overlapping gradations are impossible to trap using object trapping because you get a sharp line along the abutting edge.

Trapping artifact where blends abut

◄ **Figure 15.12** (Page 367)

The difficulty of trapping an object superimposed over a scanned photograph.

Figure 13.12

Process color screen angles keep dots from piling up on one another as in the left illustration of a dot pattern. However, as you can see in the right illustration, if you don't use the correct angles you can get a bad moiré pattern. (Also reproduced in the color section.)

First, you can't do process color without running the colors at different angles; otherwise the dots would pile up on one another in a sort of mush. The angles should make the dots appear to stand alone, so that your brain combines the dots, not so the inks mix on paper, as we've discussed. Ultimately, you want the angles to create a rosette pattern. You might think of the rosette as being almost like a super spot, a major agglomeration of halftone spots that collectively create the impression—the optical illusion—of the final mixed process color.

Second, incorrect angles create a particular kind of printing defect. If the angles are off, you get a moiré pattern. It's a sort of smeary wave effect.

Bottom Line Advice on Screening

We promised some bottom line advice and here it is.

Always have a pre-project discussion with your commercial printer. In that discussion, you will work with the printer to settle a number of technical issues you should resolve before beginning work.

As we discussed in Chapter 10, scanned images are bitmapped, resolution-dependent graphic files (usually in TIFF file format). The resolution at which those graphics are scanned by you or by your pre-press services bureau has a lot to do with the results you will obtain when your electronic paste up pages are turned into ink on paper with a printing press.

So, one item you will resolve in your conference with the printer will be the specifications for screens to make halftones. You need to know how fine or coarse a screen will be used to get good photo reproduction on the printer's presses—the line screen or screen frequency.

Your printer will tell you how fine a dot his press can hold, which in turn determines what line screen will work best on his press. Once you know the line screen, you and the printer will then be able to decide what resolution you must work in when scanning images.

In general, the advice from the printer will probably be to scan at one-and-a-half or two times the line screen. So, for a 133-line screen, common for commercial process color reproduction purposes, you would scan at 200 to 260 dots per inch. Scanning at a resolution any higher than that, in most situations, will simply be a waste of disk space. However, a great deal depends on the paper that will be used, the press, and the nature of the art being scanned (photo, sketch, line art, and so on).

Beginning with a Sketch

As we've discussed, the design for this rose company annual report was created by designer Lydia Mather. She provided us with a sketch that we adopted as a template for producing this design. It was literally adopted as a template, in fact, because we scanned it and placed it on a master page so that it provided the basis for the initial layout as you see in Figure 13.13.

Ultimately, a typeface change was made, which triggered some maneuvering of elements on the page; however, basic relationships were retained among the major components of the design as you can see with the sketch and the final design overlaid in Figure 13.14.

Remember this. Sketching a design concept on paper can be—almost always is, in fact—a crucial part of the design process. Many designers use full size sketches, or quick small sketches, to develop an idea before moving to the computer. And these concept sketches are often a good tool for working through ideas for preliminary client approval before spending expensive hours on producing the final design.

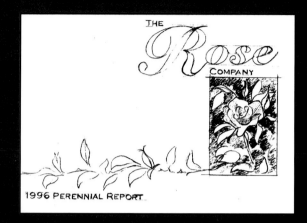

Figure 13.13

Although this design evolved somewhat from Lydia's sketch during work on the project, the lineage of the final result comes through very clearly.

Figure 13.14

The evolved final design, showing the final result overlaid on a screened back (lightened) version of the concept sketch, using the sketch as a template.

Deleting Colors

Now, armed with all this color theory, let's get ready to actually do some color work. The following quick exercises prepare the gardening company annual report project for the next chapter. There you will spend the entire chapter doing exercises that show you various techniques for applying color.

The first step in preparing your Colors palette should be to eliminate unused colors.

1. Before starting, make sure your copy of QuarkXPress is back to factory defaults by renaming or deleting the defaults file—XPress Preferences in the QuarkXPress program folder—with the program closed of course.

   Once your copy of QuarkXPress is factory fresh, open file **13BASE01.QXT**.

2. Open up the Colors palette, View>Show Colors, F12.

   It will be dim (grayed out) because you do not have any item selected that it could act upon. Click with the Item or Content tool on any of the items on the page and your palette will look like the one in Figure 13.15.

   To see the entire list of colors, you may need to size the palette by clicking and dragging its lower right corner.

   QuarkXPress's Colors palette works much like the Style Sheet palette, allowing you instant exercise of your color options. Select what you want to color and simply apply your choice of colors. Of course, you must "define" the colors you want to use before they will be listed as choices in the palette.

Figure 13.15

QuarkXPress's Colors palette.

Notice that your palette already contains some basic colors. You have the CMYK colors of Cyan, Magenta, Yellow, and Black. Plus you have Registration, White, Red, Green, Blue.

You can simplify this palette by deleting some of these colors. QuarkXPress won't allow you to delete the CMYK colors or Registration or White. However, you can delete Red, Green, and Blue. In general, it'll be pure happenstance that you might want to use these colors rather than ones you select yourself so you can reduce clutter by getting rid of them.

3. The place you control most of QuarkXPress's color features is the Colors dialog box in Figure 13.16, reached via Edit>Colors, ⬆Shift+F12. Open it now to have a look.

   This dialog box is the Grand Central Station of QuarkXPress color operations. It lists all the colors in the Colors palette, offers swatches of selected colors, and lets you remove colors or define new ones.

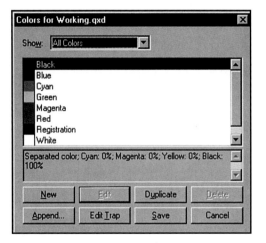

Figure 13.16

The Colors dialog box for removing or defining colors.

4. Select the color Red from the list and click the **D**elete button.

   The color will disappear from the available list of colors but it won't disappear from the Colors palette yet. That won't happen until you click the **S**ave button at the end of this exercise.

   By the way, if you had used this color somewhere in your document, QuarkXPress would have double-checked by asking you to confirm your decision before allowing you to delete it, and forcing you to choose another color to replace it wherever it was in use.

5. Finish removing unused colors by deleting Green and Blue, just like you deleted Red, selecting each one in turn and clicking the **D**elete button.

6. Complete this color deletion operation by clicking **S**ave to finalize your work.

Notice that the Colors palette no longer contains the colors you deleted, Red, Green, or Blue.

● The annual report cover as it should look at this point has been saved on the CD-ROM in a file named **13BASE02.QXT**.

Tip

Colors Palette Accepts Defaults

You can standardize your Colors palette just like most any other QuarkXPress feature. Just edit the Colors palette with no document open. That will set a default that will apply to any future new document you create.

Defining Spot Colors

Now that you have deleted the unused colors from your palette, it's time to add some. You need colors for the illustrations on the front cover of The Rose Company annual report as well as for the type. You will be selecting these colors, spot colors, from one of the libraries of standard colors that comes built into QuarkXPress.

1. Open up the color definition dialog box, but this time use a shortcut.

⌘+ Click (Mac) or Ctrl + Click (Win95) on one of the standard colors in the Colors palette. The "color" Registration would be a good choice.

Notice that this shortcut works a great deal like the Styles palette. You will be in the Color palette with the clicked color selected.

2. Click the **N**ew button to reach the Edit Color dialog box you see in Figure 13.17.

The only difference between this "new" color dialog box and the "edit" version of the dialog box is the name of the color. When you click the **E**dit button, the dialog box will open to edit whatever color was selected. The **N**ew button is set to create a new color name.

Quick search box

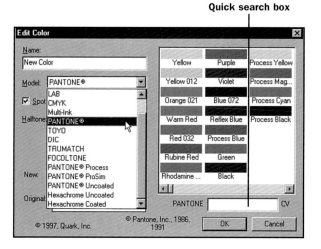

Figure 13.17

Selecting a color system.

3. Pull down the **M**odel list and select Pantone.

As you can see, QuarkXPress includes all the Pantone color libraries as well as libraries from Toyo, Trumatch, Focoltone, and others.

4. Scroll sideways through the panel of color swatches, looking for a special pink for your rose.

Select 213 and click OK.

5. Look at the Edit Color dialog box and you will notice that this color is defined as a spot color. The **S**pot Color checkbox is checked on. That means it will have an overlay—a printing press plate—all to itself wherever it appears in the document.

Tip

Work with Your Printer on Selecting a Color System

Your choice of a color matching system—an ink selection method—should always be done in collaboration with your commercial printer. The printshop manager will be able to give you perspective on all sorts of variables—from how the ink will work on your choice of paper to ways of saving money on press setup because you might use a similar ink already needed for another job.

6. Before accepting this particular color definition as final, change the name of the color so it will be easy to remember its purpose in your palette. It's also good to shorten the name so you can narrow your Colors palette on a crowded screen.

Edit the color name to read **Pink PAN 213**.

7. Click OK, then Save and the new color will be adopted into your Colors palette.

8. This will be a two color job. You need a good shade of green for the type and the vine drawing to go with this pink flower.

On your own, use the same process you just used to define a second color, Pantone number 568. Name it **Green PAN 568**.

Tip

Use the Quick Search Box to Locate Color Swatch

Type a number into the quick search box below the box of color swatches in order to scroll instantly to a particular color.

Now that you've got a good solid grasp of color theory and you've set up your color palette, you are all set to make this annual report cover bright and colorful… that's what you'll be doing in the next chapter.

The progress so far on the gardening company annual report cover has been saved on the CD-ROM in a file named **13BASE03.QXT**.

Summary

The next chapter, where you actually begin applying color to your document, will probably be more fun because it is full of exercises instead of theory. However, this chapter may be the most important of the two. Knowing how color works and the basics of halftone and screen technology will help you achieve a good collaboration with your commercial print shop and a fast, smooth color production job. Without this knowledge, you can make costly and time-consuming mistakes.

Review It

As a review of what you have learned in this chapter, please answer the following questions.

1. Name three reasons why your computer screen lies to you about color.

_____

_____

2. Which would usually be more accurate, spot or process color?

_____

_____

3. Name the three components of a digital halftone. How are they related?

_____

_____

4. If you want to quickly define a new color, or edit an existing one, what's the shortcut?

_____

_____

5. Name two things, among the many, that you must consult with your printer about early on in your publishing process.

_____

_____

6. How do colors mix in the four-color process?

_____

_____

7. Why might you still choose a spot color ink plate for a job, even if you are going to be using four-color process methods?

_____

_____

8. How can you make the "color" gray?

_____

_____

9. What factor determines the intensity of a color or the shade of gray in a halftone?

_____

_____

10. How do you set a default Colors palette?

_____

_____

Check It

Multiple Choice

Please circle the correct answer for each of the following questions.

1. In order to reproduce a color photograph you must_____.

   a.   break the picture up into dots

   b.   halftone the picture

   c.   separate the picture into CMYK colors

   d.   all of the above

2. The hierarchy of elements in a digital halftone is_____.

   a.   cell, dot, spot

   b.   dot, spot, cell

   c.   spot, cell, dot

   d.   none of the above

3. Laser printers dots, as in dpi, are equivalent to _____ in a digital halftone.

    a. dot

    b. cell

    c. spot

    d. none of the above

4. A tint and a halftone are alike in what way?

    a. Both have dots

    b. Both have been screened

    c. Both display shades of gray or some other color

    d. all of the above

5. When dealing with screen angles it is particularly important to _____.

    a. adjust them to suit the printing job

    b. leave them alone

    c. consult with your printer

    d. none of the above

6. Some colors that you can't delete from the Colors palette are _____.

    a. registration

    b. white

    c. cyan

    d. all of the above

7. When working with spot color swatches from a color matching system, such as Pantone, you can be virtually positive that _____.

    a. onscreen color will be accurate

    b. ink color will be accurate

    c. final color will be accurate

    d. none of the above

8. Each spot color gets its own _____.

    a. ink color

    b. overlay or separation

    c. press plate

    d. all of the above

9. Your computer screen and the printing press don't match because _____.

    a. RGB versus CMYK or spot color

    b. the effects of ambient light

    c. hardware variations

    d. all of the above

10. The shortcut to the Colors dialog box is _____.

    a. ⌘+ Click (Mac) or Ctrl+ Click (Win95)

    b. F12

    c. ⌘+F12 (Mac) or Ctrl+F12 (Win95)

    d. all of the above

True or False

Please circle *T* or *F* to indicate whether the statement is true or false.

T   F   **1.** Paper has no effect on the final color results of a printed piece.

T   F   **2.** You need a halftone to produce any photograph, no matter what.

T   F   **3.** It's important on every job to adjust screen angles to avoid a moiré effect.

T   F   **4.** The percentage of gray in a halftone is controlled by the size of the dot.

T   F   **5.** Press ⬆Shift+F12 to reach the Edit Colors dialog box.

T   F   **6.** You can be fairly confident of accurate color if you use a color matching system swatch.

T   F   **7.** The printing process has become so standard that you rarely need to consult with your printer prior to handing off the job.

T   F   **8.** You can set a default color palette by editing it with publication open.

T   F   **9.** Always set up your monitor in a room with neutral colors for best color accuracy.

T   F   **10.** Selecting color from a swatch book will assure you of accurate color on screen.

Design It

Work with a copy of the gardening company annual report cover and spend some time experimenting with this design. We probably tried at least twenty different variations before settling on the one used here. Try some of following questions and techniques for yourself and see if, ultimately, you would end up with the same design as we did.

- Is the word "The" in the best location? Where else might you put it in relation to the capital letter "R" in "Rose"?

- What would happen if you flipped the design around and had the rose and vine at the upper-left corner of the design? In that configuration, what would be the best location for the company name?

- Print out your variations, at least the ones you like, and tape them up on your wall. Live with them for a few days and see how you feel about them after some time goes by. Does your view of the design change over time?

If you have access to the QuarkXPress documentation in your school computer lab, take some time to preview the next chapter by reading the information on color in the QuarkXPress manual. Sometimes just having a concept explained a different way after first having been exposed to it will help you gain a deeper understanding.

Using Color

Finishing the Annual Report Cover

What You Will Learn

Actually applying color within QuarkXPress is the easiest part of the color production process. It's also the most creative, and the most fun.

While being creative and having fun in this chapter, you will:

➤ Apply the colors you have defined on your Colors palette to graphics and text

➤ Color box frames and fills

➤ Create blends of colors, gradations from one color to another

➤ Import colors by importing a colored EPS object

➤ Streamline the production process by consolidating QuarkXPress created colors and imported colors

➤ Import a scan of a color photograph

➤ Study the effects of various color techniques by printing out separations of each version of the publication

➤ Learn how to get more accurate color, on-screen and in final creation of printing plates using a color management system

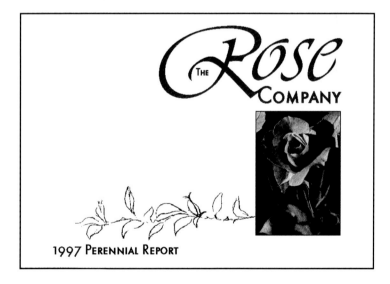

Fig. 14.1

The annual report cover for The Rose Company will go through a design evolution in this chapter. The top cover, with the hand-sketched rose drawing, has been colored using spot colors you defined in the last chapter. The center version of the cover contains an EPS graphic drawing of the rose, with colors adopted from that computer-drawn sketch. The bottom version contains a scanned photo of the rose. (Also reproduced in the color section.)

Getting Set Up

Copy all the files for this chapter from the CD-ROM to a work area on your hard drive. They are all in the **Steps** folder in the subfolder labeled **14**.

As in the last chapter, you will need to have the Vivaldi and Function Small Caps fonts installed on your computer for the exercises in this chapter.

Following each exercise in this chapter, save your project to a work area on your hard drive. Each succeeding exercise builds on the previous one, so saving at the end of each exercise will enable you to pick up where you left off if you aren't able to complete all the chapter exercises in one sitting. Also, on the CD-ROM you will find saved versions of the project as it should exist at the end of each exercise. You can fall back on those interim versions as reference points if you are having trouble with one of the exercises.

Applying Defined Colors

In this section, you put to work the colors you created in the last chapter. You will assign the pink spot color to the rose sketch and use it to highlight key parts of the text. The more muted dark green will go to the box around the rose, the vine, and the remaining text. By not doing the expected, by not using black at all, this spot ink job makes maximum use of color with only two spot colors.

1. Open file **14BASE01.QXT**. (It's the same as 13BASE03.QXT, if you are continuing on from the previous chapter.)

Applying Colors to Text

2. First, apply color to the text.

   Take must use the Content tool to do this. You can't simply select the text box with the Item tool and apply color. That would color the text box but not the text inside it.

   This works a lot like selecting text and making it bold or italic, except you use the Colors palette and color it instead.

   Select the word "Rose."

Color Selection Options

3. Take a quick glance at your alternatives for coloring the selected text.

   You have two menu choices.

   Check out Style>Color and notice the pull out list of color choices.

   And have a look at Style>Character, ⌘+⬆Shift+D (Mac) or Ctrl+⬆Shift+D (Win95). You can see that you could use the Color box to make a color choice.

4. Instead, let's use the Colors palette for this coloring job.

   In order to use the Colors palette you must tell the palette what mode it should be in. As you see in Figure 14.2, you can choose from coloring the frame, the box, and the text.

   Select the text icon.

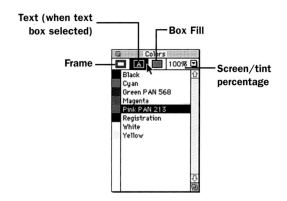

Text (when text box selected)
Box Fill
Frame
Screen/tint percentage

Figure 14.2

Selecting a Colors palette mode.

5. Click the pink color in the palette to color the selected text.

Select "1997" and color it pink.

6. Use the same Colors palette technique to apply green to "Perennial Report," and "The."

Tip

Use Color In Text Styles

One of the all-time great uses of paragraph and character styles is applying color to text. In just the same way you can define a font or some other text attribute, you can include a color in a text style definition. Not only do styles enable you to quickly assign a number of attributes to a text selection in a single step, styles also enable you to easily experiment with color choices or even to make an after the fact change to a color design for large quantities of text with a single global move.

Coloring Imported Objects

7. Now apply color to the sketches.

Click the rose picture box and have a look at the Colors palette. The text mode icon has been replaced by a new contents icon. That's because you have selected a picture box instead of a text box.

Make sure the picture box contents icon is selected.

8. Click the pink color in the Colors palette to assign that color to the rose picture.

9. Click the vine, making sure the picture box contents icon is still selected, and assign it the color of green.

Note that these are black-and-white scans, saved in the TIFF file format. That's why you can color them within QuarkXPress and also see the color on-screen. QuarkXPress will also enable you to color grayscale TIFFs.

It's important to understand that "coloring" an imported object doesn't change the underlying graphic in any way. That's why what's displayed on-screen is not relevant to your results on the printing press. Coloring the imported graphic simply tells QuarkXPress that you want that object to print on a particular spot color overlay—which means it will be put entirely on that color's printing press plate.

Coloring Frames

10. You still have to color the box around the rose. QuarkXPress boxes can have both lines around them (frames) and fill (backgrounds).

The easiest way to control which part of a QuarkXPress box you are coloring is by using the three buttons you see at the top of the Colors palette in Figure 14.2.

For this operation, with the rose picture box selected, choose the frame line mode, the button on the left.

11. Click the green color to give the frame that color.

Printing Out Spot Overlays

12. As we've discussed, spot color works by assigning the various parts of a publication to individual printing plates. In order to create those plates, you need to separate a publication into a set of overlays, one for each spot color.

You can see how this works by printing out a set of overlays using a desktop printer. They won't have high enough resolution to be suitable for actual use in producing printing press plates, but they will be good enough to give you the idea of how the system works.

Go to the Print command, ⌘+P (Mac) or Ctrl+P (Win95).

Setting Up for Separations

13. In the Document tab, turn on the Separations check box as in Figure 14.3. That tells QuarkXPress you want to separate the color in this project into color overlays.

Selecting Printer and Orientation

14. Switch to the Setup tab you see in Figure 14.4.

Choose the printer description for your desktop printer.

Choose the Landscape (horizontal) orientation.

Turn on separations

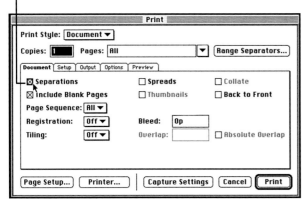

Figure 14.3

Document tab of Print dialog box to call for Separations.

Choosing Inks

15. Switch tabs again to Output.

As in Figure 14.5, turn off all the CMYK inks, leaving your defined green and pink inks.

Landscape

Choose your own printer

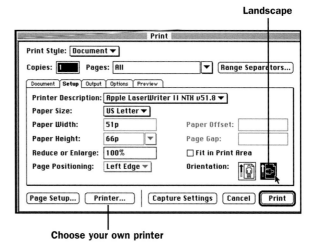

Figure 14.4

Selecting printer and page orientation.

16. Click Print, and QuarkXPress will separate the publication into overlays, sending each one to the printer. You should get two pieces of paper from the printer, one with all the green items on it and the other with all the pink items, as in Figure 14.6. Also, as you see in Figure 14.6, these overlays come together to create a color composite.

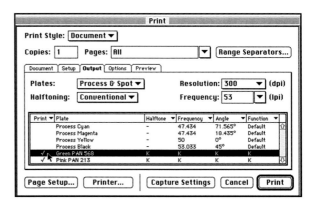

Figure 14.5

Selecting spot overlay inks.

Figure 14.6

The two "black" overlays (top and center), when burned onto printing press plates and coated with spot color inks, will come together into the color composite final publication (bottom). (Also reproduced in the color section.)

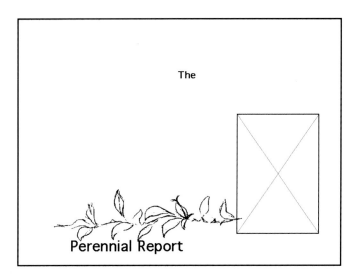

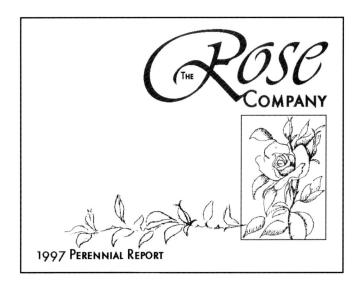

● The progress on coloring the annual report cover has been saved on the CD-ROM in a file named **14BASE02.QXT**.

Making Colored Blends

In the printing business, there must be a dozen names for blends—gradations, gradients, graduated screen tints, fountains, degradés—but the point is still the same. You can fill a QuarkXPress box with a gradual transition of color from one to the other. Or, as you will see in this exercise, you can gradually transition the same color from one intensity to another.

1. This exercise will be an experiment and you won't be saving your work at the end of it. Open **14BASE02.QXT** to get a new document that you can toss at the end of the exercise. Alternatively, do a save now of your working file so you can File>**R**evert To Saved at the end of the exercise.

2. Select the box with the rose sketch in it. You can use either the Content or Item tool.

3. Select the fill (or background) icon at the top of the Colors palette, the one on the right.

4. Color the box pink by clicking that color in the palette. (Don't worry. The rose will disappear from view, but we'll get it back.)

5. As in Figure 14.7, select one of the blend options from the pull-down list. We picked the Mid-Linear Blend.

   Notice that the #1 and #2 option buttons become available, once you have a blend chosen.

   By the way, the blend feature is also available in the Modify command dialog box but the palette is usually a lot easier to use.

6. Make sure the #1 option button is selected and choose a tint of pink in the pull-down list shown in Figure 14.8. We chose 40%. (You could type in a custom tint percentage. You don't have to pick from the list.)

7. Click the #2 option button and keep the same pink color, but set the tint to 0%.

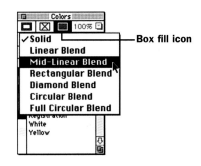

Figure 14.7

Choosing a type of blend.

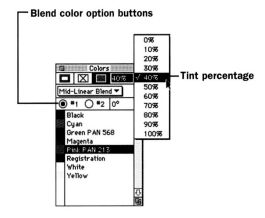

Figure 14.8

Choosing the first color and its tint.

8. Finally, set the angle of the blend at 45 degrees so that the light area in the center swipes across the rose sketch at about the same angle as the leg of the "R" up above it. (The Mid-Linear Blend goes from color #1 to color #2 in the center and then back to #1 again.)

9. Spend some time flipping between various types of blends so you can experience their effects.

   You can see in the pull-down list that there are a lot of options here. Basically the names with geometric figures in them, such as rectangular or circular, make blends from the #1 color on the outside to the #2 color in the center.

   While you are at it, experiment with the angle setting and the various levels of tints you can use for the #1 and #2 colors.

10. Frankly, the blend behind the rose sketch doesn't look very good from a design point of view, but it was important that you spend some time learning about this QuarkXPress feature.

As we indicated in the first step of this exercise, either toss this version of the annual report cover or use the Revert To Saved command to get back to where you were. Then move on to the next exercise.

Tip

Consult Your Printer on Mixed Spot Colors

Be very cautious when mixing colors. It's easy to do in QuarkXPress and may look fine on-screen but it can create a muddy, murky mess on the printing press. One pitfall would be trying to blend one spot color to another one. Another thing to watch out for is actually mixing a new color out of two spot colors in the Edit Color dialog box. You can use QuarkXPress's new Multi-Ink feature to do it, but spot color inks aren't really meant to be mixed like that. Consult with your printer before attempting to mix colors.

Importing Colors with a Graphic

When you import EPS graphics, any spot colors defined in the graphic piggy-back into your Colors palette. This is one of the most ways that colors will arrive in your publication.

Without proper handling of imported colors, you can create a spot color mess. QuarkXPress makes up a spot color overlay for every ink defined in the Colors palette, as you know from the previous exercise where you printed out each overlay. If you have already defined a particular color in QuarkXPress and you import an EPS graphic containing the same color as one of the existing ones, but with a different name, you will have more than one spot color overlay for that duplicate color when you separate the file.

Conversely, thinking ahead and organizing colors can really take advantage of piggy-back colors. If you import an EPS with piggy-back colors early in the process, you can automatically create the color palette for that job.

This exercise shows you two techniques for organizing and combining imported EPS colors.

1. With the Content tool active, select the picture box with the pink colored rose sketch in it.

Replacing a Picture

2. File>Get Picture, ⌘+E (Mac) or Ctrl+E (Win95), and double-click the file ROSE.EPS.

The new rose illustration will replace the sketch. In other words, you don't need to delete it first.

You may need to reposition the rose a bit before moving ahead.

Importing Colors Via an EPS

3. Have a look at the Colors palette and you will see that you have some new colors, as shown in Figure 14.9. They piggy-backed in on that EPS you just imported.

There are three of them: a new pink rose color, a green leaf color, and a brown stem color.

Two Methods for Consolidating Colors

Remember that having two names for the same green spot color (or any spot color) is a problem because QuarkXPress will generate two separate green plates and neither of them will include all the green objects.

There are a couple of ways to get rid of the redundant colors and assign the current ones in their place. The first one you'll try involves manually assigning the new color in place of the old and then deleting the unused color.

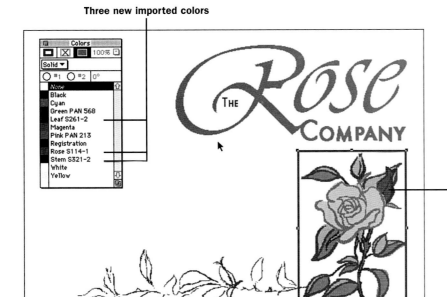

Three new imported colors

Figure 14.9

Colors palette with the additions from the EPS picture.

EPS replaced sketch

Individually Replacing Colors

4. Select the vine sketch, making sure you have the Contents icon selected on the Colors palette, and assign the vine the new color, Leaf 261-2.

5. Select the two pieces of green text and assign them the new color.

Select the word "The," the one inside the capital "R," and you should have the text icon selected at the top of the Colors palette. Color the word with the new leaf color in place of the old green one.

Select the words "Perennial Report" and color them with the new leaf color.

6. Also, select the rose drawing box and the frame icon and color them with the new leaf color in place of the old green one.

7. Do a File>Save so you can File>Revert To Saved if you need to, always a good idea before deleting colors.

⌘+ Click the Colors palette on the color Green PAN 568 and the palette will open with that color selected.

Click the **D**elete button to get rid of it.

When you click **S**ave you will be brought back to the Layout view and the old green color will be gone.

You now only have one green spot color plate for this project, but that's the tedious manual way to consolidate colors.

Merging Colors

8. The other possible approach to consolidating color overlays is to merge colors, leaving the imported EPS color intact. The advantage of this approach is its efficiency. You won't need to individually select a number of items, but you can instead do a complete replacement of a color in a single move.

Save the file in its current state so you can Revert To Saved if need be. This is important because you will be deleting a color and there's no other way to recover from that if you somehow make a mistake.

9. Select any item on the page. (You must do this before you can perform a color deletion.)

⌘+ Click (Mac) or Ctrl+ Click (Win95) the color you want to lose, Pink PAN 213.

Click the **D**elete button and you will get a dialog box like the one in Figure 14.10.

10. Choose in its place Rose S114-1 and click OK.

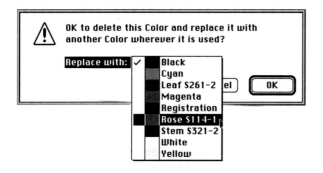
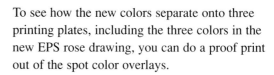

To see how the new colors separate onto three printing plates, including the three colors in the new EPS rose drawing, you can do a proof print out of the spot color overlays.

11. Use the same process you used to print separations in the previous exercise with the sketched version of the rose.

In the Print dialog box, ⌘+P (Mac) or Ctrl+P (Win95), don't forget to turn on the check box for separations and select the three new spot color inks to be printed as separated overlays.

Click Print to run your overlay proofs.

Figure 14.10

Replacing a deleted color with one of the new imported ones.

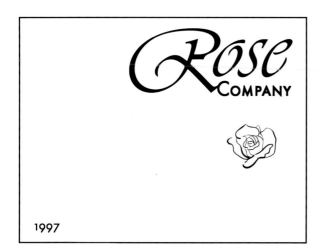
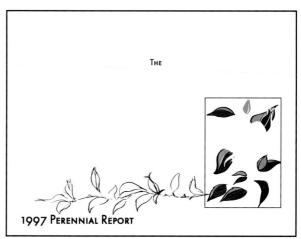
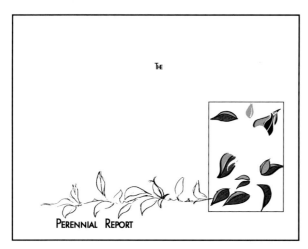
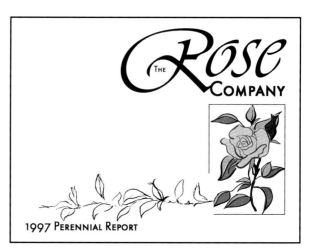

Figure 14.11

The three spot colors plates for the pink rose (upper left), green leaf (upper right), and brown stem (lower left), along with the color composite of the page with the rose drawing (lower right). (Also reproduced in the color section.)

The report cover version with the imported color sketch of the rose, the EPS graphic, has been saved in file **14BASE03.QXT**.

Working with Process Color

Up until now, all the overlays you have been printing have been spot color. In this section, you will import an actual photograph of a rose that has been scanned into a TIFF file format. You will convert your spot colors to process colors. And then you will print CMYK separations proofs on your desktop printer.

1. Select the rose drawing picture box with the Content tool.

Importing a Scanned Photo

2. Replace the rose drawing with the new photograph just as you replaced the earlier rose sketch with the rose drawing.

   Use Get Picture, ⌘+E (Mac) or Ctrl+E (Win95) and in the resulting file selection dialog box, double-click **ROSEFOTO.TIF**.

   We have also provided a smaller file called **ROSEFOTO.JPG** that you can use instead, if you like. It's a compressed version of the same photo with a slight loss of quality but a big savings in file size.

Tip

Getting a Faster, Low Resolution Display

Scanned photographs contain quite a bit of data, which is why they tend to be such large files. This can really slow down your work because all that data must be redrawn to your screen every time you make a change in the layout and the redraw takes some time. One option is to have a smaller low resolution screen preview. When importing the picture, hold down ◆Shift while clicking Open in the Get Picture dialog box.

3. Adjust the position of the green vine in relation to the photo to suit your taste.

   You could send it to the back of the photo so the edge of the frame cuts off the vine, ◆Shift+F5.

   You could keep the vine to the front and position it so it extends inside the picture box and touches a rose leaf similar to its previous position in relation to the rose drawing.

   You could use the Item tool to slide the vine to the left so it just touches the like-colored green frame around the rose photo picture box.

Converting Spot Colors to Process

4. The fact is, this publication was designed to be run in full process color. For example, you may have noticed when you imported the scanned photo that it was in the CMYK color space.

   That means it doesn't make sense to have the four CMYK process color plates on the printing press, as well as the pink and green spot colors.

   This is a great example of how important it is to know ahead of time what kind of printing process you will be using. Because we knew we would need to get to process colors eventually, the spot colors for the rose, leaf, and stem were defined in the CMYK color space.

   Because the spot colors were defined in fixed percentages of cyan, magenta, yellow, and black, it will be simple to accurately convert the spot colors (single inks) to process colors (the four process inks). The percentage of each of the process colors will stay exactly the same during the conversion.

   In Edit>Colors, ◆Shift+F12, double-click Leaf S261-2 to get to the Edit Color dialog box in Figure 14.12.

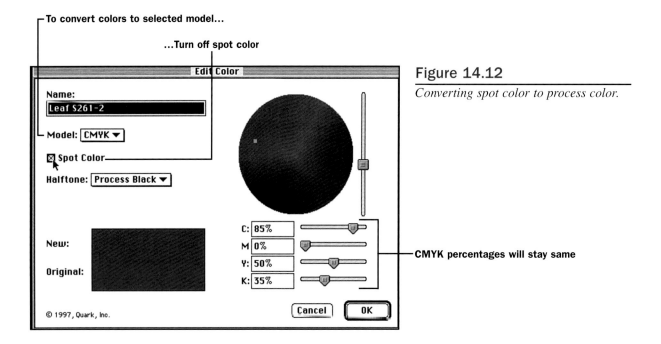

To convert colors to selected model...

...Turn off spot color

Edit Color

Name:
Leaf S261-2

Model: CMYK ▼

☒ Spot Color

Halftone: Process Black ▼

New:

Original:

C: 85%
M: 0%
Y: 50%
K: 35%

© 1997, Quark, Inc.

Cancel   OK

CMYK percentages will stay same

Figure 14.12

Converting spot color to process color.

5. Notice the mix of CMYK color percentages in the lower-right corner of the dialog box as you click off the **S**pot Color check box.

   The CMYK mix will remain the same. In other words, you haven't, in this case, harmed color accuracy by making the switch from spot to process at this stage.

   When you click OK and return to the Colors dialog box, you will see that the color description has changed from a spot color to a separated color.

Tip

Spot to Process: Watch Out!

Generally, it's a very bad idea to convert spot colors to process colors and can cause unpredictable color results. QuarkXPress and other graphic arts programs in that situation make their best guess at what CMYK mix would be best to duplicate a particular spot color. If, however, the spot colors were defined using CMYK percentages in the first place, the conversion is both easy and accurate. One particularly good solution, if you know you'll need to convert, is to use a spot color definition system, such as Pantone ProSim, that is based on CMYK colors. ProSim is specifically designed to simulate the standard Pantone colors using CMYK inks.

---

6. Perform the same spot to process conversion on the rose and stem colors. Edit the colors and turn off the Spot Color check box.

7. As in the previous color exercises in this chapter, print out separations.

   This time, however, turn on the special printer's marks that will help you tell one plate from another. These marks also put "targets" on each overlay so they can be precisely registered, as well as trim marks that enable the printer to trim the edges of oversized printed sheets to the correct page size.

   In the Print dialog box, ⌘+P (Mac) or Ctrl+P (Win95), go to the Document tab and the **R**egistration pull-down list and select Centered to turn on these printer's marks.

8. Flip to the Preview tab and you will see that you have a problem. The printer's marks take up a lot of space around the edges of the document and you only have an 8 ½" by 11" piece of paper for this 8 ½" by 11" document.

   Go to the Setup tab and turn on the Fit In Print Area check box. This will print the document smaller, but it's great for proofing color overlays from a laser printer just to see that the separations are going to the correct overlay.

9. Be sure to turn on **Separations** in the Document tab before clicking the Print button.

Still in the Print dialog box, go to the Output tab and notice that you no longer have any spot color inks, just the CMYK process colors.

When you have your separations printed, try to visualize how they all fit together. You can see what they should look like in Figure 14.13.

For example, if you think about the definition for the leaf color (cyan 85%, magenta 0%, yellow 50%, black 35%), it's obvious that most of the green information would be on the overlay for cyan but there should be none of the green text on the magenta plate.

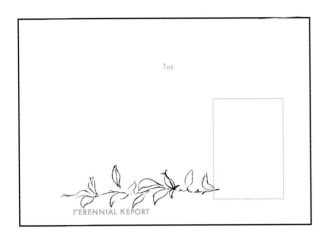

Figure 14.13

The four process colors will be used to make the printing press plates. Together, they combine to make up a full-color photograph and the former spot colors. (Also reproduced in the color section.)

The final form of The Rose Company's annual report cover has been saved in file **14BASE04.QXT**.

Introducing...Color Management

We've already discussed the color accuracy issue in an earlier chapter. Your computer screen does not show true color. Some systems show more true colors than others, but to one degree or another this basic premise holds true no matter how good your hardware.

A color management system can help—sometimes quite a bit. However, it's critical that you are aware of the limitations and don't automatically accept what you see on-screen as 100 percent accurate color. Never make color decisions based solely on what you see on-screen, even if you are using a color management system.

Color Production Is Device Dependent

Color management systems try to take account of the fact that color accuracy depends on the specific devices in the color production work flow. This includes the color management system that comes built into QuarkXPress.

We say that color publishing is device dependent. One manufacturer's scanner model will produce a different color rendition from that of another scanner

manufacturer. And the computer monitor you use to view those scans will add yet another variable to the color reproduction equation.

Let's assume that you took a picture of a brick wall, and your camera recorded the color fairly accurately. But now imagine the flow of your color work from that point forward and all the way out to the printing press and your final product:

- Your scanner may want to describe that red as a bluish-red.

- Your computer monitor may think red should be a deep red color with a touch of orange.

- Your composite proofing device, your Iris or Fiery or whatever, may see the red as having a more brownish tone.

- This string of color imperfection may deteriorate even further if, at any time during this process, you try to "correct" the color based on what you are seeing on your computer monitor or your composite proof printer. You might correct in the wrong direction.

- Finally, with all of these differences, who knows how the picture of the brick wall will actually turn out when you separate it and run it on the printing press, given the limitations of CMYK colors?

Color management tries to smooth out all these differences by electronically adjusting color as you move the graphic elements of your layout from scanner to computer screen to printing press. In each case, the color management system translates the color for the appropriate device. If it could talk to each of the devices in your system it might say something like, "I know you tend to look at brick red and see bluish-red or brownish-red or whatever. Add a pinch of this and take away a pinch of that to compensate for your color error factors."

CMS Relies on Touchstone Color Benchmark

The CMS does not make these translations by going directly from one device to the other. In the background, it constantly refers back to a sort of touchstone, a method of describing the color that is device independent. It's the CIE color model (that stands for *Commission Internationale de l'Eclairage* or in English, the International Committee on Illumination).

It's important to remember this CIE color concept because, at various times in the process of saving color bitmapped files, you have opportunities to cut yourself loose from device dependent color descriptions and save your file as a "CIE Lab TIFF."

Because color production is device dependent, one of the most important things you will do in working with color management is to specify for QuarkXPress the devices that are being used in the electronic publishing process. It needs this information so it can make the color translations between different devices. The color management system needs to be told:

■ The *source* for the digitized color image files being used in the publication, usually a scanner, although it could be a color chosen from a standard color library.

■ The video monitor you are using to *view* the color images as you work.

■ The printing device you will be using to produce a *proof* of your color publication, which is often a desktop color printer.

■ The color characteristics of the printing *press* and the device that will use the process color separations you will be generating.

Remember those keywords—source, view, proof, press.

When you make all these choices, you are selecting device profiles. These are files that electronically describe for the color management system the characteristics of the chosen device.

A number of these device profiles comes with QuarkXPress, but if one of your devices isn't listed, you'll need to use a generic choice or obtain a profile from the manufacturer. The better job you do in selecting a device profile the more accurate your color is likely to be.

Optimize Your Color Viewing Environment

Color management software aside, the single most important thing you can do to improve computer color accuracy is to improve upon the color viewing environment. The weakest part of your color management system may be the room in which you work. If you are in front of your computer, examine your environment, including your computer monitor, and see if your viewing environment may be distorting the accuracy of your color view:

■ Work with a plain gray screen desktop, with no fancy backgrounds. They may be fun, but they practically vibrate with distracting colors that zap any chance of your brain's properly reading colors for the page you are setting up.

■ The same goes for your work room. No distracting wallpaper. No wild colors. No extremes. Go for gray, and let the color happen on your monitor.

■ Have the room lighting set to a moderate level. It should not be much darker or brighter than the amount of light coming from your monitor.

■ Windows and bright sunny days are great, but they play havoc with color accuracy. Again, no wild extremes for your room lighting, and sunlight in particular is a problem. Sunlight constantly changes color, from sunrise to high noon to sunset.

Putting the Color Management System to Work

Color management, as you can probably tell, can be a very technical issue. However, it's pretty simple to implement as long as you have device profiles for all the elements in your color universe—scanner (source), monitor (view), printer (proof), and final production device (press).

In this exercise, you get a quick introduction to how color management works in QuarkXPress. If you don't have a profile or aren't sure of which one to use, that's okay. Just follow through the steps so you can get the experience of the color management system tools in QuarkXPress. In a non-classroom situation, if you are really putting color management to work, you or the company you are working for will be sure to obtain all the profiles you need.

So, in this experiment, you will set up color management defaults for this document and then apply color management to a specific imported graphic, the rose photo.

1. You can continue in your working file or, better yet, start a fresh file from the last exercise by opening **14BASE04.QXT**.

(You may need to set your screen resolution and number of displayed colors at a higher value in order to see this color test properly. If you have your screen set only to 256 colors, you will be wasting your time setting color management. Some QuarkXPress color features won't even work at that color depth setting.)

Turning on Color Management

2. Go to Edit>Preferences>Color Management to reach the dialog box you see in Figure 14.14.

Click the Color Management Active check box.

Setting Your Color Management Profiles

3. Do your best to match your equipment to the profiles offered in the various pull-down lists in this dialog box.

The most important settings are to have your monitor match the final output device that uses your color separations. Set your separations printer for SWOP Proofer CMYK Coated, and make sure that your CMYK image source is set for the same thing, so they match.

Turn on CMS

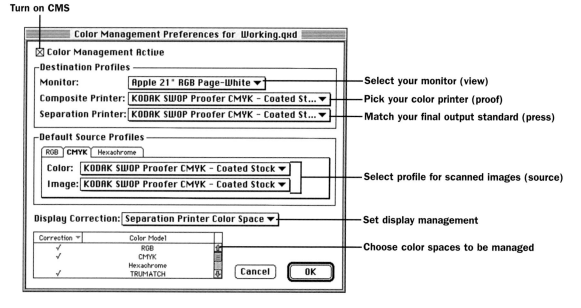

Figure 14.14
Setting up the QuarkXPress color management system.

4. When you are finished selecting profiles, click OK to put them all into effect.

Managing Your Profiles

5. It's easy to find out which profiles are in effect at any time.

   Open up **Utilities>Usage** and select the Profiles tab and have a look at the dialog box you see in Figure 14.15.

   Click Done when you are finished investigating the Usage dialog box, which you will notice is the same one you use to check on usage of fonts and graphics.

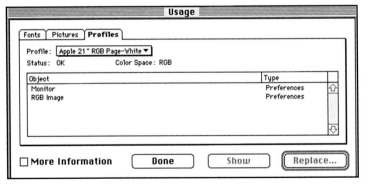

Figure 14.15

Checking profile usage.

Setting CMS on an Individual Object

6. You can set profiles for individual graphics files.

   Select the rose picture graphic and open up the Profile Information palette, from the **View** menu, as you see in Figure 14.16.

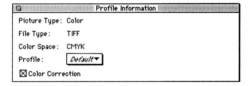

Figure 14.16

Set profiles for individual graphics with the Profile Information palette.

7. It will help you understand how profiles work if you spend some time experimenting with different settings in the Profile Information palette. See how different choices affect the display of the rose graphic.

8. When you are finished trying out different CMS profiles, you can toss this file. It was just for experimentation purposes.

Summary

You are now almost through a suite of three chapters that will help you handle color design and reproduction at a professional level. After learning the basics of getting color and color images from a digital form to the printing press in Chapter 13 (halftones and screening, defining colors), you have now added knowledge about how to apply and manage color in a QuarkXPress publication (Colors palette, importing colors, Color Management System). Coming up in Chapter 15 — handing off your publication to a prepress service bureau and commercial printer to go to press.

Review It

As a review of what you have learned in this chapter, please answer the following questions.

1. Name at least two ways you can apply color to boxes and frames in QuarkXPress.

   _____

   _____

2. Name three ways to apply color to text in QuarkXPress.

   _____

   _____

3. What key software element in the color management system describes a device?

   _____

   _____

4. What are the four keywords for color management device choices?

   _____

   _____

5. Where in QuarkXPress do you separate colors?

   _____

   _____

6. In the Colors palette, how do you control how the color gets applied to a QuarkXPress item?

_____

_____

7. How many overlays will you get if you laser proof a process color publication with two spot colors?

_____

_____

8. Name at least three of the four locations where you control the QuarkXPress color management system?

_____

_____

9. Name three key factors in your color viewing environment that would harm the accuracy of your color perceptions.

_____

_____

10. Describe the fastest way to merge two colors.

_____

_____

Check It

Multiple Choice

Please circle the correct answer for each of the following questions.

1. Before you can use the Colors palette to color text with a non-default color you must _____.

   a. select contents icon in palette

   b. select text

   c. define the color

   d. all of the above

2. If you don't have a profile for your scanner you should _____.

   a. write one

   b. modify an existing one

   c. obtain one from a manufacturer

   d. all of the above

3. You select the inks you want to output in the _____.

   a. setup tab of the Print dialog

   b. output tab of the Print dialog

   c. profile Information palette

   d. none of the above

4. To produce ink overlays you must first _____.

   a. turn on Separations check box in Preferences

   b. turn on Separations check box in Print dialog box

   c. turn off unwanted inks

   d. none of the above

5. You can merge colors by _____.

    a.   deleting old color and replacing with a new one

    b.   search and replace old color with a new one

    c.   editing two colors to same color space definition

    d.   all of the above

6. To create a blend in the Colors palette you must _____.

    a.   select the box fill/background icon

    b.   choose #1 and #2 colors/tints

    c.   select a type of blend

    d.   all of the above

7. If you import a graphic with defined spot colors _____.

    a.   the colors will be added to the Colors palette

    b.   the colors won't display in QuarkXPress

    c.   QuarkXPress will try to merge the colors into the closest existing spot colors

    d.   none of the above

8. In QuarkXPress the color management system uses _____ to adjust color for consistency.

    a.   device profiles

    b.   CIE color model benchmark

    c.   CMS preference choices

    d.   all of the above

9. To replace a graphic with another one you must _____.

    a.   delete the old one first

    b.   select the old one and Get Picture

    c.   use File>Replace Graphic

    d.   all of the above

10. When mixing two inks you should always _____.

    a.   consult your printer for advice

    b.   run a laser proof

    c.   turn on CMS

    d.   all of the above

True or False

Please circle *T* or *F* to indicate whether the statement is true or false.

T   F   **1.**   To color text select the text box with the Item tool and click the color in the Colors palette.

T   F   **2.**   To color a box frame you can use the Frame tab of the Modify dialog.

T   F   **3.**   The best place for checking color proofs is outdoors in the sunlight.

T   F   **4.**   For faster screen redraw hold down ⬆Shift while clicking OK in Get Picture.

T   F   **5.**   One efficient way to color text is with a style definition.

T   F   **6.**   You shouldn't hesitate to mix two inks to make a third color.

T   F   **7.**   It's impossible to set a CMS device profile just for one picture in QuarkXPress.

T   F   **8.**   In general, all the color reproduction we deal with in DTP is device dependent.

T   F   **9.**   When you assign a spot color to a graphic file you change its color.

T   F   **10.**   The angle setting on a tinted blend adjusts the angle of its screen.

Design It

Select one of the projects you have built in the course of this term and redesign it with color in mind. Consider that your color choices may have a big impact on the design.

- ■ Decide first what your communication goal will be for this color redesign. Do you want the piece to be more vibrant or more laid back, and why?

- ■ Will you use spot colors or process color?

- ■ If you need to match colors for design elements to existing color graphics how will you handle matching the colors?

- ■ How does it affect readability if you put text on a colored or blended background?

- ■ Show the results of your effort, or even two or three versions of the design, to colleagues or a mentor. Ask them to think like a client or a consumer. Did you meet your communications objective with this redesign?

Getting Projects Printed

15

What You Will Learn

In this chapter, you will get up to speed on the practical work of making your design into reality by moving it from a computer design to ink on paper. In the process, you will learn about:

➤ Ways you can check for typos and other copy and layout problems

➤ Packaging up your job so you can hand it off to the service bureau that will generate the high resolution imagesetter output you will need to submit to your commercial printer

➤ Choosing from your various color proofing options to make sure your publication will be color-accurate off the press

➤ Holding a coordination meeting with your commercial printer, and other methods for improving your communications with the print shop

➤ Working with your printer on choosing a line screen and coordinating the job of color trapping

➤ Why trapping is an important issue, and ways you can avoid having to deal with it yourself

Taking Basic Proofing Steps

Before going to press, you must proof your publication. To paraphrase an old adage in modern inflationary terms, "To correct a mistake costs one dollar to fix at the manuscript stage, a few dollars on the desktop, hundreds of dollars after the imagesetting run, and thousands of dollars after the pressman has pushed the button on the printing press."

Proofing needs to be a way of life for a desktop publisher; that is, if you hope to get your job done correctly, on deadline, within budget—and approved by the client.

Checking Copy

Checking the text in a publication may seem pretty basic—because it is—but it is also one of the most essential steps you must take before you submit your materials to a service bureau or commercial printer.

Some people just seem to go blank whenever they look at an easy-to-fix—and cheap—laser proof. It seems as though they don't really focus until they get to the blueline stage. (A blueline is a test print, using a process very much like an architect's blueprint, done directly from the actual film after it has been run by the service bureau and before it goes to the printer.)

The time to focus occurs long before the blueline. But last-minute changes to film or printing plates happen so often in the printing business that there's even a name for late copy changes. They are called *AAs*, for Author's Alterations. To prevent the need for AAs, consider taking the following copy-proofing steps.

- Use a spell checker, not only the one in QuarkXPress but also the one in your word processor before you get to the layout stage.

- Indexing and table of contents lists often reveal structural problems in text, as well as poor word usage and spelling problems.

- Hire a professional proofreader—an expense that may pay for itself if you avoid even one AA.

- Have two people do a proof check of complex financial tables or other similarly complex material. One person can read the text to another, or a person working alone can read text into a tape recorder and listen back while checking a laser proof for accuracy.

- Make sure that you get a written sign-off on any proofs for client approval; otherwise, you may end up paying for a botched job because there's no proof of your proofing.

Laser Printer Layout Proofing

One of the most important steps to take before submitting your files to a service bureau is to run your publication through a PostScript laser printer. Among other benefits, this step helps you check that your project pages look right and that they will run through an imagesetter. (Imagesetters are invariably PostScript devices.) In fact, most service bureaus require that a laser proof accompany your file submission.

Run Thumbnails or Reader's Spreads

Running thumbnails or reader's spreads—options available under the QuarkXPress Print command—gives you an overall feel for your multipage project, as well as a check on how it all flows together from a visual point of view. Reader's spreads, if your publication has been set up for facing pages, help you evaluate pages as they will look when finally bound together.

Composites

They aren't in color, but composite (non-separated) printouts from your laser printer tell you a great deal about the basic color design values of your pages, even multicolor layouts. If text is unreadable in shades of gray because it doesn't have adequate contrast against a background, you need to think about whether it will work in color. Composite laser proofs are also an important client sign-off step before going to expensive imagesetting and color proofs.

Listen to Your Laser Printer

If a job won't run on your laser printer, chances are high that it will fail when run through a service bureau's imagesetter.

One service bureau tells the story of a client who sent in a complex design for film output. After four hours of trying to get the job to run, the technician called the client to talk about the trouble. Asked whether he had run a laser proof (one didn't come in with the job), the client replied, "Well, I tried to run one, but it wouldn't print on my laser printer. It ran for half an hour and gave me a PostScript error." The trouble at the imagesetter suddenly became very clear: The file was unprintable.

If your file won't run through your laser printer at its relatively low resolution of 300 or 600 dpi, it almost certainly won't print at 2,450 dpi from the imagesetter.

Use a PostScript Error Checker

QuarkXPress has a PostScript error checker built right into it (see the Options dialog box of the Print command). During your laser proofing stages, you should definitely use this error checker if you are having trouble printing a file. It may give you a clue as to what's wrong. (If you are running a print to disk file, a technique discussed in the next section of this chapter, don't include the error checker unless you first get an OK from the service bureau.)

Preliminary Color Proofing Steps

Before getting into expensive color proofing, discussed later in this chapter, take a few less expensive steps to check your color publication.

Test Separations on a Laser Printer

One easy and practical color-proofing technique that won't cost you a bundle is testing your separations on your laser printer, using the same technique as you used in the Chapter 14 exercises. Run non-composite laser proofs to confirm that spot color objects and type are going to the correct layers. Also, evaluate the grayscale composite for reality testing of your colors, just to see that objects that should be dark are dark, and so on.

Run Inexpensive Color Printer Comps

Run color mock-ups of your piece on a desktop color printer. Inexpensive color printers have been flooding the market. These days, practically everyone can afford to have color output.

Even with excellent color management systems, these printers can't possibly provide you with an accurate view of your color results on press. However, when used with care, they can still play a valuable role in the proofing process. Show color composites to your client for sign-off that colors are in the right place. But consider putting some kind of disclaimer on your sign-off block indicating that the color comp is only an estimate and that there may be considerable color variation when the project goes to press.

Tip

To Control Your Project, Use the Master Checklist

Appendix D on the CD-ROM contains a master checklist for desktop publishing of over 300 items, including every item mentioned in this chapter. The checklist will help you think of all the things that even extremely experienced professionals have a tendency to forget in the heat of meeting a deadline.

Making a Decision: Native File or PostScript?

You have a tactical decision to make before you begin getting your job together for the service bureau. Do you send your native QuarkXPress file to the service bureau, or do you print the PostScript information to a file that you send to the service bureau? (This print-to-disk file is often called a *PostScript dump*.)

Your decision between these two options primarily revolves around responsibility. Who will have most responsibility for the final result? If you send a PostScript file, your service bureau will love you because you are taking them off the hook. You will be completely responsible for any wasted film, repro paper, and time on the system. On the other hand, if you send them a QuarkXPress file, they can play a part in helping you get the job done.

Being Tamper Proof

"Print to disk" means you "print" your publication to a PostScript file instead of paper. This approach dumps all the PostScript data that would normally go to the imagesetter or your desktop printer to a file on your hard drive. You hand off this file to your service bureau and the service bureau then simply downloads the PostScript file to the imagesetter.

This choice has the advantage of locking your publication into a practically uneditable PostScript file that contains all the fonts and graphics needed for the job. It has the disadvantage that the responsibility is all yours for settings, font loading, and all the other details of the imagesetter run. But if you don't want anybody altering your document, the print-to-disk method basically eliminates that worry for you.

Specific Situations Call for Print to Disk

Some specific situations favor the tamper-proof option of a PostScript dump. Perhaps you have done something special in the file, such as defining your own custom printer's crop marks and registration targets, or maybe you are nervous that the service bureau will change an unusual setting that you have implemented. Maybe you used an unusual font, and you want to be font independent so you don't have to worry about the service bureau not loading up the correct font. You may be worried about your carefully hyphenated copy reflowing on the page. In short, you could have a bunch of reasons for wanting to lock your files down.

In fact, if you will be producing your pages in the Windows version of QuarkXPress, it may always be better to send a print-to-disk file to the service bureau. If you are a Windows user, you are likely to be sending your publication into a Macintosh environment. If you don't want to have your job run on a Mac, you will need to make explicit arrangements and take special care in choosing your service bureau to make sure they run jobs on PCs.

This situation has been steadily improving. A few years back, service bureaus were virtually all Macintosh-based; it was very hard to find a service bureau that had PC capabilities, or a Mac-based one that was willing to solve cross-platform problems. These days, you should be able to find a PC-hip service bureau in your area, especially if you live in a metropolitan area. Still, veteran PC-based designers often feel safer when sending in a PostScript file for imaging.

However, be on your guard. There have been cases when a Mac-based service bureau ran a PC file through a Mac. In theory, that should be fine; however, assumptions can be very dangerous when you are dealing with an expensive job on a tight deadline.

QuarkXPress files are cross-platform compatible, and PostScript files are as well. The problem is, the two platforms use slightly different character sets in their fonts, even if the exact same typefaces are chosen. Fraction characters, a nearly universal characteristic of PC fonts, get replaced with ligatures, which are common in Mac fonts. Such a disaster would not, of course, be your fault, but trying to settle the resulting dispute with the service bureau won't be easy or fun.

Tip

PostScript Dump and EPS Are Not the Same

Don't confuse a PostScript dump with saving a page as an EPS file. The PostScript dump is a PostScript file of all the pages in a file that you generate using the PostScript driver through the Print command. You can also generate an EPS image of a single page using the File>Save Page As EPS command.

Allowing Yourself to Be Rescued

If you send a native QuarkXPress file to the service bureau, the bureau opens the file on its computers in QuarkXPress, just as you do. And the service bureau uses the Print command to send the job to the image-setter, much as you would if you were making a print-out from your desktop printer.

If you submit a native QuarkXPress file instead of a print-to-disk PostScript file, you give the service bureau the chance to rescue you if it turns out there's a problem. The prepress techs at the service bureau, who look at problem files every day, may catch problems when they preflight the project before putting it into the production queue. They may even be willing to fix small problems for you. You are ultimately responsible, of course, for problems caused by your design, but most service bureaus take some initiative to ensure that your file will run properly. They may charge something for their work, but it may save your deadline, and it is likely to be far less expensive than having to run a flawed job twice in order to make corrections.

On the other hand, the QuarkXPress file approach has one definite disadvantage. It leaves more potential for human error by someone at the service bureau who isn't familiar with how your publication is supposed to look.

Tip

Submit Original Files Just in Case

If you do decide to submit a PostScript dump, give yourself a backup option in case there's a problem when running the file. Despite your best efforts, you may have forgotten a setting. It could happen. Include on your disk a copy of the original document, hidden away in a folder titled SPARE or some such name. If a problem occurs, you can simply tell the service bureau tech to go to the original publication file and make the fix. In a way, this approach gives you the best of both worlds.

Tip

Test Your Print-To-File Publication on a Laser Printer

Test your print-to-disk PostScript files by using them in the same way your service bureau will. Download them to a PostScript laser printer if you have one to see if they print okay.

Print-To-Disk PostScript Dump Mechanics

Printing a file to disk works the same way it does for any other application, but there are some differences between the Macintosh and Windows 95 because the operating systems are constructed so differently.

Macintosh PostScript Dump Checklist

Here are the steps to generate a PostScript dump on a Macintosh.

1. Check that you have plenty of disk space. PostScript dumps are huge files, especially if you've got large graphic files in your design. (The LaserWriter 8 PostScript driver actually uses double space because it writes everything to disk and then composes the PostScript dump.)

2. You must choose a PostScript printer in the Chooser.

3. Make sure you've chosen the correct printer (usually a model of imagesetter used at your service bureau, call them to see which setting to use) in the Setup tab of the Print dialog box.

4. Check all your other settings. Remember, it will be your cost if you have the wrong settings. The service bureau won't rerun the film for free if you do this wrong. One particular thing to check is the resolution and line screen setting in the Output tab of the Print dialog box.

5. Click the Printer button at the bottom of the Print dialog box. That will take you to the Macintosh PostScript driver.

6. Click the File button (instead of printer) for your destination and click Save (which appears in the place of the Print button when you choose File mode).

7. Name the file, and complete the other settings in Figure 15.1.

   Choose all fonts if you want to be completely independent of worrying whether the service bureau will load the correct fonts or if you have used some rare ones in your design. This will make a larger file, but may be worth it.

   ASCII PostScript is more portable among devices but binary is faster. Ask your service bureau which they prefer.

   Level 1 compatible, being the original PostScript format, is also more portable than Level 2. Consult your service bureau.

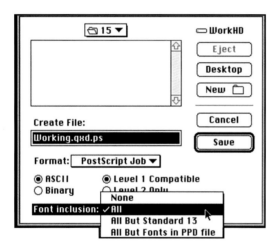

Figure 15.1

Setting up a PostScript dump for the Macintosh.

Windows PostScript Dump Checklist

Here are the steps to generate a PostScript dump on a Windows 95 machine.

1. Check that you have plenty of disk space. PostScript dumps are huge files, especially if you've got large graphic files in your design.

2. Set your PostScript printer driver to print to a file instead of the actual printer.

   You do that by going first to the Start menu and choose Settings>Printers. Right click your printer and choose Properties.

   Every printer is liable to be different but generally there will be a Details tab where you can select a port, and you want to choose "FILE" as in Figure 15.2.

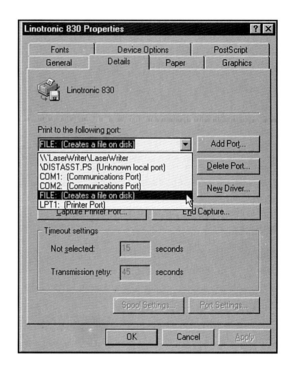

Figure 15.2

Choosing to print to file in Windows 95.

3. In QuarkXPress, in the Setup tab of the Print dialog box, make sure you've chosen the correct printer (usually a model of imagesetter used at your service bureau, call them to see which setting to use).

4. Check all your other settings in the Print dialog box. Remember, it will be your cost if you have the wrong settings. The service bureau won't rerun the film for free if you do this wrong. One particular thing to check is the resolution and line screen setting in the Output tab of the Print dialog box.

5. When you click Print, instead of sending the information off to a printer you will get a dialog box that allows you to name your PostScript dump file.

Handing Off Your Files

Whichever course you take, PostScript dump or native QuarkXPress submission, you must do a good job of handing off the files to your service bureau. You must specify exactly what you are providing to the service bureau and what you want the service bureau personnel to do with the materials.

The three top causes of bad imagesetter runs are poorly filled-out disk submission forms, missing fonts, and poor proofing practices. Avoid those pitfalls and save yourself lots of time and money in the long run by filling out the forms, including a detailed note, or otherwise including the information spelled out in this section. Although filling out forms isn't nearly as much fun as designing dynamite pages, it sure does spoil the fun of designing if your pages are problems at deadline time.

Some Sample Service Bureau Forms

Several service bureau forms are included here to give you an idea of the level of detail needed. (See Figures 15.3, 15.4, and 15.5.)

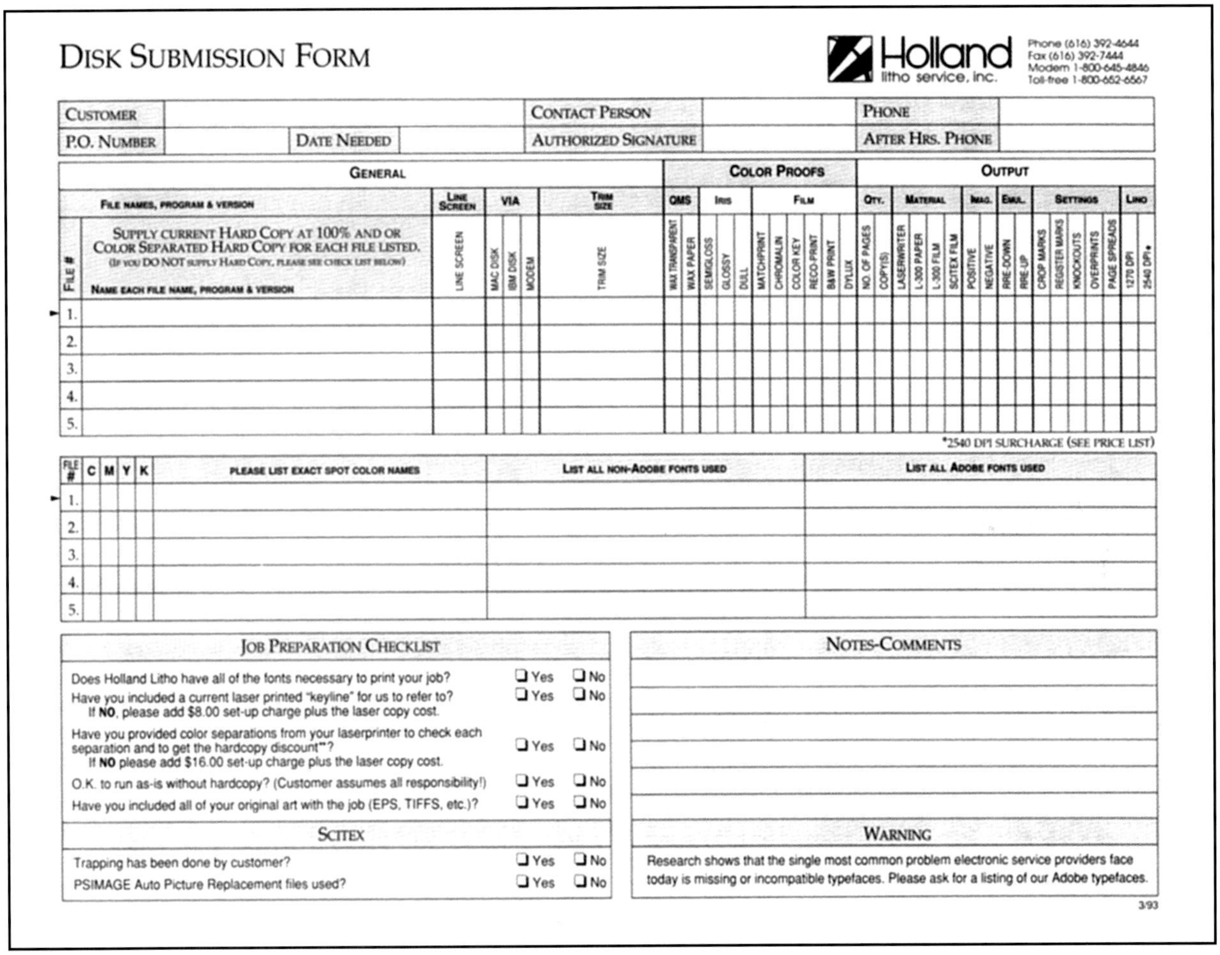

DISK SUBMISSION FORM

Holland litho service, inc.
Phone (616) 392-4644
Fax (616) 392-7444
Modem 1-800-645-4846
Toll-free 1-800-652-6567

CUSTOMER				CONTACT PERSON		PHONE	
P.O. NUMBER		DATE NEEDED		AUTHORIZED SIGNATURE		AFTER HRS. PHONE	

GENERAL							COLOR PROOFS											OUTPUT																
FILE NAMES, PROGRAM & VERSION		LINE SCREEN	VIA			TRIM SIZE	QMS		IRIS			FILM						QTY.		MATERIAL				IMAG.		EMUL.		SETTINGS					LINO	
FILE #	SUPPLY CURRENT HARD COPY AT 100% AND OR COLOR SEPARATED HARD COPY FOR EACH FILE LISTED. (IF YOU DO NOT SUPPLY HARD COPY, PLEASE SEE CHECK LIST BELOW) NAME EACH FILE NAME, PROGRAM & VERSION	LINE SCREEN	MAC DISK	IBM DISK	MODEM	TRIM SIZE	WAX TRANSPARENT	WAX PAPER	SEMIGLOSS	GLOSSY	DULL	MATCHPRINT	CHROMALIN	COLOR KEY	RECO-PRINT	B&W PRINT	DYLUX	NO. OF PAGES	COPY(S)	LASERWRITER	L-300 PAPER	L-300 FILM	SCITEX FILM	POSITIVE	NEGATIVE	RRE-DOWN	RRE-UP	CROP MARKS	REGISTER MARKS	KNOCKOUTS	OVERPRINTS	PAGE SPREADS	1270 DPI	2540 DPI*
1.																																		
2.																																		
3.																																		
4.																																		
5.																																		

*2540 DPI SURCHARGE (SEE PRICE LIST)

FILE #	C	M	Y	K	PLEASE LIST EXACT SPOT COLOR NAMES	LIST ALL NON-ADOBE FONTS USED	LIST ALL ADOBE FONTS USED
1.							
2.							
3.							
4.							
5.							

JOB PREPARATION CHECKLIST

Does Holland Litho have all of the fonts necessary to print your job?	❑ Yes	❑ No
Have you included a current laser printed "keyline" for us to refer to? If NO, please add $8.00 set-up charge plus the laser copy cost.	❑ Yes	❑ No
Have you provided color separations from your laserprinter to check each separation and to get the hardcopy discount**? If NO please add $16.00 set-up charge plus the laser copy cost.	❑ Yes	❑ No
O.K. to run as-is without hardcopy? (Customer assumes all responsibility!)	❑ Yes	❑ No
Have you included all of your original art with the job (EPS, TIFFS, etc.)?	❑ Yes	❑ No

SCITEX

Trapping has been done by customer?	❑ Yes	❑ No
PSIMAGE Auto Picture Replacement files used?	❑ Yes	❑ No

NOTES-COMMENTS

WARNING

Research shows that the single most common problem electronic service providers face today is missing or incompatible typefaces. Please ask for a listing of our Adobe typefaces.

3/93

Figure 15.3

The disk submission form used by Holland Litho Service, Inc., in Holland, Michigan.

PHONE: 310-330-3800 • **DIRECT PHONE:** 310-330-4562 • **FAX:** 310-672-3061 • **MODEM:** 310-330-4565

alan
OUTPUT WORKSHEET

Client Info

COMPANY: _____ CONTACT: _____

JOB#: _____ PHONE: _____ FAX: _____ HOME PHONE: _____

Document Info

FILE NAME: _____ NUMBER OF PAGES TO OUTPUT: _____ ☐ FLOPPY ☐ SYQUEST ☐ MODEM ☐ BERNOULLI ☐ OPTICAL ☐ DAT

SYS/APP/VERSION: ☐ MAC ☐ WINDOWS ☐ PAGEMAKER_____ ☐ QUARKXPRESS_____ ☐ FREEHAND_____ ☐ ILLUSTRATOR_____ ☐ PHOTOSHOP_____ ☐ CORELDRAW_____ ☐ OTHER:_____

☐ PROCESS (CMYK) ☐ PMS/SPOT/VARNISH:_____ LINE SCREEN:_____ TRIM SIZE:_____ OTHER:_____

ADOBE FONTS USED (INCLUDING EPS FILES): _____

NON-ADOBE FONTS USED (OR CUSTOM): _____

☐ VERIFY YOU HAVE ENCLOSED ACCURATE, FINAL COMPOSITE LASER PROOFS FOR ALL PAGES ☐ ARCHIVE ($50 PER DAT, PER YEAR) ☐ ARCHIVE & RETURN (CLIENT SUPPLIED MEDIA) ☐ ARCHIVE & RETURN (ON ALAN_____MEDIA)

SPECIAL INSTRUCTIONS: _____

Pre-Flight Info/Office Use

DATE/TIME IN: _____ DATE/TIME DUE: _____ SALES REP: _____ CSR: _____

☐ SELECTSET ☐ ACCUSET ☐ CROSFIELD ☐ RRED ☐ RREU ☐ SPREADS ☐ BLEED ☐ LASER ☐ RAINBOW ☐ TRAPWISE ☐ PRESSWISE ☐ ARCHIVE ☐ PATCH PROOF ☐ COMPOSED PROOF ☐ SCALE %_____

PRE-FLIGHT NOTES: _____

Client Checklist

• Are all the files you want output on the disk?
• Do you have a backup of all the files?
• Are all disks labeled with your name?
• *Fonts:* If non-Adobe, did you include both screen and printer fonts on disk? We have all Adobe font packages #1–325.
• Did you include a composite laser output of all your pages? We prefer proofs at 100%. If proofs are reduced, indicate output reduction on each page.

OUTPUT WORKSHEET 4/93

Images & Imported Files Checklist

• Are all imported files included on disk? (TIFF, EPS, DCS, etc.)
• If FreeHand EPS files are used, please include master FreeHand file.
• After copying files to disk for output, did you open layout file and update all links?
• If a process (CMYK) color job, are all spot (Pantone, default red, green, blue, etc.) color converted to process?
• If low resolution scans are used are they indicated as for-position-only (FPO) on proof?
• If you are using low res placement scans from us, it is not necessary to include the placement files on disk.

Hold Harmless Clause

All that appears on the enclosed disk is unencumbered by copyrights. We, the customer, have full rights to reproduce the supplied digital images.

Signature: _____

Date: _____

Please be sure to fill out worksheet completely. Jobs are often delayed due to lack of information. If assistance is required, please call your sales rep. A Pre-Flight meeting is always encouraged, only a rough comp is needed—please call!

Figure 15.4

The disk submission form used by Alan Litho in Los Angeles, California.

Please remit all payments to the main office:

Graphics Plus
3750 South Robertson Blvd, Suite 101
Culver City, CA 90232
Telephone 213 559 3732
FAX 213 559 2225

graphicsplus

Job Ticket

Invoice Date_____
TJR_____
TJD_____

B I L L   T O
_____
_____
_____
_____
_____

S H I P   T O
_____
_____
_____
_____
_____

This job ticket must be filled out in its entirety before your files will be submitted for imaging. Never "style" fonts. If you do not use Adobe screen fonts, Graphics Plus will not be responsible for the results. Your job will be delayed if the information you have given us is not accurate or incomplete.

PURCHASE ORDER	TURNAROUND	SALES REP.	TERMS	TAX EXEMPT #
Job #	❏ STANDARD ❏ 1 HR ❏ SAME DAY (FILM) ❏ 3 HR ❏ SPECIAL		❏ NET 30 ❏ C.O.D.	

TYPE OF SERVICE	DELIVERY INSTRUCTIONS	PICK-UP INSTRUCTIONS
❏ LINOTRONIC ❏ TRANSPARENCY/QMS ❏ COLORSCRIPT ❏ FILM ❏ LASERWRITER ❏ OPTRONICS ❏ SCANNING ❏ 4CAST	❏ WILL CALL ❏ UPS ❏ FEDERAL EXPRESS ❏ U.S. MAIL ❏ G+ DELIVERY	❏ MODEM ❏ DROP OFF ❏ G+ PICK-UP ❏ DISK ENCLOSED

Archive Name: _____

File name/description (columns: # of Pages | # of Copies (if not 1) | Scaling? (if yes %) | Crop & Reg. Marks? (Y or N) | Line Screen (lines/inch) | Page Size (Lt, Lgl, Tab, other) | P or F (paper or film) | Optronics | Q or F (QMS, ColorScript/4CAST) | Linotronic 300 | N or P (neg or pos) | U or D (RR emuls. up or down) | P or S (process or spot color) | # of colors per pg) — FILM OUTPUT

① ② ③ ④ ⑤ ⑥ ⑦ ⑧

SCANNING

❏ Optronics   ❏ Color
❏ Microtek   ❏ Grayscale
❏ Nikon   ❏ Line

# of Trans._____ # of Reflectives_____

SIZING/RESOLUTION

Final Size	Quantity	Image Description
2x3		
4x5		
5x7		
11x14		
16x20		

SOFTWARE APPLICATIONS USED	FONTS USED
_____	_____
_____	_____
_____	_____
_____	_____

What line screen (LPI) will you use for film output?_____
If not applicable, state other sizing/resolution info: _____

SPECIAL INSTRUCTIONS & COMMENTS
_____
_____
_____
_____

PressMatch Prints

❏ 11x14   ❏ 16x20
❏ 12x18   ❏ 20x24

$25 MINIMUM ON ALL JOBS. PLEASE READ AND SIGN THE TERMS AND CONDITIONS ON REVERSE. THANK YOU.

Figure 15.5

A disk submission form from Graphics Plus in Culver City, California.

Follow All These Steps

Include all this information to the service bureau when submitting a file for output.

- *Contact Info.* Don't just include the company name. Include the name of the person responsible for decision making on the publication and if possible include after-hours contact numbers as well. Time on the system is everything at a service bureau, and the ability to reach you at a moment's notice may keep your job from being bumped. Your deadline is at stake.

- *Time Line.* The shorter the deadline, the more the job will cost you.

- *Collect for Output Report.* Seems pretty basic but don't forget it. It includes basic document info like the file name and its size, the versions of QuarkXPress, any required XTensions, the names of all the fonts used, graphics used and their resolution, H&J specifications, colors as needed on each page, and trapping info.

- *Fonts.* One category of files that QuarkXPress won't collect for you is fonts. If you are sending fonts to the service bureau with your files, you need to gather them up by hand to make sure they're included.

- *Indicate Special Graphics File Needs.* If you have had the service bureau do high-resolution drum scans for you, be sure you note that on the form. In this situation you will have worked with low-resolution files they provide to you for position purposes, and the service bureau has been storing the graphic images in its system. They need to know this so that they can link everything back up.

Make sure the service bureau can handle the files if you send along a Photo CD for your scans. Generally, you are better off providing your shots on disk rather than on CD. In all probability, you have modified the pictures to some degree for cropping, rotation, color correction, and so on, so those Photo CD shots need to come to the service bureau on disk.

- *Clean Up Your Submission Disk.* You will almost always submit files to a service bureau on some sort of removable mass storage. Be sure to delete any old files off your Syquest cartridge (or Zip disk, or Bernoulli, or whatever you are using for removable mass storage to transport your files to the service bureau) so old files can't be confused with the current files.

- *Give Yourself a Safety Net.* Run a backup before sending your disk to the bureau; don't send your only copy.

The backup helps in two ways. First, if the file transfer has some defect, you already have a backup at the service bureau. Second, the backup can help solve any dispute about the way you set up the file if the service bureau has made a mistake in running the original.

■ *Resolution.* Coordinate with the printer. Ask your print shop what screen frequency to use for your choice of paper and printing press. (There's more on this in an upcoming section.)

■ *Type of Imagesetter.* Many service bureaus have more than one type of imagesetter, and they let you choose. Be sure you understand the choices you are making. In general, you pay more for higher resolution (dpi) and precision, as well as the imagesetter's capability to render halftone dots (usually expressed as the capability to hold a certain line screen frequency).

■ *Film and Paper Specifications.* Ask your printer (again, coordination is essential) whether you should order film with emulsion up or down, and whether the film should be right or wrong reading. The most common setting is emulsion down, right reading.

Also, ask your printer whether you should order negative or positive film or paper. Most printers in the United States prefer negative film and positive paper.

■ *Printer's Marks.* Specify the trim size of your publication and, in most cases, ask that printer's marks be turned on. If you created custom crop marks right on your pages, make sure the service bureau understands that they are to leave the automatic crop marks turned off.

■ *Delivery Method.* Help the service bureau find the file by letting them know that it is coming by modem, if that's the case. Is it on a floppy, a Syquest or Zip cartridge, or a less common disk format? Has the file been compressed to fit on the disk with WinZip (Win95), Stuffit (Mac), or some other compression program?

■ *PostScript Error Checking.* If you are printing to disk, ask the service bureau if you should click the Include PostScript Error Handler checkbox in the Options dialog box of the Print command.

■ *Send Your Laser Proofs.* At a minimum, include a composite laser print of your publication.

For a color publication, include a separated laser proof as well. If you are running a long document, however, you may not want to send proofs for the entire job. In that case, you can pull some sample pages, and, if it's a spot color job, clearly mark them with directions on how the separation layers are supposed to work. Discuss with the service bureau whether they want a long document to be submitted with a separated proof for every page. It's hard to imagine most prepress techs making much use of four-color separations of a 300-page book. (That's 1,200 pages!)

■ *Obtain Proofs.* In addition to sending proofs along with the job, you must also specify to the service bureau which proofs you want to receive.

For a black-and-white publication or simple spot-color job, you may decide against running a service bureau proof and simply double-check that each page is properly separated. The printer will probably do a blueline for you when the project has been assembled.

If it's a process-color document or a complex spot-color job requiring trapping, get a color proof and make your choice of proofing method. Certain types of proofing are better than others for evaluating trapping. There's more on this topic in the upcoming section "Using Laminate (Separation-Based) Color Proofs."

Hand Off Files to Your Partner

By now, after reading through this lengthy list of details, you may be feeling a bit intimidated. That's not the point of the list. Rather, the point is to give you all the information you could possibly need so you can do a service bureau hand-off with confidence.

This next exercise is designed to build that confidence. By the time you are finished, you will know for sure that you can manage the service bureau process. You will have, for all practical purposes, proven to yourself that you can succeed—even if you don't have an imagesetter at your disposal for practice runs.

1. Pair up with someone else in your class. You will hand off a file to your partner, and your partner will try to run it through a PostScript printer. (And you will return the favor by receiving a file from your partner and seeing if it runs by following your partner's explicit instructions.)

   The point is, coordinating with a service bureau (or a printer) is an exercise in human communications. The technology is, after all these years, pretty standard. The slip-ups take place because somebody forgets to take a step or leaves out vital information.

2. Pick a project to run. It must be a color project (requiring separation of process color, or spot color overlays).

   One way to come up with an exercise project is to use one of the independent study projects you have developed in the course, the Portfolio Builders. Or you could use one of the exercise projects, if you prefer.

3. Hand off the project to your partner, just as if your partner was a service bureau. It's okay to work together—that's the point. But start out by going through the entire checklist in the last section, spelling out your instructions. Then consult with your partner on such questions as available fonts.

4. To really make this exercise work best, your partner should be running the jobs on some other printer at the school, not just on the one you've been using all term in the computer lab.

   Try hard to make this a learning experience in which you are submitting files into a shop where you aren't familiar with the printing equipment. That's the point of this exercise; to communicate well enough that, even when sending your files into an unfamiliar environment, you can get good results. Doing it this way will help you negotiate the pitfalls of running a job through a service bureau.

   There's an excellent by-product that comes out of this exercise. When it is your turn to run your partner's job, you will experience role reversal and will understand what the service bureau goes through in taking in a file from a customer.

Proofing Color

One proofing step, a crucial one, is proofing color. It's a step that often takes place at a service bureau, where they own high-end color output equipment. Your commercial printer may also run proofs. Some types of color proofing—the most accurate ones usually—can't be done until after the service bureau has run film out of the imagesetter.

The concept of attempting to check color accuracy before going on press has a certain note of unreality to it. There isn't any way, really, to know your color results until you get ink down on paper in the printing press, as you know from discussions in previous chapters. However, you can catch many problems—especially many potentially expensive problems—by proofing color. The high end color proofing systems are very good.

You can break color proof sheets down into two types: composites and laminates (or separation-based). The choice between composite and laminate proofing methods is probably a money issue, so you need to understand the benefit that might cause you to buy into a laminate-proofing technique (the more expensive of the two).

Using Composite Color Proofs

Composite proofs have become more and more common as color desktop publishing has grown. These proofs are generated digitally, straight out of the computer into a color desktop printer—usually a rather expensive one. Some people even refer to them as *digital proofs.*

Keep in mind that much of this discussion relates to the proofing of process colors. Your color proofing process may not need to be so rigorous if you are printing in spot colors because they come from premixed ink and are therefore intrinsically accurate based on the swatch book you use to make your choice of color.

There are three basic types of composite color printers available:

■ Color copiers, which are driven with special color controller boxes. You might see one of the Canon color laser copiers, for example, driven by EFI's Fiery unit or by ColorAge's ColorQ.

■ Thermal dye sublimation printers, such as the 3M Rainbow, apply color to special glossy paper.

■ High-end inkjet printers spray ink on the paper in microscopic dots, not unlike the inexpensive color printer that you may use for color comping. You'll hear names at your service bureau such as Iris and Stork Bedford.

Your service bureau will probably offer one, or maybe several, of these printer types on their price sheet.

Two of these printer types—the color copiers and the inkjets—may be able to print to the actual paper stock you'll be using for your printed piece. Thermal dye process requires special paper.

Using Laminate (Separation-Based) Color Proofs

The most expensive type of color proofing is the best. By building proofs from layers of colors, just as it would be done on the printing press, the laminate or separation-based color proofs will reveal any trapping or moiré flaws in your piece.

You can get overlay proofs in which the color is built up from loose acetate sheets of each color, all bound together in register. If you are offered an overlay proof, it's likely to be a 3M Color Key or a DuPont Cromacheck.

The best proofs of all are the ones that are bonded together in a lamination. Your film is shot to the layers of proofing materials, processed, and registered. Then it's sealed together in one solid sheet. It doesn't get any better than this. Look for names like Cromalin (DuPont), Matchprint (3M), and ColorArt (Fuji).

Evaluating a Color Proof

To proof color, you need to set a goal. Do you need the color to be only pleasing to the eye, or must it precisely match the original subject? There may be some publications where color accuracy isn't all that critical. On the other hand, if you've got a standard product color (such as for a brand of soda pop, for instance), the printed photos of that product better be an extremely close match. When you've got the goal defined as clearly as you can state it, get a sign-off from your client (or boss, whomever the approver might be, if it isn't you) and convey the goal in your conferences with the service bureau and the print shop.

Focus on the Memory Colors

Focus on the so-called memory colors when evaluating color proofs of scanned photographs. Some colors just stick out in a person's mind instantly if they seem wrong; those are the memory colors.

Flesh tones are especially important memory colors. You need to pay particular attention to flesh tones if you have different races in the same shot, because that visual environment makes color accuracy problems even more glaring. The flesh tone memory colors may be the most important ones of all. Even Crayola finally provides a variety of flesh tones for different races. (The old so-called flesh color, the pinkish/salmon one, never looked quite right anyway, did it?)

There are other memory colors too. Blue sky, oranges, apples, hamburgers, familiar brand-name products such as soft-drink cans—any objects that are really familiar also must look real and believable.

Evaluate Colors in Controlled Light

Actors have known about this for years, of course. The color of everything, including your skin, varies depending on the lighting. Your facial color is different if you're outside at dawn, under the incandescent lights in your dining room, or under fluorescent lighting at the office. If possible, evaluate proofs under standard lighting in a color evaluation booth. Most prepress service bureaus and print shops have such lighting or have rigged up the equivalent. The booths attempt to duplicate the color of daylight at midday.

Collaborating with the Print Shop

In some ways, this section on collaborating with your commercial printer should have been the first chapter in this book. That's because your collaboration with the printer really should begin long before you get to the final stages of publishing a project. Because the printer is at the end of the publication process, he or she can tell you best how to begin.

To understand why early collaboration is so important, it helps to think of your publication process as a motor journey. It's a long drive with a deadline for your arrival, plus a budget limit on your transportation costs. The printer, your guide and collaborator, helps you draw up a map—a plan to get you to your destination. The printer also offers free advice on alternate routes that may give you better quality, plus ways to avoid potholes and other road hazards. And before this analogy wears entirely too thin, it's important to mention that the printer can make suggestions that can help you save money on fuel for the trip as well.

Your commercial printer also brings to your collaboration a quantity and quality of experience that you can't possibly hope to match. In a week, your printer sees the number of jobs that you see in a couple of months or more. Even if you've done a hundred jobs, the printer has experience and wisdom based on a thousand.

This wisdom has become extremely important in recent years. Our growing power to instantly design beauty on the computer screen has cut us adrift from the basic printing press technology that ultimately makes that beauty possible. But the commercial printer remains a bastion of practical experience, able to translate your design from the high-tech world of the computer screen into your low-tech destination: paper and ink on the printing press.

Holding a Preflight Printer Meeting

Ideally, you will hold a preflight meeting with your printer. In this utopian world, your preflight check happens before you begin to perform the electronic layout work for the job so that you can use the advice from the printer to do the job faster, cheaper, and with better quality. It hardly ever happens that way in reality, but that's the ideal timing for your initial meeting at the print shop. Try hard to meet with the printer at the stage at which you are making your fundamental design decisions about a project. It will save you money, save you problems, and save you heartbreak.

There aren't any granite solid rules for this sort of collaboration and, obviously, there's a wide range of help that your printer can offer or that you may require. You need to make your own decision about how much or how little of the information here applies to your job.

Preparing for Your Printer Coordination Meeting

Obviously, do some thinking, planning, and designing before you meet with the folks at the print shop. Stay flexible, of course, or you won't get the benefit of their expertise. At the same time, be clear about your needs and goals. At minimum, you need to have made some preliminary decisions about each of the following categories:

■ *Intents and Purposes.* When people use the phrase "for all intents and purposes," they are usually being practical. That's the essence of your preflight session. You must be able to spell out the intents and purposes—the practical aspects—of your publication. What's the audience, and what is the goal?

■ *Rough Sketch, Comp, Mock-Up.* Use this early version of your publication to convey the basic format of your publication to the printer

Your rough sketch may be on the back of an envelope, but at least go into the preflight meeting with some idea of what your publication will look like. Your collaboration will work best if there's something specific as a basis for discussion. Sketch out the layout in rough blocks or thumbnails so you have a visual representation of all the other issues in this list.

If you can, mock up the job. For a brochure, for example, fold a piece of paper the way you think the panels should go, and draw in the blocks of information. This can help both you and the printer get a good idea of what you need in the way of bindery services (sewing, folding, scoring, insertions, perforating, and so on).

Tip

Use Samples for Communication

Samples are great tools. Collect them incessantly. There really isn't much that's new in the world of publication design. Samples can aid your communication in the preflight meeting if you can say things like, "I saved this gold-embossed piece I got in the mail the other day because it has just the effect I want." Or perhaps, "Here's a pamphlet I picked up at the Eggplant Eaters' Rights Rally the other day. I like this deckled-edge paper that they used."

■ *Size of Run and Budget.* A process of negotiation is ahead of you, so you don't want to name the price that you are willing to pay. Maybe you'll be able to improve the financial bottom line. However, you can save both yourself and the printer lots of time by suggesting your rough expectations at the preflight session. If you ask to do four colors and 5,000 pieces for a one-sheet flyer, it's going to cost more than $1.98.

■ *Quality.* Keep in mind your overall needs for quality. Again, this has a lot to do with how the piece will be used. If it's a sales presentation and the product costs several thousand dollars a pop, the quality will be different from a church newsletter done on a volunteer basis and funded out of the weekly collections.

■ *Deadline.* How soon does the job need to be done, and how long before you can get your design firmed up? When does the printer need to get the job in order to deliver on time? What's the last possible day? What's the optimum day to get the best price and quality?

■ *Ink and Varnish.* How many inks do you think you will need? Have you planned to do process   Have you thought about how a couple of spot colors might do the job just as well? What color matching system do you prefer (as opposed to what the printer might actually support)?

■ *Paper.* The way the piece is used has a lot to do with your paper requirements, so bring along some paper swatches, if you can. Do you need covers as well as paper for body text? Do you want a special finish on the paper? Do you need envelopes printed? Paper companies are usually happy to provide you with samples, especially if you let them know that you are putting together a job with a printer that already buys paper from them.

■ *Special Sensitivities and Crazy Ideas.* What are the touchy spots? Does a product shot need to be precisely matched for color? Does the client (or do you) have a phobia about some previous bad experience with a print job?

Almost any creative task involves a fair amount of brainstorming. That's the fun part, and you will be well-served to let your printer have some of the fun, too. Go to the preflight session with whatever crazy ideas have spun through your imagination. Maybe the printer will find a way to pull off one of those ideas—maybe even within your budget.

Beginning the Collaboration

Armed with all your preparation, go to your meeting with goals and questions clearly in mind and state them right up front, as follows:

■ *Electronic Publishing Experience.* Does the printer have experience working with desktop publishing output? There's no sense doing a publication in QuarkXPress and then taking it to someone who doesn't understand the first thing about digital art.

■ *Reality Testing.* You want a reality check. Ask the printer to look at what you are attempting and to point out any problems that you are building for yourself. Print shops are in business to accomplish things for people, but they are, above all, bastions of practicality—at least the good ones are. Printers know that clients tend to hold them responsible for problems, whether the problems are the fault of the printer or not. Printers have a vested interest in steering you through the tough spots, and they usually welcome this "reality check" question.

■ *Quality.* Aside from suggestions about preventing problems, does the printer have any suggestions for improving quality (and how much will it cost)? You should have some ideas of your own about what level of quality is appropriate for your publication.

Keep in mind that printers are set up to deliver a range of quality, and that your job may not fall in their range. A quick printer may be great for running stationery or forms but would be completely out of the question for running a four-color, hardbound book. Some of this has to do with the kind of press equipment a shop owns. It also has to do with the way the shop has carved out its customer base. For example, quick printers usually build their business on small print runs, quick turnaround, and heavy volume from walk-in customer traffic.

■ *Time.* Are there suggestions about scheduling? Would it help if the covers were delivered first so they can be embossed, foil stamped, varnished, and scored while the rest of the job goes through collation?

■ *Money.* What suggestions does the printer have for saving on the budget? Maybe you have in mind a paper that only comes in a size that wouldn't be efficient when trimmed to the size of your publication. The printer may suggest a similar paper that would allow you to fit more pages on a sheet, making for big savings.

Developing Tactics on Working with the Print Shop

Here's the most vital aspect of your preflight session. Don't leave without developing a tactic for how you will work with the print shop. Aside from all the other pre-bidding brainstorming you see in this section, you need to resolve the following essential prepress and logistics issues:

■ *Color Matching and Ink Strategy.* If you are going to use spot colors, you must know what color matching setups your print shop supports. It's probably going to be Pantone, the most commonly-used system in the United States.

Whatever color matching setup you and the printer agree to use, you'll need to decide on paper. The libraries and swatches differ, for example, between coated and uncoated paper stocks.

Work with the printer on inking strategy. If you combine spot and process colors, for example, it may make a lot of sense to go with a process color-based color-matching system.

Also, ask the printer to give some thought to the order in which the inks are laid down on the paper. That may help you make choices when you design reverses, knockouts, and overprinting.

■ *Line Screen.* Given the paper you plan to use and the press that's probably going to be used, what's the optimum line screen? This frequency has a major impact on how you handle photo scans and blends, among other things.

Does the printer have any other advice on specifications for you or the prepress service bureau when scanning photos? Discuss issues such as compensating for dot gain; for color photos, you need to know about undercolor removal and gray component replacement.

For more about line screens, see the section later in this chapter, "Choosing a Line Screen with Your Print Shop."

■ *Trapping.* Trapping means slightly overlapping different inks around the edges of objects on the page. It's necessary because no printing press runs perfectly in register. Paper stretches. The press slips around as it runs. The result is misregistration, and trapping helps cosmetically cover up the gaps between colors that result. In your printer collaboration meeting, you need to decide who will do the trapping, if it's needed at all. Does the printer see any ways to slightly modify your design approach so the need for trapping can be eliminated?

We'll talk about trapping in detail later on in this chapter.

■ *Imposition.* In your preflight session, make sure that you get clear agreement on who will be responsible for imposition. (Most print jobs are printed in "multiple ups" in which many pages of the publication are combined onto a large piece of paper. *Imposition* is the process of folding this paper just right, and then trimming the edges so the page numbers all work out correctly.)

■ *Specifications for Mechanicals.* Given all the other decisions you are making, what does the printer want to see in the way of mechanicals? Will high-resolution laser output be okay for this job? Or do you need imagesetter output? Should the image-setter output be positive resin-coated paper or negative film? Fine line screens in the range of 133 and above almost demand films.

If you do films using a service bureau, what directions do you need to give the bureau? Will it be emulsion down or up, negative or positive, and right or wrong reading? You need to ask the printer for these specifications, so you can give them to the service bureau. If you are interested, and lucky, the printer may take time to show you how all these things work when it comes to putting your projects on press.

Will the printer work directly with the service bureau on other prepress issues, such as trapping specifications, and other technical considerations, such as compensating for dot gain and handling imposition? Or maybe you will decide to have the print shop handle those and other prepress tasks in-house, which would make many of the coordination issues moot.

■ *Proofs.* At the preflight, get an agreement on proofing procedures. Will there be a press check? Will the print shop accept the service bureau's color proofs? The shop may want to do the proofs on their own system because they know how it relates to their presses.

Choosing a Line Screen with Your Print Shop

One crucial consultation with the printer is the choice of a line screen. The print shop can only guarantee that halftone spots will remain distinct up to a certain point. After that point, you get dark mush instead of detailed grayscale. The finer the halftone screen (the more lines per inch), the more critical this becomes. You need the printer to give you this recommended setting for the lines per inch of your halftone screen. A lot depends on your paper choice and the capabilities of your printer's presses.

Understanding the Effects of Dot Gain

The printer calculates this line screen mush point, for the most part, based on the anticipated dot gain. When the ink hits the paper from the press, the paper absorbs the thick, greasy ink just as a sponge or a blotter soaks up a spill. You can imagine what happens to the tiny spaces between the dots of ink in a halftone. They are liable to clog up. That's why you can usually depend on a halftone to print darker than it looks from the service bureau's proof. Why? Because dot gain means you get bigger dots, and as a practical that means it appears higher up on the grayscale.

What to Do with the Line Screen Information

When you have the printer's recommended line screen, you are armed with the data for two vital action steps: scanning resolution and output line screen setting.

When you scan a photograph, the dots-per-inch (dpi) setting sets the intrinsic resolution—for a given size—of your digitized photograph. There's no sense collecting any more resolution in the scan than your line screen can deliver on the press. You just waste precious disk space with a file that's much larger than necessary.

Be really clear on one point: The pixel resolution of the photo is being discussed here, and that's not the same as the halftone resolution. The photo hasn't been screened at this point (or at least, it shouldn't have been).

Anyway, when you know your line screen, you know the resolution you need to use when you scan a photo or edit a previously scanned one. Most experts say it's a waste to scan at any more than twice the lines per inch of your halftone screen. If you work with 85 lpi on the press, scan at 170 dpi. If you will be at 133 lpi, scan at 266 dpi.

Some folks claim that scanning at double the line frequency still wastes time and disk space for no significant gain on the press. They recommend scanning at one and a half times the line screen. Check with your printer and your service bureau for more advice on the specific challenges of your piece, given the types of photos you are running and the issue of dot gain.

Now, for line screen setting: You need your printer's line screen recommendation so you can tell your service bureau what line screen setting to use when they output your job. You'll also know what setting you should use if you are doing your own output.

Some Line Screen Guidelines

A given paper produces a given dot gain on a given press, and nobody can tell you what line screen to use

for each press and paper combination better than the person who runs that press. However, Table 15.1 shows some widely accepted guidelines that you can use in a pinch.

Table 15.1 Guidelines for choosing a line screen for given paper and press conditions

Paper/Press	Lines Per Inch
Newsprint	65 to 85
Standard Coated	85 to 133
Better Press/High Grade Coated Paper	133 to 175
Superior Paper and Press Conditions	175 +

Print Shop Proofs and Checks

After your film has been run, it goes to the print shop. At this stage, you can still take some steps to prevent expensive errors on the printing press. Or, rather, your print shop can help you take some steps.

Printer Inspection of Films

Nobody may be better qualified to inspect your imagesetter output than the person doing the printing. Even if the service bureau has checked the films, have the press people run another analysis with those experienced eyes that have been watching stuff come off the press for hundreds, maybe thousands, of print runs. The more eyes the better, and odds are high that your print shop folks have the best of all.

Blueline

By checking a blueline proof, you can verify that the print shop understood your trimming and folding instructions. It's also the only proof you'll get that indicates how fronts and backs go together—obvious for book jobs, not always so obvious for multifold brochures, or a postcard that might have a horizontal front and a vertical back.

A blueline is made basically the same way a blueprint is. Light-sensitive paper gets exposed to light in a one-to-one contact print with your actual stripped-together films—the flats about to be used to make up your printing press plates. It's the most intimate and close to the press method of proofing—outside of the press check itself—and tells you whether the print shop has properly collated all the separations for your job. A blueline is, well…blue.

Dummy

If you are creating a multipage document, your print shop may provide you with an *imposed proof*, a dummied-up copy of how all the flats will be folded when they are printed to paper and then trimmed. The *dummy*, usually made from the blueline, shows you the spreads and how they will all fit together when bound.

If you need one, ask for it in your initial meeting or at least let the printer know you'll want one if you award the job to them. Dummies are also sometimes used to test how differing text and cover stock look together, and to gauge the thickness of the spine for book binding.

Press Check

Do a press check at least once in your life, even if you aren't working on color critical publications. It's magical to see your design coming to fruition, and there's no better way to fully understand the process of getting images onto paper from a printing press.

When you arrive, you'll go to the press room where the press will be ready to roll—or close to it. When the crew hits the button, a lot of waste, called *make ready*, results. Sheet after sheet of paper (if it's a sheet-fed press) or yards of paper (if it's a web press) roll along as the printing crew adjusts everything.

When they are satisfied, they'll shut down the press and bring a sample to you before rolling the press again to finish the job. This is no time to discover a typo that should have been caught long ago. You are

there to see that the colors are accurate and that no obvious defects exist in the work. If you are happy, you'll be asked to sign the proof, and the crew will use it as a standard for evaluating the rest of the pieces off the press for the rest of the run.

What do you look for at the press check? Ask a lot of questions and look—really look—at the piece as it comes off the press.

- Ask the crew to share their technical check with you. If you aren't familiar with some of their tools, you can't do better than ask them to explain what they are and how they work. The new knowledge will help you understand the relationship between what you create on the computer screen and the ink the press puts on paper.

  How did dot gain look on the star targets? These spoke wheel-like patterns look a little like a miniature TV test pattern.

  What did the densitometer show about how the inks are laying down on the page? Have them explain what they discovered as they examined the color and grayscale density bars.

  The press crew will already have done this, but take the extra care to double-check that all the registration marks are lined up.

- Go through the piece and check that colors are as you want them to be, suited to the color accuracy goal on which everyone agreed. If there are critical items for color matching, such as product shots or color matching system swatches, make sure that they are there at the press check and use the standard light table to make a comparison. Don't work from memory.

- Look for physical defects caused by the printing process. Wrinkles, print-through from the back side of the piece, impurities such as hair or dust sticking to the plate and printing on the piece, smudges, and blotting from undried ink transferring between stacked sheets are the kinds of defects you need to look for.

Understanding Trapping

For designers, trapping may be the most misunderstood—yet most often performed—aspect of getting a publication ready to go on press. As a result, many jobs go to the printer with many trapping errors. In this section, you will learn what trapping does, and you will learn why it is so easy to do a bad job at it. You'll also get an introduction to the right way for you to go about doing your own trapping if you feel determined to do so.

The Problem

Basically, trapping exists because there's no such thing as a perfect printing press. As the paper screams past the plates at high speed (or even at low speed), it shifts around. It slips from side to side. It stretches. The paper changes dimensions as it soaks up wetting solution and ink. And, after all, a press is a mechanical device, and you can't expect anything made out of iron to roll all day without a little slop.

A little slop might be okay when you are working with only one color. But slop is absolutely not okay if you are laying down multiple colors. The colors ought to align properly (*register* with one another). The chances are pretty strong, however, that anywhere two colors meet on the page, a little sliver of white paper will show through between them unless you trap the point where those colors meet (see Figure 15.6).

Figure 15.6

The dreaded little sliver of white, the reason you need trapping. (Also reproduced in the color section.)

White paper shows through

You can see there are two problems caused by this misregistration. First, there's that sliver of pristine white paper showing through between the two brilliant cyan and magenta plates. Also, the misregistration has caused the creation of a third "accidental" color on the left side where the two ink colors overlap.

To trap the triangle and its background color together, one or the other of them must expand or shrink so they have a very slight overlap.

That's what trapping is, the intentional overlapping of two ink colors. It's a cover up. Trapping doesn't make the press register correctly. It merely covers up the misregistration with an overlap of ink.

Lately, trapping has somehow become the responsibility of the designer, not of the printer. The designer didn't always have to fret about press registration problems. In times past, the printer and the stripping crew did the fretting. You generated your mechanicals, delivered them to the printer, and they came back looking great. The folks who worked on the light table with Xacto knives and masks and Rubylith worried about registration problems. You may have learned to avoid certain design elements in order to make your printer's job easier, but you as a designer never had to seriously concern yourself about trapping.

Now we have the power to produce pages all stripped together electronically, ready to go to final film and be burned to plates. That means we can skip the expensive and time-consuming step of hand-stripping at the light table. When put that way, saving time on deadline and saving money on the budget really sounds great.

But as deadline approaches, reality sets in, and maybe it doesn't sound so great any more. Now it's you who pops the aspirin, instead of the printer. When you take on trapping responsibility, you have only yourself to blame if the job looks a mess. And it will be your bill to pay.

Fundamental Trap Construction

The easiest of all the trapping concepts to understand is the *choking* and *spreading* technique. You choke an object to make it smaller, and that's why chokes are sometimes called *shrinks* or *thinnies*. Spreads, also called *grips* or *fatties*, are the reverse. (See Figure 15.7.)

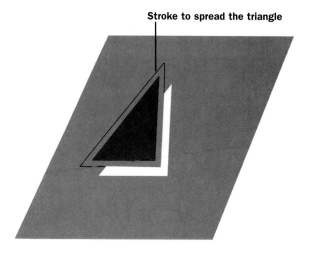

Stroke to spread the triangle

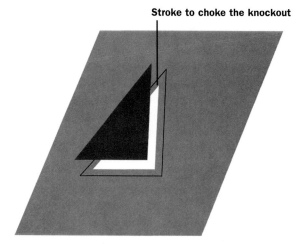

Stroke to choke the knockout

Figure 15.7

The spread is on the top, and the choke is on the bottom. (Also reproduced in the color section.)

Ideally, you always trap using the lighter color. You spread (or choke) the color that is lightest.

Trapping creates its own problems because the two colors overlap. You get a line that adds the two colors where the inks overlap. The resulting artifact of the trapping process can be an unsightly dark line that looks even worse than the dreaded sliver of white it covers up. However, by working only with the lighter colors, you minimize the effects of the dark line. As a rule of thumb, when the inks are laid down on paper, the dark color will dominate the overlapping light color.

Three Trapping Methods

How do we actually accomplish this spreading and choking? You have three techniques to choose from: the way it used to be done (mechanically on a light table), the object trapping method, and the high-end pixel edge trapping method sometimes called *raster trapping*. Those techniques are the subject of the next few sections.

The Way It Used to Be: Mechanical Trapping

To understand how all this trapping business works, it may help to have a look at the traditional, non-computer techniques used to create traps.

Printers used to create traps by using what you might call a "light sandwich" in order to make a contact print from a film of the original image. Printers placed a thin filling of clear material, such as plastic, between the original film and the contact film. This sandwich filling of clear plastic allowed the light to spread out so it created an overlap (a spread type trap) on the receiving negative film. The amount of the trap could be varied by using different thicknesses of clear material and by altering the amount of light used for the exposure (see Figure 15.8).

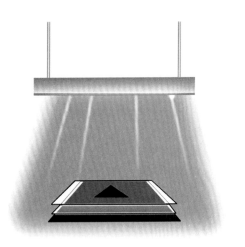

Figure 15.8

The light sandwich method used by strippers to create a trap. (Also reproduced in the color section.)

Some areas of a complex design might need different traps. To create varying traps on a page, the stripper photographically (not literally) carved up the mechanical into different zones with masks made of Rubylith and opaque material. Each zone was then exposed as needed and the final trapped flat was then used to expose the lithographic plate.

This dependable technique has worked well for a long time. However, the technique takes time, and that means money, that you or your client must pay. Also, it does go against the grain to carefully paste up your pages electronically and then have a stripper use old-fashioned razor blade-based trapping techniques on them.

Object Trapping

QuarkXPress's built-in automatic trapping uses electronic object level trapping methods.

Object trapping involves drawing a line around the object that needs to be trapped. For that reason this trapping technique is sometimes called *stroking* (Figure 15.9).

Notice that the object knocks out the background, the normal behavior for a graphic object in any PostScript-based program, including QuarkXPress. The stroke line, however, has been set to overprint so it can overlap the background. Also, the lighter of the colors has been used for trapping.

The choice of the trapping color can be pretty mind-boggling. If you are working with spot colors, you simply select the lighter of the two abutting colors. Process colors, however, can combine to make some really weird and garish third colors, called *trapping artifacts*. If you design yourself into such a corner, get advice from your printer. Better yet, have someone else do the trapping unless you are an experienced hand.

Raster Trapping

Raster or edge trapping beats one of the big problems with object trapping. Object trapping requires that you be able to access the object from within QuarkXPress. That's fine for a QuarkXPress box or some text or some other object created within the program, but if you need to trap an imported graphic you've got a problem. No desktop layout program, including QuarkXPress, can do any trapping on the areas inside that image. For trapping imported graphics, you would need to go back to the drawing or photo-retouching program used to create the graphic.

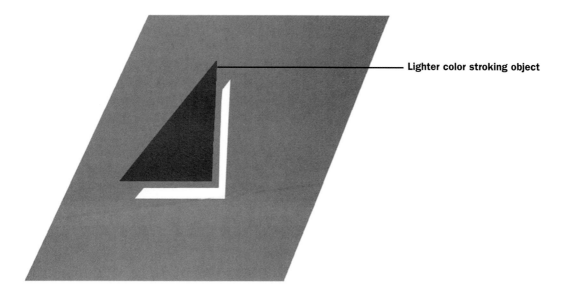

Lighter color stroking object

Figure 15.9

An object stroked with a trapping line, a spread, drawn around the object being trapped. (Also reproduced in the color section.)

What to do? There's no better trapping available than raster edge trapping. If you have designed a job that QuarkXPress's built-in trapping can't handle or if you are apprehensive about taking the trapping risk, you may need to send your job to a service bureau or printer that offers raster trapping.

Several software packages for trapping are out there, and most of them have one thing in common—a purchase price of thousands of dollars. In the hands of a skilled operator, these systems can do excellent trapping work, but they aren't the kind of thing most of us are likely to install in our own studios.

A high-end trapping system goes into your completed QuarkXPress file, sorts it out right down to the pixel level and automatically works out traps for everything on the page. That includes imported EPS graphics and virtually all the other trapping problems laid out in the upcoming section, "Deciding Whether to Do Your Own Trapping." Raster trapping does a good trapping job quickly, no matter how convoluted those abutting color objects may be.

The two big names in raster trapping are TrapWise from Luminous Corporation and Scitex FAF (FAF is for Full Auto Frame). You don't need to care very much about what system is used, as long as your service bureau delivers a good looking job on time.

Design Away the Need for Trapping

If your print job permits, you can develop a design that does not require trapping, or at least avoid the worst of the trapping risks.

Overprinting Black

If you have black type to run over a colored background, just let it print right on top of the background since the black ink will generally cover most anything. Make sure you check with your print shop about the amount of ink being applied to the page, because you could end up with too much.

Avoid such obvious legibility and design problems as putting black type on a midnight blue background. (In this situation, the type would be unreadable.) Check contrast by having a look at the page design with your monitor set in grayscale mode (Mac) or printing out a composite grayscale proof (Win95 or Mac).

Sharing CMYK Colors

As long as abutting process colors share a common process color, you don't need to trap them. For example, perhaps the adjacent objects both contain at least

10 percent or 20 percent of cyan. (Check with your printer on the minimum amount of common color, but 10 percent is a typical figure.) If the other colors slip on the page, the cyan ink fills in the gap, and you see no dreaded white sliver of paper showing through due to the misregistration. The sliver is cyan blue instead, but many designers and printers believe that's less noticeable than white.

This trick doesn't work with spot color inks. However, process color-based spot color specification systems work just fine. Check with your printer.

Frame the Untrappables

Consider running a frame around the edge of an item that might otherwise be untrappable, such as a color photo. Simply put an intentionally visible frame around it as part of the design. You need to decide whether you like the idea of doing this to your design, but it does (literally) cover any misregistration.

Avoid Trapping Nightmares

If you design your publication to include any of the following situations, you can be sure to have trapping nightmares. No desktop publishing program, QuarkXPress included, can handle these trapping challenges.

- *Imported and Resized Graphic Objects.* If you resize an imported EPS that was trapped in its originating program, you will probably ruin its trapping. For example, if you make the item bigger, the resizing pulls apart the elements in the drawing, opening up chokes and spreads (see Figure 15.10).

- *Abutting Blends.* If you design overlapping blends—anything that doesn't have a sharply defined edge—QuarkXPress object trapping won't help you (see Figure 15.11).

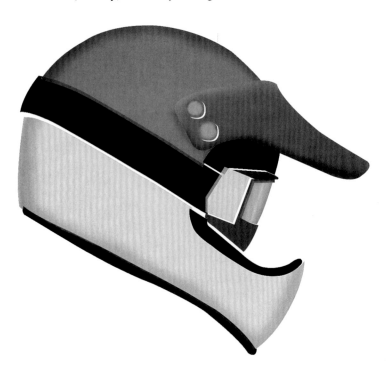

Figure 15.10

You must trap imported graphic objects in the programs that created them. (Also reproduced in the color section.)

Figure 15.11

Overlapping gradations are impossible to trap using object trapping because you get a sharp line along the abutting edge. (Also reproduced in the color section.)

——Trapping artifact where blends abut

This example of two different-colored and abutting blends was poorly trapped by simply adding a solid color along the edges of the blends. The result is a trapping artifact line.

Another approach would have been to trap the blends by the common color method mentioned earlier in this section, but that still gives you a trapping artifact. In both cases, the problem arises because the color of a blend gradates along its edge. The trapping color must track exactly with the colors of the blends, creating sort of a sliding trap.

■ *Objects Overlapping Halftones.* One of the toughest trapping challenges is an object such as text superimposed over a photograph. You simply have no way to stroke your object against the picture, because all the colors are changing underneath the object, similar to the problems you face in trapping a gradation. See Figure 15.12.

Figure 15.12

The difficulty of trapping an object superimposed over a scanned photograph. (Also reproduced in the color section.)

Deciding Whether to Do Your Own Trapping

Basically, except for the simplest of jobs, you probably shouldn't do your own trapping. The information in this text has been included because you do need to understand it. Trapping requires a lot of experience and knowledge, and traditionally it has been performed by the printer. The printer knows his or her own press, which is what determines the need for trapping. The temptation will be there to do your own trapping because QuarkXPress offers some simple trapping capabilities. But consider the following when deciding whether to do it yourself:

- *Money and Time.* How much is your time worth, and how much will it cost to rerun a job if you mess up the trapping? How much less would it cost to pay the printer to do the trapping?

- *Risk Versus Benefit.* Are you willing to risk the mistakes you might make when trapping? If you take responsibility for the trapping and it comes out badly, you might be reaching into your bank account for some not-so-petty cash to pay for those 10,000 color catalogue sheets the client rejected.

- *Are You a Film Stripper or a Designer?* Do you really want to sit in front of the computer making trapping decisions? Or, would you rather be designing another job?

- *Quality.* How good will the job be when you get done? Is the piece important or complex enough that it deserves high-end raster trapping? Do you have all the skills and experience needed to handle this particular trapping job properly?

- *Design to Avoid Trapping.* Is it possible to design around the need for trapping? If no colors touch one another, there's no need to trap. Or maybe you can use the common color method if you are working in process colors, and design abutting objects to share one of the four process colors.

- *Job Complexity.* Is doing the job yourself with object trapping techniques even technically possible?

Controlling QuarkXPress Trapping

Although we've given you some advice against doing your own trapping, you do need to know how to control it. If nothing else, you need to be able to turn it off.

Setting a No Trapping Default

Here's how to make sure that your new QuarkXPress documents do not have trapping turned on.

1. Start up QuarkXPress with no document open.

2. Get to the trapping controls through the Document Preferences dialog box, ⌘+Y (Mac) or Ctrl+Y (Win95), and choose the Trapping tab as you see in Figure 15.13.

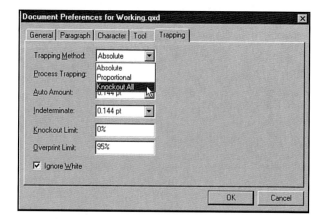

Figure 15.13

Knockout All turns off trapping.

3. With no document open, set your preferences for no trapping in the Trapping Method pop-up menu for no trapping by choosing Knockout All.

While you are here, take a moment to check out some of the trapping controls QuarkXPress provides.

Absolute trapping setting tells QuarkXPress to use the settings in this dialog box (or in the Trap Information palette for individual items) to calculate traps. It looks at whether an object color is darker or lighter and either chokes the item (darker) or spreads it (lighter). It uses the trap width you set in **A**uto Amount.

Proportional trapping basically does the same thing, except it adjusts the trap based on the relative luminance of the two inks for the items that are being trapped.

If QuarkXPress can't figure out which object is lighter or darker, it judges the situation indeterminate and traps the object based on whatever you enter in the Indeterminate box in this dialog box.

Tip

If You Trap, Collaborate

If you eventually decide to do your own trapping, the most important item on the list of technical things you need to know is the width of the traps you want QuarkXPress to set for you. Ask your printer for that information. He or she knows the looseness of the press, the line frequency of your screens, your paper, and the dot gain. From that information, your printer can determine the trapping amount. The amount of ink overlap will probably range from 0.1 to 2.2 points (QuarkXPress's default is .144 points), and there may be a different amount for black ink and all the other color inks.

You may see standard guidelines for trapping technical specifications, but it's just plain silly to trap without asking the printer what the trapping parameters are for the particular press that will be used. Trapping is, after all, something you are doing to compensate for misregistration on the press, and it varies a great deal from press operation to press operation.

Tip

Don't Do a Half Trap Job

Don't run QuarkXPress trapping if your design includes even one of the trapping nightmare situations illustrated in this chapter. Handing the printer films that have been trapped in some areas but not in others will make it impossible for the printer to complete the job. Trapping software like TrapWise and traditional printing darkroom techniques for trapping usually work over the entire area of a page, which creates a sort of all-or-nothing situation. Running trapping software over your existing QuarkXPress-generated traps would give you double traps in some spots—not a good outcome.

4. When you are done looking around, click OK and close QuarkXPress to save your new default preferences.

Summary

The technical and logistical side of getting a job ready to go on press really requires a lot of attention to detail. That should be evident from reading this chapter. Hopefully the detailed lists of steps and needed information we've provided here—along with the master desktop publishing checklist on the CD-ROM in Appendix D—will help you avoid some of the mistakes it can be so easy to make when rushing to finish a job.

Review It

As a review of what you have learned in this chapter, please answer the following questions.

1. Name two layout evaluation views you can get through the Print command.

   _____

   _____

2. Name three reasons why you should run a laser proof before going to a service bureau for imagesetting.

   _____

   _____

3. What's the difference between a composite and laminate color proof?

_____

_____

4. When evaluating a color proof, what types of colors should you be checking?

_____

_____

5. Name two kinds of proofs the print shop will often give you before finishing a job.

_____

_____

6. When should you begin collaborating with your commercial printer?

_____

_____

7. Why is it so important to find out from the printer about the proper line screen for your job?

_____

_____

8. What are the primary considerations in favor of handing off a PostScript print to disk file to a service bureau?

_____

_____

9. Why would you choose to go with a native QuarkXPress file, instead of a print to disk file?

_____

_____

10. What causes the need for trapping?

_____

_____

Check It

Multiple Choice

Please circle the correct answer for each of the following questions.

1. Black-and-white laser proofs of color files are good for _____.

   a. checking spot color separations

   b. judging grayscale values in composite proofs

   c. seeing if the PostScript will run okay

   d. all of the above

2. You can create a PostScript dump by _____.

   a. setting printer driver to print to file

   b. checking the File option in Print dialog

   c. using File>Save As EPS

   d. all of the above

3. When handing off files, always include _____.

   a. font list

   b. contact information

   c. all publication and graphics files

   d. all of the above

4. The best possible color proofing is done on a _____.

   a. dye sublimation printer

   b. laminate proofing system

   c. color laser printer

   d. none of the above

5. You should hold a collaboration meeting with your printer when _____.

   a. you are starting a design

   b. when you are first planning a job

   c. when you have produced film

   d. none of the above

6. Dot gain happens when _____.

   a. laser printer output is used for final art

   b. trapping is set too high

   c. ink blots into paper on the press

   d. none of the above

7. If your publication will be run at a 150 line screen, _____ resolution would be best for a scan.

   a. 150 dpi

   b. 300 dpi

   c. 2450 dpi

   d. none of the above

8. When designing to avoid trapping you can _____.

   a. design so there are no abutting colors

   b. allow shared process colors to overlap

   c. let black overprint

   d. all of the above

9. To turn off trapping in QuarkXPress, you set it for _____.

   a. absolute

   b. proportional

   c. knockout All

   d. none of the above

10. The best trapping method of all is _____.

   a. raster trapping

   b. QuarkXPress trapping

   c. object trapping

   d. none of the above

True or False

Please circle *T* or *F* to indicate whether the statement is true or false.

T   F   **1.** To avoid the need for trapping, make sure to use overlapping spot colors.

T   F   **2.** At a press check, bring along your color memory aids.

T   F   **3.** A dummy proof tells you how pages go together.

T   F   **4.** The advantage of submitting a PostScript dump to the service bureau is that it is tamperproof.

T   F   **5.** The advantage of a native QuarkXPress file submission is that the service bureau can correct errors you make.

T   F   **6.** A normal line screen for a newspaper would be 175.

T   F   **7.** A choke is where the trap expands to cover a color seam.

T   F   **8.** A spread is where the trap widens an object.

T   F   **9.** Since pre-trapped vector graphics are EPS there's no harm to resizing them.

T   F   **10.** A laminate proof can't show you traps, although its color accuracy is quite good.

Design It

To fully understand the process of producing a printed piece, you need to spend a bit of time at two types of places—a service bureau and a commercial print shop. Make contact with one of each in your city and see if they'd be willing to let you watch for an afternoon.

- At a service bureau, ask to see the high-end scanning department where drum scanners are used to produce nearly perfect photo scans.

- Spend some time at the service bureau in the room where they run the imagesetters and process the film output.

- At a print shop, you want to see the presses, of course. But try to manage an invitation to be there for a complete process from setting up the press to running a job.

Presentation

Advice—Telling Your Story Creatively

David Rozansky: For each sample of my work, I have a little caption printed out that explains the job. For instance, my specialty is tight deadlines, so my captions show how I gather great stories or lay out difficult pages in only an hour or two. My captions explain what techniques I used on a piece that may not be obvious. One explains how I did layout in a tent in a dusty wind, showing my resourcefulness. These captions get better readability than the samples themselves.

I would say using captions like this would greatly help a student portfolio. The reviewer would know it is a new designer, but could see why the project brought out unique talents. For instance, the caption on an ad might state that the class assignment was to develop a compelling poster with as few words as possible which persuaded people to volunteer some time each week, and how the designer used her experience from her inner-city background to find imagery that rang true with the proposed audience.

Mike Cotterell: From the other side of the desk, I have found portfolios interesting when interviewing job applicants. A portfolio often helps to put them at ease when they are asked to talk about their work.

The way the work is presented makes a big difference. I don't mean whether it's in a nice case but whether the applicant has thought through how they are going to present the work—what they are going to say about each item. Three main faults I've seen are when a student plops the portfolio down on the desk and just says, "Well, there it is." Or when they fill the portfolio with everything they own and then say about many of the items, "Well, this one isn't very good…." And the worst is when they appear totally unprepared, look at the pieces as if it's the first time they've seen them and respond to questions about them with "Err…dunno…can't remember."

Exercise—Packaging and Rehearsal

The contents of your portfolio will normally be only half of the story you are telling. The other half is you, talking about the portfolio.

- Find a way to rehearse your portfolio presentation in a realistic way. Present the portfolio to someone you trust and ask for their feedback.

- Make sure your test audience knows that you want a workout. Set them up to ask questions about you and your work.

- You might even consider asking them to create a hypothetical design situation so you can test how you will respond to the situation using your portfolio to tell your story.

- Decide how you will physically package up the portfolio to help tell your story. Labels or story-telling caption are one technique. Another issue is the physical look of your portfolio. You are a designer so your presentation should be well designed. It, too, is part of how you illustrate yourself.

Index

Printer button, 348
printers, dot gain, 359
printing
    bluelines, 344
    colors
        blending, 327-330
        Color Swatch, 317
        gray, 307-308
        halftones, 305, 307-309
        PMS (Pantone
            Matching System),
            304, 307
        process, 305
        screens, 307
        separations, 305
        spot, 303-305
        trapping, 362-367
        trapping, methods,
            364-365
    cross platforms, 346
    documents, print-to-disk, 346
    dot gain, 359
    files, 354
    halftones, gray, 311
    images, screening, 313
    options, choosing, 325
    overlays, 324-325
    pages, 44
    print shops
        collaborating with,
            356-358
        line screens, 359-360
        samples, 357
        specifications,
            358-359
    screens, angles, 312-313
    spot colors, defining,
        316-317
    SWOP (Standard for Web
        Offset Printing), 337
process cameras, 309
process colors, 305, 331-334
    screens, angles, 312-313
    separating, 305
    spot colors
        converting from,
            331-334
        deciding between, 307

Profile Information palette, 338
proofing
    colors, 345, 354, 356
        composites, 355
        laminates, 355
    composites, 344
    documents, 344-345
    error checking, 345
    master checklist, 345
    thumbnails, 344
proofs
    blueline, 360-361
    colors, evaluating, 355-356
    dummies, 361
    imposed, 361
    press checks, 361
proportionally spaced type, 56
publications, *see* documents

Q-R

QuarkXPress
    defaults, 20-22
    em space measurement, 57
    preferences, 20-21
QZXT file extension, 7

range kerning, 94
raster
    graphics, 233
    trapping, 364-365
reader's spreads, 9
Rectangle Picture Box tool, 13
Rectangular Text Box tool, 13, 61,
    89, 107, 124
register, colors, 362-363
rejoining boxes, 289
relationship points, items, spacing,
    280-281
Replace button, 8
replacing
    characters, invisible, 142
    documents, 137-138
    words, 147
reports for service bureaus,
    generating, 352-353

resolutions
    dependent, 233-235
    dpi (dots per inch), 235
    independent, 233
        jaggies, 233-234
    low, photographs, 331
    photographs, pixels, 360
reversing out, text, 125
Revert To Saved command (File
    menu), 141, 167, 244, 265, 327
RGB (Red, Green, Blue), 337
right-aligning text, 76
rotating
    graphics, 243-244
    text, 271-272
Rotation tool, 13, 271-272
Rounded-Corner Picture Box tool,
    13
ruler guides
    setting, 42, 90-91
    snapping, 42
    visibility, 207
rules, paragraphs, establishing,
    78-80
Rules command (Style menu), 79
runarounds
    Auto Image, 246
    editing, 246-248
    text, 214-215, 240-246
    tolerance, settings, 246

S

Sabon font, 200
sans serif fonts, 27
Save As command (File menu), 9,
    244
Save command (File menu), 9
Save Page As EPS command (File
    menu), 346
saving
    documents, 8
    files, 8
        automatically, 58
    libraries, autosaving, 238
Savoy font, 201

MACMILLAN COMPUTER PUBLISHING USA

A VIACOM COMPANY

Technical Support:

If you cannot get the CD/Disk to install properly, or you need assistance with a particular situation in the book, please feel free to check out the Knowledge Base on our Web site at **http://www.superlibrary.com/general/support**. We have answers to our most Frequently Asked Questions listed there. If you do not find your specific question answered, please contact Macmillan Technical Support at **(317) 581-3833**. We can also be reached by email at **support@mcp.com**.

By opening this package you are agreeing to be bound to the following:

The CD-ROM runs on both Macintosh and Windows 95 platforms. For information, please double-click the README file in the root directory of the CD-ROM.

The CD-ROM includes:

➤ Font Management (Appendixes A and B)

➤ Glossary (Appendix C)

➤ Master Checklist for Desktop Publishing Projects (Appendix D)

➤ Fonts

➤ Chapter-by-Chapter Folders (which contain the text, graphics, and step/exercise files within the chapter.)

➤ Adobe Acrobat Reader 3

Minimum System Requirement to run the CD

Windows®	Macintosh®
i486™ or greater processor	Macintosh computer with 68040 or greater processor
8M RAM, 16 recommended	8M of RAM, 16 recommended
Windows 3.1x or higher	Apple® System Software 7.1 or higher
256-color display monitor, thousands of colors recommended	13-inch or larger 256-color display monitor, thousands of colors recommended
Sound card	2X CD-ROM drive
2X CD-ROM drive	
Mouse required	